0445064775

Governing the soul

Governing the soul

The shaping of the private self

Nikolas Rose

Routledge
London and New York

First published 1990
by Routledge
11 New Fetter Lane, London EC4 4EE
29 West 35th Street, New York, NY 10001

© 1990 Nikolas Rose

Page-set and laser printed directly from the publisher's w-p
disks by NWL Editorial Services, Langport, Somerset.

Printed and bound in Great Britain by
Mackays of Chatham PLC, Chatham, Kent

British Library Cataloguing in Publication Data

Rose, Nikolas, 1947 –
   Governing the soul: the shaping of the private self
   1. Psychology
   I. Title.

ISBN   0 – 415 – 02856 – 6

*Library of Congress Cataloging in Publication Data also
available*

It would be wrong to say that the soul is an illusion, or an ideological effect. On the contrary, it exists, it has a reality, it is produced permanently around, on, within the body by the functioning of a power...on those one supervises, trains and corrects, over madmen, children at home and at school, the colonized, over those who are stuck at a machine and supervised for the rest of their lives.

Michel Foucault

Contents

Preface

This book is about the powers that have come to bear upon the subjective existence of people and their relations one with another: political power, economic power, institutional power, expert power, technical power, cognitive power. I use historical investigations to demonstrate the incentives that have, over the course of the last fifty years, led power to infiltrate subjectivity and intersubjectivity, and the concerns, mechanisms, and goals of the human technologies that have been invented. But it has not been my intention to write a historical book. I have tried to use history to help myself and others think through the meaning and consequences of the new devices that have been invented for the government of the self, and to unsettle some of our comfortable illusions about their truthfulness and humanity.

Psychology and psychologists have important roles in my narrative. But it has not been my aim to write a history or a critique of psychology as a body of knowledge or as a group of professionals. Instead I have tried to show the ways in which the government of human subjects has become bound up with innovations and developments in a number of scientific discourses that have rendered knowable the normal and pathological functioning of humans. I have tried to make manifest some of the ways in which these ways of knowing have taken up and transformed problems offered by political, economic, and moral strategies and concerns, and how they have made these problems thinkable in new ways and governable with new techniques. In the course of these events these ways of knowing have profoundly and irreversibly transformed political rationalities, institutional life, moral discourse – and personal existence itself.

Critiques of psychology have been plentiful over the past twenty years. They have frequently argued that psychological theories and practices are concerned merely with the isolated individual and with his or her social adaptation. I take a different view. The psychologies that are important in contemporary social regulation do not treat the subject as an isolated automaton to be dominated and controlled. On the contrary, the subject is a free citizen, endowed with

ix

personal desires and enmeshed in a network of dynamic relations with others. The very psychological theories and practices promoted by 'progressive' critics of 'adaptationist' psychology – dynamic and social psychologies, psychotherapies, family therapies – in stressing the significance of subjectivity as the key to our humanity, in elaborating techniques that enhance subjectivity through self-inspection and self-rectification, have underpinned the ways in which subjectivity has become connected to networks of power.

The first part of the book, 'People at War', concentrates upon World War II. The practical involvement and research activities of psychologists and others involved with the human problems of wartime were of crucial importance in shaping the post-war technologies for the regulation of subjectivity. After a brief account of the role of psychology in World War I and the inter-war years, I consider a number of distinct but related areas of psychological activity: morale on the home front, psychological warfare, the selection of servicemen and officers, and the rehabilitation of psychiatric casualties and prisoners of war. Two overriding themes emerge: the argument that psychological expertise is vital for the maximization of the use of human resources in institutional life, and the birth of the notion of the group as a fundamental field of analysis, therapy and regulation. While World War I had stimulated the development and deployment of intelligence tests, World War II led to the invention of a range of different devices for the assessment of the psyche, in the context of demands for more accurate techniques of recruitment and promotion, and more efficient ways of choosing between policy options. New dimensions of subjectivity, especially 'attitudes' and 'personality', were grasped in thought and utilized in practice. With the development of new languages for speaking about subjectivity, and new techniques for inscribing it, measuring it, and acting upon it, the self became calculable and manageable in new ways. Psychological expertise staked its claim to play a key role within any practice for management of individuals in institutional life.

World War II was a war of morale. One needed to analyze the bonds between individuals, the relations between internal mental states and external relations with others, if one was to understand what made a fighting unit efficient, what maintained the resolve of the civilian population, or what promoted recovery in the neurotic serviceman or the demoralized prisoner of war. The war produced a new set of social psychologies, psychotherapies and psychiatries that sought to document, interpret, and utilize these social relations in different ways, from assessing the state of public opinion or the attitudes of servicemen, through the use of training and propaganda to build up the morale of allied servicemen and civilians and undermine that of the enemy, to the systematic utilization of group relations for therapeutic purposes. The group would have a great future in psychological thought and regulatory practice in the post-war years.

Nowhere were these two inventions, the maximization of human resources and the role of the group, more important than in industry. These are the issues I examine in the second part of the book, 'The Productive Subject'. In the pre-war years, the National Institute of Industrial Psychology and the work of the Industrial Health Research Board had made a limited impact in vocational guidance and in the study of such issues as fatigue. In each of these areas, methods of assessment and analysis had been predominantly based upon the analysis of individual capacities. In the post-war period, the new ways of thinking and acting on the group and on human resources were deployed in debates about labour productivity, about industrial unrest, and about maximising the commitment of the worker and his or her integration into the enterprise. Additionally work has been given wider, non-economic significance. Employment has become construed as an essential element in individual psychological health, family stability and social tranquillity.

Work is now seen as an imperative as much psychological as economic. It is not merely that productivity is hampered by pathological psychological characteristics of the worker, or the misallocation of square pegs to round holes. It is also that the yield of the enterprise in terms of productivity, profit and satisfaction can be enhanced by the judicious adjustment of the temporal, spatial and interpersonal relations of the workplace according to a knowledge of the subjectivity of the worker. In the new developments in management thought, work is no longer an obligation imposed upon individuals, nor an activity only undertaken for instrumental reasons. Work itself is a means of self-fulfilment, and the pathway to company profit is also the pathway to individual self-actualization.

In the third part of the book, 'The Child, the Family and the Outside World', I consider the strategies that have linked the 'private' sphere of the family with the objectives of government. For perhaps a century and a half, social and political concerns have linked the rearing and well-being of children with the welfare of society at large. Social ills from crime and juvenile delinquency to military defeat and industrial decline have been connected with incorrect or ignorant practices of child care within the family. Around the child, lines of force have been established between the objectives of government and the minute details of conjugal, domestic and parental behaviour.

Since World War II, psychology has increasingly provided the language in which these concerns with the rearing of children have been phrased, the means of identifying problems and the types of expertise capable of putting them right. Emphasis has gradually but decisively shifted from a concern to prevent psychological maladjustments through correct procedures of child rearing to new objectives: maximizing both the emotional adjustment and the cognitive efficiency of the child through proper management of early relations with the parents and the environment.

Critical discussions of family regulation have tended to concentrate on social work intervention into poor families, non-nuclear families and the families of ethnic minorities. Such mechanisms remain significant. But for the vast majority of families regulation operates by other means. Coercion, the disabling of the family unit by the removal of the child or the threat of such removal, plays a minor role. Family practices are increasingly aligned with social objectives not through coercion but through acting upon the wishes, desires, and aspirations of adults. Psychology has played a key role here, in establishing norms of desirable childhood development and behaviour, and in providing new means of visualizing and understanding the nature of childhood, its normalities and pathologies. These psychological norms and languages have been disseminated not only through the education of social workers and health visitors, but also through the terms of popular literature and debate in the mass media, in advertising and in culture generally. In the inevitable gaps between the behaviours of actual children and the ideals of these norms and images, anxiety and disappointment are generated in parents, anxiety that is the occasion for seeking professional guidance to manage the discrepancy between the experienced and the desired.

In the final part of the book, 'Managing Our Selves', I consider the nature and implications of the proliferation of psychotherapies and the emergence of what one might term 'the therapeutic culture of the self'. Anthropologists and historians long ago recognized that the category of 'the self' was not universal, that different cultures and different historical periods specified human capacities differently and individualized humans in ways foreign to our own. Sociologists too have suggested that the free, rational, conscious, choosing, autonomous self is a creation of western capitalist democracies. Two features of the history and anthropology of the self have, however, been less studied. The first concerns the relations between cultural categories and beliefs and the actual existence of individuals as selves. The second concerns the emergence of new conceptions and techniques of the self in the recent period: the desiring, relating, actualizing self is an invention of the second half of the twentieth century. Psychological theories have played a key role in the birth of this new concept of the self, and psychological techniques have had a crucial role in the development of those practices and techniques through which modern selves are constructed, sustained and remodelled.

The development of dynamic and social psychologies in the post-war years, and the emergence of new notions of personality, have gone hand in hand with the development of new techniques for the reshaping of selves by systematic management under the guidance of psychological expertise. Behavioural technologies have been one paradigm. These technologies gained a foothold first of all in relation to problems that were not those of mental illness but of maladapted personalities – alcoholism, phobia, anorexia, bulimia, obsessions. They were rapidly joined by other techniques that could be utilized in every area in which human action was to be shaped up in relation to specified goals. From giving up smoking to the management of anxiety, from sex therapy to assertion training, from reformatory techniques for the kleptomaniac to cognitive restructuring of values, psychological techniques can be applied.

Psychological expertise now holds out the promise not of curing pathology but of reshaping subjectivity. On every subject from sexual satisfaction to career promotion, psychologists offer their advice and assistance both privately and through the press, radio, and television. The apostles of these techniques proffer images of what we could become, and we are urged to seek them out, to help fulfil the dream of realigning what we are with what we want to be. Our selves are defined and constructed and governed in psychological terms, constantly subject to psychologically inspired techniques of self-inspection and self-examination. And the problems of defining and living a good life have been transposed from an ethical to a psychological register.

The present book is, in many ways, a development of the arguments I made a few years ago in *The Psychological Complex* (London, Routledge & Kegan Paul, 1985). It extends the analysis to the present and widens it to deal both with economic life and personal existence. In order to make my argument here self-contained, I have sometimes discussed and rectified the account given in that earlier book. But, in the main, I have tried to focus on events in Britain, and to a lesser extent the United States, from the 1930s onwards. While I regard the processes I have documented to be general to liberal democratic societies, it will be for others to judge the extent to which they have resonances outside the domains I have studied.

In preparing this book I have drawn upon many sources and many people. Most notably, my way of thinking about the questions that concern me has been shaped by the researches and analyses of Michel Foucault, whose memory deserves better than the industry of commentary that has thrived upon it. I have also made much use of secondary histories in the many areas I cover. While I have tried to acknowledge these in detailed references, I thank in advance all those who detect the influence of their ideas in my writing. Some of the arguments in this book have been presented in earlier versions elsewhere, but appear here in substantially reworked and corrected form. I have also drawn upon the interviews I have conducted with Peter Miller in the course of our research into the intellectual and social history of the Tavistock Clinic and Tavistock Institute of Human Relations, work that is assisted by a grant from the Lever-hulme Trust. I must also thank Brunel University and especially the Faculty of Social Sciences for granting me two terms of study leave in the academic year 1986-87 in which to conduct the initial research for this book.

Many people have assisted me in the writing of this book, by sending me material, talking to me about the issues involved, commenting on seminar papers in which I presented early thoughts, supplying me with references, and guiding me through materials. I am especially grateful to all the organizations that supplied me with information used in the preparation of Part IV. I hope they will forgive me for the use to which I have put it. A number of people kindly read and commented on drafts of some of the material: I am grateful for their advice, even that which I ignored. I would particularly like to thank Paul Hirst, Phil Jones and Peter Seglow, who each generously helped me with one or more chapters. Many of the ideas for this book have arisen out of discussions with Peter Miller, who has also commented on parts of the draft and gently directed me away from blind alleys and onto more productive paths. Diana Adlam has, as always, been my first and best critic, discussed the issues with me throughout, given generously of her extensive knowledge of the history of psychology, and helped eliminate many errors and confusions in the text. But while most credit for what may be good in the book is owed to my friends, culpability for the final product remains mine.

London

July 1988

Introduction

> I don't think that we should consider the 'modern state' as an entity which was developed above individuals, ignoring what they are and even their very existence, but on the contrary as a very sophisticated structure in which individuals can be integrated, under one condition: that this individuality would be shaped in a new form, and submitted to a set of very specific patterns.[1]
>
> Michel Foucault, 1982

Our intimate lives, our feelings, desires and aspirations, seem quintessentially personal. Living at a time when we are surrounded by messages of public troubles that appear overwhelming – war, famine, injustice, poverty, disease, terrorism – our mental states, subjective experiences and intimate relationships offer themselves as perhaps the only place where we can locate our real private selves. There is, no doubt, much comfort to be afforded by such a belief. But it is profoundly misleading.

Our personalities, subjectivities, and 'relationships' are not private matters, if this implies that they are not the objects of power. On the contrary, they are intensively governed. Perhaps they always have been. Social conventions, community scrutiny, legal norms, familial obligations and religious injunctions have exercised an intense power over the human soul in past times and other cultures. Conduct, speech and emotion have been examined and evaluated in terms of the inner states that they manifest, and attempts have been made to alter the visible person by acting upon this invisible inner world. Thoughts, feelings and actions may appear as the very fabric and constitution of the intimate self, but they are socially organized and managed in minute particulars.

The management of the contemporary self is distinctive, however, in at least three respects. First, the personal and subjective capacities of citizens have been incorporated into the scope and aspirations of public powers. This is not only a link at the level of abstract political

1

speculation. It is also a link at the level of social and political strategies and institutions and techniques of administration and regulation. While it would be too much to claim that our rulers now construe their tasks wholly or even largely in terms of the interior lives of citizens, subjectivity now enters into the calculations of political forces about the state of the nation, about the problems and possibilities facing the country, about priorities and policies. Governments and parties of all political complexions have formulated policies, set up machinery, established bureaucracies and promoted initiatives to regulate the conduct of citizens by acting upon their mental capacities and propensities.

The most obvious manifestation has been the complex apparatus targeted upon the child: the child welfare system, the school, the juvenile justice system and the education and surveillance of parents. But the regulation of subjective capacities has infiltrated wide and deep into our social existence. When ministers, civil servants, official reports and the like concern themselves with military efficiency and think in terms of fitting the man to the job, when they construe industrial productivity in terms of the motivations and satisfactions of the worker, or when they pose a social problem of the growth of divorce in terms of the psychological stresses of marriage, the 'soul' of the citizen has entered directly into political discourse and the practice of government.

Second, the management of subjectivity has become a central task for the modern organization. Organizations have come to fill the space between the 'private' lives of citizens and the 'public' concerns of rulers. Offices, factories, airlines, colleges, hospitals, prisons, armies and schools all involve the calculated management of human forces and powers in pursuit of the objectives of the institution. Many ingredients clearly enter into the management of organizational life. But, to a greater or lesser extent, bosses, military commanders, educationalists and so on are now obliged to attend to the subjectivity of the employee, soldier or pupil in achieving their objectives. When, for example, the army seeks to minimize indiscipline and the breakdown of troops, and to increase fighting efficiency, through the rational allocation of individuals to activities in light of a knowledge of their intelligence, personality or aptitudes, human subjectivity has become a key element in military power. When industrialists seek to increase productivity and harmony by adapting working practices in the light of considerations of group dynamics, intersubjectivity has become central to managerial authority. Organizational life, that is to say, has taken on a psychological hue.

Third, we have witnessed the birth of a new form of expertise, an expertise of subjectivity. A whole family of new professional groups has propagated itself, each asserting its virtuosity in respect of the self, in classifying and measuring the psyche, in predicting its vicissitudes, in diagnosing the causes of its troubles and prescribing remedies. Not just psychologists – clinical, occupational, educational – but also social workers, personnel managers, probation officers, counsellors and therapists of different schools and allegiances have based their claim to social authority upon their capacity to understand the psychological aspects of the person and to act upon them, or to advise others what to do. The multiplying powers of these 'engineers of the human soul' seem to manifest something profoundly novel in the relations of authority over the self.

These new ways of thinking and acting do not just concern the authorities. They affect each of us, our personal beliefs, wishes and aspirations, in other words, our ethics. The new languages for construing, understanding and evaluating ourselves and others have transformed the ways in which we interact with our bosses, employees, workmates, husbands, wives, lovers, mothers, fathers, children and friends. Our thought worlds have been reconstructed, our ways of thinking about and talking about our personal feelings, our secret hopes, our ambitions and disappointments. Our techniques for managing our emotions have been reshaped. Our very sense of ourselves has been revolutionized. We have become intensely subjective beings.

The studies that follow attempt to trace some of the ways in which a central role has come to be accorded in modern societies to these subjective aspects of the lives of individuals as they conduct their commerce with the world, with others and with themselves. The investigations I undertake try to describe the conditions within which new networks of power have taken form, the hopes and fears that lay behind them, the new ways of thinking and acting they have introduced into our reality. My approach differs from those that have become most influential in recent sociological literature.[2] This literature is characterized by its use of a limited set of interpretive and critical tropes: the moral entrepreneurship of professional groups; the medicalization of social problems; the extension of social control; the ideological nature of knowledge claims; the social interests of scientists; the psychological sciences as legitimating domination. This paradigm of 'socio-critique', if I may be forgiven the term, certainly highlights something significant about the rise of this new knowledge and these new techniques. But I find this perspective upon the relations between the psychological sciences, the psychological professions and the organization of political power limited in a number of important ways.

Socio-critique implies that this knowledge of subjective life is, in some significant sense, false or wanting; perhaps, even, that it is because it is false that it can have a role in systems of domination.

3

Knowledge, that is to say, is evaluated in epistemological terms. My concern is different. It is not with truth in some philosophical sense, but with the ways in which systems of truth are established, the ways in which true statements are produced and evaluated, with the 'apparatus' of truth – the concepts, rules, authorities, procedures, methods and techniques through which truths are realized. My concern is with the new regimes of truth installed by the knowledge of subjectivity, the new ways of saying plausible things about other human beings and ourselves, the new dispensation of those who can speak the truth and those who are subject to it, the new ways for thinking about what might be done to them and to us.

Socio-critique implies that the psychological sciences and their practitioners are socially effective to the extent that they participate in a domination of the subjectivity of individuals. Subjectivity, here, appears as an essential datum; societies are to be evaluated according to the extent to which they repress it or respect it. I would like to pose the question the other way round: How has subjectivity itself become, in its different guises and conceptions, the measure of political systems and power relations? The relations between power and subjectivity are, from this perspective, not confined to those of the constraint or repression of the freedom of the individual. Indeed, the distinctive features of the modern knowledge and expertise of the psyche have to do with their role in the stimulation of subjectivity, promoting self-inspection and self-consciousness, shaping desires, seeking to maximize intellectual capacities. They are fundamental to the production of individuals 'free to choose', whose lives become worthwhile to the extent that they are imbued with subjective feelings of meaningful pleasure.[3]

Socio-critique views psychological knowledge and techniques as supporting power relations. Perhaps they do, but their role is more fundamental than this implies. For this way of thinking fails to capture the new effects they produce, the novelty of the connections they establish between the aspirations of authorities and the projects of individual lives. Hence their role is much more that the legitimation of power. They forge new alignments between the rationales and techniques of power and the values and ethics of democratic societies.

Socio-critique tends to suggest that the origins and success of this knowledge and techniques can be explained in terms of the functions they serve for the state. I see matters rather differently. Instead of speaking in terms of the state, I would prefer to talk in terms of 'government'. Government, in the sense in which I use the term, refers neither to the actions of a calculating political subject, nor to the operations of bureaucratic mechanisms and personnel. It describes, rather, a certain way of striving to reach social and political ends by acting in a calculated manner upon the forces, activities and relations of the individuals that constitute a population.[4] During the nineteenth and twentieth centuries, the national territories of Europe and North America have become criss-crossed by programmes for the management and reconstruction of social life in order to produce security for property and wealth, profitability and efficiency of production, public virtue, tranquillity and even happiness. And subjectivity has become a vital resource in the managing of the affairs of the nation.

Governmentality, as Michel Foucault has termed it, has become the common ground of all our modern forms of political rationality, insofar as they construe the tasks of rulers in terms of a calculated supervision and maximization of the forces of society. Governmentality is 'the ensemble formed by the institutions, procedures, analyses and reflections, the calculations and tactics, that allow the exercise of this very specific albeit complex form of power, which has as its target population'.[5] For all systems of rule in the west since about the eighteenth century, the population has appeared as the terrain of government *par excellence*. Not the exercise of sovereignty – though this still plays its part. Nor the management of the life of the nation as if it were a family, though the family itself is a vital instrument of rule, but the regulation of the processes proper to the population, the laws that modulate its wealth, health, longevity, and its capacity to wage wars and to engage in labour and so forth. Rather than the state extending its sway throughout society by means of an extension of its control apparatus, then, we need to think in terms of the 'governmentalization of the state' – a transformation of the rationalities and technologies for the exercise of political rule.

With the entry of the population into political thought, rule takes as its object such phenomena as the numbers of subjects, their ages, their longevity, their sicknesses and types of death, their habits and vices, their rates of reproduction. The actions and calculations of authorities are directed towards new tasks: how to maximize the forces of the population and each individual within it, how to minimize their troubles, how to organize them in the most efficacious manner. The birth and history of the knowledges of subjectivity and intersubjectivity are intrinsically bound up with programmes which, in order to govern subjects, have found that they need to know them. The questions posed by governmentality come to mark out the territory on which the psychological sciences, their conceptual systems, their technical inventions, modes of explanation and forms of expertise will come to play a key role.

Two features of government are of particular significance in understanding the part that these sciences have played in linking subjective and intersubjective life to systems of political power. The first is that government is dependent upon knowledge. On the one hand, to govern a population one needs to isolate it as a sector of reality, to identify certain characteristics and processes proper to it, to make its features notable, speakable, writable, to account for them according to certain explanatory schemes. Government thus depends upon the production, circulation, organization, and authorization of truths that incarnate what is to be governed, which make it thinkable, calculable, and practicable.

On the other hand, governing a population requires knowledge of a different sort. To make calculations about a population necessitates the highlighting of certain features of that population as the raw material of calculation, and requires information about them. Knowledge here takes a very physical form; it requires the transcription of such phenomena as a birth, a death, a marriage, an illness, the number of persons living in this or that house, their types of work, their diet, wealth or poverty, into material upon which political calculation can work. Calculation, that is to say, depends upon processes of 'inscription', which translate the world into material traces: written reports, drawings, maps, charts and, pre-eminently, numbers.[6]

The invention of programmes of government depended upon and demanded an 'avalanche of printed numbers', which rendered the population calculable by turning it into inscriptions that were durable and transportable, that could be accumulated in the offices of officials, that could be added, subtracted, compared, and contrasted. The term given to these practices of inscription was 'statistics'. From the seventeenth, through the eighteenth and the nineteenth centuries, statistics – the science of state – began to transcribe the attributes of the population into a form in which they could enter into the calculations of rulers. Persons in the land, their ages, their places and forms of habitation, their employment, their births, illnesses, and deaths – all these were noted and transcribed. They were turned into figures, and collected together at central points; the unruly population was rendered into a form in which it could be used in political arguments and administrative decisions.

The transformation of the population into numbers that could be utilized in political and administrative debates and calculations was to be extended, in the nineteenth century, into new realms. The statistical societies in Britain were to compile charts and tables of domestic arrangements, types of employment, diet, and degrees of poverty and want.[7] And moral topographies of the population were to be constructed, mapping pauperism, delinquency, crime, and insanity across space and time and drawing all sorts of conclusions about changing rates of pathology, their causes and the measures needed to ameliorate them. The capacities of subjects were becoming pertinent to and available for government in a new way.

The dependence of government upon knowledge, in these two senses, enables us to appreciate the role that psychology, psychiatry, and the other 'psy' sciences have played within the systems of power in which human subjects have become caught up. The conceptual systems devised within the 'human' sciences, the languages of analysis and explanation that they invented, the ways of speaking about human conduct that they constituted, have provided the means whereby human subjectivity and intersubjectivity could enter the calculations of the authorities. On the one hand, subjective features of human life can become elements within understandings of the economy, the organization, the prison, the school, the factory and the labour market. On the other, the human psyche itself has become a possible domain for systematic government in the pursuit of sociopolitical ends. Educate, cure, reform, punish – these are old imperatives no doubt. But the new vocabularies provided by the sciences of the psyche enable the aspirations of government to be articulated in terms of the knowledgeable management of the depths of the human soul.

The psychological sciences played another key role, for they provided the means for the inscription of the properties, energies, and capacities of the human soul. They enabled human powers to be transformed into material that could provide the basis for calculation. The examination formed the model for all psychological inscription devices.[8] The examination combined the exercise of surveillance, the application of normalizing judgement and the technique of material inscription to produce calculable traces of individuality. The examining mechanisms of the psychological sciences – of which the psychiatric diagnosis and the intelligence test are two paradigms – each provided a mechanism for rendering subjectivity into thought as a calculable force. The examination not only makes human individuality visible, it locates it in a web of writing, transcribing attributes and their variations into codified forms, enabling them to be accumulated, summated, averaged and normalized – in short, documented. Such a documentation of the psyche enabled the elements of any individual life that were pertinent to the authorities to be assembled into a dossier, enshrined in an archive, or transmitted to a central place where the traces of individuals can be compared, evaluated, and judged. Traces can be amalgamated into a knowledge of the psychological characteristics of the population as a whole, which can in turn be utilized to calibrate the individual in relation to that population. Psychological inscriptions of individuality enable government to operate upon subjectivity. The psychological assessment is not merely a moment in an epistemological project, an episode in the history of knowledge: in rendering subjectivity calculable it makes persons amenable to having things done to them – and doing things to themselves – in the name of their subjective capacities.

Innovations in knowledge have thus been fundamental to the processes by which the human subject has entered into the webs of government. New languages have been invented for speaking about human subjectivity and its political pertinence, new conceptual systems have been formulated for calculating human capacities and conduct, and new devices have been constructed for inscribing and calibrating the human psyche and identifying its pathologies and normalities. These ways of knowing have made it possible to assemble 'human technologies': ensembles of forces, mechanisms, and relationships that enable action from a centre of calculation – a government department, a manager's office, a war room – upon the subjective lives of men, women, and children.[9]

Human technologies involve the calculated organization of human forces and capacities, together with other forces – natural, biological, mechanical – and artefacts – machines, weapons – into functioning networks of power. Within such a composition, elements are brought together that might appear, at first sight, to belong to different orders of reality: architectural designs, equipment and technical devices, professionals, bureaucracies, methods of calculation, inscriptions, reformatory procedures and the like. Thus theoretical knowledge renders the soul thinkable in terms of a psychology, an intelligence, a personality, and hence enables certain types of action to be linked to certain types of effect. Techniques, from the layout of buildings to the structure of timetables, organize humans in space and time in order to achieve certain outcomes. Relations of hierarchy, from age to educational qualifications and accreditation, locate individuals in chains of allegiance and dependency, empowering some to direct others and obliging others to comply. Procedures of motivation, from moral injunction to payment systems, direct the conduct of children, workers or soldiers to certain ends. Mechanisms of reformation and therapy provide the means whereby self-regulatory techniques may be reshaped according to the principles of psychological theory. As networks form, as relays, translations and connections couple political aspirations with modes of action upon persons, technologies of subjectivity are established that enable strategies of power to infiltrate the interstices of the human soul.

Such ramifying technologies of subjectivity have had radical consequences for economic life, social existence and political culture. But this does not require us to locate their origin or principles of explanation in the state or to view these events as the implementation of a rationally invented and coherent programme to secure class domination. As Michel Foucault has suggested, we need to install chance in its rightful place in history. Innovations have frequently been made in order to cope, not with grand threats to the political order, but with local, petty and even marginal problems. Programmes for enhancing or changing the ways in which authorities should think about or deal with this or that trouble have sometimes issued from the central political apparatus, but more characteristically they have been formulated by other forces and alliances: clergymen, philanthropists, doctors, policemen, lawyers, judges, psychiatrists, criminologists, feminists, social workers, academics, researchers, bosses, workers, parents. Effecting these programmes has sometimes involved legislation, and sometimes entailed setting up new branches of the political apparatus, but it has also been the work of charities, foundations, trusts, employers' organizations, trades unions, churches, or professional bodies. The innovations made have sometimes arisen from radically new inventions, but at other times they have involved the ad hoc utilization, combination, and extension of existing explanatory frameworks and techniques. Sporadic innovations like these have often come to nothing, failed or been abandoned or outflanked. Others have flourished, spread to other locales and problems, and established themselves as lasting and stable networks of thought and action. And out of these small histories, a larger pattern has taken shape in whose web we all, modern men and women, have become entangled.

Thus the psychological sciences are intimately bound up with programmes, calculations, and techniques for the government of the soul. The twentieth century development of the psychological sciences has opened up new dimensions for our thought. Simultaneously, it has made possible new techniques of structuring our reality to produce the phenomena and effects that can now be imagined. The translation of the human psyche into the sphere of knowledge and the ambit of technology makes it possible to govern subjectivity according to norms and criteria that ground their authority in an esoteric but objective knowledge.

Psychological knowledges certainly addressed problems that arose in specific social circumstances, but these circumstances did not, themselves, predestine or determine the types of solutions they proposed. Conceptual systems, explanatory philosophies, and conventions of evidence and proof exerted their own effects, engaging with and transforming the initial problems and questions, feeding back their languages of classification, discussion, and evaluation into social debate. Of course, as so many commentators have recognized, the discipline of psychology is far from homogeneous: it is riven by competing schools and fuelled by rivalry between incompatible explanatory models, tacitly or explicitly founded upon opposed philosophical bases. This diversity and heterogeneity of psychology has been one of the keys to its continued inventiveness at the conceptual level and to its wide-ranging social applicability. Far from undermining its truth claims, it has allowed a fruitful differentiation in its points of application, enabling it to operate with a diversity of contexts and strategies for the government of subjectivity – different ways of articulating social power with the human soul.

The expertise of subjectivity has become fundamental to our contemporary ways of being governed and of governing ourselves. This is not because experts collude with the state in trapping, controlling and conditioning subjects. Liberal democratic polities place limits upon direct coercive interventions into individual lives by the power of the state; government of subjectivity thus demands that authorities act upon the choices, wishes, values, and conduct of the individual in an indirect manner. Expertise provides this essential distance between the formal apparatus of laws, courts, and police and the shaping of the activities of citizens. It achieves its effects not through the threat of violence or constraint, but by way of the persuasion inherent in its truths, the anxieties stimulated by its norms, and the attraction exercised by the images of life and self it offers to us.

The citizens of a liberal democracy are to regulate themselves; government mechanisms construe them as active participants in their lives. No longer is the political subject thought to be motivated merely by a calculus of pleasures and pains. No longer is the individual, as far as the authorities are concerned, merely the possessor of physical capacities to be organized and dominated through the inculcation of moral standards and behavioural habits. Whether it be in the home or in the army or factory, the citizen is actively thinking, wanting, feeling and doing, relating to others in terms of these psychological forces and affected by the relations that others have with them. Such a citizen subject is not to be dominated in the interests of power, but to be educated and solicited into a kind of alliance between personal objectives and ambitions and institutionally or socially prized goals or activities. Citizens shape their lives through the choices they make about family life, work, leisure, lifestyle, and personality and its expression. Government works by 'acting at a distance' upon these choices, forging a symmetry between the attempts of individuals to make life worthwhile for themselves, and the political values of consumption, profitability, efficiency, and social order. Contemporary government, that is to say, operates through the delicate and minute infiltration of the ambitions of regulation into the very interior of our existence and experience as subjects.

Technologies of subjectivity thus exist in a kind of symbiotic relationship with what one might term 'techniques of the self': the ways in which we are enabled, by means of the languages, criteria, and techniques offered to us, to act upon our bodies, souls, thoughts, and conduct in order to achieve happiness, wisdom, health, and fulfilment.[10]

Through self-inspection, self-problematization, self-monitoring, and confession, we evaluate ourselves according to the criteria provided for us by others. Through self-reformation, therapy, techniques of body alteration, and the calculated reshaping of speech and emotion, we adjust ourselves by means of the techniques propounded by the experts of the soul. The government of the soul depends upon our recognition of ourselves as ideally and potentially certain sorts of person, the unease generated by a normative judgement of what we are and could become, and the incitement offered to overcome this discrepancy by following the advice of experts in the management of the self.

The irony is that we believe, in making our subjectivity the principle of our personal lives, our ethical systems, and our political evaluations, that we are, freely, choosing our freedom. If the studies that follow have one underlying aim, it is to contribute to the writing of the genealogy of that freedom.

Part one

People at War

Chapter one

The Psychology of War

All war, no doubt, is fought out in the minds of the combatants as well as across their flesh and their territory. In World War II this battle for the mind was to include not only soldiers but civilians. It was to become the province of special organizations, expertise, and techniques. Warfare produced new ways of thinking about the functioning of organizations in terms of 'human engineering'; the rational utilization of the human factor in the management of institutions and society appeared an urgent and real possibility. Warfare also gave rise to new ways of construing institutional life in terms of 'human relations' and 'the group'. Emotional and personal relations between individuals became central to psychological theory and expertise. Ways of calibrating psychological factors were invented, such as 'personality' and 'attitude', producing new ways of calculating the relations between human subjectivity and administrative objectives, not only in the military, but also in the factory, the family, and the population at large. In the process, new relationships were established between psychologists, psychiatrists, anthropologists, and sociologists, and new ground established upon which they would collaborate. The conceptual and practical innovations that were made, the technologies that were invented, and the experts who used and understood them, were to have a major impact upon the post-war world.[1]

It is widely accepted that the experience of war led to fundamental changes in post-war Britain, stimulating an expansion of the state machinery and economic planning and the revamping of social policies that is associated with the reforms of 1945.[2] Some authors, however, have expressed scepticism as to whether these changes were in any meaningful sense a *result* of the wartime events, arguing that they came about in response to more fundamental processes of social development; the war might have crystallized these, but it did not initiate them.[3] Most agree, however, that the war did at least provoke technological innovation and the deployment of scientific resources for social and national objectives. Science and technology are usually understood, in this context, to signify *natural* science and *physical* engineering.[4] But the transformations in the social role of the *human* sciences, and the implications of the wartime experience for *human* engineering, were at least as significant. Their impact on our everyday lives may have been even more profound.

Discussion of warfare in psychological terms is now routine: the psychological causes of war, the psychology of conflict and of fighting, the effects of warfare upon the psychological states of combatants, survivors of concentration camps and civilians, and the psychological consequences of war for the development of culture.[5] In a different vein, Peter Watson's study of 'the military uses and abuses of psychology' uncovered an enormous and hidden continent of military psychology, mainly developed since the end of World War II, and concentrated for the western bloc in Fort Bragg in North Carolina, which is the base for the US Army's special warfare school. He found that

> Everything you could think of – from the psychology of the cell structure of underground insurgencies to the psychological effects of weapons, from the selection of men to work behind enemy lines to the ways to induce defection, from the way to stop men chickening out of battle to how to avoid being brainwashed, from tests to select code-breakers to the use of ghosts to harry tribal peasants – had been investigated in remorseless detail and the relevant psychological research drained of any military application it might have.[6]

Watson seeks to show how some of these developments might make war more likely, how others are problematic because they involve deception of or harm to their subjects, how others involve the dehumanization of the enemy or the debrutalization of killing, and, in general, how free and open debate of the political and ethical implications of military psychology is prevented by obsessive secrecy.

No one can doubt the significance of such questions. My concern with the relations of psychology and warfare is, however, rather different. It is not so much with how psychology altered the nature of warfare, but how, through its involvement in World War II, the nature of psychology and its relation with social life were themselves altered, how the experience of war has transformed our ways of thinking about and intervening in the organization of human beings within military and non-military spheres alike.

These transformations were not merely a product of personal biographies. Nonetheless, a glance through the volumes of *A History of Psychology in Autobiography* reveals the extent to which so many of the major figures of post-war psychology were involved in war work.[7] As far as America is concerned, the relationships range from the bizarre to the fundamental. B.F. Skinner, for example, received a defence grant in 1944 for a project that attempted to train pigeons to guide missiles onto targets; Jerome Bruner worked in the unit monitoring foreign broadcasts to provide information on enemy intentions and morale.[8] Of the figures who participated in the far-reaching work of the post-war Department of Social Relations at Harvard University, Gordon Allport was centrally involved in the study of civilian morale, Samuel Stouffer spearheaded research into the attitudes of the American soldier, Henry Murray directed the assessment staff of the Office of Strategic Services and Clyde Klukhohn was co-director of the Foreign Morale Analysis Division in Washington.[9]

As for Britain, Donald Broadbent, Philip Vernon, and Hans Eysenck are among the most influential of the post-war psychologists whose early career was shaped by the tasks of 'psychological warfare' in its broadest sense. Aubrey Lewis, Tom Main, Maxwell Jones and other key figures in the movement for a new 'social psychiatry' that took off after the war, integrating themes from social psychology, psychiatry and psychoanalysis, were similarly involved with the mental problems of warfare.[10]

So too were those who reshaped the Tavistock Clinic and founded the Tavistock Institute of Human Relations immediately after the war: the intellectual formation and social vocation of John Bowlby, J.R. Rees, Henry Dicks, Elliot Jaques and many others were forged in the study of war and its consequences. The post-war transformations in the rationales and technologies for the government of the human soul are impossible to understand without recognizing the ways in which the experience of warfare transformed the conceptual apparatus, practical techniques, and professional aspirations of those involved.

This experience was split into a number of relatively distinct areas – selection and training of military personnel, the attitudes of warriors, morale on the home front, 'sykewar', the problems of wartime industrial production, the neurotic soldier, the returning serviceman. But two themes run across them all: the need to systematically utilize the human factor and the psychology of the group. In order to appreciate the novelty of these themes, it is necessary to relate them to the previous role of psychology in warfare.

Prior to the outbreak of World War II, the involvement of the professionals of psy with the problems of warfare in Britain and the United States was limited. In World War I two issues had emerged that were of considerable significance. The first was the use of intelligence tests in the screening of recruits. The prehistory of intelligence testing in the United States has been widely discussed, as has its relations with the eugenics movement and its racist bases and implications.[11] Proponents of the military use of intelligence testing argued that it could perform three crucial tasks: segregating and eliminating the mentally incompetent; classifying men according to mental ability; selecting competent men for responsible positions.[12] By the end of the war they appeared to have achieved considerable success. The famous alpha and beta group tests of intelligence had been developed – the former required ability to read, the latter was nonverbal – and by 1918 their use had been extended to the whole army. In the course of the war tests were administered to some 1,750,000 recruits; over 7,800 were recommended for discharge because of mental inferiority and over 19,000 recommended for either labour or development battalions. Robert Yerkes, president of the American Psychological Association at the outbreak of war and a leading figure in the eugenics movement, who had made the initial proposal for the testing programme, claimed that this demonstrated the feasibility of large-scale testing, that it could produce a huge increase in the efficiency of large organizations and save millions of dollars.

Franz Samelson provides a rather more sober evaluation of the role of psychology in the US military in World War I.[13] He argues that psychologists' recommendations were a relatively small factor in rates of rejection and discharge, or in decisions as to allocation. Other criteria based on military judgement appear to have been more influential, and there was considerable scepticism about the utility of the tests. This was manifested in, and reinforced by, the weak strategic position of the mental testers themselves, who were located neither in the Medical Corps nor in the US Adjutant General's Office, but in the Sanitary Corps. And after the armistice the evaluation of psychology in the army was unenthusiastic. It was asserted that, whatever the contribution that the military had made to science, all that was required for military purposes was a simple screening test for the rejection of the mentally unfit, which need not be administered by skilled psychologists. In 1919 the US War Department abolished the psychological service, and with it, concludes Samelson, psychological work by and large disappeared from the army.

A far more significant contribution of psychology than the intelligence test, according to Samelson, was a development that appears both mundane and bureaucratic – the introduction of a specialized personnel system. Walter D. Scott, who was responsible for the rationalization of the personnel system, received the Distinguished Service Medal after the war. Under his direction, tables of occupational requirements for different units were constructed and the specialist skills of individuals were registered. The system thus had the capacity to link the one with the other and to distribute the skilled specialists in a systematic and rational manner to the places where they were required.

Samelson remarks wryly, 'A cynic might even say that the psychologists' greatest contribution to the war effort was the introduction of a system of colour-coded celluloid tabs indicating occupational skills on the army's personnel cards.'[14] But the significance of such an achievement should not be minimized. One of the major contributions of the psychological sciences to our modernity has been the invention of techniques that make individual differences and capacities visible, through devising means whereby they can be inscribed or notated in legible forms. The routine inscription of personal capacities into documentation enables the individual to become simultaneously calculable – individual capacities can be thought about and planned into the running of organizational life – and practicable – individuals can be distributed and allocated in such a way as to make use of their capacities to minimize malfunctioning of the institutional machinery and to maximize its efficiency or profitability. In this sense coloured celluloid tabs and intelligence test results are equivalent: both render the human individual into the field of knowledge and the scope of management of institutional life. Irrespective of the fate of psychological testing itself, the systematic management of the human factor in military life was now on the agenda.[15]

In Britain there was no such mass psychological testing of recruits to the armed forces in World War I. A small grant aided committee was appointed by the psychological sub-section of the British Association to consider what assistance psychologists could give in war time, and there were attempts to develop tests for specific capacities such as night vision in pilots or for the selection of other specialist occupations.[16] Such military applications came to little in the inter-war years. It was in Germany that the full scale psychologization of warfare appeared to be a possibility. Modelling itself on the US Committee for Psychology set up by the National Research Council in 1917 when the United States entered the war, in the 1920s and 1930s a comprehensive apparatus of military psychology was established. By 1936 there was a central laboratory in the War Ministry, staffed by over eighty psychologists, under whose direction worked psychological laboratories attached to every army corps. Indeed, while within the German universities there was a respectable academic psychology, this remained very much under the aegis of philosophy; it has been suggested that psychology scarcely existed as an autonomous discipline in Germany until the Wehrmacht provided a specific occupational demand.[17]

Max Simmonheit, who Burt referred to as 'the doyen of military psychology in Germany', described the tasks of military psychology as sixfold: job analysis and adaptation of machinery and equipment, characterology and personnel selection, training, morale, propaganda and psychology of foreign nations, and the conduct of war.[18] The major activity of these psychologists was, however, the analysis of character or psychological diagnosis. Increasingly the techniques used shifted, from standardized tests favoured in Britain and the United States to diagnoses of character more in keeping with the doctrines of Nazism. Yet the military status of psychologists was to be short lived. Whether because of conflicts with the judgements of the military, or because of disputes over particular officer candidates favoured by Goering and von Rundstedt but not by the psychologists, the growth of German military psychology suffered a sudden reverse. All psychological sections in the German army and air force were dissolved by an order of the high command in December 1941; all relevant documents were recalled and destroyed; the psychologists were either called up for military service or found other occupations.[19] But despite its fate the pre-war machinery of German psychology was to serve as something of an example for the British and Americans, regularly invoked by the advocates of the expertise of the psyche.

If the psychologization of recruitment and personnel allocation had a rather difficult time in Britain and the United States prior to World War II, there was another area of warfare where psychological developments did not suffer the same setback.[20] The first few months of World War I saw an alarming number of casualties suffering not from obvious physical injuries but from a condition generally termed 'shell shock'. Whatever the difficulties in interpreting the statistics, it was estimated by December 1914 that 7 to 10 per cent of officer casualties and 3 to 4 per cent of casualties from other ranks came into this category. Special hospitals were set up for the treatment of shell-shock cases, and some estimates put the number of those discharged from active service on the grounds of shell-shock as high as 200,000.[21] Be that as it may, the number of cases of shell-shock over the war as a whole was officially estimated at 80,000 and some 65,000 ex-servicemen were still receiving disability pensions for shell-shock by 1921.

As far as psychiatry was concerned, the experience of shell-shock had profound effects. Numerous young doctors were exposed to work with individuals with well developed psychiatric symptoms, yet whose background was apparently normal. Further, good results were claimed by the use of psychotherapeutic techniques broadly derived from the work of Freud and Janet, ranging from rational re-education, through persuasion, suggestion and hypnosis to a kind of psychoanalysis. This work and its success led in two directions.[22] In the first, it appeared to support a dynamic conception of psychological processes, with such characteristics as an unconscious and repression, but to disprove the Freudian argument for a specific sexual aetiology of mental disturbance; this tended to be replaced with a theory of multiple instincts that came into conflict with one another because of contradictory social pressures. The latter appeared to be evidence for the social significance of minor mental disorders, and for their treatability, thus challenging the previous focus upon gross insanity requiring prolonged incarceration, mainly considered to be of organic origin and untreatable. The mental hygiene movement was to take up this cause, stressing the importance of such 'functional' nerve disorders and their role in social problems from crime to industrial inefficiency, and seeking to promote mental health and welfare by early intervention, out patient treatment and prophylactic measures.[23]

In this seemingly peripheral area of concern, a new way of conceiving of the relation between madness and society was being born. Within this new conception, it would not be a question of organic predispositions, exciting causes, and virtually incurable lapses into insanity. Madness was now thought of in the terms of social hygiene. Mental health could be maintained by proper adjustment of the conditions of life and work; poor mental hygiene and stress could promote neurosis in large numbers of people. The effects were not those of social scandal and florid symptomatology, but unhappiness, inefficiency, incompetence, maladaptation, and antisocial conduct. The effects of this on institutional efficiency were considerable; skilled advice could prevent inefficiency, restore the maladjusted, and promote efficiency and contentment. In the inter-war years these ways of thinking and acting proliferated, although not within the military machinery itself. But, as we shall see, as hostilities became conceivable, possible and then inevitable during the 1930s, the psychiatric experiences of World War I were extrapolated into the future, with dire predictions as to the effects of such functional nerve disorders upon the efficiency of the fighting forces and upon the mental health and morale of military and civilian alike. Winning the war was to require a concerted attempt to understand and govern the subjectivity of the citizen.

Chapter two

The Government of Morale

For the first time in history a government has officially recognized that the state of public opinion is as important an index of the health of the community as a full anamnesis in the case of individual illness...the Ministry of Information has established that group feeling is a medico-psychological concern and that it calls for instruments of precision in diagnosis.[1]

Edward Glover, 1940

Edward Glover, director of the London Clinic of Psychoanalysis and of the Institute for the Treatment of Delinquency, may have announced the birth of social psychiatry in the *Lancet* of August 1940 in florid language. But his enthusiasm was part of a much wider analysis, which saw winning the war as highly dependent upon the success of the authorities in discovering and regulating the mental states and subjective capacities and orientations of the population – both in and out of uniform, both that of the allies and that of the enemy. If one word came to stand for this concern, a word that 'haunted the politicians, the civil servants and the generals', it was 'morale'.[2]

It was, of course, no new thing for governments to be concerned with 'the condition of the people'; with debating it, monitoring it, calculating its social, industrial and military consequences, seeking to alter it by more or less conscious political action.[3] The extension of the apparatus of government in the late nineteenth and early twentieth centuries should be understood in terms of the rise of a political rationality conceived in these terms. In the early decades of the twentieth century, government was extended to the petty details of personal life. The new social medicine sought to produce a healthy and efficient population through engaging individuals in a hygienic programme for managing themselves and their relations with others, educating them in the detailed techniques of body maintenance, sanitation, diet, child rearing, and so forth, and monitoring health through health visitors and school inspections, as well as through clinics for tuberculosis, venereal diseases, and child welfare.[4]

The experience of shell-shock during World War I was, as we have seen, a forceful stimulus for the government to extrapolate this programme of the health of the population to the hygiene and welfare of the mind via the concepts of neurosis and functional nerve disorder. Insanity, crime, and delinquency, as well as industrial and other social inefficiency were construed as indices of the mental hygiene of the population. Such social ills did not result from personal evil, immoral character or degenerate constitutions inherited down a family line. Rather, they resulted from, or at least were precipitated by, poor mental hygiene in the family and in society at large. The implication was that psychiatrists should not simply concentrate upon major insanities; they should focus instead upon the minor troubles of the mind. These were not only the signs and precursors of major problems to come, they also led to all sorts of personal unhappiness and inefficiency, and were susceptible to early treatment. As the Royal Commission of 1926 put it, the problem of insanity was essentially a public health problem to be dealt with on public health lines.[5]

A new kind of scrutiny was being applied to the mental state of the population, and this mental state was being linked to the objectives of government in a new way. Morale signalled an extension of this concern to a wider and more complex subjective territory. Morale was a powerfully mobile notion, linking up the psychiatric register, the notion of public opinion, the control of news and propaganda, public support for civilian and military authorities, the consequences of policy changes in army life, and much more. The first clear focus of such concern was the prospect of air war – or rather of its consequences.[6] As early as 1934, Churchill was bringing these to the attention of the House of Commons:

> No less formidable...than these material effects are the reactions which will be produced in the mind of the civilian population. We must expect that, under the pressure of continuous air attack upon London, at least 3,000,000 or 4,000,000 people would be driven out into the open country around the metropolis. This vast mass of human beings, numerically far larger than any armies which have been fed and moved in war, without shelter and without food, without sanitation and without special provision for the maintenance of order, would confront the Government of the day with an administrative problem of the first magnitude, and would certainly absorb the energies of our small Army and our Territorial Force. Problems of this kind have never been faced before, and although there is no need to exaggerate them, neither, on the other

hand, is there any need to shrink from facing the immense, unprecedented, difficulties which they involve.[7]

These consequences of air attack were not merely an accidental by-product of raids upon targets of military or industrial significance. The prospect, according to Titmuss, was of 'a war to be conducted by the enemy first and foremost upon the unorganized, un-uniformed and undisciplined section of the nation with the object of breaking its morale to the point of surrender'.[8] From 1924 onwards it was accepted almost as a matter of course that widespread panic and neurosis would ensue among civilians as a consequence of air war. This was based upon little more than some limited reports on the behaviour of civilians under air attack in World War I. Nonetheless, it informed the assumptions of planning committees throughout the rest of the 1920s and 1930s; they prepared themselves for the task of controlling mass exodus from the cities and mass panic among the population.

Mental health professionals supported and intensified this belief. The report prepared by leading psychiatrists from London teaching hospitals and clinics, which was presented to the Ministry of Health in 1938, encapsulated the dominant expert view. Psychiatric casualties of air raids would, it seemed, exceed physical casualties by three to one: there would be some 3 million to 4 million cases of acute panic, hysteria, and other neurotic conditions during the first six months of air attack. A complex organization must be set up; it should be able to provide immediate treatment in bombed areas, twenty-four-hour out-patient clinics on the outskirts of cities, special hospitals, camps and work settlements in safer areas, mobile teams of psychiatrists and mobile child guidance clinics.[9]

Psychiatrists and psychologists schooled in psychodynamic theory compared the position of the civilian in war unfavourably with that of the soldier. While for the latter training and discipline acted as checks upon the desire for self-preservation, the former were isolated, unattached, unorganized and without such checks. Civilians could not be expected to suppress their urge for self-preservation in continuing their mundane and inglorious labour. As Hugh Crichton Miller put it, 'there is a real danger that [the civilian] will seek, not security, but infantile security'.[10]

These anxieties proved to be unfounded.[11] The air raids of 1940–41 actually led to a decrease in attendances at mental hospitals and clinics. There appeared to be a fall in drunkenness and disorderly behaviour in public places, though juvenile delinquency did increase. There was no evidence of any significant increase in neurotic illness or mental disorder in Britain during the war. It was bed-wetting by children, rather than mass public hysteria and panic, which was provoked; a problem made visible by, and thought to be caused by, the evacuation of children and their separation from their families. This would be a theme that would be of some significance for psychology in the immediate aftermath of the war.[12]

But the anxiety about the possible epidemic of neurosis produced its own consequences. A sustained effort was made to chart the neurotic topography of the population. Aubrey Lewis, an early promoter of social psychiatry, collected and analyzed statistics for the early war years in a report for the Medical Research Council published in the *Lancet* in August 1942. Carlos Blacker gathered together even more statistics in his *Neurosis and the Mental Health Services*, published in 1946. Philip Vernon surveyed psychologists, psychiatrists and doctors to collate their experiences of the effects of bombing. C.W. Emmens examined the factors influencing morale in the bombed cities for the Research and Experiments Branch of the Ministry of Home Security, and the Ministry of Health also sought to draw conclusions from the relationship between admission to special hospitals and air raids. The mental state of the population was beginning to be translated into a calculable form: inscribed, documented, and turned into statistics, graphs, charts, and tables that could be pored over in political deliberations and administrative initiatives.[13]

Studies of reactions to air war suggested that practical organizational measures, rather than psychiatric services, were most useful in promoting the capacity to adjust. It might appear to be self-evident that good and clear information should be provided as to what to do and where to go, that food, shelter, and social services should be equitably distributed, and so forth. But the desirability of these arrangements was now not merely a matter of fairness and efficiency. They were also desirable because they furthered a psychological objective. Additionally, some psychologists argued that the lack of panic and neurosis could be explained if one reversed the pre-war analysis made by the experts. War could offset the circumstances that provoked the onset of neurosis, it relieved the sense of inferiority and failure consequent upon the normal unhappiness of civilian life, marriage, employment, unemployment, and so forth. Each individual was now a wanted, contributing member of a cohesive society.[14] Social solidarity and psychological relations were becoming the central terms in accounting for mental health. Even the disproof of a psychiatric prediction could enhance another type of psychiatric explanation.

The issue of civilian response to air raids was but the most specific of a range of wartime programmes for the government of morale, whose key administrative centre was the Ministry of Information. Immediately after the German invasion of Poland in September 1939, it was the Home Publicity Division of the Ministry of Information that met to discuss possible panic from air raids.[15] The Ministry of Information had been set up following a recommendation of a subcommittee of the Committee of Imperial Defence in 1936 to present the national case to the public at home and abroad in time of war. Its career was a chequered one – ridiculed and accused of inefficiency in its early years, it settled into a more workmanlike but lower key operation after Brendan Bracken succeeded Lord Macmillan and John Reith as Minister of Information in July 1941.

It would be misleading, however, to think that the existence and operation of this ministry inaugurated a wholesale programme for the psychological management of the civilian population. Indeed the relations of professional psychologists, and of psychological concepts, theories, or methods, to morale work on the home front was rather limited. In the inter-war period and the early years of the war, psychologists were writing about morale, and some of their concepts entered into the policies of the ministry, penetrating into general lines of thought of officials, affecting the language and interpretations provided by some of their informants and influencing the survey methods used to obtain information.[16] But few psychologists were professionally involved in morale work on the home front. The 'experts' called upon by the ministry were drawn, instead, from the ranks of the great and the good, or, on occasion, from advertising. The significance of the strategy of government for the fate of psychology was, if anything, the other way 'round – the emergence of subjectivity as a key concern of government offered a problem to psychology that it would later strive to claim for its own.

It was in the early years of the war, before Bracken took office in 1941, that the ministry sought to make morale governable. It utilized posters, handouts, and leaflets, usually of an exhortatory character: 'Freedom is in Peril – Defend it with all your Might'; 'Our Fighting Men Depend on You'. It held public meetings and wrote letters to the press. It engaged itself in a campaign to fight the destructive effects of rumour on morale. But while the psychology of rumour would be a central field of work in the later years of the war, especially in the United States, the campaign waged by the ministry owed little to the dominant psychoanalytic conceptions of the nature and effects of rumour.[17] For example, Tom Harrisson of Mass Observation argued that the most favourable condition for the origin and spread of rumour was dread without knowledge, and analyzed rumour in quasi-psychoanalytic terms. It was suggested that people unconsciously projected onto the fifth columnist the phantasy rumours that are produced from fear or despair to explain the facts or expectations of the moment. The ministry, however, took advice on its anti-rumour campaign from an advertising agency. The series of posters it produced sought to produce shame, guilt, and condemnation, rather than seeing rumour as arising from specifiable psychological conditions; they vilified those who speculated about the war or discussed rumours. The unfavourable public and political response to these posters helped to discredit the very idea of explicitly and directly trying to manage morale.

Yet however clumsy its operations, the ministry realized that, in order to govern morale by whatever means, one required information. Somehow the nebulous, ambiguous, and ill defined notion of the morale of the population had to be inscribed and transformed into information that could be transmitted to the centre, where it could be examined, evaluated, compared, and contrasted with other information and with data from earlier moments in the war, and used as the basis of calculation. How else was one to gauge what public concerns were, or how effective this or that campaign technique was?

Opinion testing by the government was not new, although it was not yet properly British. George Gallup's American Institute of Public Opinion was one paradigm for later mechanisms for transcribing 'public opinion' into political debate. Its significance seemed to be demonstrated when Gallup predicted Roosevelt's election victory in 1936. Public opinion, for Gallup, was not some supra-individual social conscience, but the outgrowth of the opinions of individuals, hence calculable by polling those opinions, aggregating them, and presenting them to government and public alike. The public opinion poll was a crucial new instrument for taking 'the pulse of democracy', establishing the vital two-way connection between citizens and their representatives.[18] In the inter-war years in the United States enthusiasts argued not only that the opinion and consent of the policy was a vital legitimating force for any system of rule, but that a direct link should be opened between public opinion and government policy which would supplement or even supplant the ballot box.[19] Earlier psychological conceptions of the mass psychology of the mob or the crowd as a potentially dangerous and irrational political force gave way to a notion of the populus as an aggregate of individuals with views and wishes that could be investigated by precise techniques and communicated to government by experts.[20]

The new science of democracy also drew upon a new way of thinking about individual will. No longer was the will merely an element in a speculative philosophical anthropology, it consisted in a number of specifiable and measurable attributes of individuals. Individuals were moved by 'attitudes' or 'sentiments', internal states that shaped the ways in which an individual apprehended and evaluated events and objects and directed them towards certain types of actions.[21] Attitudes thus bridged the internal world of the psyche and the external world of conduct; or rather, they enabled the latter to be made intelligible and predictable in terms of the former. The advantage of the notion of attitude was that it provided a language for talking about the internal determinants of conduct and a means for thinking out how these determinants could be charted. Hence the 'attitude survey' or 'morale survey' became a key device for making the subjective world of citizens, employees, voters, and so forth inscribable and calculable. The public will could be turned into numbers and charts that could be used in formulating arguments and strategies in the company, in the political party, in the army – indeed anywhere where individuals were to be governed 'by consent'.[22]

In Britain, opinion testing had developed since World War I from the ad hoc collation of views of civil servants and MPs into a relatively methodical system. This was based upon government departments and used techniques of social investigation and market research in addition to monitoring press reports and interpreting the data supplied by the networks of the Special Branch and the secret intelligence services. Middlemas argues that, over this period, the political elite superimposed a system of 'continuous contract' upon the traditional cycle of general elections and party warfare. He suggests that 'the fine measurement of opinion and its careful management by propaganda, together with the creation of a degree of mystification about the political process' achieved public submission to the dominant political ethic, encapsulated in such fictions as 'government objectives' and 'national interest'.[23] However that may be, the programme for the management of consent through the monitoring and channelling of opinion was greatly elaborated in the conditions of war.

The ministry utilized three main sources to turn morale into writing and make it legible. The first, and consistently most used, source of information was that derived from the investigations of the home intelligence section of the ministry. This section prepared regular and frequent reports based on a range of sources that reveal just how extensive was the link being forged between the need to govern and the need to know.[24] Information was gathered by regional staff from officials at shops, cinemas, transport organizations, and Citizens' Advice Bureaux. Bodies such as the Brewer's Society completed questionnaires. Data were obtained from the BBC Listeners' Research Unit, from officials of political parties, from police duty room reports passed on by the Home Office. And weekly reports were provided to the section from Postal and Telegraph Censorship, whose staff numbered 10,433 in May 1941, and who sometimes scrutinized up to 200,000 letters a week.

A further source of information that was used, despite some disquiet concerning its methods, was mass observation.[25] Mass Observation was able to supply regular reports on such subjects as the incidence of gas mask carrying, current rumours, the size of the shelter population, shopping habits, reactions to new films and the ministry's propaganda, and investigated particular events such as by-elections and conditions in recently raided towns.

A third source was the Wartime Social Survey. The planning of the survey was conducted through the London School of Economics, though it was placed under the auspices of the National Institute for Economic and Social Research. Its earliest intentions were to interview about 5,000 people per month as a representative sample of the population of Britain, and to obtain answers about 10 simple questions designed to test attitudes to the war situation, as well as to carry out more specific investigations of attitudes to particular issues. But these early attempts were attacked by psychologists, and criticized in press and Parliament as 'snooping'; the survey was only to continue in a less ambitious form. The explicit investigation of morale appeared not only technically difficult, but intrusive and un-British.

When Brendan Bracken became minister, in 1941, the role of the ministry altered. Morale propaganda and morale investigation per se were abandoned – morale, it was said, could be left to the good sense and natural resilience of the English. The ministry concentrated instead upon the management of news, and censorship, negotiating a relationship with the press about the form and timing of publicity of defeats, victories, plans, and so forth. It also sought to co-ordinate campaigns aimed, not at morale directly, but at purveying information of a practical and hygienic nature: 'Coughs and Sneezes Spread Diseases', 'Post Before Noon', and so forth.

This British history should be counterposed to American wartime enthusiasm for the scientific study and regulation of morale. By 1939 the US Department of Agriculture had established a public opinion research organization, under Rensis Likert. Likert was also active in the studies of enemy morale, and of the attitudes of American soldiers discussed below; his Likert scale was to become one of the principal devices for rendering 'attitude' inscribable and quantifiable. After the United States entered the war, the psychological study of morale really took off. The Society for the Psychological Study of Social Issues devoted its yearbook of 1942 to morale, the Committee for National Morale sponsored a study entitled *German Psychological Warfare*, published in 1942; the Harvard Seminar in Psychological Problems of Morale prepared worksheets that were widely circulated among government agencies, the Bureau of Intelligence of the Office of War Information made surveys for particular government agencies, as did the National Opinion Research Centre, the Office of Public Opinion Research, and commercial organizations like Gallup and Fortune. Floyd and Gordon Allport studied the effects of news and rumour on civilian morale. In light of such studies both government and private groups embarked on programmes for the maintenance of morale, especially among industrial workers, conceiving military power as dependent upon such phenomena as absenteeism, turn-over, conflict among workers, and the adjustment of minority groups.[26] The morale of the American civilian population had become the object of knowledge; the success of administrative decisions was from now on to be construed as dependent upon information about the public mind.

But while the British programme could not match this, it should not be thought that the new policy of the Ministry of Information after 1941 meant the end of the attempt to transform the petty details of the moral and psychological state of the population into information. Not only did monitoring continue through the Home Intelligence Section and mass observation, but the Wartime Social Survey was transformed into a more limited but precisely targeted set of enquiries, under the guidance of a respectable scientific advisory panel containing such notables as Seebohm Rowntree, Aubrey Lewis, A.M. Carr Saunders, Launcelot Hogben, F.C. Bartlett, and Cyril Burt. Using accredited methods of sampling, interviewing, and analysis, 101 surveys had been carried out by October 1944, involving 290,000 interviews on topics requested by other departments ranging from household methods of cooking food through methods of getting to work to coverage and effectiveness of publicity media.[27]

From being criticized by the psychologists, the survey now won their praise for its contribution to the war effort; it had made itself so much a part of the thinking of government that it was incorporated after the war into the Office of Population Census and Surveys.[28] The survey provided the means for translating the psychological state and well-being of the population into the calculations of government agencies. As McLaine puts it, 'Never before had government involved itself so intimately with the minutiae of British working class life.'[29] While Middlemas suggests a fundamental opposition between manipulative opinion management and popular democracy, this argument is tendentious.[30] For one can see here the birth of a new conception of democracy, one that recognizes the intimate link between knowledge and citizenship, and the key role of scientific investigation in providing the mediations between the two. This relationship, conceived as the cornerstone of modern, enlightened democratic government, was to be a fundamental principle for much post-war social psychology of opinion and attitudes, in both Britain and the United States.[31] On the one hand the public need to be given information in order to discharge the duties of citizenship; on the other hand the government needs to obtain information on the needs, wants and attitudes of the public, on its psychological as well as its physical state, in order to adjust its administrative methods and objectives and gain public co-operation. The citizen is an active element in the modern polity, no longer the passive recipient of instructions or injunctions, he or she is to be actively engaged in the maintenance of political order and social harmony. Information and happiness go together in the new science of government as much as in the old science of police.[32]

If diagnosis of public opinion was one side of the coin, propaganda was the other. Propaganda on the home front took a number of different forms. First, a particular image of the enemy was constructed. This had the aim of limiting the demoralizing effects of German victories and instilling the certainty of eventual German defeat. The techniques used were consistent with psychological advice, although McLaine suggests that, for the most part, the ministry studiously avoided consulting psychological experts.[33] Hate, it was argued, was a poor basis for raising morale; rather than hatred, the images purveyed of the Germans concentrated upon demonstrating the flaws in the national character, its weakness, rottenness, bully complex, vulnerability beneath the bluster, and so forth. This work was not only the focus of meetings and papers during the war, it would be followed in the post-war years by a number of sustained psychological projects to calibrate, document and explain national character.[34]

A more problematic issue concerned propaganda stressing the positive aims of the war. The Ministry of Information had recognized early in the war that there was a link between civilian morale and war aims or peace aims – the prospect of the Britain that would be built after victory and for which we were fighting. A War Aims Committee was set up, and numerous memoranda on the topic were produced, circulated, and shelved. Churchill was a powerful opponent of war aims propaganda, asserting that the emphasis must be entirely upon the task of winning the war, and that discussion of the world following victory was a distraction from this fundamental and all encompassing objective. Furthermore, the line was very thin between arguing that the fight was for democracy, freedom from want, equality, housing, work, liberty, and so forth – which is what the various statements of war aims proposed – and the accusations of socialist propaganda.[35]

At the most obvious level, the ministry did avoid the use of its propaganda machinery to persuade the population of the legitimacy of its fight through inculcating a commitment to the aims of the war. Its posters and leaflets shifted, after 1941, from exhortation to the dissemination of information. This too was consonant with the arguments of the psychologists; truthful information, forcefully purveyed is the best propaganda and the only form consistent with a democracy.[36] However elsewhere, the aims of the war, with all their socialist implications, were being powerfully promoted in a sustained intervention into morale that came not from posters and leaflets but through films. In the United States, the Morale Branch or Information and Education Division of the army produced the *Why We Fight* series of educational films, aimed initially at increasing the efficiency and commitment of soldiers, though ultimately defining America's war objectives for military and civilian personnel throughout the world. The British film movement worked rather differently.[37] The Films Division of the Ministry of Information commissioned and funded documentary films stressing the themes that the pre-war conditions shall never return, and spelling out the advantages of turning the wartime experience of planning the economy and society to the advantage of all in the coming peace.

Whatever the extent to which these films were produced without the explicit consent of ministers and others, their implications for present purposes are clear. Citizenship had acquired a subjective form. From this point forth, winning the war, and winning the peace, required the active engagement of the civilian in the social and political process, a shaping of wills, consciences, and aspirations, to forge social solidarity and individual responsibilities in the name of citizenship and democracy. As citizenship became a psychological matter, the psyche of the citizen was discovered as a new continent for psychological knowledge and for the deployment of the professional skills of the technicians of subjectivity.

Chapter three

The Sykewarriors

> In this war, which was Total in every sense of the word, we have seen many great changes in military science. It seems to me that not the least of these was the development of psychological warfare as a specific and effective weapon.... I am convinced that the expenditure of men and money in wielding the spoken and written word was an important contributing factor in undermining the enemy's will to resist and supporting the fighting morale of our potential Allies in the occupied countries.... Without doubt psychological warfare has proved its right to a place of dignity in our military arsenal.[1]
>
> Dwight D. Eisenhower, 1945

Total war required the explicit waging of war upon the mind of the enemy – psychological warfare.[2] And psychological warfare required both a knowledge of the subjectivity of the enemy population and a mechanism for acting upon it. In developing this knowledge and technique, new meaning would be given to the notion of national character, new conceptions developed of the influences upon it, and new technologies invented for acting upon it in the interests of policy.

In the Allied strategy in World War II, psychological attack was thus, as Daniel Lerner puts it, 'integrated with the instruments of violence'. Psychological warfare was waged through a number of loosely coordinated agencies.[3] Responsibility for psychological warfare against Germany in the campaign in north-west Europe lay with the Psychological Warfare Division (PWD) of the Supreme Headquarters Allied Expeditionary Forces (SHAEF). PWD was formed to tie together US and British policies in propaganda, but both Britain and the United States had their own independent propaganda structures. The British structure, which was closely copied by the Americans,

33

was under the overall control of the Political Warfare Executive (PWE), which was a small policy committee designed to coordinate the enemy propaganda activities of three other agencies, the British Broadcasting Corporation, the Ministry of Information (whose US parallel was the Office of War Information (OWI)), and the Political Intelligence Department of the Foreign Office (PID). Like its parallel in the US Office of Strategic Services (OSS), PID was charged with the gathering, evaluation, and dissemination of intelligence data. Richard Crossman, subsequently a senior Labour cabinet minister, is perhaps the best-known individual engaged in this work, first as director of political warfare against the enemy in PID, then as a member of the joint Anglo-American staff of PWD.

What was the rationale of this complex system? It has become conventional to divide its activities into two broad types: 'white' and 'black' propaganda. White propaganda was that which was openly admitted to; it obeyed the principles of democratic propaganda openly expounded by psychologists and politicians alike. Crossman puts them thus: '(a) Honesty is overwhelmingly the best policy; and (b) if you want to achieve results, you must get inside the other fellow's skin, feel his feelings and think his thoughts.'[4] The psychological warfare that Crossman and other 'white' propagandists engaged in thus promised nothing and threatened nothing that was not true; it stuck to the alternatives of continued resistance or unconditional surrender to Anglo-Saxon mercy and justice.[5] Propaganda thus exposed German boasts as lies and stressed the inevitability of Allied victory and the integrity and decency of the democratic world in contrast with the corruption and untrustworthiness of the Nazi leaders.

The two principal media for such propaganda were radio and leaflets. Radio, mainly news but also entertainment, sought to create a state of mind among civilians in Germany and the occupied countries required for the various stages of the campaign, demoralizing them, bringing home the implications of German defeats and Allied victories, issuing instructions as to how to act when the Allied troops neared, and conveying the impression that others were carrying out such instructions.

The principles behind the leaflet campaigns were similar. Leaflets, disseminated by specially designed shells and bombs, were of different sorts varying from dissemination of advice to soldiers and civilians as to how to surrender, to those in the form of 'safe conduct passes' that soldiers could keep and use when they surrendered. Such passes promised nothing but the conditions that would in any event be provided for prisoners of war, but, again, were intended as reassurance of the humanity of the Allies and as reminders of the stark choice between death and surrender. PWD dropped over *three billion* leaflets of various types in north-west Europe between D-Day and the German surrender; and almost *six billion* leaflets were distributed over the Continent in all by aircraft based in Britain. The leaflet campaign in the north-west European theatre alone involved approximately 4,000 bombs and 1,000 tons of paper per *month*: a war on the mind of an immense scale.

But if the principle of white propaganda was its objectivity, the use of the truth in such a way as to make it credible by the enemy, so-called black propaganda worked by other techniques.[6] The credo adopted was: 'To approach the German mind through... elaborately sustained fictions, calculated to throw it off its guard and to appeal to the selfish, disloyal, individualist motives in the [German soldier and civilian].'[7] Black propaganda attempted to 'drive a wedge between the Nazi leaders and the people, and to create an intensification of war-weariness and defeatism by every means, open and clandestine.'[8] It operated principally through rumour, planted by agents and sympathizers with the Allies in Germany and the occupied countries, spread by radio broadcasts to the troops purporting to be from German dissident organizations and so forth.

Black propaganda merged into the strategy of deception, inspired by the belief that, as Churchill put it; 'In wartime, truth is so precious that she should always be attended by a bodyguard of lies'.[9] The policy of deception was born at the meeting between Churchill, Stalin and Roosevelt at Teheran in December 1943 when they formulated the common strategy against Hitler, which was to culminate in the Allied landings in Normandy in spring 1944. It sought to plant large numbers of fragments of information – whispers, rumours, activities of double and triple agents, sacrificial operations, wireless games, creation of fictitious armies, manipulation of resistance forces – which, when assembled by enemy intelligence, would form a plausible and acceptable, though false, picture of Allied military intentions, especially leading to the belief that the Allies would not attack at Normandy but elsewhere.

Deception is generally regarded as having played a major part in the Allied victory; the evaluation of black propaganda is more equivocal. Lerner not only suggests that there was no real difference between black and white propaganda, but also that the claims for the effectiveness of black techniques are dubious. Indeed he suggests that rumour was not only a difficult weapon to control, but that the spreading of false rumours may have been counter-productive, easily detected to be false, increasing the anger and determination of the enemy and undercutting belief in the essential honesty and forthrightness of the allies.[10] But whatever their military pay-off, these propaganda campaigns acted as a psychological laboratory and testing ground of considerable significance.

Given the undeveloped state of British academic psychology at the outbreak of the war it is hardly surprising that in the British contribution, psychologists were outnumbered by financiers, politicians, diplomats, writers and artists. The British academics involved were typically from the natural sciences or humanities – historians and political scientists. None the less, psychological and psychiatric expertise did play a significant role. A team of British psychiatrists from the Directorate of Army Psychiatry (War Office), headed by H.V. Dicks (Professor of Psychiatry at the University of Leeds School of Medicine and subsequently of the Tavistock Clinic), worked with PWI in London and made some field studies to supplement its data. Dicks' most significant study, in which he was aided by a sociologist in the form of Edward Shils (Professor of Social Science at the University of Chicago and Reader in Sociology at the University of London), was an analysis of German political attitudes in terms of personality types.[11] Based upon statistical analysis of interrogations with prisoners of war, Dicks divided German males of military age into five categories: fanatical 'hard-core' Nazis (10 per cent); modified Nazis 'with reservations' (25 per cent); 'unpolitical' Germans (40 per cent); passive anti-Nazis (15 per cent); active anti Nazis (10 per cent). The virtue of this analysis was that it shifted the debates over the nature of the German population from an interminable dispute about the existence of 'good' and 'bad' Germans into a precise set of categories with defined subjective characteristics. The propagandists who had to prepare leaflets and broadcasts could thus target them upon specific sectors of the population in light of this knowledge of their psychological state. The personal and interpersonal characteristics of the population were made thinkable and calculable, they could now enter into the strategies of war and peace.

Dicks and Shills were jointly responsible for the rationale of the intelligence section of PWD. This entailed the analysis of verbal and written statements gleaned from prisoners of war, from German civilians, from intelligence agents and others in contact with Germany, from German radio and press and from captured German documents. Prisoners of war were given the Dicks questionnaire, which made up for the fact that none of the PWI interrogators in the field were professional psychiatrists.[12] Documents were subject to detailed textual analysis to reveal not only German military intentions but also the state of German morale and likely German reactions to Allied activities. The prime movers in technique here were Harold Lasswell, who directed the Experimental Division for Study of Wartime Communication at the Library of Congress; while German propaganda was studied by the research Project on Totalitarian Communications at the Graduate Faculty of the New School for Social Research in New York.[13]

Indeed, as far as the United States is concerned, by the end of 1942 the majority of social scientists in general and social psychologists in particular were in government service either full time or acting as consultants on particular projects.[14] The investigation of morale, the analysis of attitudes, the interpretation of the dynamic relations between individual and group – these formed the matrix for a plethora of distinct but interrelated investigations that blurred disciplinary boundaries, as social psychologists, anthropologists, sociologists and psychiatrists worked together to chart and understand the social, cultural and interpersonal determinants of the resistance of the enemy, and the conduct of the fighting forces.

Rensis Likert complemented his work on home morale with a programme conducted under the auspices of the Morale Division of the United States Strategic Bombing Survey. This systematically appraised the effects of strategic bombing on the will of countries to resist. Cartwright singles out this work for particular praise. 'Especially noteworthy,' he concludes, 'is the excellent research design involved in this project.... Because it is the first quantitative comparative analysis of the values and motives of people in different countries, this project will stand as a milestone in the history of social psychology.'[15]

The morale of the enemy was to be investigated in many ways. After the Japanese attack on Pearl Harbour in 1941, a listening centre was established at Princeton and was later developed into the Foreign Broadcast Monitoring Unit (subsequently the Foreign Broadcast Intelligence Service).

Paul Lazarsfeld, Jerry Bruner, Harold Lasswell, and R.K. White developed systematic tools for the analysis of spoken and written texts, and analyzed foreign broadcasts to provide intelligence reports on military intentions and enemy morale. This approach, the counterpart of the work on home morale, was to be supplemented from a rather different perspective, one that focused upon the culture of the enemy and its links with the personality of the civilian and soldier.

Clyde Kluckhohn, whose principal anthropological experience had been in the pre-war study of the Navaho of New Mexico, and Alexander Leighton, a psychiatrist who had assisted in these studies, were appointed Joint Chiefs of the Foreign Morale Analysis Division in Washington. Leighton had previously been working at the Japanese Relocation Camp at Poston, Arizona, where he had concluded that, in times of stress, individuals appeared to behave according to belief systems: they were conditioned by the patterns and attitudes of their culture that had been deeply ingrained in them through their upbringing.[16] In these terms, Kluckhohn and Leighton sought to understand the morale of Japanese soldiers and civilians. Basing themselves upon reports of interrogations of prisoners of war, captured personal and official documents, and transcripts of monitored press reports and radio broadcasts, they searched for flaws in morale that could be exploited in propaganda.[17] Not that they could do much to counter the belief among US policy makers that Japanese resistance to defeat was fanatical and would prevail unto death. Despite the strong evidence of flagging morale by 1945, the US Secretary of State for War still considered the bombing of Hiroshima and Nagasaki the only way to ensure unconditional surrender.[18]

One outcome of this work, however, was a remodelled psychological conception of national character that was to provide the conceptual starting point for a series of studies of 'culture and personality' in the post-war years.[19] The notion of national character was not a new one, but the experience of wartime enabled its translation into psychological techniques for the empirical investigation of national populations and expert advice in political calculations. A wave of quasi-psychoanalytic anthropological studies were published in the closing years of the war, in sufficient quantities to warrant a bibliography of work relevant to the Japanese alone, edited by H.M. Spitzer and Ruth Benedict and published by the US Office of War Information in 1945.[20] These most frequently described different national character structure of enemy nations in the language of psychoanalysis, posing the possibility that it was both formed by early experiences, and could be modified by a psychoanalytically informed intervention into early life.

After the war this would be developed into a psychoanalytic investigation of America's own problematic national populations. The US Bureau of Indian Affairs funded and supported the influential series of studies by Kluckhohn, Leighton, and Erikson into the relationship between child-rearing practices and adult character structure, which took as its focus the Indian tribes, who were thought to be obstinate, demoralized, degenerating, and resistant to re-education.[21] And further afield, the Rand Corporation, established by the air force in 1946 to continue the partnership between the military and university scientists that had developed in wartime, funded studies of soviet culture that were drawn upon by Margaret Mead and Martha Wolfenstein in their project that eventually produced *Childhood in Contemporary Culture*. This project was inaugurated by Ruth Benedict through her research at Columbia University on contemporary cultures, which was itself grant aided, like the American Museum of Natural History Studies in Contemporary Culture, by the Human Resources Division of the Office of Naval Research.[22] The social importance of this psychologization of childhood and personality was to go far beyond the military concerns that had provoked it.

The US wartime morale workers were to give an institutional form to their new interdisciplinary modes of thought: the Department of Social Relations at Harvard University which was established in 1946. Among those central to the department in its early years were Gordon Allport, Edward Shils, and Clyde Kluckhohn, together with two figures we will encounter presently – Henry Murray, who headed the assessment staff at the Office of Strategic Services, and Samuel Stouffer, who directed the research branch of the Information and Education Division of the War Office. The experience of war had temporarily breached the powerful internal policing mechanisms and boundary-maintaining devices of the disciplines of sociology, anthropology, psychology, and psychiatry. Parsons' general theory of action integrating personalities, social systems, and cultural systems would be perhaps the most academically prestigious child of this new relationship.[23]

In the period immediately following the end of the war, the more immediate fruits of this American labour on the public psyche were to become widely available.[24] A host of books were published reflecting on the experience of wartime and seeking to develop from it a theory of propaganda, public opinion, and the psychology of rumour.[25] The precise details of this work will not concern us here. What is important for our purposes is the translation of the public mind into a domain accessible to knowledge via psychological expertise, to calculation via psychological theory, and to government via psychologically informed propaganda. This psychologization of the polity, of its attitudes, solidarities, and oppositions, its interpersonal transactions, was to establish the platform for the most significant developments of psychological expertise, and the most important transformations of the rationales of government, in the post-war years.

Chapter four

Groups at War

Service psychology has the positive aim of making the most effective use of human resources. Service psychiatry is more concerned in preventing human waste; hence it gives first place to preventive measures. In both spheres of activity, the starting point is the fact of individual differences. The object of psychology and psychiatry alike is to ascertain these individual differences so that the unfit can be detected and the fit placed where they can function in a most useful way to the Service and satisfactory to themselves...in modern warfare it is no longer a question of 'measuring Guardsmen by the yard'.[1]

Privy Council Office, 1947

The expert committee that reported on service psychology at the end of the war stressed the significance of the psychology of individual differences to the war effort. But the expert attention to the subjective state of the fighting forces did not merely revive the strategy of intelligence testing that had taken off in the United States in World War I. First, individual differences came to concern personality as much as intelligence. But, more importantly, the minds of service personnel became active elements in the life of the forces by means of the refinement of the notions of morale and attitude. Crucially, the role of the individual was increasingly viewed from the perspective of a larger entity – the group. The birth of the group constituted the most profound effect of the experience of war upon the government of subjectivity.[2]

From the start of the war, procedures of selection, allocation, and promotion increasingly deployed psychological and psychiatric criteria, seeking to act upon the efficiency of the fighting forces by administrative means. The mechanisms were both negative and positive. Careful selection and allocation of individuals to tasks could eliminate those whose presence posed a danger to the efficiency of the services – the mentally defective or the unstable or unreliable individual whose training would consume energy and time uselessly, or who might even endanger lives if placed in important posts. On the positive side, proper allocation of personnel – the principle of matching the man to the job and the job to the man – could minimize the risk of breakdown and maximize the use of the human factor. This was true for the ranks; it was even more true for promotion to officer level.

Psychological involvement in recruitment and allocation was not accepted with open arms in the British forces. Despite the US experiments, the recommendations of the official committee of enquiry, and the fact that about 120,000 people were still in receipt of pensions or had received final awards for psychiatric disability arising from World War I – about 15 per cent of all pensioned disability – little attention was paid to selection of personnel in the inter-war years. Instead the Ministry of Pensions expressed the intention of not providing pensions for cases of neurosis developed during active service, but providing treatment instead, hoping thereby to combat the possibility of an epidemic of 'war neurosis'.[3] In April 1939 J.R. Rees of the Tavistock Clinic and Alec Rodger of the National Institute of Industrial Psychology (NIIP) submitted a memo to the medical authorities at the War Office calling for a preliminary experiment to assess the contribution to the speed and quality of the training of conscripts that might be made by psychological and psychiatric assessments.[4] This memo drew attention not only to the past experiences of the fighting services but also to the results of research in industrial psychology, which had sought to demonstrate the contribution of psychoneuroses to days lost from work and poor industrial efficiency, and to show the value of special aptitude tests in allocation of individuals to specialized tasks.[5]

It is not clear why the scheme was rejected, though Rees remarks that psychiatrists were often accused of being fifth columnists, assisting those who wanted to evade service.[6] However, in September 1939 Rees was invited to act as consultant for the army at home; Henry Yellowlees was made consultant to the British Expeditionary Forces and after the commencement of war was followed abroad by a small staff. From April 1940 psychiatric involvement in the army increased, first with the appointment of command psychiatrists attached to the medical headquarters of each command in Britain and, by 1941, with the attachment of up to fifteen area psychiatrists to each of these. The navy also established a psychiatric service early in the war; the RAF did rather less, though it did publish a number of studies based upon the characteristics of those referred to neuro-psychiatrists. For present purposes, the experience of the army is most significant.[7]

Virtually as soon as the command psychiatrists were appointed they began agitating for a scheme for the selection of recruits.

Ronald Hargreaves, also formerly of the Tavistock Clinic, carried out experiments with J.C. Raven using the Penrose-Raven Progressive Matrices and other tests. Professor Godfrey Thompson, an early proponent of group testing, co-operated with the command psychiatrist in Scotland. By 1940 testing had been introduced in certain establishments and units, with much of the work being done by Eric Farmer of the Cambridge Psychological Laboratory and Alec Rodger. More pressure by Rees and Hargreaves led eventually to the establishment of an Advisory Committee on Mental Testing early in 1941 consisting of Professor J.H. Drever together with Dr. C.S. Myers of the NIIP and Dr. S.J.F. Philpott. By June 1941 a Directorate of Selection of Personnel was set up under the Adjutant-General.

A system of intelligence testing was introduced at all recruitment depots, using the Progressive Matrices, supervised by industrial psychologists, with all those who were assessed as mentally dull or backward being referred to psychiatrists. Soon it was psychiatrists, rather than commanding officers, who were making the recommendations about the posting of these men. By 1942 a new intake scheme was introduced, in which all men on entering the army were taken into a General Service Corps where they were subjected to a series of intelligence and aptitude tests, interviewed by trained personnel selection officers, and referred to psychiatrists if they were in the lowest selection group, were stammerers, had a history of psychiatric illness or special schooling, presented with abnormal behaviour or bizarre test results, or showed an apparent lack of 'combatant tendency'. Some 14 per cent of the total intake were referred to the psychiatrist who could recommend transfer to a non-combatant arm or an armed or unarmed section of the Pioneer Corps, admission to hospital, or discharge. Later, as maximization of manpower resources became critical, the work of selection and allocation was extended to army selection centres, which received 'misfits' from the army and those transferred from the other forces.[8]

The Directorate of Selection of Personnel was not only concerned with weeding out the dullards and the unstable. Its aims were not merely negative but positive. As Rees put it:

> The Directorate for Selection of Personnel had undertaken a complete job analysis of the multitudinous tasks in the different arms of the Service, and as a result was able to lay down the standards of intelligence and other aptitudes necessary for each job, thus providing a basis for the correct posting of men in certain proportions to each type of unit. The accomplishment of this work produced a revolutionary change in the Army's utilization of manpower and has set a standard which will certainly be applied in industry and in social life in the post-war world. The matching of

men to suitable work is as valuable a means of psychiatric prophylaxis as anything that could well be devised.[9]

This issue was to be taken up with enthusiasm in the United States in the immediate post-war period. General Dwight Eisenhower, later US President, established a Conservation of Human Resources Project at Columbia University, with sponsorship from organizations as varied as the Ford Foundation, General Electric, the Radio Corporation of America, Coca-Cola, Standard Oil, and the Bigelow-Sanford Carpet Company. Eisenhower was stimulated by his own experience of marked shortages of manpower during the North African campaign and in the European theatre at the Battle of the Bulge; he knew that, at the same time, large numbers of young Americans were being rejected for military service or being prematurely discharged because they were judged to lack the mental and emotional qualities that made a good soldier. Some 20 million men had been examined during the war as to their suitability for military service, of whom 14 million were enlisted, and there were records giving not only their test results but also details of their performance in military life and some indication of how they performed in civilian life prior to recruitment and after discharge. The Columbia project aimed to make a systematic analysis of these wartime personnel records in order to investigate the nation's human resources as a basis for future planning, not only of the armed forces but also of the nation as a whole.

The project, directed by Professor Eli Ginzberg, published a number of studies based upon its analysis.[10] Its conclusions were that the armed forces had paid a high price because of their lack of knowledge of the characteristics of the manpower pool, of their future requirements, of the potential of the recruits, and of the capacity of those with apparent deficiencies to perform adequately in particular tasks or with specific assistance. In particular, selection was inadequate without being accompanied by proper training and assignment to fit the individual into the organization so that he could perform effectively. This had been insufficiently recognized. The result had been a loss to the army of two and a half million men, or the equivalent of over fifty divisions. The lesson was clear: organizational policy could improve the performance of large organizations by taking account of personality and motivation. The full use of the nation's resources now required government to have a manpower policy conceived and organized in psychological terms.

A further wartime research project was of great significance for the development of psychological techniques – the surveys of the attitudes of American troops conducted by the research branch in the Information and Education Division of the US War Department. This study, directed by Samuel A. Stouffer, published its results in four volumes in 1949 and 1950, under the general title of *Studies in Social Psychology in World War II*.[11] The research branch carried out some 200 to 300 large- and small-scale surveys during the war at the request of other departments. These concerned attitudes to such issues as the war, the medical services, civilians, leisure activities, army jobs, blacks, the recruitment of women, and demobilization procedures.

The work of the research branch appeared to show that what was crucial, from the point of view of the smooth running of an organization and the morale of individuals, was not so much the objective characteristics of the situation, but the subjective relation of the individual to his or her situation. The significance of the concept of attitude was that it grasped this subjective relationship. It enabled any individual's multitudinous and diverse tastes and prejudices to be rendered into thought in the form of a value on each of a small number of dimensions. The inscription of attitude was by means of a new device for mental calibration: the scale. The scale was a technique of constructing questions such that an individual's response to a particular item allowed their responses to all other items on a particular dimension to be predicted. Developed in the work on Stouffer's project done by Rensis Likert and Louis Guttman, the technique of scaling brought a new subjective dimension of the human condition into the sphere of knowledge and regulation. The correlative development of the concept of attitude and the technique of the scale opened this dimension up for management; attitudes could be investigated, measured, inscribed, reported, and calculated, and administrative decisions made in that light. A knowledge of attitudes made it possible to conceive of a mode of administration in which the soldier would be both contented and efficient, efficient because contented.

It seemed that this contentment had little to do with the soldier's commitment to the objectives of the war. Stouffer and his researchers could not find, in their soldier subjects, any clear thinking about, let alone belief in, the principles for which the struggle was being waged. What was crucial, for the maintenance of morale and efficiency, was the group:

> The group in its informal character, with its close interpersonal ties, served two principal functions in combat motivation: it *set and enforced group standards* of behaviour, and it *supported and sustained* the individual in stresses he would otherwise not be able to withstand.[12]

Behaviour during combat thus appeared to be a matter of the strength of the bonds between the soldier and his buddies, strengthened by loyalty to their immediate leadership, rather than arising from the unreal and distant principles and causes of the war. Paradoxically, the American soldier was mobilized by exactly the same forces as his German enemy, whose main motivation, according to Shils' interpretation of his research with Dicks, also derived from his loyalty to his primary group and its leader, rather than to the army as a whole or higher authorities.[13] In their discovery of the primary group as the key element in the relations between the individual and the organization, the American wartime social scientists reinforced the theses that the American psychologists of industry had elaborated in the 1930s: management of the army, like the factory, was to be achieved through acting upon the bonds of the primary group and aligning individuals through this mechanism with the objectives of the organization.[14] Social psychology could become a science of administration.

At a more mundane and immediate level, psychological investigation could inform very detailed military decisions. For motivation and contentment appeared to be a product of the issues and exigencies of everyday existence: status, comfort, minimum exposure to danger, and training to assist the individual after discharge. Attitude research enabled these general desires to be specified in terms amenable to administration: how to organize leisure, where to deploy women or blacks, how to avoid discontent through the careful phasing of demobilization. Psychological expertise had become the key to organizational harmony.

Of no less concern than the psychological state of recruits was that of officers. Officer selection began to pose a problem in the early years of the war.[15] First, there was much concern about the apparently high rate of psychiatric breakdown of officers, partly thought to result from the commissioning of men with a history of maladjustment or neurotic disorders. Second, there was a high rejection rate from officer cadet training units, exacerbated by the fact that the boards selecting candidates for officer training, in the words of Rees, 'found themselves rather at sea' once the supply of young men from the universities and public school began to dry up; they were used to selecting individuals with whose background and outlook they were familiar. In unfamiliar waters they found themselves accepting for training many who would fail, and rejecting many who might succeed. This fuelled the existing suspicion, damaging to morale and to applications from the ranks, that class bias was influencing decisions of promotion. Given the recognition of the importance of leadership to the happiness, welfare, and efficiency of the fighting units, something had to be done.

Rees and Eric Wittkower, also from the Tavistock, together with the Scottish Command Psychiatrist T.F. Rodger, carried out experiments from 1941 that led to a permanent system of War Office Selection Boards (WOSBs) in 1942, together with a Research and

Training Centre that investigated ways of improving techniques. Each board was staffed by a president – a senior army officer – and advised by a psychiatrist, a military testing officer, and a psychologist or sergeant tester. Candidates were investigated over a period of about three days, during which they filled in a biographical and medical questionnaire, were given various intelligence and personality tests, were interviewed by the president or his deputy, and given a series of lectures and practical tests by the military training officer. A proportion were interviewed by the psychiatrist.

The role of the psychiatrist on the WOSBs was contentious.[16] Originally psychiatrists interviewed every candidate, as well as giving an opinion on the results of the psychological tests, thus not merely identifying the unstable but acting as general experts on personality.[17] While the first restrictions on these procedures came from lack of trained staff and problems of numbers of candidates, there was a more profound hostility from many army officers. It was thought the psychiatrists were exerting an influence out of proportion with their status, that they were recommending rejection of suitable candidates on the basis of far fetched beliefs about the importance of such things as sexual adjustment, and that any benefit that may have arisen from their activities was outweighed by the damaging effects of the resentment aroused in candidates, not simply by their sometimes insensitive questions but also by their very presence. As a result of such criticisms, their role was reduced to that of interviewing those thought potentially abnormal; when the war was over the Crocker Committee, which enquired into the work of the WOSBs, recommended that they were no longer necessary as permanent members of the boards. Nonetheless, a new possibility had been placed on the agenda: the psychiatrist not as a keeper of lunatics but as an accredited guide to the territory of subjectivity: an all-purpose advisor on the utilization of the human factor in institutional life.

As far as the psychologists were concerned, testing was still the order of the day. But the lack of trained psychologists meant that most of the work of testing was carried out by trained sergeants acting as assistants to psychiatrists who interpreted the results of the test. The bulk of the professional psychologists were confined to the research and training centre; they had more difficulty in finding an effective foothold within the institutional procedure than did the medically qualified psychiatrists. But this was not only because of their small number and generally lower status. It was also because officer suitability appeared to be chiefly a matter of character and personality, and these features of psychological life had proved resistant to quantification in the pre-war period.[18] The war itself was to enable this to be transformed, principally through work done in the United States.[19] Large populations were available for psychological investigation, funding was plentiful, and advanced statistical techniques could be applied. The outcome of this work, such as the Minnesota Multiphasic Personality Inventory, which measured hysterical, neurotic, and schizoid attributes, and the Cattell Sixteen Factor Personality Questionnaire, was too late for the war effort. None the less, the latter did for the personality what the former had done for intelligence – enabled it to be visualized, materialized, inscribed, calculated, and administered.

While the United States provided the techniques for the standardization of personality, Britain innovated in the use of real-life situations for the assessment of capacity – the observation of candidates while they performed the various tasks set them. The psychological rationale for this lay partly in the influence of the field theory approaches of American social psychologists, in particular Lewin and Moreno.[20] Traits, it appeared, were not constant qualities of the individual that all successful officers possessed, and which existed independent of context. Leadership was not a quality inherent in the individual that could be displayed both in tests and in real life.[21] Personality was an organized whole, a system of tensions or needs that interacts dynamically with the varying demands of different situations. 'Officer quality' should, therefore, be analyzed and assessed in terms of the main roles that future officers would be called on to play, the most crucial being that of leadership in a small group, giving the group direction, and maintaining its cohesion and solidarity against disruptive forces from within or without.

This form of reasoning led to Wilfred Bion's famous invention, the leaderless group test. Bion's own account is worth quoting at length:

> The essence of the technique which was evolved, and which has since become the basis of selection techniques in many different fields, was to provide a framework in which selecting officers, including a psychiatrist, could observe a man's capacity for maintaining personal relations in a situation of strain that tempted him to disregard the interests of his fellows for the sake of his own. The situation had to be a real life situation. The situation of strain, and the temptation to give full rein to his personal ambitions was already there.... The problem was to make capital of this existing emotional field in order to test the quality of the man's relationships with his fellows.... The actual task of the test is merely a cloak of invisibility for the testing officers who are present.... It is not the artificial test, but the real life situation that has to be watched – that is, the way in which a man's capacity for personal relationships stands up under the strain of his own and other men's fear of failure and desires for personal success.[22]

The concept of the group was to become the organizing principle of psychological and psychiatric thought concerning the conduct of the individual. From the wartime years onward, social and institutional life was increasingly to be conceived as intersubjective emotional relations, the interplay between social solidarities and individual personality dynamics. It was not the static traits of a character that were at issue, but the ways in which individuals resolved personal conflicts in the context of group decisions, directions and cohesiveness. The invention of the 'group', the conception of 'social' or 'human' relations as key determinants of individual conduct, were the most consistent lesson of the psychological and psychiatric experience of war.

The approach to assessment developed in the WOSBs was to be exported to the United States, where 'situational testing' was to be the basis of the technique used by the US Office of Strategic Services for the selection of personnel, under the direction of Henry Murray.[23] But further, operating in these terms, psychiatric expertise could also transform techniques for the training and management of soldiers. Solidarity was the key here. Soldiers would not be trained to fight efficiently by instilling hatred of the enemy or by hardening them to savagery by exposing them to blood and gore. Some conditioning to the rigours of warfare could help – such as 'battle inoculation' in which exposure to bomb blast and sound was administered in gradually increasing dosages. But the spirit of a fighting unit was largely dependent on other things. What was crucial were the psychological bonds and relations between its members, the solidarity of the group. This was not a matter of external discipline, of obeying orders and following rules. It was a matter of internal discipline, of the pride of each individual in the order of his group, of his sense of worth and belonging, and of the value and significance of his own contributions to group life. The efficiency of the whole was construed in terms of the psychological relations of its members, simultaneously producing a new way of scrutinizing and representing the likely efficiency of a collection of individuals directed towards a task, and a new way of regulating and maximizing it.

This, too, was the abiding significance of the various experiences of rehabilitation of soldiers suffering from psychoneurotic symptoms and returning prisoners of war developed by Bion, John Rickman, and Tom Main and Maxwell Jones – the principal protagonists of the social psychiatry that would take off in the post-war period.[24] Bion and Rickman were drafted into Northfield Military Hospital near Birmingham in 1943 to deal with unruly conditions that had developed in its Training Wing. Rickman used group discussion to highlight the relations of the individual to the group to the patients themselves, developing a conception of the 'good group spirit' as the aim of the process. The group needed a common purpose; it should recognize itself, its boundaries and the position, the function and contribution of each individual within it; it must develop the capacity to face and cope with discontent within itself.

Bion sought to produce self-respecting and socially adjusted men able to accept responsibility by uniting the individuals on the ward into a group tackling a common problem.[25] The problem to tackle, he decided, was precisely the existence of the neurosis that threatened the successful rehabilitative working of the institution. Hence the group itself was to be persuaded to attack neurotic disability as a communal problem destroying happiness and efficiency. The training of the Training Wing was actually to become a course in understanding and resolving problems of interpersonal relationships. In this way the group itself would be able to resolve the neurotic symptoms of its members and bring them to a state of personal responsibility.

Bion's tactics were to act upon the conduct of the men through manipulating authority relations in the wing. The neurosis was first made visible by relaxing the authoritarian framework that had provided both the framework of community life and the structure for resistance to it. When the men themselves had to take responsibility for organizing tasks and for defining and disciplining miscreants, they would learn that the disruption was not grounded *in* authority but in their psychological relations *to* authority. When the group realized the psychological origins of its distress, it could release its full energies in self cure. It is difficult to overstate the conceptual, tactical, and strategic implications of this reflexivity for the therapeutic activity of the post-war years. The cure was no longer to lie in the hands of another, but to be introjected into the sick themselves, who would cure themselves under the authority of expertise.

Although this experiment ended after six weeks, it was followed by a second 'Northfield experiment'. In this, Main sought to produce what he referred to as a 'therapeutic community' in which the hospital was to be used

> not as an organization run by doctors in the interests of their own greater 'technical efficiency, but as a community with the immediate aim of full participation of all its members in its daily life and the eventual aim of the resocialisation of the neurotic individual for life in ordinary society ... a spontaneous and emotionally structured (rather than medically dictated) organization in which all staff and patients engage.[26]

For such a reformatory technology, the institutional regime was construed as a system of relations that were more emotional than technical. There was also a shift in relations of expertise. The role of the doctor was no longer direction but interpretation. All those around the sick person – patients, domestics, nurses – were drawn into the field of the illness and its cure. The social relations of group life were now conceived not only as a means of treatment of neurosis, but also the field where neurosis was manifested and may be exacerbated: the origin of neurosis itself was to be discovered in problems of social relations.

At the same time, a parallel experiment was developing an analogous technology.[27] In 1942 Pat Wood, a cardiologist, and Maxwell Jones, a psychiatrist, became joint directors of a 100 bed unit for the treatment of 'effort syndrome'. The Mill Hill Neurosis Unit was one of two establishments for the treatment of war neuroses run by the Ministry of Health with staff drawn from the Maudsley Hospital. While the other unit utilized short-term treatments like modified insulin, ether abreaction, continuous narcosis and narco-analysis, at Mill Hill the emphasis was on the application of sociological and psychological conceptions of treatment.

The investigators concluded, after detailed cardiological examination, that effort syndrome – breathlessness, palpitations, left chest pain, postural giddiness, occasional fainting attacks and fatigue – was not related to heart disease. On the contrary, it was deemed a psychosomatic complaint. A discussion procedure involving nurses was developed to explain to the patients the physiological mechanisms that produced their symptoms, seeking to allay the anxiety that exacerbated the problem and to change patients' attitudes to their symptoms. These discussion groups soon expanded, beginning to deal with problems raised in life on the ward and elsewhere, and taking the form of group discussion and, often, dramatization of the problems. It gradually appeared that the whole of hospital life could affect the illness, provoking deterioration in the condition or participation in therapy. Further, the patient's reactions to the hospital community mirrored his reactions to the community outside. Hence the latter could be affected by working upon the former. Group psychotherapy had been born.

These notions of pathology as a group phenomenon and cure as a matter of rehabilitation of asocialized individuals were further developed in the units that were set up for returning prisoners of war. These were part of the massive exercise in labour resettlement undertaken by the Ministry of Labour when the war ended. Twenty civilian resettlement units were established, with the aim of rehabilitating ex-prisoners of war for civilian life. In these 'transitional communities for social reconnection', Adam Curle, Eric Trist, and Tommy Wilson extended and refined the techniques and analyses that would later be applied in the group therapies of the post-war period.[28] Maxwell Jones was made responsible for the unit set up at

Southern Hospital, Dartford, in Kent, and reused the procedures developed at Mill Hill, additionally seeking to connect the 'transitional community' with the local community that surrounded it. Where rehabilitation had previously been a mere adjunct to therapy conducted by other means – mediating between life under the dominance of medicine and life as a private matter – it now became continuous with, indeed the essence of, the therapeutic intervention itself. The relational life of the group had become both the field of the illness and the domain of the cure.

These procedures were extended beyond the returning prisoners of war to many other categories of socially maladjusted individuals. The problems of disabled labourers prompted the establishment of an elaborate social apparatus in the immediate post-war period.[29] The Disabled Persons (Employment) Act had been passed in 1944; at the beginning of 1950 just under 1 million persons were registered disabled, there were 366 full-time and 1,450 part-time disablement resettlement officers, and twelve industrial rehabilitation units located in the big cities, containing workshops with factory-like conditions. As far as the National Advisory Council on the Employment of the Disabled was concerned, the most troublesome aspect of the problem was the hard core of chronic unemployed. While only around 50,000 registered disabled persons were classed as psychiatric, for this hard core, whatever their diagnostic label, unemployment had led to the development of antisocial attitudes. Hence their problem had become a psychiatric one, a problem of maladjustment requiring rehabilitation.

The Roffey Park Rehabilitation Centre had utilized community treatment for maladjusted industrial workers with some success; the Industrial Neurosis Unit at Belmont Hospital was set up in 1947 to investigate methods of treatment and resettlement of this hard core to feed back into general planning for rehabilitation of inefficient or maladjusted workers. The population of chronic unemployed neurotics it received from all over England included inadequate and aggressive psychopaths, schizoid personalities, early schizophrenics, various drug addictions, sexual perversions, and chronic psychoneurotics. To this unpromising and heterogeneous population, unified only by their social inefficiency and maladjustment, were applied all the community techniques for restoring the neurotic to adjustment to his environment in order to maintain functional efficiency. Through these devices sexual, criminal, industrial, or social deviants, whose behaviour was now construed as a manifestation of an underlying personality disorder, were to be managed back to a state of adjustment in which they could function smoothly within the institutional regimes they had previously disrupted.

In the years immediately following the end of the war, the problems of economic reconstruction would insert these issues of the group into the heart of economic debate, managerial practice and psychological innovation. Not only could mental capacities be aligned with institutional roles, but it appeared that organizational pathology could be prevented and efficiency could be promoted by acting upon the psychological relations that traversed organizational life. Solidarity and morale could be produced by administrative means. The group had become a crucial means of conceptualizing the social behaviours of the individual, of analyzing the efficiency of all manner of social practices, of promoting individual contentment and organizational efficiency, and of conducting the business of the cure.

A vast territory had been discovered that would be explored in the post-war period: experts of subjectivity and intersubjectivity would seek to stake their claims in all institutions of society.

Part two

The Productive Subject

Chapter five

The Subject of Work

Work. The very word, for many, conjures up a vision of the more or less direct exercise of power upon the body of the worker: coercion, exploitation, discipline, control. In work, it would appear, the worker is no more than a factor of production, just one factor among many caught up in a process whose sole rationale is profit. The aim of the boss, and the task of the manager, is to maximize the labour extracted from the body of the worker while at the same time minimizing the opportunity for, and likelihood of, worker resistance to company goals of efficiency and productivity. From this standpoint, whatever changes may have occurred since the nineteenth century critiques of Marx, Engels, and others – in the types of work people do, in rates of pay, hours of work, working condition, styles of management, and the like – at the heart of work under capitalism the fundamental conflict remains.

At one pole stand the labourers and those allied with them in the trade union and labour movement. With nothing to sell but their labour power, the interests of workers short of a fundamental reorganization of society lie in boosting wages, keeping employment high, reducing hours of work, minimizing the effort of labour, and imposing constraints upon exploitation by fighting for better conditions of employment and firmer legislative constraints upon the freedom of the bosses. At the opposite pole stand the bosses and their functionaries and apologists in management, personnel, and occupational psychology. Their interests are tied to increasing profit through raising productivity, keeping work rates high and wages low, weakening the collective power of workers through unions, and reducing their capacity to disrupt work, while at the same time casting a cloak of legitimacy over the fundamentally exploitative nature of the employment relation.

From such a perspective, no amount of re-jigging of the details of work, the organization of the enterprise, the conditions of the labour process, or levels of reward could transform the basic alienation that lies at the heart of work. Workers work because they have to, they work at the behest of others in a process they do not control, to produce goods or services they do not enjoy. It is the wage, not the pleasure of work, that drives them to the production line, the office desk, or the shop floor each morning. Work ultimately is that which is required to earn the means to satisfy needs and desires in the world beyond work - for food, clothes, housing, consumption, family life, and self fulfilment. As far as the worker is concerned, it would seem, work is made up, principally, of the elements of obedience, self-denial, and deferred gratification – it entails an essential subordination of subjectivity.

In nineteenth century capitalism – in mine, mill, and manufactory – work seems easy to picture in these terms. But over the course of the present century, types of work and conditions of working have radically changed; in addition, industrialists, managers, philanthropists, psychologists, and others have initiated a series of reforms of the workplace, claiming to be able to radically restructure the working relation, to make work pleasureable for the worker at the same time as it is profitable for the employer. These different attempts to transform work see the subjectivity of the worker not only as a value to be respected rather than subjugated, but also as a central determinant of the success of the company. In various ways they have questioned the view that work is undertaken only to satisfy desires that it itself frustrates. On the contrary, they have argued that correctly organized, productive work itself can satisfy the worker; the activity of working itself can provide rewarding personal and social relations for those engaged in it; good work can be a means to self-fulfilment.

Employers and managers equipped with these new visions of work have thus claimed that there is no conflict between the pursuits of productivity, efficiency, and competitiveness on the one hand and the 'humanization' of work on the other. On the contrary, the path to business success lies in engaging the employee with the goals of the company at the level of his or her subjectivity, aligning the wishes, needs, and aspirations of each individual who works for the organization with the successful pursuit of its objectives. Through striving to fulfil their own needs and wishes at work, each employee will thus work for the advance of the enterprise; the more the individual fulfils him or herself, the greater the benefit to the company.

The subjectivity of the worker has thus emerged as a complex territory to be explored, understood, and regulated. Management has become dependent upon an objective knowledge, a scientific expertise and a rational technology of the personal and interpersonal. A range of somewhat ill-defined and overlapping subdisciplines and specialities have been born – occupational psychology, industrial psychology, organizational behaviour, vocational guidance, ergonomics, human engineering, and so forth. Both management and industrial relations have tried to establish a knowledge basis for their expertise, drawing in different ways upon theories of the subjectivity of the worker. There has been a correlative growth in the practical involvement of psychological expertise in the enterprise, the organization and the labour market, with psychologically trained functionaries carrying out such tasks as selection, promotion, job evaluation, performance appraisal, work design, job enrichment, and so forth, either as permanent employees or through the mechanisms of consultancy. And, in the past decade, there has been a growth in private outfits offering training, counselling and guidance to ambitious managers, hard-pressed or frustrated executives, and would-be high fliers, not only in the ways of managing for excellence in one's company, but also in the techniques for achieving excellence in oneself.

Sociological analysts of the labour process in capitalist society have, in the main, subjected these psycho-technologists of work to a harsh critique: they are no more than servants of power, engaging in the manipulation of workers in their attempts to adjust them to exploitative working conditions. [1] Their analyses of industrial unrest in psychological terms, as signs of emotional immaturity or maladjustment, mystify and legitimate oppression in work. For all their talk of the importance of the contentment and fulfilment of the worker, they have not fundamentally altered the situation inaugurated by the birth of scientific management in the early decades of this century. Thus the writings of F. W. Taylor serve as a paradigm for analysis of future 'scientific' interventions on work.[2] Functional organization of the factory was to optimize efficiency. Work study would define the best way to carry out each task; selection would assign the appropriate man for each job; training would inculcate the discipline of following the methods laid down; scientific delineation of a fair day's work would allocate rewards to tasks to minimize dispute and maximize effort. The whole would be enforced by rigorous management of the minutiae of the workplace. Systematic knowledge of production was thus part of a strategy to vest complete control over the process in the hands of management, treating the worker as merely the possessor of physical powers to be deployed and utilized under strict control and in the service of a pure logic of efficiency.

Critics of developments in the psycho-technologies of management since Taylor acknowledge that the worker is no longer viewed simply as an automaton, a more or less productive body, but is now seen as a person with subjective and inter-subjective attributes that are pertinent to work. But they argue that the skills and capacities that mass production transferred to technology and management have not been restored to the worker. Nor have the vast disparities in financial rewards that characterize the organization of production been substantially ameliorated: at root, the rationale of production remains profit for the owners. And, whatever changes may have been made in work organization, workers do not manage themselves. Ultimately the workplace remains hierarchical, with power exercised from above, by bosses and managers, upon those below, whether they are stuck at a machine, behind a desk, or 'servicing' the needs of others.

These critics are aware that the programmes and techniques for the humanization of work – from the industrial psychology of Charles Myers through the human relations approaches of Elton Mayo to contemporary movements for the quality of working life and quality circles – have represented themselves as liberal, democratic, and egalitarian transformations of the activity of production. However, these representations are dismissed as disingenuous or politically naïve, ignoring the inequalities of power and financial interests in the sphere of production, as merely attempts to justify the self-interested ambitions of the experts in work. Whatever their professed concerns, the psychologists of organizations and occupations have colluded in the invention of more subtle ways of adjusting the worker, based upon the happy but not altogether innocent illusion that industrial discontent, strikes, absenteeism, low productivity and so forth do not derive from fundamental conflicts of interest but from ameliorable properties of the psychological relations of the factory. The apparent discovery of a fortunate coincidence between personal contentment of the worker and maximum efficiency and profitability for the boss is merely yet another dissimulation of the fundamental conflict between capital and labour. By concentrating upon theories and techniques that would sell it to managers, the psychological expertise of production has inevitably adopted a managerial perspective. The 'industrial relations problems' it promises to resolve are in fact, from the workers' perspective, solutions, even if temporary and defensive, to the basic injustices of their role, status, and rewards.

There is much truth in these critical analyses. The symbolism and authority of scientific languages and techniques have certainly helped to continually re-establish the legitimacy of the private enterprise and the hierarchies of power and reward at work. The ideal pictures of management and of workplace relations purveyed in the scientific textbooks have, no doubt, been discrepant from the realities of work. Much of the new technology of employee participation has scarcely veiled the hope that a direct relationship between employee and company will attenuate the power of the trade unions and their prerogatives for the representation of collective interests and the defense of collective rights. But to regard these scientific, psychological discourses as ideological suggests a particular way of explaining their existence and operation: the knowledge claims are false; they serve a social function and answer to a set of economic needs; it is because they are false that they can serve this function and answer to these needs; the historical origins of the knowledges or techniques in question are sufficiently explained by pointing to the function they have served.[3]

The new languages and techniques of management have certainly arisen in political contexts, and have had political consequences. But they are not merely functional responses to, or legitimations of, given economic needs, static political forces or pre-existing social interests. The changing conceptions of work and the worker, the changing vocabularies and techniques of management, do more than legitimate the conditions and relations of production in the face of concerns about inhumanity, inefficiency, profitability, democracy, accountability and the like. As Miller and O'Leary have shown, while 'Taylorism' was certainly not simply the logical outcome of the need to co-ordinate tasks in the large corporation, as suggested by some orthodox historians of management, neither was it merely the effect of some inner need of capitalism for increasing control over the workplace.[4] Rather, it was part of a wider family of political programmes that sought to use scientific knowledge to advance national efficiency through making the most productive use of material and human resources. It shared with other members of this family a belief in the improvement of the efficiency of persons through the application of expertise. And, like concerns with the physical state of the population and its mental capacities, it did this by constructing norms and standards that accorded a visibility to previously obscure and unimportant aspects of the activities of persons, and by calibrating and governing these minutiae of existence in accordance with these norms – of hygiene, of intelligence and so forth. Taylorism was also part of a new attention to individual differences among persons, seeking to know them and managing them from the perspective of social and institutional goals and objectives, an attention that enmeshed the individual within a complex of calculative practices. And it was the first of many attempts to bring the internal life of the enterprise into line with the values of democracy, providing a legitimacy for management by giving it a rational basis and according it the capacity to eliminate waste and thus promote the national interest.

Managerial thought and the psychological expertise of work play an active part in the formation of new images and mechanisms, which bring the government of the enterprise into alignment with cultural values, social expectations, political concerns, and professional aspirations. At the level of political thought, these new ways of construing production provide novel ways of connecting the interior life of the enterprise with calculations concerning the economic well-being of the nation, changing the very notions of the proper sphere of politics and the activity of the state. At the level of policy the new images and techniques are embedded in previously unthinkable strategic interventions into the enterprise to promote particular economic and social objectives. In these processes, new groups come to identify themselves, conceive of their interests in terms of these new words and images, formulate their objectives through them, and mobilize to put them into action. Within the enterprise itself, changes in ways of construing, documenting, and acting upon the internal organization of the factory, office, shop, or airline actually transform the meaning and reality of work. And the new ways of relating the feelings and wishes of individual employees to the fate of the enterprise are key elements in the fabrication of new languages and techniques to bind the worker into the productive life of society.

The changes in the conception, organization, and regulation of work and the worker over this century involve relations between many aspects of thought and practice: the history of the large corporation; the changing relations of manufacturing and non-manufacturing industry; the elaboration of an expertise of management; innovations in the rationale and techniques of accounting to incorporate the human resources of the enterprise; transformations in macro-economic policy and much more. I view these events from one particular perspective: that of the subjectivity of the worker. Hence I examine the relations between governmental rationalities, social strategies, human technologies, and techniques of the self that have been brought into being by these new ways of thinking and acting on the economy, the workplace, and the worker. They have provided means for linking changing political objectives, the ceaseless quest of business for profitability, the demands for a source and basis for managerial authority, and the psyche of the worker. Through them new networks of power have been established, a web of calculations and technologies connecting macro-economic policy, the management of the enterprise, and the design of the labour process with human subjectivity itself.

Chapter six

The Contented Worker

> Business efficiency and the welfare of employees are but two sides
> of the same problem.[1]
>
> E. Cadbury, 1912

Employment, in its fundamental capitalist form, implies a purely
contractual relationship between two isolated economic actors. The
worker enters into an agreement to alienate a certain quantum of
labour power in exchange for a wage; the capitalist agrees to part with
a certain quantum of money in exchange for the right to deploy a crucial factor of production within the labour process.[2] No doubt this
stark picture captures much of what was essential to the mode of
production in early capitalism. But since the earliest struggles over
the length of the working day and the conditions of employment, the
worker has come to be seen as something more than an expendable
and endlessly replaceable commodity. Initially it appeared that it was
the strength, the health, the virtue, and the moral rectitude of the
worker that required conservation, and that such considerations
would have to be imposed upon the employer by law. Some see the
imposition of such obligations on employers through the nineteenth
century Factory Acts as the outcome of campaigns by enlightened
philanthropists; others regard them as the product of labour militancy. Marx himself viewed such legislation as the means by which the
state, acting in the interests of capital as a whole, stimulated concentration and monopolization by setting conditions that small
manufacturers found hard to meet, and safeguarded the supply of a
vital factor of production – workers themselves. However this may be,
by the first decade of the twentieth century the contractual relation
between employer and employee was encumbered by certain
statutory requirements and constraints. Work became a key element
of *social* economy.

Over the course of this century employment was to be further socialized. It was to be situated within a wider network of relations be-

tween the worker, the employer and the state. This network took shape along four intertwined pathways: welfare, security, harmony, and productivity. Welfare denoted a concern with the conditions of labour, and their effects on the health and well-being of the worker, later growing to encompass not only the selection and allocation of workers but also all those conditions in the production process, in the organization of the workplace, and in the make-up of the workers themselves that could impede or promote efficiency. The imperative of security addressed itself to securing, for society as well as for the individual, the conditions of orderly life for the labourer and his or her dependents outside the wage relationship. This initially took the form of voluntary, collective, or industrially based techniques but ultimately, at least until the 1980s, social insurance came to be the crucial mechanism – pensions, unemployment, sickness benefit and so forth provided through socially funded and bureaucratically organized mechanisms. The search for harmony entailed a range of initiatives that sought, in one way or another, to mitigate the antagonistic possibilities in the employment relation, by integrating the worker within networks of obligation in the enterprise; schemes of industrial democracy, joint consultation, communication, and share ownership were the most common. And the desire for productivity led to the maximization of the contribution of the worker to the objectives of the enterprise, its output, efficiency, and profitability. The financial incentive of the wage came to be supplemented by a range of physical, technical, and psychological interventions upon the capacities, motives, enthusiasm, and commitment of the worker.

It was in the first decades of the twentieth century that the subjectivity of the worker began to be connected with the imperatives of economic policy, the search for social integration, the management of industrial harmony and the quest for business efficiency. The majority of firms prior to World War I had remained relatively indifferent to the conditions of the labourer.[3] But Quaker employers such as Rowntree at York, Cadbury at Bournville, and Lever at Port Sunlight perceived a fundamental relationship between the obligations of philanthropy and the pursuit of profit. The 'industrial betterment principle' was a new rationale and technique for organizing the reciprocal duties and obligations of employer and employee, in which industrial labour was no longer an isolated economic exchange but was located within relations of solidarity and ties of community. The efficiency of production, it appeared, was directly related to the 'welfare' of the labourers.

Industrial betterment operated on two fronts. The first concerned relations outside the workplace, the second concerned conditions within it. Outside the workplace, model villages, public baths, recreation clubs, libraries, and other techniques were used to improve the culture and standards of living of the worker. Within the workplace, the relationships that the employee had to the activities of work – selection, training, working conditions, and standards of reward – were to be organized to ensure the good health and orderly habits of the worker. The key figures in this new network were the 'social secretaries' or welfare workers. Some acted as extra mural visitors to the families and homes of the workers, advising them on ways of conducting their affairs, managing their budgets, and coping with sickness or other crises. Others operated within the factories themselves, watching over health and behaviour, especially of women workers, in the light of the possibly degrading consequences of the physical and social conditions of employment upon their health and morals. Welfare workers thus acted as vital go-betweens, establishing links between the workplace, the home, and the cultural milieu, relaying advice and information, supervising each from the perspective of the health, hygiene, and morality of the worker.

But this unitary and embracing strategy, based upon the integration of workers and their families into bonds of social solidarity that had the workplace as their hub, was isolated and short lived. In large part the limits on this strategy arose from the way in which, in the first twenty years of the twentieth century, 'the state' extended its scope to the government of the 'social economy'. Networks of power were formed that brought every individual into the view of the public authorities and their field of action. From medical inspection of schoolchildren to aid in the prevention of physical deterioration of the population, through public health measures directed at the moral and hygienic conditions of home and family, to compulsory universal education to moralize and instruct the future workers and citizens, the responsibilities of rule were extended to embrace positive promotion of the social good through acting upon the conduct and habits of each member of the population.[4]

Many new social devices were invented to connect the quotidian affairs of citizens with the powers of the authorities. Economic life was no exception. Since at least the early nineteenth century the significance of work for public order had been as important as its directly economic function – its moralizing effect upon the worker, its capacity to enmesh the individual in the network of expectations and routines that make up the social body. Hence the social consequences of the economic conditions of those outside the wage relation, temporarily or permanently, were prime objects of social economy. Labour exchanges were, perhaps, the first technical solution to this linked problem of economy and subjectivity, aiming to establish not only a free market in labour for the genuine unemployed, but also to expose the industrial malingerer to deterrent sanction. Even more far reaching in their significance were the new devices to safeguard the economic existence of workers and their families outside the relationship of individual worker to particular boss. These were the mechanisms of social insurance. Social insurance would incorporate into society those sectors of the population not directly and immediately in receipt of a wage – the young, the old, the sick and the unemployed – through establishing a set of direct economic relations between each citizen and the state. Further, the state would directly intervene as a third party in the contract of employment between the labourer and the boss, thus writing a social contract of security into the individual wage contract. The employee was to be, at the same time and by the same token, an insured citizen.[5]

Social insurance, from the first National Insurance Act of 1911 to the present, institutes a direct relation between the insured citizen and the state in which both parties have their rights and their duties. This new relation was intended to entail a definite reduction in the general social and political consequences of economic events – industrial conflict, unemployment, and so forth – by ensuring that, working or not, citizens became, in effect, employees of society. The significance of the vocabulary of insurance for the initiators of the schemes was primarily moral. The relation between contributions and benefits was political rather than actuarial, in that the amount of each was the product of a political calculation and the contributions of the insured person did not so much pay for their benefits as qualify them to receive them. Nonetheless, the language of insurance was chosen for its psychological effects, its resonances of 'security, respectability and virtuous providence' were to bind the citizen subjectively into the obligations of the social order.[6]

The principle and mechanisms of national insurance led to the decline or demise of other systems of security for the worker: Friendly Societies, community- or union-based provisions, or those, such as the Quaker schemes, based directly on the enterprise. Further, the wage relation was encumbered by other provisions of social economy: health and safety legislation and, in some sweated industries, wages boards to set minimum rates of pay. In the factory, the office, and the shop, government began to extend itself to the social bonds of labour. The paths of industrial welfare and social security bifurcated. While some welfare workers severed their links with the enterprise and installed themselves in the network that began to be established between the social insurance system and the domains of home and work, the 'industrial welfare workers' were to integrate themselves into the technology of management within the physical locale of the plant. Their destiny was to be profoundly affected by World War I.

The economic necessity for the management of the human resources of industrial life was thrown into sharp relief by the strains on production imposed by the rate of expenditure of munitions on the bloody battlefields of France. Most extravagant in its demands was the Somme front. Almost 3 million rounds of artillery ammunition were accumulated at the front prior to the battles of 1916, not to mention the volume of ammunition required to fuel the mechanized and industrialized lethality of the Maxim machine gun.[7] Many boys and women were working up to 70 hours a week; some men worked over 100 hours. The pace and intensity of war work was having effects on the health and behaviour of munitions workers, and this in its turn was taking a toll in productivity and efficiency. It was of vital military importance to discover ways in which these effects might be minimized, and the labour process so organized to maximize efficiency and minimize fatigue, accidents, and illness.

The issues that had inspired the Quaker philanthropic employers took on a new significance. Seebohm Rowntree was appointed to establish a Welfare Department at the Ministry of Munitions, and a Health of Munitions Workers Committee was set up. While this committee was disbanded at the end of the war, the concerns that had animated it remained. It was replaced by a new Industrial Fatigue Research Board, 'to consider and investigate the relations of hours of labour and other conditions of employment including methods of work, to the production of fatigue, having regard both to industrial efficiency and to the production of health among the workers.'[8] This board was later placed under the auspices of the Medical Research Council and collaborated in research with the Department of Science and Industrial Research. The nature of this concern with the productive body can be gathered from the kinds of reports the board produced on hours of work and ventilation in munitions and tinplate factories, on efficiency and fatigue in the iron and steel industry, on the speed of adaptation to different hours of work, on the effects of rest pauses, and on individual differences among operatives in the cotton industry, as well the investigations it conducted on the causation of industrial accidents and the principles of time and motion study and vocational guidance.[9]

These early studies of industrial fatigue, by and large, construed the worker as a physiological apparatus whose attributes were to be analyzed, calculated and adjusted to the design of work – lighting, rest, pauses, bench layout and so forth – in order to minimize fatigue and maximize efficiency. But by the 1920s it became apparent that fatigue, inefficiency and accidents were not explicable in purely physiological terms. 'The physiological factors involved in purely muscular fatigue', wrote C. S. Myers, 'are now fast becoming negligible, compared with the effects of mental and nervous fatigue, monotony, want of interest, suspicion, hostility, etc. The psychological factor must therefore be the main consideration of industry and commerce in the future.'[10] In the inter-war years these psychological factors were to become the basis of a new matrix of relations between economic regulation, management of the enterprise and psychological expertise. The organizing institution of this matrix was the National Institute of Industrial Psychology under the direction of Charles Myers.

Myers was an exemplary figure in the British psychology of the inter-war years.[11] While a pupil of W. H. Rivers at Cambridge, he had accompanied him and fellow pupil William McDougall on A. C. Hadden's 1898 expedition to the Torres Straits, a turning point in the attempt to use scientific techniques in the study of 'man'. After completing the Natural Sciences tripos at Cambridge and qualifying in medicine, Myers returned to Cambridge where he became director of the Psychological Laboratory in 1912. His interests ranged from music to experimental psychophysiology and the role of psychology in practical problems; his pupils included virtually all the central figures in British psychology in the inter-war period: F. C. Bartlett, Eric Farmer, C. A. Mace, W. J. H. Sprott, R. H. Thouless, C. W. Valentine, and many more.

During World War I Myers left Cambridge and 'proceeded on his own initiative to France in October 1914 to do what he could to help the war effort'.[12] He was soon appointed psychological consultant to the British forces in France, where he virtually coined the term 'shell shock'. After supplementing his services to the military with advice on sound localization techniques in submarine detection, he was appointed to co-ordinate psychological work in neurological centres for shell-shock cases. Crucially, like so many others, he became convinced of the key importance of psychoneurotic factors, not only in shell shock, but also in mental inefficiency in general.

As late as 1930 Myers was asserting his opposition to behaviourism by stating that 'the fundamental subject matter of psychology is conscious experience, not conduct'.[13] But it was precisely 'conduct' that was to come to concern him, and lie at the heart of the 'human factor' technologies that he and his co-workers were to invent and promulgate from the National Institute of Industrial Psychology: personality assessment, aptitude testing, vocational guidance, staff selection, work study, personnel management, training and much more. In 1918, Myers had given a series of lectures on *Present Day Application of Psychology with Special Reference to Industry, Education, and Nervous Breakdown*, where he argued for the establishment of 'institutes of applied psychology in each of our largest cities'. Urged on by leading industrialists, supported by virtually the entire caucus of British psychologists from Cyril Burt to Susan Isaacs (then Brierley), and funded by Rowntree, Cadbury, Cammell Laird, and the trustees of Carnegie and Rockefeller, the National Institute of Industrial Psychology was the outcome. Established under his direction in 1921, it was to carry out fee-paying work for public and private organizations and individuals. But it would also proselytize for a new way of thinking of the relations between human subjectivity and organizational life.[14]

At the National Institute of Industrial Psychology, Myers and his colleagues addressed the problems that were now becoming standard fare – fatigue, industrial accidents, 'lost time' – but they propounded a view of the nature of the productive subject, the origins of industrial discontent and the role of industrial psychology that related the subjectivity of the worker to the demand for productivity in a new way. The worker was neither a mindless brute nor a psycho-physiological machine, but an individual with a particular psychological make-up in terms of intelligence and emotions, with fears, worries, and anxieties, whose work was hampered by boredom and worry, whose resistances to management were often founded in rational concerns, and whose productive efficiency was highly dependent upon sympathy, interest, satisfaction, and contentment. If this were the case, Myers argued:

> it becomes the function of the industrial psychologist not merely to investigate methods of payment, the movements of the worker, and the length of hours of his work but also to attempt to improve the mental make-up of the worker, to study his home conditions and to satisfy his native impulses, so far as they are satisfiable under modern industrial conditions where, despite longer education and increasing culture, industrial specialization tends to reduce him to the status of a small wheel working in a vast machine, of the nature of which he is too often kept in complete ignorance, and towards which consequently he is apt to develop apathy or actual antagonism.[15]

The subjectivity of the worker was to be opened to knowledge and regulation in terms of two notions which were central to psychological thought and strategy in the period after World War I: individual differences and mental hygiene.[16] Firstly, workers differed among themselves, not merely in intelligence but also in emotional make-up, and these differences had important industrial consequences. Farmer and his colleagues had shown, for example, that liability to accidents could be predicted by a study of individual psychological characteristics.[17] Hence there was no 'one best way' to organize production, suitably for all tasks and workers. It was a question, rather, of fitting the job to the man and the man to the job. The worker, that is to say, was to be individualized in terms of his or her particular psychological make-up and idiosyncracies, the job analyzed in terms of its demands upon the worker, and human resources were to be matched to occupational demands. Vocational guidance and selec-

tion would adjust recruitment to work through a psychological calculation of suitability; movement study and analysis of periods of rest
and work, the design of tasks and materials and so on, would adjust
work to the psycho-physiology and psychology of the worker.

Second, the human being was not to be analyzed in terms of a
superficial analogy with a piece of engineering machinery, and to be
degraded to a servile mechanism of management – such an attitude
was not only bound to produce an entirely rational antagonism from
the worker, but was also based on faulty psychology. The worker had
a complex subjective life that needed to be understood if industry was
to truly take account of the human factor. The terms of this understanding were derived from 'the new psychology'. The subjectivity of
the worker was the outcome of the shaping of instincts by forces and
constraints in early family life; the conduct of the worker was to be explained through the relationship between the personality so formed
and the industrial surroundings in which work took place.[18] Adjustment, that is to say, required the successful resolution of conflicting
instinctual forces and their harnessing to the particular requirements
of social and industrial life. And the corollary was that social and industrial inefficiency and unhappiness were the outcome of failures of
adjustment of the internal life of the individual to the external reality
in which he or she lived and worked – in short, they were the outcome
of maladjustment.

In work the individual sought not merely financial returns but
gratification of the particular pattern of instinctual wishes and
desires that comprised their unique character or temperament. It was
through the satisfaction of these instincts and the matching of work
to temperament that workers would be induced to give of their best.
Hence the worker was not to be forced to work against his will, but to
be encouraged by removing the obstacles and difficulties that
prevented him from giving the best to his work. The worker was certainly not motivated purely by financial incentives. Men may continue to work when they are rolling in wealth; they may continue to
loaf while they are well nigh starving from poverty.

At least as important, then, as methods of payment is the mental
atmosphere of the works, that character of which is largely dependent
on management and leadership on the one side, or loyalty and com-
radeship on the other, and on the satisfaction of each worker's instincts and interests, which are by no means confined to what money
will buy him or her outside the factory.[19]

But not all problems could be resolved by judicious adjustment of
the mental atmosphere of the workplace, or by fitting the man to the
job. Some individuals had become maladapted as a consequence of
the formation of their temperament in early life. Such maladapted individuals were both personally unhappy and socially inefficient.

Maladaption led to social discontent, industrial inefficiency, and individual neuroses; if untreated it could even result in delinquency, crime, and full-blown insanity. At work, unconscious conflicts, unsuccessful repression of thwarted instincts, and unexpressed emotions could be found at the root of many industrial problems. Psychoneuroses, that is to say, were at least as important as rest pauses, posture, illumination and the like. The question of industrial efficiency was, at root, one of mental hygiene – the diagnosis and treatment of the minor mental troubles of the manager or the worker before they produced major and disabling problems; the promotion of correct habits in light of a knowledge of the nature of mental life; the organization of the factory itself so as to minimize the production of symptoms of emotional and mental instability and enhance adjustment.

Myers characterized bad managers in terms of their psychodynamics. The egotistical emotional type reacts not to situations but to the emotions that they arouse in him, is therefore apt to be unjust, lacking in balanced criticism, producing anxiety or indifference in his workers. The over-anxious manager is always grumbling and finding fault, depressing subordinates and denying them pleasure in their work. The manager with absorbing interests or absurd prepossessions also produces a bad state of discipline, for when workers pander to his whims they tend also to pander to their own. A psychotherapeutics of management was necessary for selection and for cure.

But more crucial, perhaps, was the problem of the maladjusted worker. By 1927 Eric Farmer and others were clear that industrial inefficiency was not simply a question of individual difference, it was rooted in mild psychoneuroses. 'Telegraphist's cramp', for example, was merely one among other manifestations of such minor mental disturbances in the worker. The maladjusted worker lacked self-confidence, felt ill at ease with people, was frightened by authorities, and was anxious about unrealistic events. Under conditions of telegraphic work such a worker would develop the disorder of telegraphist's cramp, but this was only a symptom of the psychoneurosis. Not merely explanation but also prophylaxis, prevention and cure for worker inefficiency, appeared possible through the application of psychological knowledge to industrial problems.

In 'human factor' psychology, the worker was no longer conceived of as a set of psycho-physiological capacities and reactions, but as a subjective being with instincts and emotions. But while the mental hygienists talked in terms of the mental atmosphere of the factory and the emotional relations between workers and managers, the focus of their techniques was upon the maladjusted individual, upon efficient allocation of manpower through selection and vocational guidance, upon identifying the characteristics of the normal worker in contradistinction to the neurotic, upon treatment and prophylaxis of psychoneuroses. Developments in the United States, amplified by another experience of war, would place the inter-subjective relations of the workplace at the heart of the psycho-technology of industry.

In the United States, too, the maladjusted worker had been discovered.[20] Maladjustment, it appeared, was at the heart of dissatisfactions expressed in ways ranging from petty jealousy, through lack of cheerful co-operation, poor work performance, tiredness, irritability, distractibility, nausea, abnormal fears, and neuroses to labour agitation. It was estimated that half of the annual cost of labour turnover to industry resulted from emotional maladjustment, and that the effectiveness of about half the labour force was impaired by emotional maladjustment requiring investigation and treatment. However this concentration on the maladjusted worker and the industrial misfit in the United States was accompanied by a rather different way of linking the subjective world of the worker with the demands of production, construed not in terms of the individual but of the group. It came to be identified with the writings of Elton Mayo and the notion of 'human relations'.[21]

Mayo had initially been concerned with the body as a psycho-physiological mechanism – the effects of rest pauses and the conditions of the workplace upon fatigue, accidents and labour turnover. But the conclusions he drew from the long series of studies of the Hawthorne Works of the Western Electric Company conducted between 1923 and 1932 were to provide a new language for interpreting the links between the conditions of work and the efficiency of production.[22] What was now of significance was neither the objective exigencies and characteristics of the labour process – levels of light, hours of work, and so forth – nor even the maladjustments and psychoneuroses of individual workers, but the human relations of the enterprise; the informal group life that made it up, and the subjective inter-relations which comprised it.

Productivity, efficiency and contentment were now to be understood in terms of the *attitudes* of the workers to their work, their *feelings* of control over their pace of work and environment, their *sense of cohesion* within their small working group, their *beliefs* about the concern and understanding that the bosses had for their individual worth and their personal problems. This was not simply a matter of drawing attention to a complex domain of informal organization in any plant that existed in tension with its formal organization. It was also that a range of new tasks emerged to be grasped by knowledge and managed in the factory.

On the one hand, the subjective features of group relations had to be rendered into thought and made amenable to calculation. The device used here was the non-directed interview. The Hawthorne investigations, for example, involved some 20,000 interviews whose initial purpose had been to obtain objective information. But their value, as the studies progressed, appeared to be very different: they provided, rather, a way into the emotional life of the factory, the emotional significance of particular events in the experience of the worker. Thus complaints could be analyzed into their 'manifest' content and their 'latent' content, distinguishing their 'material content' from their 'psychological form'; they were not 'facts in themselves' but 'symptoms or indicators of personal and social situations which needed to be explained'.[23] One could thus get at the thoughts, attitudes, and sentiments among workers, foremen, supervisors and so on that gave rise to problems, dissatisfactions, and conflict. As we have seen in a previous chapter, these devices were to have a far-reaching significance, beyond the world of the factory, in rendering the subjective features of social and national life thinkable and governable.[24] The analysis used by the theorists of human relations construed the emotional life of employees in terms analogous to those used by British human factor psychologists, but located these personal sentiments within a new perception of the workplace as a social organization. The factory was a pattern of relations between those in particular organizational positions, symbolized through social distinctions, embodying certain values and expectations and requiring delicate interpretations among all involved. Problems arose, then, not only as a result of individual maladjustment, but also where these values came into conflict with one another, or where the social equilibrium was disrupted by management seeking to impose changes without recognizing the sentiments and meanings attached to the old ways of doing things. Given that the management were predominantly moved by the logic of cost and efficiency, while the workers tended to operate in terms of the logic of sentiments and the inter-human relations of the plant, it was no wonder the two so often came into conflict.

But once they had been conceptualized and studied, these subjective features of work could themselves be managed to promote organizational harmony. The interviews and surveys of workers themselves had a role here, for the airing of grievances was often therapeutic in itself. But more generally, the task for management was to manage the enterprise and change within it in light of a knowledge of the values and sentiments of the work force, and to act upon these so as to make them operate for, rather than against, the interests of the firm. Personnel workers had a key role here, not only in documenting values and sentiments, but also in working out plans in light of them, advising supervisors, and diagnosing problems of the group and individuals within it. 'Communication' became a vital instrument for realigning workers' values with management objectives, through explaining the situation, clearing up misunderstandings, and allaying fears and anxieties. Personnel workers also had a role in counselling individual workers about their difficulties to assist them in adjustment to the social organization. By such techniques management could create the internal harmony that was the condition of a happy and productive factory. The minutiae of the human soul – human interactions, feelings, and thoughts, the psychological relations of the individual to the group – had emerged as a new domain for management.[25]

The network of interpersonal relations that constituted the group within the workplace came to accrue a significance that went beyond work. On the one hand it could satisfy the needs of the individual for human association, and have a direct relation not only for productivity and efficiency, but also for mental health. On the other hand it had a social function. Increasing division of labour had fragmented the ties of solidarity that bound individuals together; the state was too distant from individuals to bind them into the life of society at the level of their individual consciences; hence the working group was a crucial mechanism for dragging otherwise isolated individuals into the 'general torrent of social life'.[26] From Mayo to the present day, the social significance of employment and unemployment, its function for individual health and social solidarity, was to be cast in this subjective form.

Before and during World War II, British management thought came to accept the economic advantages of fostering the loyalty of employees through human relations styles of management: the emphasis on the need for the integration of the worker, on the social functions of group relations, on the effectiveness of participative managerial leadership.[27] As the challenge of trade unionism to the power relations of the workplace began to recede after the General Strike, fundamental questioning of the authority of management was consigned to political extremes. Management came to represent itself as an expert profession, and to claim that it was not capitalist discipline but industrial efficiency that required skilled managerial control over the process of production. The legitimacy and authority of management were to depend not only upon its basis in practical experience, but also upon a scientific knowledge that would cast this experience within the framework of technical rationality. And to manage rationally one now required a knowledge of the worker.

The language and techniques of human relations were thus one element in the managerial claim to a specific knowledge base for its expertise. They also underpinned the argument that management was independent of the simple interest the boss had in maximizing profit. Management could represent its authority as neutral, rational, and in the worker's interest. In return for the acceptance of such authority

by workers and their representatives, the worker would be treated
equitably, justly, honestly, fairly. The language and techniques of
human relations allowed British management to reconcile the apparently opposing realities of the bosses' imperative of efficiency with
the intelligibility of the workers' resistance to it, and to claim the capacity to transform the subjectivity of the worker from an obstacle to
an ally in quest for productivity and profit.

In the inter-war years in Britain, the human relations role of management intersected with developments along a rather different path
along which the subjective commitments of the worker were to be incorporated within the objectives of the firm. Again, crucial conditions for this development arose as a consequence of World War I. In
1917, in response to a series of strikes in industries vital to the war effort that were thought to be fuelled by Marxists and other subversive
political elements, especially in the Shop Stewards Movement, Lloyd
George had established the Industrial Unrest Commissions 'to
remove justifiable reason for unrest'.[28] The urgency for some
measures to restore industrial concord was highlighted by the success
of Bolshevism in Russia and the rising tide of government crisis and
militant working-class struggle in Germany and France. Industrial
politics was rapidly transforming, as intellectuals and politicians of
the Left debated nationalization and workers' control, and skilled
and white-collar workers increasingly sought unionization and affil-
iation with the TUC and began to envisage campaigns of direct
action.

Whitley Councils, which had originated in a reconstruction sub-
committee chaired by J.H. Whitley, sought to provide just such a reconstitution of industrial harmony. They were to be 'composed of
representatives of employers and workers in each industry'; were intended to discuss everything – not just wages and conditions, but participation, job security, technical education, and improvement of
management – 'affecting the progress and well-being of the trade
from the point of view of those engaged in it, as far as this is consonant with the general interests of the community'.[29]

The problem that had to be resolved was two faceted. On the one
hand, how could certain features of the national economic situation
be controlled and harmonized without threatening the private
ownership of the enterprise and the economic autonomy of the boss?
Whitleyism could accomplish this through voluntary agreement to
arbitration schemes and the adherence of industries and firms to decisions made through joint discussion. On the other hand, how could
the worker be integrated into the enterprise while leaving intact the
basis of authority within it? Such considerations underpinned the
deliberate separation between these mechanisms and the established
machinery of collective bargaining.

73

While the take-up of Whitleyism among employers was not particularly enthusiastic, there was some extension of works council schemes, and these often paid lip service at least to ideas of industrial democracy and joint control. As management sought to establish itself as a third element intervening between the owner and the worker that was not to be identified with the interests of capital, Whitleyism seemed an element consistent with its vocabulary of democratic control, social responsibility, and humanitarianism. But this conception of the managerial vocation was in decline by the mid-1920s. Whitleyism itself had proved somewhat of a disappointment. Commonly management would use works councils to talk about production problems, while workers made more or less rude suggestions as to what should happen to the foreman.[30] As unemployment grew and industrial militancy subsided, the philanthropic and humanitarian conceptions that had infused management thought with themes from Quakerism, liberalism, and socialism began to give way to the notion of management as a specialized form of neutral scientific expertise. More and more came around to Sidney Webb's point of view that 'Under any social order from now to Utopia management is indispensible and all enduring.'[31] Whitleyism fell into decline, the joint councils that survived became not so much mechanisms for sharing control as instruments of industrial welfare, managing contentment through symbolizing the values of communication and participation.

With the increasing concentration of industrial activity over the 1920s and 1930s, the growth of new industry and the increase in size and complexity of plants, policies for the management of the human relations of the firm began to appear necessary to many large corporations, no longer for ethical reasons but to minimize industrial disharmony and maximize efficiency. Gradually, during the inter-war years, welfare workers extended their concerns from issues such as selection, the education of young workers, working conditions, first aid, and groups, to embrace all these new aspects of management that concerned the well-being of the employee and its relation to the organization of the workplace. The Welfare Workers Association, founded in 1913, was to become the Institute of Labour Management in 1931. It was to be further transmuted, in the 1940s, into the Institute of Personnel Management.

The events of wartime were again to provide crucial conditions for the development of new rationales and technologies for the government of the individual. For the demands upon industry imposed by total war were to force a consolidation and generalization of the networks of power that linked the duties of government, the objectives of business, and the techniques of management with the subjectivity of the worker.

Chapter seven

The Worker at War

> There existed, so to speak, an implicit contract between government and people; the people refused none of the sacrifices that the government demanded from them for the winning of the war. In return they expected that the government should show imagination and seriousness in planning for the restoration and improvement of the nation's well-being when the war had been won.[1]

W. Hancock and M. Gowing, 1949

Historians have waxed lyrical about the new political contract opened between government and citizen during World War II and its positive implications for post-war social and economic reform. Those of a radical persuasion have taken a less favourable view, tending to see the wartime experience as a crucial phase in the growth of 'corporatism' in British politics. In the 'contract' for wartime production, argues Keith Middlemas, one observes the marshalling of business through employers' organizations, the working class through the elite of the trade unions, and the government through ministers and civil servants into agents of a managerial state. Such corporatism, it is argued, operates not according to doctrines of parliamentary sovereignty or those of irreconcilable conflicts of class interests, but by a technocratic logic committed to unquestioned objectives of efficiency, rationality, and productivity.[2] The critical function of the notion of corporatism is certainly valuable – it debunks the political fictions of constitutionalism on the one hand and class struggle on the other. But it tends to obscure what was being positively constructed in these events – the elaboration of a new rationale of government, a new way of formulating the tasks of public authorities, a new way of conceiving and regulating the links between the citizen and his or her productive activity.

When Ernest Bevin was appointed Minister of Labour by Churchill in May 1940, he set himself a threefold task:

to meet the needs of the forces and raise productivity speedily and efficiently to its maximum capacity by the full use of each citizen; to help men and women to tolerate the efforts they were called on to make; and to safeguard the rights of the individual as far as possible.[3]

The government of production was both direct and indirect. By 1943 the Ministry of Supply was the country's largest employer. Its 42 Royal Ordnance factories had 300,000 employees. But the Ministry of Labour under Bevin also took powers over manpower in private industry of an unprecedented scope: to mobilize and control the recruitment of labour, to determine wages irrespective of the wishes of employers, to reduce excess profits via taxation, to prevent strikes. Conciliation machinery sought to ensure fairness in the wages and conditions of employment of workers in controlled occupations and to resolve disputes without strikes and lock-outs. While voluntary collective bargaining remained, a National Arbitration Tribunal became the final court of appeal. Essential Work Orders sought to limit labour turnover by controlling the conditions under which a worker could be dismissed or leave, but which introduced in return a series of restrictions on the authority of the boss for which unions had long been campaigning: minimum periods of notice for dismissal, minimum wage levels for employees, conditions of employment of a level established centrally, and satisfactory arrangements for welfare and training.

The objectives of this enhanced involvement of political authorities in the productive life of the nation were straightforward – the construction of the machinery of warfare such as tanks, planes, ships, weapons and the like, the maintenance of supply of material, and the production of the necessities of life on the home front. But the mode of government it entailed was novel. A manpower policy was required to ensure the most effective allocation of human resources to the various branches of the war effort in the fighting forces and in the factories. Maximum efficiency and productivity needed to be maintained, over a long period without deleterious effects on the physical or human resources of production. Interruptions to the production process by strikes, disputes, lock outs, illness, labour turnover, absenteeism, or slacking had to be minimized. And all this had to be done in a manner that maintained morale at home and did not infringe the principles of liberty and democracy upon which this morale depended.

The techniques deployed in each of these areas were not new, but their interlinking in a coherent programme transformed each, and established the conditions for the emergence of a new conception of work and its regulation in the post-war period. On the one hand, the issue of the welfare of employees became, as it had in World War I, a matter of national military importance. In his annual report of 1941 the Chief Inspector of Factories put the matter thus:

> In recent years, it has been increasingly appreciated that the welfare of employees implies attention not only to their physical comfort but to their mental and psychological make-up also and that accordingly good personnel management in an establishment is the primary object to be aimed at.[4]

The wartime strategy transformed this appreciation into a set of statutory requirements and devices surrounding the relations of employer and employees. The Factory (Welfare and Services) Order of July 1941 gave the Chief Inspector of Factories powers to secure medical and welfare services in war factories; pretty soon all matters concerning the conditions of the worker were concentrated in the Factory and Welfare Department of the Ministry of Labour. By 1943 the Royal Ordnance factories alone employed 600 labour officers, and the Chief Inspector of Factories estimated in 1942 that, in firms employing over 250 people, 5,500 welfare officers were employed. The contract between employer and employee became, on the one hand, regulated by public powers; on the other, it required the attention of expert knowledge deployed by apparently independent professional agents.

Through an amalgam of political necessity, industrial calculation, and professional ambition, a new branch of management had come into existence. As the Institute of Labour Management put it in 1943:

> Personnel management is that branch of the management function which is primarily concerned with the human relationships within an organization. Its objective is the maintenance of those relationships on a basis which, by consideration of the well-being of the individual, enables all those engaged in the undertaking to make their maximum personal contribution to the effective working of that organization.[5]

The role and power of the welfare officer were determined neither by whether the plant was privately or publicly owned, nor by responsibility to a particular employer, but by a relationship enshrined in law and conducted under the auspices of specialized knowledge. Through this new attention to the welfare of the worker, the workplace, in crucial respects, ceased to be a private domain; it entered the sphere of government by expertise.

During World War II, these transformed concerns for the welfare of the worker were accompanied by a renewed search for harmony in the workplace, with the hope of decreasing labour problems and hence increasing productivity. This took the form of attempts to integrate the worker into the enterprise by according him or her a share in the responsibility of its decisions. The revival of the Whitley strategy of joint consultation during World War II was within a programme to construct a kind of partnership for production at all levels of economic activity from the plant to that of national economic planning. At the national level a Joint Consultative Council was set up with representatives of the unions and of employers' associations, chaired by Bevin. The Joint Consultative Council became a primary instrument of government policy, negotiating agreement on such contentious issues as dilution and procedures for negotiation and arbitration over wages. 'In political terms', Middlemas writes, 'these arrangements created something close to parity between unions and employers, and elevated their joint body, the JCC, to the status of an unofficial government department.'[6]

This 'partnership in the national enterprise of war' at the national level was paralleled in joint consultative procedures in national and regional production committees.[7] Whitley Councils were rehabilitated, and forty-six new councils were created. Wages boards were extended to cover the pay of over 15 million workers by the end of the war. At the plant level, Joint Production Committees spread, initiated in the Royal Ordnance factories; by the end of 1942 there were 2,000 of these exchanging views and information on methods of production and seeking to produce co-operation for greater efficiency. A new relationship between the worker and the activity of production had been created, overlaying the purely financial exchange of the wage contract. New layers of responsibilities, obligations, rights, and duties were being created between the government, the industrialist, and the working citizen.

Security of the citizen, welfare of the employee, integration of all actors in production in a joint partnership for productivity, management of the human relations of the enterprise in the name of happiness and productivity – these were the elements of the new rationale for the government of labour that had taken shape by the end of World War II. Each of these elements, in their different ways, sought to forge a link between the subjectivity of the worker and the activity of production. Work was to be more than merely a contractual relationship between the individual and the employer, in which the former suffered the pains and deprivations of labour in exchange for the wage, and the latter sought to extract the maximum profit from a worker viewed as a mere function in the labour process. Work was the means by which the individual achieved a relationship with society at large, and entered into the bonds of social solidarity and mutuality. In work, the same relation was to obtain as in the polity at large – no longer antagonistic and irreconcilable opponents, the worker and the boss would go forward together in a partnership of production. Democracy had extended itself to the workplace.

Chapter eight

Democracy at Work

Is the psychological nexus between the industrial worker and his production, broken by modern industrialism, to remain forever shattered? Is there no way of providing the workingman with new status, new dignity and what is perhaps most crucial, new responsibility, without destroying the ultimate supremacy of community needs?.... [As] the actions of the Labour government demonstrate, the subordinate status of the worker is not a product of any particular form of industrial ownership; the worker's status is inherent in industrial technology and an interdependent economy.... Will the worker ultimately become as discontented with his status under socialism as he is under capitalism?... Or will British socialists develop methods, such as the widespread use of consultative devices, that will integrate the workingman psychologically into the productive process without weakening the ultimate control of the community over economic policy? On the answers to these questions, it is no exaggeration to say, the prospect of social peace in Western Europe may well depend.[1]

Robert Dahl, 1947

Democracy, productivity and contentment – in the years following the end of World War II in Britain it appeared that these three values could be fused together in a new way of thinking about and organizing work. The experience of the war, together with the knowledge and practices of the pre-war years, appeared to give the lie to the belief that there was an antithesis between the pleasure of the worker and the productivity of the enterprise. The worker's interest in work was more than merely that of maximizing wages and minimizing the severity of labour in terms of effort and hours. Through work, the worker obtained psychological and social benefits: fulfilment and a feeling of belonging. And as a corollary the productive worker was one who felt satisfied and involved in work. Hence the bosses' interest in the labourer should not be restricted to the technical organization of the labour process, and the establishment of effective systems of command, authority, and control. It had to encompass the happiness of the worker, the human relations of the enterprise.

A policy for the transfer of ownership from the private sector to the state did not itself address the problems of the human relations of the workplace. In the first place, there was no immediate prospect of public ownership of all industry. In the second place, as debates within the Labour party in the inter-war years revealed, there was a clear opposition between those who saw public ownership as a mechanism for national economic management by government and those who saw it in terms of control of the organization by those who worked within it. And the political argument had been won by those who saw socialism as a means of economic planning.[2] Even the TUC, after some controversy, came to adopt such a position. Its *Interim Report on Post-War Reconstruction,* published in 1944, proposed workers' control for the regulation of *private* industry, but opposed it for public industry, in order to allow the continued operation of the trade union as the means of representing the workers' interests.[3] After Labour's election victory, control of coal and transport was vested in boards of experts, with no particular provision for either worker representation on the board, or for consultation with trade unions concerning their composition. It seemed that the status of the worker in a democracy must be addressed through different mechanisms.

In the post-war years the growing band of occupational psychologists capitalized upon the lessons of wartime. One message of the wartime experience, built upon especially by the National Institute of Industrial Psychology, stressed the efficient allocation and utilization of human resources – fitting the man to the job and the job to the man by vocational guidance, systematic selection and promotion procedures, job design, equipment design, and so forth. Such psycho-technologies for the management of the human factor could now draw upon the new respectability conferred upon psychology and psychologists by the war, and upon the new techniques that had been developed. Psychologists now had at least some authoritative approval and a range of more effective devices in their toolbags for calibrating character and mathematizing potential. Intelligence tests, projective tests, aptitude tests, factorized personality tests, and so forth were all advocated with enthusiasm.[4]

But alongside these old individualistic methods of selection, the ex-wartime psychologists began to promote the application of their group techniques in civil life, and a small number of self-consciously 'progressive' firms adopted them. Unilever was a key locus for the industrial development of these techniques, employing Ronald Hargreaves of the Tavistock wartime group in a series of initiatives, beginning with the use of the procedures of the War Office Selection

Boards for recruitment and development of managers.[5] The psychology of group relations elaborated its theories around the new language of the workplace: solidarity, morale, leadership, communication, attitudes, the primary group, motives and purposes. It was not simply that certain sorts of work experience caused sickness in the worker. Nor was it simply that industrial inefficiency – low productivity, absenteeism, accidents, rapid labour turnover – stemmed from the lack of mental hygiene in the factory. It was also that certain ways of organizing work were conducive to mental health, to industrial efficiency, to social adjustment *and* to social democracy. This psychology of the worker as a social subject was explicitly fused to a radical project for transforming the conditions of labour and the authoritative relations of the workplace in the name of ethical principles, political beliefs, industrial efficiency, and mental health.

It would be misleading to see these post-war debates over the organization of work as 'objectively' about different ways of soft-soaping the labourer into docile acceptance of exploitation and alienation. What was at issue was the proper relations that ought to obtain between employer and employee, between leader and led, between manager and worker, in a democracy. In the first place the worker was, after all, a citizen inside as well as outside the workplace. But, in the second place, pleasure in work, and productivity of work, were fundamentally linked to the stake that the worker felt he or she had in the enterprise of work – the goals of the company, its products, and its decisions. Democratic styles of leadership, communication, and consultation within the enterprise and so forth were of significance not only because of the values they embodied, but also because of their consequences for efficiency and productivity, through the links they established between the feelings and aspirations of the worker and those of the enterprise.

In the aftermath of World War I, government concern with industry, and the arguments concerning the role of mechanisms of participation and consultation, had centred upon the risk of industrial strife if not insurrection. In the aftermath of World War II the focus was a problem that appeared more narrowly economic – productivity. As Jim Tomlinson points out, interest in joint production committees was already declining at the end of the war.[6] Attention in the labour movement was directed towards other economic issues, such as nationalization and full employment. The organizational base of joint production committees was weakened by the disruption of their strongholds in the munitions and engineering industries, as the focus of production switched from war supplies, and the wartime labour force was replaced by demobilized servicemen. And indeed, the economic crisis of 1947 appeared to *result* from the difficulties of full employment. If there was little possibility of firms recruiting more labour, and if they could not spur their labour force to greater efforts with the threat of dismissal, how was productivity to be increased? To this question the new social psychology of industry appeared to promise an answer.

Stafford Cripps, who became prominent in economic policy making in 1947, had already shown his enthusiasm for the new science of work by establishing the Production Efficiency Board in 1942 when Minister of Aircraft Production.[7] And in 1947 the National Joint Advisory Committee, which had taken over from the Joint Consultative Council in 1946, recommended to employers and unions that joint production committees should be set up on a voluntary, advisory, and industry-by-industry basis for the regular exchange of views between employers and workers on production questions.[8] Cripps, as 'supremo of the production drive', construed the link between productivity and joint production in psychological terms.[9] It was in these terms that the Human Factors Panel of the Cabinet Committee on Industrial Productivity was conceived – to advise on how research on human factors in industry could help to increase productivity.[10] The chairman of the panel was Sir George Schuster, himself the author of a book entitled *Christianity and Human Relations in Industry*; among the projects sponsored were studies of the role of the foreman and of joint consultation undertaken by the National Institute of Industrial Psychology, and of human relations in one company, carried out by Elliot Jaques for the newly founded Tavistock Institute of Human Relations – the famous Glacier Metal studies, to which I shall return.

Enthusiasm for these attempts to establish industrial harmony through techniques of joint consultation was certainly muted, as far as the parties to it were concerned.[11] Employers resisted the notion that productivity was a function of such structures and the implications which they held of workers' control and a political challenge to managerial authority. Unions, while more enthusiastic, were anxious lest such arrangements cut across their traditional pre-eminence in representation and bargaining. The Ministry of Labour, unlike Cripps, saw joint consultation principally in terms of good industrial relations rather than productivity; they were reluctant to speed its growth through compulsion for fear of upsetting the existing industrial relations system. But despite the relatively slow growth of joint consultation *mechanisms* over the 1950s, a self-consciously 'new' *vocabulary* had been forged for describing the enterprise, its problems and possibilities, and the rationale for its government. The writings of management theorists – Urwick and Brech on the Hawthorne experiments, Northcott on personnel management, Munroe Taylor on foremanship – were joined by more directly psychological works – in particular those of J.A.C. Brown, G.R. Taylor, and R.F. Tredgold – to proselytize for a *new* image and a *new* style of management, and a *new* conception of the worker.[12]

As far as the psychologists were concerned, this new perception of the enterprise resulted from the merging of the language and analysis of the mental hygiene movement, with its concern for the positive mental health of the worker, with the human relations picture of the organization as a network of sentiments, attitudes, meanings and values. Brown's *Social Psychology of Industry*, published in 1954 and reprinted ten times in the 1950s and 1960s, was probably the most influential example of this new British approach to the subjectivity of the worker.[13] Brown adopted much of the vocabulary of human relations, but gave the notions of attitude, sentiment, and group life an explicit conceptual foundation in the American social psychology of Gordon Allport, Kurt Lewin, J.L. Moreno, Muzafer Sherif and others, and in the sociology of the Chicago School.

What this meant, first of all, was that '*the unit of observation is the social relationship rather than the individual*'.[14] The primary group was not a mob. When well integrated, its actions were likely to be disciplined and controlled, and to be logical in relation to the situation as that group perceived it. It was to this group that the worker would give his loyalty; if he felt the interests of the firm to clash with those of the primary group 'no amount of propaganda or pleading or "discipline" will cause him to develop feelings of loyalty towards that firm'.[15] While the formal structure of the enterprise had some importance, the informal working group was the main source of control, discipline, and values of individual workers. To manage the individual worker thus required, first and foremost, management *through* the informal group.

For the worker enmeshed in his or her working group, work was not a simple financial necessity, his or her need for work and relation to it did not begin and end with the wage packet. The notion of a 'Protestant work ethic' was misleading; work played a vital role in the mental life of the individual, a source of satisfaction as much as frustration, of self-realization as much as self-denial. As Taylor put it:

> we must consider the factory not so much as a place where things are produced as a place in which people spend their lives: an environment for living.... The work situation meets many basic human needs in a way which no other situation can approach. If the factory runs into trouble it is because it has created a work situation which frustrates these needs.... In short, the problem with which we are faced is the *humanization of work*.[16]

To consider work in human terms revealed what would spur the worker to high output or lead him or her to slack. Not physical conditions themselves, such as lighting and ventilation, nor organizational arrangements per se, nor even financial rewards. It was social rewards, personal contentment, and the sense of belonging that were crucial here, not objective conditions themselves but the workers' *attitudes* to those conditions:

> The concept of attitude postulates a hypothetical mental structure in order to explain what goes on between stimulus and response, what causes the stimulus to be experienced in the way that it is. When, for example, the employees in a certain department show resentment because they have seen two supervisors talking together, it is obvious that their response cannot be fully explained in terms of the objective stimulus. It must be assumed that they have an *attitude* of suspicion towards management which makes them feel in such a situation that they are being discussed and adversely criticized.[17]

Hence for the British social psychologists of industry, like their American counterparts, the attitude or morale survey was not just a technique of social research, it was a powerful new device for management. It could uncover sources of irritation among employees at an early stage to enable them to be put right. The opinions expressed could be used when policies were being formulated, changes made and innovations such as new worker amenities planned; and the 'mere fact that opinions and resentments can be expressed in this way acts as a safety valve which, even in a factory with rather poor morale, may drain away such resentment', though it would of course be wrong to use this mechanism unless it was intended to do something constructive about any grievances that were revealed.[18]

The internal world of the factory was becoming mapped in psychological terms, and the inner feelings of workers were being transmuted into measurements about which calculations could be made; the management of the enterprise was becoming an exercise in the management of opinion.[19] Consent to management could be produced through the adoption of the correct techniques of circulation, presentation, and discussion of information. And it was in the financial interests of management, as well as part of its social responsibility for the creation of high productivity and low industrial conflict, to create the right attitudes, the right atmosphere, the right culture.

Attitudes could be governed in two ways: communication and leadership. The concept of communication opened up the semantic life of the enterprise for investigation and regulation. The worker did not exist in a realm of brute facts and events, but in a realm of meaning. In the same way as low productivity could often be traced not to physical conditions but to the workers' feelings about such conditions, so much discontent could be traced not to the actual decisions and actions of management, but to the meanings they had for workers. Hence the 'wise manager should hesitate to criticize unless he has asked himself whether he has treated his employees fairly and whether he has taken the trouble to explain the situation fully to them and allowed them to discuss it fully with him'.[20]

This was not just a matter of formal channels of communication. Humans search for the meanings and intention behind messages, so 'an order, however unpleasant, and even hated, is not resented if the situation is seen to necessitate it; whereas even a reasonable order may be bitterly resented if it is thought to give expression to a feeling of contempt'.[21] In the absence of explanations, workers imparted their own meanings to such events as alterations in pay, changes in working practices, staff re-deployment and so forth, and often put the worst interpretation upon them. To cater for this need for meaning, the misunderstandings and failures of communication that were so often at the root of industrial strife needed to be minimized by establishing mechanisms for the flow of information. The flow needed to be two ways, both downward, to make clear the intentions and objectives of management, and upwards, to make known to managers any actual or potential causes of industrial discontent. The foreman came to be seen as the crucial junction in the information network between the shop floor and the boardroom.

The foreman was crucial, too, for the second way of managing attitudes: leadership. Low productivity, high absenteeism, accidents, and labour turnover were rarely the product of the individual personalities of workers; if they were, how could one explain the way in which they affected one plant but not another. No, the worker who idled in the day was the same person who dug their allotment without stint in evenings and weekends – their poor working performance did not emanate from their inherent laziness or inefficiency. But social psychology had shown that the style of leadership, of the managers, supervisors and foremen, *was* crucial, for this could create or destroy the atmosphere of common purpose and high morale upon which productivity depended. Brown, for example, drew on Lewin, Lippitt, and White's pre-war experiments on leadership styles in boys' clubs. The effects of leadership operated irrespective of the individual personalities of leaders or led. While autocratic leadership produced aggression or apathy and *laissez faire* leadership produced chaos, democratic leadership produced not only feelings of loyalty and belonging but also the most work of the highest quality. Democratic leadership was not only good ethics, it was also good psychology and good business.[22]

The new social psychology of industry thus promised an astonishing transformation of industry, reducing friction and increasing the technical efficiency of production in terms of the numbers of hours contributed by a given labour force as well as output per man hour:

It is probably not too much to say that Britain could expand her national income by one-half within five years without any additional capital investment if such methods were universally adopted....

And none of this at the cost of driving the employee harder: on the contrary, the ordinary worker would certainly be freer and happier. Indeed these two things are inseparably connected. It is the frustrated and driven worker who is most likely to strike or restrict output. It is precisely by working to remove these pressures and frustrations that the desired result is to be achieved. The paradox of industry is that if you simply aim for higher output, you get neither output nor contentment. If you work for personal happiness and development of the employee, you get this and output too.[23]

The enterprise thus became a microcosm of democratic society, with the need for respect for the feelings and values of the individual, with the focus upon the interdependency of leader and led, with the emphasis upon communication up and down the power hierarchy and the management of opinion. The new human technologies of subjectivity aligned the management of the enterprise with images of the enlightened government for which the war had been fought and the values of freedom, citizenship, and respect for the individual that had underpinned victory. Democracy walked hand in hand with industrial productivity and human contentment.

This new perception formed the matrix for a host of psychological investigations of industry during the 1950s and 1960s. In addition to the large general literature along human relations lines, we can roughly separate out three other lines of investigation.

The first was a concern with the mental health of the worker. This focused upon the interrelationships between morale, fatigue, sickness, neurosis, and industrial accidents. In the immediate aftermath of war, Fraser had concluded, from a survey of 3,000 workers in light industry, that there was a 10 per cent incidence of disabling neurosis, and further 20 per cent incidence of minor neurosis, and that neurosis was responsible for up to one-third of absence due to sickness. And these figures did not include the loss of efficiency consequent on neurosis prior to breakdown.[24] Tredgold was not alone in concluding that 'These figures sound a clear challenge to a country the survival of which is constantly said to depend upon its power to produce.'[25] But it was not simply 'a question of deciding whether a worker has neurosis – it is whether he is at his maximal mental health, happiness or efficiency, or a fraction below it'.[26] The elimination of neurosis becomes just one part of a more general project of striving for the positive mental health of the worker.

At one extreme this concern was linked to the older attempts to elaborate a psycho-physiological science of work. Psychologists working along these lines remained both distant and somewhat skeptical of the enthusiasm of human relations, while continuing the themes of the wartime research on the sensory and informational capacities of humans. Thus F. C. Bartlett, Donald Broadbent, and others in Cambridge continued to work on vigilance and attention in vision and hearing, work deriving from the wartime problems of continuous scanning of radar screens.[27] Radar also produced the problem of decision making on the basis of probabilities in conditions of uncertainty. Bartlett's work on the relations between skill and fatigue developed into K. J. W. Craik's conception of the human operator as an engineering system. Mackworth's work on the effects of environmental stress on tasks requiring vigilance brought stress into psychological focus as a versatile means of conceptualizing the linkages between environmental, psychological and physiological processes. Thus psychologists pursued the goal of fusing the psychological and sensory capacities and peculiarities of human workers with the technical design of equipment to produce an optimally productive and efficient labour process. Ergonomics or human engineering was to become a routine aspect of the design of the production process.

At the other extreme this concern with the mental health of the worker merged into another, which we might term a *psychoanalysis of the organization*. The most significant proponents of this work were the group associated with the Tavistock Institute of Human Relations.[28] In the period immediately following the end of the war, a number of those who had operated the new group techniques for selection, resettlement, and therapy in the military sought to apply their experience and expertise to the problems of a peacetime community. Funded by the Medical Sciences Division of the Rockefeller Foundation, they established the Tavistock Institute of Human Relations, and when the Tavistock Clinic became part of the National Health Service in 1947, the Institute established itself as a separate, non-profit-making association. From its inception, the Institute was closely linked with Kurt Lewin's Research Centre for Group Dynamics, which transferred in 1947 from the Massachusetts Institute of Technology to the University of Michigan. From 1947 onwards Lewin's group carried out a series of studies funded by the US Office of Naval Research into the links between morale, teamwork, supervision, and productivity – studies inspired by the Harwood experiments, which had appeared to show that employees' resistance to change could be overcome if they were involved in its planning and execution.[29] With the Research Centre the Tavistock founded a quarterly journal, *Human Relations*, whose defining characteristic was the application of social science expertise from a range of disciplines –

psychiatry, psychology, sociology and anthropology – to the practical problems of group life.

A psychoanalytic version of human relations came to define the Tavistock approach. Industrial problems from labour turnover, through low productivity and industrial accidents, to absences attributed to physical and neurotic illness could all now be analyzed within a single framework: the psychodynamic relations of the group and the ways in which these played across the psychodynamics of the individual. One significant theme deployed Melanie Klein's concepts of paranoid and depressive anxiety in analyzing the pathologies of group life. Thus labour turnover, absence and accidents were all forms of unconsciously motivated withdrawal from the work situation. But these would not readily respond to the anodyne recipes of much human relations optimism, for they were rooted in the ways in which difficulties of relations in the work situation called up all sorts of anxiety and hostility that had developed in the earliest years of the individual's life. Only a few exceptionally well adjusted individuals would be able to cope without some form of withdrawal. Different group relations, different phases in working life, and different social roles would trigger personal anxieties in different ways. These difficulties could be analyzed and overcome, but only by working in a new way upon the subjectivities of all employees, from the highest reaches of management to the lowest labourer.

Tommy Wilson stated the new rationale in his introduction to the report of the research project on the Glacier Metal Company carried out by Elliot Jaques:

> [F]irst, that each one of us, in the course of development, has painfully worked out a set of assumptions as to what is real and what is important in determining our behaviour; secondly, that these assumptions give meaning to our lives and offer some protection from fear and uncertainty; and, thirdly, that even personal attempts to modify such deeply-rooted assumptions arouse anxiety and resistance which can only be overcome by serious psychological effort. Finally, under certain definable conditions – particularly those of professional work dealing with practical human and social problems – the need to overcome a difficulty, that is, the need for change, may offset anxiety and resistance to both assess and change, and permit first-hand observation of important areas of behaviour.[30]

Despite the fact that the Institute carried out some seventy projects in its first four years, its concerns predictably came to be dominated by the issue of productivity. The Glacier Metal study was one of the programmes funded by the Human Factors Panel. Joint consultation was its initial focus, though as the work developed stress came to be laid on conflicts of roles and statuses as underlying determinants of many organizational difficulties, on the significance of confusions in powers and responsibilities, and so forth. In his later works Jaques would develop his ideas into a full-scale theory of bureaucracy, and a new set of proposals for equitable linkages between pay and work by means of an assessment of the levels of discretion attached to particular jobs. But what is more important here is the mode of intervention into the enterprise that was developed in this research.

The psychoanalysis of the organization entailed, first of all, a new role for the expert that combined research, consultancy, and therapy. The research team investigated a problem at the behest of the organization, it worked with the organization, but it was the organization itself that had to find its way to change. What soon became clear was that many of the apparently maladaptive confusions of role actually had psychological functions. 'Role confusion', argued Jaques,

> is an unconsciously motivated defence to which individuals have recourse in order to avoid the anxiety produced by disjunctions between their personalities and the demands of the roles they carry. If this picture of role confusion is correct, one must expect that the task of obtaining flexibility in organizational structure will be hampered by strong opposing forces.[31]

Group work enabled the psychological relations of the organization to be opened for attention in a new way, and these opposing forces to be overcome by the process of 'working through'. The researcher produced psychoanalytic interpretations to the group in order to increase its insight and capacity for change. It became clear, in many cases, that the apparent problem about which the organization was concerned was only a symptom of a deeper difficulty. For example, meetings between representatives of management and workers at Glacier kept straying off the point and came to naught, apparently to the intense frustration of everyone involved. The cause was relationship problems that had to be resolved before the wage question could be tackled. The workers were deeply suspicious of management, management feared that workers' representatives would behave destructively, the whole department feared domination from higher up, workers' representatives distrusted one another, and there was no unity on the shop floor. The apparent side issues that frustrated discussion of the wages problem had unconscious functions – the parties were actually testing each other out. Interpretation by the researcher, while initially resulting in denial or projection, eventually allowed working through. Working through by group discussion and interpretation built upon the constructive forces within individuals and the organization. As a result of a successful analysis the factory as a whole could become more flexible and healthy.[32]

Jaques himself left the Tavistock to join Glacier Metal as an independent consultant; it was Eric Trist, together with Ken Bamforth and A. K. Rice, who coined the concept that was to mark the next phase in the Tavistock initiative: that of the socio-technical system. The introduction into the coal mines of the so-called longwall system of working, modelled on mass production techniques in industry, was not producing increased productivity without problems. Instead it appeared to be accompanied by all sorts of difficulties in working relationships and in personal health. For Trist and Bamforth these problems were intelligible; they could be interpreted in terms of the group.[33] Their initial ideas were framed principally in terms of Lewin's field theory, and based on their observations of a new way of group working that had been introduced at Elsecar colliery, where Bamforth's brother-in-law was pit manager. This 'all-in' method, according to the older miners, reawakened the old work traditions that had been lost in the new ways of working. The autonomous working groups it involved appeared to threaten both managerial prerogatives and union practices and beliefs. But, for the Tavistock researchers, the implications of not recognizing their significance were stark. The informal groups that had arisen out of the disruption of the small, primary work groups that characterized the earlier methods of coal mining were often manipulative in character; they led to a range of other 'symptoms' such as reactive individualism, mutual scapegoating, and compensatory absenteeism. The reconstruction of autonomous working groups not only reawakened the group relations that had characterized the lost traditional ways of mining; they also held within them the secret of a much more general transformation of work.

The National Coal Board initially hesitated both about the research and about the new methods of working. But political concern about the effects of the new organization of coal mining mounted, and by 1953 Trist was funded by the Department of Scientific and Industrial Research to direct a programme of research into the organization of work in the mines, though still encountering coal board resistance. What was distinctive about the concept of a socio-technical system that was developed in these studies was the way in which it overlayed a meticulous dissection of the labour process, its stages, divisions and relations of command, with an equally fine-meshed network of intra-psychical, inter-individual, and inter-group forces, tensions, conflicts, and anxieties. Trist and his colleagues thus claimed that the technology did not *determine* the relations of work – there were social and psychological properties that were independent of technology. Hence organizations could choose how tasks should be organized to promote the psychological and social processes that were conducive to efficient, productive, and harmonious relations. The analytic procedure could, as it were, be reversed to conceptualize and construct the details of a labour process that would be in line with both technological and psychological requirements.

It was not merely that a new language was being formulated for speaking about the internal world of the enterprise, factory, plant, mine, or hospital. It was rather that the microstructures of the internal world of the enterprise (the details of technical organization, roles, responsibilities, machinery, shifts, and so forth) were opened to systematic analysis and intervention in the name of a psychological principle of health that was simultaneously a managerial principle of efficiency. Through the conception of the autonomous working group, it became possible to fuse together technical requirements, managerial imperatives, and psychological mechanisms. The group would provide a technological mechanism through which the subjectivity of the individual could be integrated into the objectives of the organization.

With hindsight we may feel that this concern with the human relations of industry was naïve in its denial that conflicts of interest in the working relation derived from macro-social and macro-economic conditions outside the workplace, and its belief that psychological maladjustments or psychodynamic problems underlay accidents, unrest, and low productivity. But to dismiss these authors as witting or unwitting servants of power would be to lose sight of the new images, values, and ethics of work they were seeking to forge, and of the new politics of work they explicitly sought to inaugurate.

When the Glacier Project stressed the importance of material and psychological contracts between individuals or representatives in order to reduce ambiguity, clarify boundaries and maximize the chances of harmonious relations at work, it did so in the name of a constitutional form for the employment relation, which would enshrine the values of equity and justice in the organization of work.[34] Other social psychologists of industry shared some of these goals. Thus Brown urged a policy of decentralization for democratically run enterprises; with the Tennessee Valley Authority and Unilever as examples, he argued that large organizations should be broken into units of a size consistent with the social psychology of the group, with powers of decision vested to a large extent in those in each plant.[35] Taylor also sought to forge an image of work consistent with the values of democracy. The real basis of industrial democracy, he argued, is the 'grassroots democracy' established by effective communication, appropriate managerial attitudes, and so forth, 'compared with which the much advertised democracy of the consultative committee, and the even more tenuous satisfactions of ownership by public boards, are of insignificant importance'.[36] Hostility of unions to management merely institutionalized the dichotomy between them and hampered the progress towards a life of self-fulfilment at work based upon genuine co-operation.

Reconstruction of the internal world of the factory was thus linked to reconstruction of the economy and society at large. If work was a fundamental human experience and was vital for the satisfaction of human needs, if the group experience of working life was a fundamental element in the satisfaction of such needs, if the large concern, whether private or state controlled, would continue to exist, if the formal ownership of a factory by state or individual did not alter the basic properties of its internal environment, if management was a specialized function and therefore hierarchies of authority were inevitable, what organization of work was consistent with both the imperatives of productivity and efficiency and the ethics of humanization, fairness, justice and democracy? For almost two decades in Britain after the end of World War II it appeared as if psychology held the answer.

Chapter nine

The Expertise of Management

[There is] a set of industrial relations 'problems' from consideration of which the arguments of virtually all advocates of reform begin...

(i) The strike problem: the increase from the later 1950s onwards in the frequency of unofficial and unconstitutional strikes in all major industries except mining.

(ii) The restrictive practices problem: the relative inefficiency in labour utilization in British industry, traceable in some important part to over-manning, rigid job demarcation, the systematic control of output and other forms of work regulation upheld by groups of rank-and-file employees with, or more often without, the official support of their unions.

(iii) The wage- or earnings-drift problem: the uncontrolled upward movement of earnings, and thus of labour costs, which results from bargaining at plant level producing increases in earnings much in excess of those which would follow simply from increases in nationally negotiated wage rates.[1]

John Goldthorpe, 1974

The link between democracy and productivity, between justice and contentment, began to be displaced in the Britain of the 1960s. The problems of production came to be posed in a new way, in the context of the development of strategies for the rational and systematic regulation of the national economy in the interests of national productivity. The solidaristic relations of the enterprise came to appear as either irrelevant or counter-productive to the pursuit of industrial efficiency. What was necessary for economic health, it appeared, was the reconstruction of the rational relations between pay and production, and the reconstitution of proper relations of authority and responsibility in the life of the workplace. Management needed to be skilled, to be organized on the basis of a knowledge of the particular requirements of different production processes, to be structured by clear principles of hierarchy and responsibility, and to operate according to explicit and agreed objectives. In this new rationality of production, the psychologists of work would find a different role, providing a vocabulary and a technology for rendering the labour of the worker visible, calculable, and manageable, enabling it to be integrated into the rational economic calculus that was now to be the fulcrum of the relationship between the employee and his or her working life.

By the late 1950s, human relations were already ceasing to define common sense for most British researchers into work. The early studies which the National Institute of Industrial Psychology carried out for the Human Factors Panel had analyzed foremanship and joint consultation in the familiar terms of human relations: autocratic versus democratic leadership, the centrality of feelings and attitudes, the atmosphere of the firm, the need for a sense of common purpose, the centrality of the foreman in linking workers to the firm, the direct relation of all this to production.[2] The Human Factors Panel ceased its work in 1953, but it was succeeded by two separate committees under the joint auspices of the Department of Scientific and Industrial Research and the Medical Research Council, but funded by American 'Conditional Aid'. The Committee on Human Relations in Industry was concerned with such issues as incentives, management organization, technical change, production, and industrial education. It included among its members Tommy Wilson of the Tavistock Institute of Human Relations, Aubrey Lewis of the Maudsley Hospital, and Nancy Seear, who had worked with the production efficiency board of the Ministry of Aircraft Production before going to lecture on personnel management at the London School of Economics. The nineteen projects it supported ranged from Tom Burns' study of change and adaptation in industry at Edinburgh, through Tommy Wilson's comparative study of mining systems at the Tavistock, to Richard Titmuss' investigation of the effects of the mother's employment on family life – a theme to which we will return in a later chapter. When the committee submitted its final report in 1957 it suggested that, while 'human relations in industry cannot be judged solely on the extent to which they affect productivity' and 'work in industry should satisfy other than purely economic needs', 'since improved industrial efficiency is a widely accepted social objective', it should remain an important object of study.[3] The link between productivity and human relations, which had for a time seemed so clear, was becoming rather difficult to formulate.

The sister committee, on Individual Efficiency in Industry, was chaired by Sir Frederick Bartlett, and included James Drever and C.

B. Frisby, then director of the National Institute of Industrial Psychology. Its projects ranged from studies on equipment design and working conditions to factors influencing learning and training and industrial engineering. But it also funded Frisby to undertake a study of the adjustment of the individual to the job. And this study seldom found the links proposed by the doctrines of human relations between events in the inner world of the factory and such indices as labour turnover and absence. It was, rather, in the outer economic world that the key influences were to be found, in particular in the levels of local unemployment.[4] By 1960 even the author of an American book entitled *The Human Side of Enterprise*, Douglas McGregor, was to base his argument on a rejection, not a reactivation, of human relations philosophy:

> It has become clear that many of the initial strategic interpretations accompanying the 'human relations approach' were as naïve as those which characterised the early stages of progressive education. We have now discovered that there is no answer in the simple removal of control – that abdication is not a workable alternative to authoritarianism. We have learned that there is no direct correlation between employee satisfaction and productivity. We recognize that 'industrial democracy' cannot consist in permitting everyone to decide everything, that industrial health does not flow automatically from the elimination of dissatisfaction, disagreement, or even open conflict. Peace is not synonymous with organizational health; socially responsible management is not coextensive with permissive management.[5]

It is thus not surprising that when the Ministry of Labour published the third revised edition of its *Industrial Relations Handbook* in 1961, its previous exhortations concerning the importance of goodwill, integrity, mutual confidence, and the responsibility of management for the well-being of each individual were dropped; the personnel manager was now merely an advisor to the board and to management.[6]

The 1960s and early 1970s did not seem propitious for those who hoped that psychology could make its contribution to the efficiency and humanity of the workplace. A British textbook written at the end of this period goes so far as to speak of a 'moral and professional crisis' in occupational psychology.[7] The attacks on the image of work and the worker that had been proffered by human relations thinkers came from a number of different directions. But despite their incompatibilities they combined to undercut the truth claims of its language and analyses. Radicals and socialists criticized its managerial orientation, its justification of managerial manipulation of the worker, its denial of conflict in the workplace, and its repression of differences in power and distinctions of interest. Psychologists and sociologists criticized the methodology of the research and the logic of the arguments that had grounded the doctrines. Research evaluations appeared to show that there was no evidence for the propositions of human relations, and that its strategies were ineffective: supervisory training programmes had had little effect back in the factory, there was no consistent relationship between type of supervision and levels of morale or productivity, and employees could gain as much satisfaction at work by defiance of managerial rules as by involvement with them.[8]

The image of economic man that human relations appeared to have laid to rest was now resurrected. It appeared that industrial workers did not, after all, seek 'social' rewards in work or look to the organization to provide a sense of belonging. Monetary rewards, systems of payment, promotion opportunities, and other 'traditional' factors were now reinstated as determinants of employee behaviour and opportunities for management. Even the Hawthorne findings themselves could be reinterpreted, it seemed, in the old-fashioned terms of financial incentives, firm leadership, discipline, and the pursuit of economic interests, which were now to be revived.[9]

It appeared that industrial relations were a function of factors far removed from the atmosphere of the workplace; the psychological life of the enterprise no longer formed the matrix for all analyses of its problems and their resolution. For some, it was the technology of the manufacturing process that was most important; for others, the crucial variables were size and relations with other organizations.[10] But either way, it was these non-subjective factors that determined the frameworks of discipline and control in the factory, the human relations it manifested, and the types of managerial authority it required.

The worker was also discovered to have a life and a culture outside work. Sociological investigations relocated the worker in a set of activities, values, and priorities that derived from whether he or she lived in town or country, from religion, ethnicity, age, class, and such like. Additionally the worker was influenced by such factors as the conditions of the labour market, the demand for the products being fabricated, and the strength of unionization. The internal world of the factory was recast as a domain within which oppositions of interests, beliefs, and values that came from elsewhere were played out, and where behaviour answered to imperatives that lay outside the factory walls.

As far as the task of managers was concerned, the informal norms of the workplace and the solidarity of the workers no longer appeared to be a boon that could be used to increase productivity and efficiency; once more they were construed as *obstacles* to achieving formal organizational goals. In the series of official papers and reports on the problems of British industry during the 1960s, these themes determine the analysis: the detrimental effects of solidarity, the problems engendered by technical organization of production, the consequences of the organization of economic incentives, and the links between the values of the enterprise and the outside world.[11] The powers of employers and trade unions to regulate industrial relations in an orderly manner, to negotiate centrally over pay and conditions, and to produce a mechanism for rational economic management were under threat. The threat came from the rise of the shop stewards movement and the custom of workplace bargaining. These informal and plant-based agreements encouraged over-manning, irrational demarcation, the use of overtime to boost pay levels, and practices that were detrimental to industry. They resulted in the sacrifice of productivity, profitability, and adaptability in the name of peace within the plant, in the face of the solidarity of informal groupings of workers and the weapon of the unofficial strike. Control had slipped from managers to shop stewards, bonuses and overtime earnings had virtually severed the link between pay and effort or efficiency. Managerial weakness, combined with full employment, had produced the chronic sluggishness of British industry and our lack of international competitiveness.

Whatever the solution was, it could not be derived from the doctrines of human relations, which encouraged and applauded precisely the plant-based solidarities that were at the root of the problem. According to the Donovan Report, whatever the advantages of the growth of shop stewards and workplace bargaining, the disadvantages were acute:

> [The] tendency of extreme decentralization and self-government to degenerate into indecision and anarchy; the propensity to breed inefficiency; and the reluctance to change. All of these characteristics become more damaging as they develop, as the rate of technical progress increases and as the need for economic growth becomes more urgent.[12]

The problem for the management of production was to re-articulate the informal structure of the enterprise with its formal structure, and hence to reassert order, rationality and the discipline of collective bargaining over the industrial relations of the workplace. This re-articulation was not to be achieved by law, but through the activities of competent managers reasserting their authority on the basis of rational structures and technical skills. Incentive schemes were to be controlled, hours actually worked were to be regulated, job evaluation was to be used to rationalize pay differentials, restrictive work practices were to be bargained away, and the link was to be re-established between pay and performance. For if economic incentives were now to be seen as a central determinant of industrial behaviour, economic planning and managerial authority alike required that leap-frogging and special pleading should be avoided and that pay differentials should be regulated according to scientific criteria.[13]

Not that this was a new task for occupational psychologists and personnel managers, but it was a task that acquired a new political and industrial salience. Work study had actually been introduced to Britain in the 1930s by the US firm of Bedaux; the initial response of the unions had been industrial action. Nevertheless, the consulting firm of Urwick Orr had been set up before World War II with, as its staple fare, the installation of systems of payment by results on the basis of work study. By 1959 the British Standards Institution was issuing a standard glossary of terms used in work study. There was work measurement, which sought to establish the time for a qualified worker to carry out a specified job at a defined level of performance. And there was method study, which sought to calibrate and record existing and proposed ways of doing work as a means of developing and applying easier and more effective methods of reducing costs.[14]

In the 1960s and 1970s personnel managers were to become experts in industrial relations and manpower planning, forecasting requirements, debating systems and philosophies of payment, implementing schemes for the rationalization of wage differentials and the appraisal of performance; simultaneously occupational psychologists were to be increasingly called upon to provide the technical expertise and scientific credibility for the new economic calculability of the workplace. Payment by results, job evaluation, work study, measured day work, productivity bargaining, and so forth became candidates for this re-calibration of reward. New systems were devised, research undertaken, professional opportunities burgeoned, consultancy and employment flourished. The labour of the worker was to be made inscribable, calculable, and manageable through the application of technical expertise.

The post-war image of the workplace as a nexus of psychodynamic group relations was not completely erased. A network of research centres, conferences, and training activities was taking shape that would translate the doctrines of group dynamics into a series of skills that could be taught to all those who held managerial positions in organizations; skills that would not only help them manage better but also make them better persons. The two key nodes in this network were the National Training Laboratory in the United States and the Tavistock Institute for Human Relations in Britain. The Research Centre for Group Dynamics of the Institute of Social Research at the University of Michigan, under Lewins' direction until he died in 1947, had developed the training group, or T-group, as a method of revealing the dynamics of small groups experientially to participants, by

conducting these under the guidance of specialists in specially structured meetings or 'laboratories'. The method arose out of one strand
in the post-war American social-psychological conceptual and practical assault on prejudice. The Connecticut State Inter-Racial Commission asked Lewin to conduct research and train leaders in
combatting racial and religious prejudice. In the conference that followed the staff apparently discovered 'the role of direct feedback to
people of information on the way they have been behaving, as observed and interpreted by an experienced and impartial outside person'.[15] The T-group method, which was formalized out of this insight,
provided a technology and a vocabulary through which participants
could render inter-subjectivity into thought and make it manageable,
learning to examine

> assumptions, expectations, attitudes and goals, and to project
> themselves into the roles of others in order to gain a measure of
> objectivity and detachment in considering their own ways of relat-
> ing to others. The assumption is that increased insight will lead to
> increased competence in leadership and in obtaining cooperation
> from others.[16]

T-groups were thus more than merely instrumentally advantageous to their participants; they effected a fundamental transformation in their ways of speaking about and relating to others, they made
them more insightful people at the same time as they made them better managers. Hence the enthusiasm arose not only from firms wishing better leaders and managers, but from individuals wishing to
master these new techniques of the personal and interpersonal self.
The methods were institutionalized in the National Training Laboratory in Group Development at Bethel, Maine, in 1947, and spun off
into allied institutions such as the Western Training Laboratory of
the University of California, and Arden House in New York City. By
1957 over a thousand people – executives from industry and government; members of the armed forces; people from the churches, trade
unions, and educational organizations; community leaders; and academics – had passed through the Bethel training sessions.[17] In Britain
they attracted the interest of a range of parties. The European Productivity Agency was keen to arouse European interest in improved
methods of industrial training modelled on the US examples. Academics at Leicester University were keen to develop a residential
course in group dynamics for social workers. Approached from these
sources, and with further interest aroused from the British Institute
of Management, the Industrial Welfare Society, the Ministry of Labour and National Service, the National Coal Board, Esso Petro-
leum, and the Council of the Church Training Committees, the

Tavistock Institute of Human Relations established the first of a series of Leicester Conferences in group relations.

These conferences were to continue throughout the 1960s and into the 1970s. Despite the change in the overall climate of industrial relations and management thought in Britain, they were to attract participants from industry, civil service, churches, prisons, child care organizations, and academia. Their methods combined the concepts of Lewin's T-groups with those of Bion's leaderless groups, under the conceptual auspices of Tavistock psychoanalysis. Thus groups would meet without any external task to be done, but with 'the specific task of examining the kinds of feelings and attitudes that arise spontaneously, these feelings and attitudes being those which each individual brings to any group situation, or which develop within it independently of whatever the external task may be.'[18] The role of the consultant to these study groups was to interpret group forces and processes to the participants, to produce a 'culture' within which such aspects of social life are noted, rendered into language, and re-incorporated into the modes of self-evaluation, self-presentation and social competence of the members. Thus they will become 'more tolerant and understanding of the emotional aspects of the groups within which they work – and of their own 'personal equations' as members of those groups' and 'more likely to mobilize the positive forces which lie within them'.[19]

Management now appeared to require not only that managers and leaders understand and utilize the psychological forces of those who they directed, but that they transform their own modes of personal existence in order to be adequate to wield responsibility and to lead effectively. Such processes could not, however, be merely imposed upon them by their bosses, nor were they simply devices to ensure their legitimacy and advancement. They were to become a part of the self-evaluations and self-judgements of each individual. The aspirations of management and the conditions of effective functioning at occupational tasks had been fused with the pathway of the individual to self-awareness.[20]

Chapter ten

The Production of the Self

> The possibility of self-actualization in work means a shift away from the idea that management has to offer certain kinds of extrinsic rewards (e.g. financial and social ones)...in exchange for work. Instead, the rewards are to be found in the work itself. The manager is therefore concerned primarily with making the work as interesting and satisfying as possible and arranging for it to have meaning for the individual worker. This will mean a constant effort to discover what has meaning and challenge for a particular worker and the attempt to introduce this into his work situation. More than ever, the manager becomes a facilitator providing for the employee a path to self-fulfillment through work.[1]
>
> Peter Ribeaux and Stephen Poppleton, 1978

Over the past decade the most powerful images of the economic functions of the citizen have decisively altered. The old economic ethics, the much vaunted 'Protestant work ethic', had proclaimed a set of values for the worker in which hard work was a moral, personal, and social good, where dedication to labour was to be maintained and gratification deferred, and where a stable pattern of expectations over a working life was ensured by the reasonable certainty of continued employment in a single industry, rising wages, and a predictable life cycle of youthful independence, marriage, and family. But such an ethic is out of kilter with the obligations that are now accorded to the citizen in social life and work.

The primary economic image offered to the modern citizen is not that of the producer but of the consumer. Through consumption we are urged to shape our lives by the use of our purchasing power. We are obliged to make our lives meaningful by selecting our personal lifestyle from those offered to us in advertising, soap operas, and films, to make sense of our existence by exercising our freedom to choose in a market in which one simultaneously purchases products and services, and assembles, manages, and markets oneself. The

image of the citizen as a choosing self entails a new image of the productive subject. The worker is portrayed neither as an economic
actor, rationally pursuing financial advantage, nor as a social creature
seeking satisfaction of needs for solidarity and security. The worker is
an individual in search of meaning, responsibility, a sense of personal
achievement, a maximized 'quality of life', and hence of work. Thus
the individual is not to be emancipated *from* work, perceived as merely a task or a means to an end, but to be fulfilled *in* work, now construed as an activity through which we produce, discover, and
experience our selves.

Projects for the reform of work have, once more, tried to align this
new image of the individual at work and outside it with the human
technologies for the government of the enterprise. Work itself could,
it appeared, be reformed and managed so that it could become an element in a personal project of self-fulfilment and self-actualization.
The reformers claimed, in familiar terms, that if work were reshaped
according to a knowledge of the subjectivity of the worker, not only
would the psychological needs and strivings of individuals be met, but
efficiency, productivity, quality, and innovation would all be improved.

The imperatives of the new technology, the pace of technological
change, competition from the Third World and Japan, and the crucial
importance of continual stimulation of consumption had all combined to require that production take as central the values of adaptability, innovation, flexibility, excellence, sensitivity to consumer
pressures and the demands of the market. A revamped psycho-technology of the workplace could, it seemed, act as a relay between the
new ethics of the producer and these changing requirements of production in the enterprise and in the economy as a whole. A new psychology of work, and the worker, a new set of psychological doctrines
for managers, and a new breed of psychological consultants to the enterprise would burgeon in the attempt to forge a link between the
new imperatives of production and the new mentalities of the employee.

This revived concern with the management of the productive subject was to proceed in two dimensions, ideologically opposed but conceptually compatible. The first was through a reactivation of the
project of human relations as transformed by the Tavistock notion of
socio-technical systems. This was to give rise to a new, international,
and self-consciously progressive politics of the workplace, whose
name was 'arbetsmiljö', 'humanisierung des Arbeitslebens', 'amelior-
ation des conditions de travail', 'humanization of work', or, more
generally, 'improving the quality of working life'. The second was to
take shape around a new psychological picture of the employee as a
self-actualizing ego whose personal strivings could be articulated into

the organization of the enterprise. This was to be promoted in a new doctrine of management, located particularly in the United States, in the largest and most successful corporations, which could be termed 'the management of excellence'.

The movement – for it saw itself as that – which went under the banner of 'the Quality of Working Life' or simply QWL, saw the task of 'humanizing work' as a 'priority goal' of the 1970s.[2] The values it proclaimed do not, at first sight, seem all that novel: security, equity, individuation, and democracy. But the old language of human relations was inflected, even radicalized. There was an explicit concern with the deleterious social and political consequences of alienation at work brought about by the dehumanizing industrial culture, and anxiety about this culture spreading further to the personal services and even the professions. There was a vision of the advance of technology, with its possibilities for the destruction of jobs and the subordination of people to machine on the one hand, but the prospect of the rosy dawn of a post-industrial society liberated from repetitious and uncreative labour on the other. Underpinning this were some profoundly humanistic aspirations. These certainly stressed the virtues of social solidarity provided through work. But they sought to align these with a new image of the employee as a unique individual seeking a personal meaning and purpose in the activity of labour. Hence the need for integration of the dispossessed and powerless into society, for the autonomy of the worker to be respected in a democracy, for governments to honour their responsibility for the welfare of each and all through the provision of legal protections and social benefits at the macro-level, down to interventions into the details of workplace organization.

For the promoters of QWL these values were to be realized not in the form of airy declarations but in the detailed restructuring of social, economic, political and technical arrangements. Security for the worker was not a matter of philanthropy but of legally enforceable rights that would eliminate damaging anxieties over health, safety, income, and employment. Equity would not only embrace respect for each person in the organization, but would remove disproportionate income differentials and unjustified hierarchies, through rational evaluations of the contributions of different workers to the services or product, and even through equitable profit sharing. Individuation would respect individuals through redesigning work to maximize autonomy, to allow scope for craftsmanship, to provide meaning by allowing workers control over their own work. Democracy entailed arrangements ranging from participatory management on the one hand to co-operatives, workers' control and self-management on the other.

Of course, those who promoted QWL stressed that it would enhance productivity, efficiency, flexibility, quality and so forth. But at the same time its principles described 'a system that is constructed to optimize the worker's well-being and, correspondingly, that of society. Such a system would develop in the worker a sense of hope, activeness and productiveness, alleviating symptoms of discontent, mental illness and despair.'[3] The optimized autonomous subjectivity of the worker was to be the keystone in an arch spanning the protection of the social fabric and the revitalization of economic life at the one end and the reconstruction of the minutiae of technical, financial and power relations in the workplace on the other.

The sources of this new vision of work lay in Europe, in the links established between the socio-technical expertise of the Tavistock Institute of Human Relations and the democratic corporatist political rationales that became influential in a number of Scandinavian countries in the 1960s. Thus the Tavistock joined forces in an initiative with the Norwegian Work Research Institutes, sponsored jointly by the Confederation of Trades Unions and the Confederation of Employers, which recommended not a simple increase in workers' participation, but a profound democratization of the workplace in order to improve the quality of working life. In Norway this strategy spread from five experimental firms to a project in which a group from the Tavistock sought the redesign of a whole industry – the Norwegian Merchant Marine.[4] The work of Fred Emery, Eric Trist, and others from the Tavistock Institute of Human Relations played a key role in bringing together the initiatives that began to proliferate, on the basis of the Norwegian examples, into a coherent movement. A network of researchers and action research centres began to form and stabilize in the Netherlands, Sweden, Denmark, France, and Ireland, as well as in the United States. Sweden was at the forefront of the articulation of democratic corporatism on a national scale, with representatives of government, employers, and trade unions brought together in an industrial democracy joint council, experimenting in ways of reforming work organizations, enhancing workers' power, promoting a new role for unions, and establishing new methods of management in the interests of democracy, efficiency, productivity, and equality.[5]

By the early 1970s the movement was receiving enthusiastic support not only from researchers, consultants, employers, and politicians, but also from such radical bodies as the International Labour Organization. The themes of job enrichment, job rotation, autonomous work groups, participation and self-management, design of work systems, and divisions of labour and responsibility linked the emancipation of the worker to the quality of the product through a new subjectivity of work. Finding meaning and dignity in work, workers would identify with the product, assume responsibility for production, and find their own worth embedded, reflected and enhanced in the quality of work as a product and an experience.

However, enthusiasm for the radical version of QWL in England was largely confined to a few researchers and evangelists; its destiny was to be reabsorbed into a managerial technology for promoting worker commitment and contentment. Thus the report of the Department of Employment, under the title *On the Quality of Working Life,* actually arose out of a NATO Committee on the Challenges of Modern Society, which requested Britain to enquire into problems of work motivation and satisfaction, and their opposites. And despite the co-operation of some of the exponents of QWL, the report written under the guidance of the chief psychologist of the Department of Employment was, indeed, merely to recycle the nostrums of human relations in their old form.[6]

None the less, the 1970s did produce quite a flurry of activity. An international conference was held in New York in 1972 and an international council was established to integrate the national 'nodes' of the movement into a supportive and expanding network that could put pressure on government and establish the necessary expertise. A variety of experts and professionals joined together under the auspices of this movement for the restructuring of work under the direction of expertise. Managers, supervisors, and trade unionists were concerned not merely with working conditions, but with the content of jobs, the organization of work, and the design of equipment. They were attracted by the possibility of redesigning production in such a way that, without diminishing efficiency,

> it will take into account the rising proportion of employees who are seeking, in their work, a decrease in stress or boredom and an increased satisfaction of such natural needs as a continuing opportunity to make fuller use of their capacities – and to develop them.[7]

Technologists and engineers concerned with automation found a language in which to promote their designs for new production systems, including the use of robots, which would modify and humanize tasks. Systems theorists found new conceptual and practical allies for their re-conceptualization of organizations as 'open' socio-technical systems of a dynamic character, in which the production system had to be designed with a recognition of its continuous transaction with a changing environment and the consequent need for flexibility. Accountants and economists discovered, in QWL, a further argument to support the introduction of new techniques such as social audit methods and human resources accounting, which would align their expert role with contemporary values. Doctors and others preoccupied with the safety and health of the worker in the workplace and the consequences of work for physical and mental health found a new impetus for their somewhat unfashionable concerns. And social researchers, industrial consultants, and specialists in industrial relations found a new vocabulary for their activities and a new justification for their expertise that was simultaneously social, political, economic, and ethical. The power of the language of QWL to establish and stabilize a network of thought and action appeared to be manifest in 1981, when a conference in Toronto on prospects for the 1980s attracted over 2,000 participants. 'The academic advocates of QWL were now vastly outnumbered, by over a thousand managers, two hundred and fifty trade unionists, and substantial contingents of government officials and efficiency consultants.' [8]

Gurus of QWL like Eric Trist were to go so far as to propose a new philosophy of work, in which people would be considered as a resource to be developed, not extensions of machines but complementary to them, not requiring external controls but regulating themselves, building the conditions for collaboration and collegiality rather than competition, for commitment and involvement rather than alienation, for innovation rather than the avoidance of risk, for fusing the purposes of the organization with those of its members and of society at large.[9] He was not alone in seeing, in the reform of work under the banner of the quality of working life, the first step in a process where workers would increasingly come to recognize their own competence and challenge not only the authority of managers but the very denial of rights fundamental to capitalist economic relations.[10]

But despite its explicit emphasis on union participation and emancipatory values, the criticisms levelled at human relations doctrines were redirected at the Quality of Working Life.[11] It was suggested that the schemes had the hidden purpose of inoculating workers against unionism, that they were only resorted to where managers had exhausted all other ways of resolving grave financial problems, and that they disguised an attempt to pacify workers.[12] Further, it was claimed that the popularity of these techniques among managers stemmed from their wish to protect their own status and authority, to symbolize their own caring and competence, and to reinforce their sectional claims and legitimacy within the workplace.[13]

There is more than a germ of truth in these criticisms. But the significance of the notion of Quality of Working Life was not merely its capacity to disarm, disguise, and legitimate. It lay, on the one hand, in the new image and meaning of work it articulated for workers, unions, managers, bosses, and politicians trying to programme a reorganization of work to cope with the 'turbulent environment' brought about by technological change, international competition, and the new aspirations of citizens.[14] And it lay, on the other hand, in its capacity to translate these socio-economic and psychological concerns into practicable programmes for the reform of the technical, financial, and political microstructure of work. Work was becoming aligned with a new image of the citizen, and a new mode of government of economic life was being formulated.

While the language and concerns of QWL were to be reintegrated into the routine activities of personnel managers and other experts on work, and routine references made to the Swedish experience, Volvo, self-regulating working groups, and the like, implementation of the programme in anything like its full form was limited to a few hundred organizations in the United States and even fewer elsewhere. The alignment it sought to forge between the nature, conditions, and objectives of work and the values of advanced democratic societies, the economic imperatives of technological change and international competition, and the new desires and aspirations of workers would be articulated in another way. For this explicitly democratic and progressive discourse on the quality of working life turned out to be surprisingly consonant with a refashioning of the psychological imperatives of the workplace that came from a very different culture and conceptual basis – the doctrines of the self-actualizing worker.

In Britain in the 1960s, dissatisfaction with the doctrines of human relations had been part of a move to *rationalize* the utilization of the human resources of industry. In the United States analogous dissatisfaction with management values of solidarity, security, and contentment were to be expressed. William H. Whyte's *The Organization Man* was the most popular account of the transformation in the ethics of work. Whyte argued that belief in the virtues of thrift, hard work, independence, property, security, and competition no longer supplied the ethical basis for the behaviour of those who spend their lives within the large organization. In place of this Protestant ethic, a 'social ethic' had been born. This stressed that meaning was to be found through the group. It celebrated calm, order, and security within the organization, it thus directed the individual to fit harmoniously into the routines of work, to conform and co-operate. The social ethic fostered adjustment without question, and redefined success in terms of a safe career, integration with one's peers, and dependence upon the company. For Whyte, the psychology of human relations had much to answer for; it was the scientific counterpart of, and managerial justification for this celebration of organizational conformity at the expense of individual imagination.[15]

But on the continent of the ego, the response was not simply to reinstate a norm for management based upon an image of the worker as a rational maximizer of financial returns. The worker was to be managed in terms of a new conception of 'human nature' derived from the writings of Abraham Maslow, Carl Rogers, Viktor Frankl, Eric Fromm, and others, one that would allow a translation between the social and cultural values of advanced liberal democracy on the one hand and the demands of industry on the other.[16] In this new image the subjectivity of the individual was conceptualized in terms of motivation, self-direction, and responsibility. Thus Allport's view of motivation questioned the belief that the basic need of people was tension reduction, and Frankl argued, on the basis of work with concentration camp survivors, that struggling for a goal was indispensible to mental well being. Lewin showed that people had the capacity to develop aspirations leading to a life of increasing but realistic challenges; Maslow laid stress on the person as a self-actualizing being; Rogers emphasized the importance of striving to function fully; Allport wrote of the importance of 'becoming'; Bruner discovered the intrinsic value of striving to grow. And Fromm, Frankl, and others fused psychiatry and ethics in asserting that responsibility was a condition of mental health and a good life. Hence, as Argyris put it, the trend was away from 'keeping people happy'. Happiness, morale, and satisfaction were not highly relevant guides to understanding and managing the relations of individuals and organizations: 'Individual competence, commitment, self-responsibility, fully functioning individuals, and active, viable, vital organizations will be the criteria that we will keep foremost in our minds.'[17]

Argyris, Victor Vroom, and Frederick Herzberg were perhaps the foremost American expositors of this new perception of the worker. There were a number of different versions on offer. Vroom stressed the need for management to motivate the worker through the setting of clear, attainable, and desirable objectives.[18] Individuals, it was pointed out, strove to obtain what satisfied them, and were strongly motivated to do something if they had a high expectancy that it would lead to an outcome that they valued. In short, their efforts were directed to goals. If management recognized this simple fact, it could make use of it. It could make the link between action and outcome clear, and install its own desired processes as intermediaries between individuals' motives and their goals. Hence the personal quest for satisfaction could be channelled through institutional practices that would produce efficiency, profitability, and adaptability.

Frederick Herzberg, on the other hand, began by asking what made people feel good at work.[19] Thus he sought to find out what led to dissatisfaction and what led to satisfaction, and argued that management should base its actions on the minimization of the former and the maximization of the latter. Herzberg termed the first type 'hygiene' factors. These pertained to such aspects of work as adequate salary, job security, good working conditions, and so forth. When these were absent, people became dissatisfied; however their presence alone did not produce satisfaction. Satisfaction was provided by the motivators. And the motivators were not physical or material, but psychological. Interesting work, feelings of achievement, feelings of personal growth, responsibility, and recognition – these were what made people happy, these were what motivated them to work at their maximum levels. Thus management should not be concerned solely with the adjustment of the 'hygiene' of the workplace; high commitment and performance could only be obtained by engaging the individual at the level of his or her personal psychological motives for self-fulfilment. Complex and demanding jobs, requiring skill and devolving control, did not threaten managerial authority. On the contrary, they strengthened it by linking the employee with the objectives of the company at the level of his or her most powerful strivings. The individual would come to take on the responsibility for advancing the interests of the company because, at the same time, they would serve to fulfil his or her own deepest needs.

Similarly, Douglas McGregor attacked the assumptions about human motivation that were implicit in the traditional conception of management – that individuals disliked work and needed to be coerced, controlled, directed and threatened in order to do it, that they preferred direction, avoided responsibility, had little ambition and sought security – a combination he characterized as 'Theory X'. His 'Theory Y' painted an alternative image of the worker, as an individual who *wanted* to work:

> The expenditure of physical and mental effort at work is as natural as play or rest. The average human does not inherently dislike work.... External control and the threat of punishment are not the only means for bringing about effort towards organizational objectives. Man will exercise self-direction and self-control in the service of objectives to which he is committed.... Commitment to objectives is a function of the rewards associated with their achievement. The most significant of such rewards, e.g. the satisfaction of ego and self-actualization needs, can be direct products of effort directed toward organizational objectives.... The average human being learns, under proper conditions, not only to accept but to seek responsibility.... The capacity to exercise a relatively high degree of imagination, ingenuity and creativity in the solution of organizational problems is widely, not narrowly, distributed in the population.... Under the conditions of modern industrial life, the intellectual potentialities of the average human being are only partially utilized.[20]

Where employees are lazy, indifferent, unwilling to take responsibility, intransigent, uncreative, uncooperative, Theory X offered management an easy rationalization; Theory Y implied that the causes lay within management itself. The task for management was thus 'to create conditions such that the members of the organization can achieve their own goals *best* by directing their efforts towards the success of the enterprise'.[21]

The significance of the new model of the subjectivity of the worker assembled in the 1960s ran in two directions. On one hand it could lead to the development of managerial devices to stimulate the self-actualizing forces in employees, releasing individual senses of responsibility, creativity, and potential, inserting motivators into the policies and practices of the company – a kind of refurbishing of the conceptual architecture and techniques of human relations. On the other hand, it could lead to a shift in attention from the interpersonal relations of small groups to the design of the organization itself. Here the American pathway through the ego was to come into a sort of symmetry with the European concern for the quality of working life; each sought to reshape the internal world of the organization so as to release the autonomous subjectivity of the worker in such a way that it aligned with the aspirations of the enterprise, now construed in terms of innovation, flexibility, and competitiveness.

The writings of Argyris trace out the connections made along this second pathway. As early as 1952 Argyris, in a report for the Controllership Foundation entitled *The Impact of Budgets on People*, had sought to extend the language and calculations of human relations to the financial sphere. Management needed to concern itself with 'the point where men and budgets meet' in order to enhance control by gaining acceptance of its standards and goals. It seemed that the suspicion and hostility that certain budgeting practices produced in individuals led to the formation of groups resistant to managerial objectives, while techniques such as bargaining and communication could ensure acceptance rather than rejection. The psyche of the worker and the intersubjectivity of the group were to be incorporated into the domain of accounting.[22]

By 1957 Argyris was sketching a picture of the organization, not in the old colours of human relations, but incorporating the new image of self-actualizing subjectivity and its interaction with the systematic creation of organizational dependency by management. It appeared that such principles as specialization of work, chains of command, unity of direction and span of control – typical of formal organizations and administrative control systems – created demands that tended to require individuals to experience dependence and submissiveness and to utilize only a limited number of their abilities, especially at the lower levels.[23] The managerial implications of this analysis were summarized for a British audience in 1961 in the *Research News Bulletin* of the National Institute of Industrial Psychology. Four fundamental shifts were required in the management of personnel:

From policies that emphasise employee satisfaction, morale and happiness to policies that emphasize internal commitment, self-responsibility and productiveness. From the idea that individuals are the most important part of the organization to a realization that the importance of the individual varies under different conditions. From the requirement that subordinates be developed by their superiors to an acknowledgment that no man can develop another and that the door to development is locked from the inside. From executive development programmes aimed at changing a manager's behaviour to programmes whose objective is to help the manager become more aware and more accepting of himself and therefore of others.[24]

Management was to work on the ego of the worker itself. For organizations to get the most out of their workers, from lowliest employee to highest manager, they should not seek to manage social relations to ensure maximum contentment. Instead, the organization should be reshaped so as to release the psychological strivings of its members, so that adaptability, innovation, responsibility, and commitment could be channeled into organizational success. The apparent contentment of employees under the old style of management (involving peace, security, low levels of interpersonal involvement) was actually pseudo-health, and the apparent managerial efficiency in such organizations was only pseudo-effectiveness. It was a system of complicated defensive mechanisms that disguised such activities as apathy, indifference, and goldbricking at lower levels and conformity, mistrust, and rivalry at higher levels, and protected them, locking them into the organizational structure in a repetitive and compulsive fashion. Policies that promoted real positive mental health of employees (richness of self, self-acceptance, growth motivation, investment in living, unified outlook on life, regulation from within, independence, and adequacy of interpersonal relations) would also stimulate genuine organizational effectiveness; achieving its objectives, maintaining its internal system, and adapting to the external environment.[25] Organizations had to transform practices that reinforced defensiveness and dependency so that they would positively utilize the psychological energy of individuals, increasing their experience of psychological success, by allowing them to 'strive continuously to find and create opportunities in which they can increase the awareness and acceptance of their selves and others', and enabling the individual to 'define his immediate goals, define his own path to these goals, relate these to the goals of the organization, evaluate his own effectiveness, and constantly increase the degree of challenge at work'.[26]

Organisations, it seemed, were systems that 'learned', and management needed to adopt a style of management based upon 'Model II learning'.[27] The typical organization operated by 'Model I' learning. The stress on defining and achieving goals produced defensiveness and self-centredness on the part of the actor; the focus on winning and not losing led to a stress on defining and controlling what is done; a prejudice against the expression of negative feeling resulted in the elaboration of defensive norms such as mistrust, conformity, and power-centred competition, the imperative of rationality constrained freedom of choice by careful calculations of commitment and risk. The outcome for such organizations was bleak: even when things appeared to change, they actually stayed as they were. Not so with Model II learning. Here the stress is on striving for information, collaboration, facilitation, openness, trust, risk taking, shared responsibility, choice, learning, open competition – in other words a Model II organization can learn and change.

As with human relations, the new conceptions of organizations and their management enabled the techniques for government of the internal world of the enterprise to be made consistent with, on the one hand, prevailing American cultural values and, on the other, the personal projects of individual employees. These new views of management were to be promulgated widely, in investigations that appeared to show that they did indeed characterize 'America's Best Run Companies'.[28] *In Search of Excellence* was the title of the book by Peters and Waterman, of the management consultants McKinsey and Company, that became an 'international best-seller' on its publication in 1982, and spawned a host of spin-offs and imitations. Peters and Waterman had apparently discovered that the bosses and managers of the companies considered by experts to be innovative, excellent, and top financial performers in their industrial sector (IBM, 3M, Tupperware, Hewlett-Packard, Texas Instruments, Procter & Gamble, Cheseborough-Ponds, Johnson & Johnson, McDonalds and others) shared significant elements of a managerial strategy that was the key to their success. They had recognized that the pace of technological change and international competition required a form of managerial and industrial organization that was diametrically opposed to the models of rationality and bureaucratic efficiency so stressed in the 1950s and 1960s. The 'old paradigm' of management stressed values like big is better, economies of scale, elimination of overlap, and formal coordination. It believed in low-cost production. It sought to analyze everything, and to use market research, cash-flow analysis, budgeting, forecasting, planning, and targets to avoid risk and make the unpredictable predictable. It eliminated disturbers of the peace, fanatics, and disrupters of the plan. The manager's job was that of taking decisions, analyzing financial statements, and aligning people, products, and services to get good financial results. Managers treated people merely as factors of production. They sought to control everything in the organization through job descriptions and a complex structure of accountability. Productivity was to be enhanced through high financial incentives for top performers and weeding out the dead wood. Workers were controlled by issuing strict orders, backed up through rigorous inspection procedures and quality control. Growth was all important, from managing the cosmetics of the balance sheets to expanding into ever newer industries when opportunities in one dried up.

But this managerial paradigm did not, it appeared, characterize 'excellence'. It was inherently conservative, and even heartless. Its narrow rationality was negative. It did not value experimentation. It led to over complexity, inflexibility, caution, and paralysis-by-analysis. It abhorred informality and denigrated the importance of values. Fundamentally, it was based upon a narrow over-rational view of what made people work. The management of excellence operated on radically different principles. It valued flexibility, adaptability, initiative, ad hoc groupings, cross-divisional collaboration, experimentation, informality, and a personal commitment to the excellence of the product. At root it was based on a different image of the person. People were not that rational, they were self-centred, they liked to think of themselves as winners not losers. While the old paradigm berated people for failure, the new constantly reinforced people for success. It makes most people feel that they are winners. Psychological theory, from the social psychology of attribution to B.F. Skinner's behaviorism had shown that the mere association with success led to higher motivation while stress on failure produced the reverse. High performance was not ensured by rewards but by intrinsic motivation. Lasting commitment could be obtained only by fostering conditions that built intrinsic motivations, for when people felt that a task was inherently worthwhile they would commit themselves to it.

The best companies did not suppress what is non-rational in people, they used it. Their managers spontaneously drew on the holistic and intuitive qualities that psychologists had shown to comprise one-half of our brains. They reasoned by stories as much as by data, they solved problems by gut feeling in an innovative and creative way never possible through rational decision making structures. They allowed for the emotional, more primitive side of human nature, implicitly recognizing that

> businesses are full (100%) of highly 'irrational' (by left brain standards), emotional human beings: people who want desperately to be on winning teams ('seek transcendence'); individuals who thrive on the camaraderie of an effective small group or unit set-

ting ('avoid isolation'); creatures who want to be made to feel that they are in at least partial control of their destinies. [29]

The task of the leader was thus not to force individuals to comply, but to raise them to higher levels of motivation and morality, to be an expert in the promotion and protection of values, to 'give lots of space to employees to take initiatives in support of those values – finding their own paths, so making the task and its outcome their own'.[30] Man is 'waiting for motivation'. Action, innovation, entrepreneurship, excellence, initiative, and the rest can be released by a company that fosters autonomy, values, experimentation, creativity, and risk, which learns by innovation and evolution.

The point here is not whether this research is a valid or invalid, accurate or inaccurate portrayal of the top companies. Nor is it whether such practices do, indeed, produce results. Rather, what is important is the forging of a new image of work, based upon a new image of the worker, and a new role for psychology within this complex. No longer is there to be an antithesis between the motives of the individual and those of the organization. The citizen, at work as much as outside it, is engaged in a project to shape his or her life as an autonomous individual driven by motives of self-fulfilment. Individuals produce themselves in work; the organizational culture is to be reshaped in the name of a new psychological image of man.

The managerial doctrines of excellence were accompanied by a range of individual portraits of the successful entrepreneur, the high achiever, the peak performer in sport and arts as much as in industry.[31] The entrepreneur, it seems, was actually quite like us: we *could* all be entrepreneurially successful, we could all learn to be self-realizing, if we learned the skills of self-presentation, self-direction and self-management. One must cultivate the image of the winner and actualize it in the management of the interpersonal relations upon which winning depends. Fortunately the new modes of self-management could themselves be taught and learned. A new breed of psychological consultants to the organization came to operate in these terms, training managers in sensitivity, awareness, trust, openness, and sharing. Managers could be taught to understand and work upon their motives and those of others around them; firms could and should train their managers in these new techniques. Economic success, career progress, and personal development intersected upon this new psycho-therapeutic territory.

The expertise of productive subjectivity used all the techniques of the self that were being invented within the therapeutic culture of the 1960s. These devices were not so much for curing ills as for managing one's self to happiness and fulfilment through techniques of self-inspection, through adjustment of self-images, through the remodelling of modes of self presentation by restyling behaviour, speech, and vocabulary, through learning new ways of construing situations and persons, indexed by such terms as awareness and sensitivity and involving a new vocabulary of the emotions. These new techniques claimed the authority of science, for they were backed by elaborated psychological theories and conducted by qualified technicians of the self. They answered to the logic of profitability, for they promised to improve both personal and company performance. They chimed with cultural images of autonomous and self-motivated individuality, hence avoiding the stigma attached to such techniques as psychoanalysis. And they were attractive to the individuals concerned, for they promised them a better self.[32]

While Britain may have lacked its Peters and Waterman and company, and may have been rather short of the likes of Victor Kiam, Warren Avis, and Lee Iacocca, key elements from these new technologies for the management of productive subjectivity were to be imported and promoted. The new techniques of management did, indeed, seem to characterize those British companies that had 'the winning streak'.[33] Seven of Goldsmith and Clutterbuck's eight factors that divide successful companies like Marks & Spencer, Saatchi and Saatchi, United Biscuits, Plessey, and GEC from their unsuccessful rivals had the same flavour: leadership with a mission, autonomy, stressing delegation all down the line and the taking of risks; involvement of employees in the company, including a social programme and genuine respect for the individual; emphasis on the market and high quality as guides to what and how to produce; sticking to the basic values of the company; removal of barriers to innovation and change; and integrity to employees, suppliers, and customers. In other words, it was the corporate culture that counted.

The British authors, in posing the matter in this way, enabled the ethics of self-actualization to be made congruent with the messages of inspiration and anxiety that came from elsewhere – Japan.[34] For while some images of the Japanese corporation painted the worker as anything but self-actualizing, with an almost feudal attachment to the company, the submerging of the individual into the corporate culture, and so forth, those who purveyed the lessons of Japan for British management did so in different terms. The myth of the Japanese success as grounded upon a radically distinct national character, valuing group harmony over individuality, espousing the virtues of hard work, company loyalty, and so forth was to be laid aside. The aim was to define transferable working practices that could be incorporated into British management and assure us of the same success as them. Once again, industrial success was to be based upon the utilization of expert technologies for the management of subjectivity.

Experts in personnel management claimed that what made

Japanese companies successful, competitive, peaceful, innovative, efficient, and the like was not so much 'Japanese social groupism' but their 'consideration for the self-esteem of employees'.[35] Hence the need to establish a corporate culture of 'mutual trust, cooperation and commitment in which all employees can identify with the aims and objectives of the company and which encourages and recognizes the individual contribution of all'.[36] The human technologies required are to incorporate the strivings of the individual into the activities of a team, building bonds between team members by allowing them to select and train their own members, organizing communication on a face-to-face basis within the team, giving teams total responsibility for the quality of products, and tapping the enthusiasm of the team and its members by encouraging them to innovate and improve working methods and giving them autonomy and responsibility. The new vocabulary of team-work, quality consciousness, flexibility, and quality circles thus reconciles the autonomous aspirations of the employee with the collective entrepreneurialism of the corporate culture.

These new images of work and the worker may seem no more than the dreams of academics, researchers, consultants, and other professional entrepreneurs, themselves in search of a sense of fulfilment, personal advancement, and a fast buck. And it is important to stress the gulf between the rhetorical hype and the realities of productive life in industry, in the 'service sector' or on the dole queue. But what can be observed here is more than the froth of ideology. Once again we can see the ways in which connections and symmetries are forged, at both the conceptual and practical levels, between political concerns about the government of the productive life of the nation, the concerns of owners of capital to maximize the economic advantages of their companies, and techniques for the governing of the productive subject. Experts on work play a crucial role in linking these distinct concerns into a functioning network. In doing so they come to have a key role, constructing a language and set of techniques simultaneously based upon an esoteric scientific knowledge they possess, realized through detailed technical prescriptions and devices they can construct and operate, and consonant with national economic health, increased organizational effectiveness, and progressive and humanistic values.

With the rapprochement of the self-actualization of the worker and the competitive advancement of the company, the new psycho-technology of work comes into alignment with the new psycho-technology of subjectivity. No longer was work required to satisfy the needs that it itself frustrated and exacerbated. In the psychologies of human relations, work itself could become the privileged space for the satisfaction of the social needs of individuals. In the psychologies of self-actualization, work is no longer necessarily a constraint upon the freedom of the individual to fulfil his or her potential through the strivings of the psychic economy for autonomy, creativity and responsibility. Work is an essential element in the path to self-fulfilment. There is no longer any barrier between the economic, the psychological, and the social. The antithesis between managing adaptation *to* work and struggling for rewards *from* work is transcended, as working hard produces psychological rewards and psychological rewards produce hard work. The government of work now passes through the psychological strivings of each and every one of us for what we want.

Part three

The Child, the Family, and the Outside World

Chapter eleven

The Young Citizen *

Childhood is the most intensively governed sector of personal existence. In different ways, at different times, and by many different routes varying from one section of society to another, the health, welfare, and rearing of children have been linked in thought and practice to the destiny of the nation and the responsibilities of the state. The modern child has become the focus of innumerable projects that purport to safeguard it from physical, sexual, or moral danger, to ensure its 'normal' development, to actively promote certain capacities of attributes such as intelligence, educability, and emotional stability. Throughout the nineteenth century and our own, anxieties concerning children have occasioned a panoply of programmes that have tried to conserve and shape children by moulding the petty details of the domestic, conjugal, and sexual lives of their parents.

Along this maze of pathways, the child – as an idea and a target – has become inextricably connected to the aspirations of authorities. The environment of the growing child is regulated financially, through benefits and allowances to the family, and pedagogically through programmes of education directed at the parent-to-be. Legislative obligations are imposed upon parents, requiring them to carry out social duties from the registration their children at birth to ensuring that they receive adequate education up into their teens. Health visitors exercise a surveillance, in principle comprehensive and universal, over the care of young children in their homes. Child protection legislation has imposed powers and duties upon local authorities, requiring them to evaluate the standards of care being provided to children by their parents through the agencies of social work, and to intervene into the family to rectify shortcomings, utilizing legal mechanisms where necessary. To adjudicate upon a child accused of a crime now requires scrutiny and evaluation of family life as

---

* I take the title of Part III from Donald Winnicott's book of the same name (Harmondsworth, Penguin, 1964)

a condition of the possibility and legitimacy of judgement. Doctors in general practice and in hospital have professional, if not legal obligations to scrutinize the children they see for whatever reason for signs that they may be 'at risk' and notify statutory authorities of their suspicions. And universal and compulsory schooling catches up the lives of all young citizens into a pedagogic machine that operates not only to impart knowledge but to instruct in conduct and to supervise, evaluate, and rectify childhood pathologies.

Thus, over the present century, a new visibility has been accorded to the child in its life within the household and outside it, and the 'private' family has been opened up to social powers and allocated social duties. Reflecting upon these events, among others, in his 1949 Alfred Marshall Lectures at Cambridge, T.H. Marshall argued that what had occurred amounted to the extension of citizenship to the child. Citizenship denoted 'a kind of basic human equality associated with the concept of full membership of a community'; the developments in techniques and conceptions of government since the eighteenth century showed its gradual progress or evolution over the last two and a half centuries.[1] As far as children were concerned, while they were not citizens in the sense of having political rights to participate in the exercise of political power, and perhaps were only beginning to gain civil rights necessary for individual freedom such as liberty of the person and the right to justice, they had gained social rights. The educational system and the social services extended to each child the right to a modicum of economic welfare and security, to share in the social heritage and live the life of a civilized being according to the standards prevailing in the society at large. Universal education, for Marshall, was a decisive step in the re-establishment of social rights of citizenship in the twentieth century, for it was an attempt to stimulate the growth of citizens in the making. Education was a personal right for the child irrespective of his or her parents' wishes, but it also recognized and imposed a social and collective right – the duty of each individual to improve and civilize themselves for the benefit of the social health of the community. Other sociologists have developed this argument, suggesting that special protective legislation and other forms of social provision for children in the nineteenth century were also developments of citizenship, recognizing the claims of the child, as citizen *in potentia*, upon the social collectivity.[2]

Now Marshall and his followers acknowledged that citizenship imposed obligations as well as rights, obligations both on the community and on the individuals who made it up. But, nonetheless, endowing children with the status of citizenship, making them full and equivalent members of a community, was a profoundly progressive recognition of a principle of equality, and one ultimately in conflict with the principles of inequality that lay at the heart of a capitalist economic system. Since the 1960s, however, most sociological analysts of the welfare state have interpreted these developments differently.[3] Even the most sanguine of these commentators see the apparatus of welfare as ambiguous and contradictory, and regard welfare as having more to do with the disablement of conflict than with the recognition of rights. For more than a century and a half, it is argued, the poor and oppressed, supported by progressive elements of the bourgeoisie, have campaigned and struggled to get the state and the powerful to recognize their social obligations – in the form of education, health care, social support in times of sickness and hardship, and so forth. However, the policies and practices vouchsafed were the minimum necessary to buy off the discontented; far from being inspired by a recognition of collective social obligations, their goal has been to preserve the efficiency of those who provide necessary labour power and military might, to provide antidotes to social unrest, and to ward off demands for truly progressive measures of equalization of wealth and status. The policies and practices of welfare, far from extending citizenship in any benign sense, have in fact functioned to maintain inequality, to legitimate existing relations of power, and to extend social control over potentially troublesome sectors of society.

Further, it appeared that the extension of social regulation to the lives of children actually had little to do with recognition of their rights.[4] Children came to the attention of social authorities as delinquents threatening property and security, as future workers requiring moralization and skills, as future soldiers requiring a level of physical fitness – in other words on account of the threat which they posed now or in the future to the welfare of the state. The apparent humanity, benevolence, and enlightenment of the extension of protection to children in their homes disguised the extension of surveillance and control over the family. Reformers arguing for such legislative changes were moral entrepreneurs, seeking to symbolize their values in the law and, in doing so, to extend their powers and authority over others. The upsurges of concern over the young – from juvenile delinquency in the nineteenth century to sexual abuse today – were actually moral panics: repetitive and predictable social occurrences in which certain persons or phenomena come to symbolize a range of social anxieties concerning threats to the established order and traditional values, the decline of morality and social discipline, and the need to take firm steps in order to prevent a downward spiral into disorder. Professional groups – doctors, psychologists, and social workers – used, manipulated, and exacerbated such panics in order to establish and increase their empires. The apparently inexorable growth of welfare surveillance over the families of the working class had arisen from an alignment between the aspirations of the professionals, the political concerns of the authorities, and the social anxieties of the powerful.

Feminists argued that the regulation of children had to be located within a wider history, in which 'the family' had become a key mechanism of social control and ideological support for a patriarchal capitalism that maintained both women and children in a state of dependency.[5] 'The family' was an ideological mechanism for reproducing a docile labour force, for exploiting the domestic labour of women under the guise of love and duty, for maintaining the patriarchal authority of men over the household. The notion of the family as a voluntary arrangement – entered into out of love, suffused by positive emotions, naturally wishing to have and to cherish its children, the site of self-realization for mothers and of mutual regard and protection of family members – was an ideology that disguised the oppressive relations within this intimate sphere, and the social and economic coercion upon women to enter into family life and motherhood. The function of this familial ideology was to mask the realities of family life, and to preserve a social institution that provided vital economic functions for capitalism: reproduction of the labour force, socialization of children, exploitation of the unpaid domestic labour of women, compensation to men for the alienating nature of their work, and so forth.

Radical criticism of the techniques of family regulation came to focus on the notion of the family as a 'private' domain, seeing this as the central element in the ideology masking the social and economic role of the family.[6] The language of privacy disguised and legitimated the authority of men in the household over both women and children, and obscured the extent to which the state actually shaped and controlled relations in the intimate sphere for public, political ends. The division of public and private is, of course, central to liberal political thought, demarcating the boundaries between the domain over which the powers of the state and law can properly be exercised and that where they have no place. Within these terms the family represents the private sphere *par excellence* – indeed it is doubly private, not only being outside the proper authority of the state but also outside the scope of market relations. The division between public and private is traced back in political and social philosophy at least as far as Aristotle's distinction between *polis* and *oikos* and up to the natural rights theories of John Locke. However, in the eighteenth and nineteenth centuries the distinction was posited in terms of the division between home and market. It was given a philosophical foundation in the liberal political philosophy of J.S. Mill and his followers, with the opposition between the realm of legitimate public regulation and the realm of freedom from intrusion, personal autonomy, and private choice. Writers point to the particular associations in these texts between the public sphere (the world of work, the market, individualism, competition, politics, and the state) and men, and the corollary association of women with the private, domestic, intimate, altruistic, and humanitarian world of the home.

Critics argued that this public/private divide, and the conception of the private that it uses, has always functioned to sustain a particular and oppressive set of relations between men and women. However, developments within capitalism in the nineteenth century reworked this public/private divide to suit the interests of a ruling, property owning male elite. This accounted for the emergence of the cult of domesticity with its idealization of motherhood. While allowing that this allotted certain powers to women, it did so only in their status as mothers confined to the private sphere, and hence failed fundamentally to challenge either the patriarchal separation of realms, or the economic power that men wielded over the family unit.

Analyses of the legal regulation of marriage, divorce, sexual behaviour, and domestic violence were deployed to show that the ideology of individual choice and personal freedom in the private domain of home and family legitimated a refusal by public authorities to intervene into certain places, activities, relationships and feelings. Designating them personal, private, and subjective made them appear to be outside the scope of the law as a fact of nature, whereas in fact non-intervention was a socially constructed, historically variable, and inevitably political decision. The state defined as 'private' those aspects of life into which it would not intervene, and then, paradoxically, used this privacy as the justification for its non-intervention.

Like *laissez faire* in relation to the market, the idea that the family could be private in the sense of outside public regulation was, according to these critics, a myth. The state cannot avoid intervening in the shaping of familial relations through decisions as to which types of relation to sanction and codify and which types of dispute to regulate or not to regulate. The state establishes the legal framework for conducting legitimate sexual relations and for procreation, and privileges certain types of relation through rules of inheritance. Further, the state, through public law, set up complex welfare mechanisms especially those surrounding the proper development of children. And however potent is the legal ideology of family privacy, in decisions as to the best interests and welfare of children in cases concerning care and custody, and in the division of family property and other aspects of family disputes, legal functionaries operate according to ideological and patriarchal beliefs as to morality, responsibility and family life and what is best for children. On the one hand, the state, representing dominant male interests, chooses the nature and objectives of public regulation; on the other, a domain is constituted outside legal regulation and designated 'private', where welfare agencies enforce the ideology of motherhood, and where male power is not even subject to limited protections of the rule of law.

These analyses have much to commend them. But in designating the public/private division as an ideology that disguises the hand of the state and has primarily a social control function in relation to women, they fail to register or come to grips with two key issues. The first concerns the way in which the privacy of the family was a vital element in the technologies of government that made liberal democratic rule possible, allowing a fundamental transformation in the scope and responsibilities of 'the state' and the organization of power. The second concerns the ways in which these new rationales and technologies of government did not simply control individuals through the family but played a constitutive role in the formation of citizens of such democracies, acting at the level of subjectivity itself.

'Familialization' was crucial to the means whereby personal capacities and conducts could be socialized, shaped, and maximized in a manner that accorded with the moral and political principles of liberal society. The languages of the regulatory strategies, the terms within which they thought themselves, the ways in which they formulated their problems and solutions, were not merely ideological; they made it possible and legitimate to govern the lives of citizens in new ways. In doing so, they actually brought new sectors of reality into existence, new problems and possibilities for personal investment as well as for public regulation. If the familialization of society worked, it was because it both established its political legitimacy and commanded a level of subjective commitment from citizens, inciting them to regulate their own lives according to its terms.

The emergence of an institutionally distinct political domain, the sovereign state, entailed the gradual concentration of formal political, juridical, and administrative powers that had hitherto been dispersed among a range of authorities – guilds, justices, landowners, and religious authorities.[7] This concentration, and the concomitant legitimation and delimitation of political authority by the doctrines of 'rule of law', entailed the conceptualization of certain domains that were freed from the threat of punitive sanction and detailed internal regulation. These developments coincided with the major transformations in the lives of the working population associated with the growth of urban capitalism, and hence with the decomposition of the extensive mechanisms by which the church, the local powers, and the community had specified, monitored, and sanctioned the detailed aspects of personal, conjugal, sexual, and domestic conduct. The private family was to emerge as a solution to the problems of regulating individuals and populations and of producing social solidarities that were posed by these ruptures in socio-political relations.[8]

The private family did not reactivate the independence of patriarchal authority and political allegiance of the pre-liberal household, but nor did it require the extension of the scope and prerogatives of the state into the details of everyday existence. The domesticated private family was both to be distinguished from political life and to be defined and privileged by law; it was to be both freed from detailed prescriptions of conduct and to be permeable to moralization and normalization from outside. It was to become the matrix for the government of the social economy.

The reconstruction of the working-class family in the nineteenth century took place not through the activities of the state, but through an initiative that maintained a certain distance from the organs of political power – philanthropy. Philanthropic activity was certainly mobilized by the perceived threats posed to the wealthy by the dangerous classes, the amalgam of crime, indigence, pauperism, and vice that appeared to be multiplying in the cities. But it was a response unlike either repression or charity, for it sought a prophylactic mode of action, endeavouring to promote certain kinds of moral conduct by coupling the provision of financial aid with conditions as to the future conduct of recipients. In England and France philanthropists sought not to 'preserve' the families of the urban masses – for family life was widely believed to be virtually unknown in the rookeries and at the heart of the great towns – but to organize the conjugal, domestic, and parental relations of the poor in the form of the domesticated family. Assistance was thus conditional upon marriage, good housekeeping, sobriety, moral supervision of children, and the search for wage labour.[9]

Throughout the nineteenth century a multitude of little and large projects were undertaken, each using the human technology of the family for social ends. It appeared that the family could play a vital role in eliminating illegality, curbing inebriety, and restricting promiscuity, imposing restrictions upon the unbridled sensualities of adults and inculcating morality into children. Bourgeois women sought to recruit their working class sisters as allies, arguing that marriage, domestic hygiene, and so forth were not only moral in their own right, but would further women's interests by increasing their powers *vis-à-vis* their menfolk. The legal relation of marriage was to promote emotional and economic investment by both men and women into the home, cathecting domesticity at the expense of street life, public bawdiness, and vice. Such campaigns served a vital function, operating as relays through which the imperatives of social regulation could become linked with the wishes and aspirations of individuals for security and advancement.

In such campaigns, public authorities were seldom centrally involved, although they did provide a legal framework for philanthropic action and often supported private campaigns with funds and information. A more significant ally of philanthropy, which operated not so much by *moralization* as by *normalization*, was medicine. Medico-hygienic expertise began to elaborate a set of doctrines concerning the conditions for rearing healthy children and to pose many issues of moral conduct – (drunkenness, debauchery, viciousness, masturbation, insanity) – in medical terms. They not only were detrimental to individual health but arose from weaknesses incurred through faulty government in childhood and could themselves be passed down from parents to children in the form of a susceptible constitution. Such advice was disseminated through literature and personal contact, principally into the homes of the well-to-do; its message was that the preservation of the lineage depended upon the active concentration of mothers upon the rearing of their offspring. In their turn, hygienists and philanthropists took this message into the homes of the poor, to reinforce the demands of morality with the norms of medicine. Thus a set of standards for family life began to be established and generalized that were grounded neither in political authority nor religious duty; the norms of medicine appeared to arise directly from life itself.

Philanthropists and hygienists campaigned to have their strategies enshrined in law and their expertise linked to the activities of social institutions such as courts, hospitals, prisons, and schools. By the start of the twentieth century the family was administered and policed by practices and agencies that were not 'private' (many of their powers were constructed legally, they were often recipients of public funds, and their agents were frequently publicly accredited by some form of licencing), but nor were they organs of central political power. Their operations and objectives were not specified by the decrees and programmes of political forces but operated under the aegis of moral principles and, increasingly, by professional expertise underpinned by the power of a claim to truth. In France and England, however, the turn of the twentieth century saw the linking of these moralizing and normalizing projects more centrally into the calculations and policies of the political authorities. What was involved here was not so much an expansionary project on behalf of the ruling classes, as an attempt to resolve some rather specific social troubles. The remit of the public power was to extend to the government of the physical, moral, and mental capacities of citizens. The autonomy of the poor family was not to be destroyed but re-modelled through enhancing and modifying the family machine.

A web of legal powers, social agencies and practices of judgement and normalization began to spread around troubled and troublesome children.[10] These were linked to the formal government machine at three principal points. The medical apparatus of public health extended its scrutiny to all children from birth, in their homes and in the schools, through registration of births, infant welfare centres, health visitors, school medical officers, education in domestic sciences, and schools for mothers, using legal powers and statutory institutions to provide a platform for the deployment of medico–hygienic norms and expertise, seeking to turn the school into a medical station and the home into a site of prophylaxis. Around the juvenile court, new powers of judgement and scrutiny were brought to bear upon the families of troubled and troublesome children, utilizing the legal process as a kind of case conference or diagnostic forum and deploying social workers and probation officers to scrutinize and report upon the homes of their cases, and to undertake at least a part of the normative assessment and reformation of children and their families. And the child guidance clinic acted as the hub of a programmatic movement for mental hygiene, drawing together the powers of the courts over children who had done wrong and parents who had wronged them, the universal and obligatory scrutiny of conduct in the school, and the private anxieties of family members about the behaviour of their children, into a powerful network linked by the activities and judgements of doctors, psychologists, probation officers, and social workers. These technologies of government, which Donzelot terms the 'tutelary complex', enabled the difficulties posed by working-class families and children to be acted upon with a degree of force, universality, and certainty but without disabling the family mechanism. Families would neither be lured into dependency by especially favourable treatment, nor forced into resistance by measures that were frankly repressive. Through the ministrations of expertise in the service of health, hygiene, and normality, the family would be returned to its social obligations without compromising its autonomy and responsibility for its own members and destiny.

Expertise also resolved a further problem at the junction of the family mechanism and the goals of government. This was that of achieving a harmony between the private authority, self-concern, and aspirations of the autonomous family and the best procedures for the socialization of its members. Donzelot refers to the techniques along this dimension as 'the regulation of images'. The representations of motherhood, fatherhood, family life, and parental conduct generated by expertise were to infuse and shape the personal investments of individuals, the ways in which they formed, regulated and evaluated their lives, their actions, and their goals. Of course, the construction of subjective values and investments was the aim of many of the familializing projects of the nineteenth and twentieth centuries. It was an explicit rationale of the moralizing philanthropy of the nineteenth century, and of the arguments for universal education. The concern for the health and welfare of children in the early twentieth century certainly sought to utilize 'the family' and the relations within it as a kind of social or socializing machine in order to fulfil various objectives – military, industrial and moral – but this was to be done not through the coercive enforcement of control under threat of sanction, but through the production of mothers who would want hygienic homes and healthy children. The promotion of hygiene and welfare could only be successful to the extent that it managed to solicit the active engagement of individuals in the promotion of their own bodily efficiency.

The family could come to serve these new social objectives only to the extent that it would operate as a voluntary and responsible machine for the rearing and moralizing of children, in which adults would commit themselves to the task of promoting the physical and mental welfare of their offspring. Once such an ethic came to govern our existence, the images of normality generated by expertise could come to serve as a means by which individuals could themselves normalize and evaluate their lives, their conduct, and those of their children. The means of correct socialization could be implanted in families concerned with the self-promotion of their members without the threat of coercion and without direct intervention by political authorities into the household. Such families have come to govern their intimate relations and socialize their children according to social norms but through the activation of their own hopes and fears. Parental conduct, motherhood, and child rearing can thus be regulated through family autonomy, through wishes and aspirations, and through the activation of individual guilt, personal anxiety, and private disappointment. And the almost inevitable misalignment between expectation and realization, fantasy and actuality, fuels the search for help and guidance in the difficult task of producing normality, and powers the constant familial demand for the assistance of expertise.

To be sure, the contemporary disquiet about the powers of welfare professionals in relation to the family have an old fashioned *laissez faire* ring. But the extent that they can be reactivated in the late twentieth century is testament to the success of the socializing project of the last hundred years, to the incorporation of the expert doctrines for the government of children into our own free will. Socialization, in the sense in which we see it here, is not the anthropological universal beloved by functionalist sociologists; it is the historically specific outcome of technologies for the government of the subjectivity of citizens.

The notion of the normal child and family has an ambiguous status in these technologies of subjectivity. Normality appears in three guises: as that which is natural and hence healthy; as that against which the actual is judged and found unhealthy; and as that which is to be produced by rationalized social programmes. Criteria of normality are simultaneously used to construct an image of the natural child, mother and family, to provide a more or less explicit set of instructions to all involved as to how they should identify normality and conduct themselves in a normal fashion, and to provide the means of identifying abnormality and the rationale for intervention when reality and normality fail to coincide.

Yet our conceptions of normality are not simply generalizations from our accumulated experience of normal children. On the contrary, criteria of normality are elaborated by experts on the basis of their claims to a scientific knowledge of childhood and its vicissitudes. And this knowledge of normality has not, in the main, resulted from studying normal children. On the contrary, in tracing the genealogy of normality we are returned to the projects of the government of children that provided the platform for the take-off of expertise. It is around pathological children – the troublesome, the recalcitrant, the delinquent – that conceptions of normality have taken shape. It is not that a knowledge of the normal course of development of the child has enabled experts to become more skilled at identifying those unfortunate children who are in some way abnormal. Rather, expert notions of normality are extrapolated from our attention to those children who worry the courts, teachers, doctors, and parents. Normality is not an observation but a valuation. It contains not only a judgement about what is desirable, but an injunction as to a goal to be achieved. In so doing, the very notion of 'the normal' today awards power to scientific truth and expert authority.

Since World War II psychologists have increasingly provided the vocabularies with which the troubles of children have been described, the expertise for diagnosing and categorizing such children, the languages within which the tasks of mothers and fathers have been adumbrated, and the professionals to operate the technology of childhood regulation. Psychology has played a key role in establishing the norms of childhood, in providing means for visualizing childhood pathology and normality, in providing vocabularies for speaking about childhood subjectivity and its problems, in inventing technologies for cure and normalization. Through the connections established between the norms of childhood and images of family life, parenting, and motherhood, the psyche of the child and the subjectivity of the mother have been opened up for regulation in a new way. It has become the will of the mother to govern her own children according to psychological norms and in partnership with psychological experts. The soul of the young citizen has become the object of government through expertise.

Chapter twelve

The Gaze of the Psychologist

For a long time ordinary individuality – the everyday individuality of everybody – remained below the threshold of description. To be looked at, observed, described in detail, followed from day to day by an uninterrupted writing was a privilege.... [The disciplinary methods] reversed this relation, lowered the threshold of describable individuality and made of this description a means of control and a method of domination.... This turning of real lives into writing is no longer a procedure of heroization; it functions as a procedure of objectification and subjectification.[1]

Michel Foucault, 1979

It was once the privilege of the wealthy, the noble, and the holy to have their individuality remarked upon, described, documented, recorded for posterity in image and text. But during the nineteenth century the individualizing gaze alighted upon those at the other end of power relations – the criminal, the madman, the pauper, the defective were to be the target of many laborious and ingenious projects to document their uniqueness, to record it and classify it, to discipline their difference.[2] Children were to become favoured objects and targets of such programmes of individualization. Psychologists were to claim a particular expertise in the disciplining of the uniqueness and idiosyncracies of childhood, individualizing children by categorizing them, calibrating their aptitudes, inscribing their peculiarities in an ordered form, managing their variability conceptually, and governing it practically.

Michel Foucault argued that the disciplines 'make' individuals by means of some rather simple technical procedures.[3] On the parade ground, in the factory, in the school and in the hospital, people were gathered together *en masse*, but by this very fact they could be observed as entities both similar to and different from one another. These institutions function in certain respects like telescopes, microscopes, or other scientific instruments: they established a regime of visibility in which the observed was distributed within a single common plane of sight. Second, these institutions operated according to a regulation of detail. These regulations, and the evaluation of conduct, manners, and so forth entailed by them, established a grid of codeability of personal attributes. They act as norms, enabling the previously aleatory and unpredictable complexities of human conduct to be charted and judged in terms of conformity and deviation, to be coded and compared, ranked and measured.

The formation of a plane of sight and a means of codifiability established a grid of perception for registering the details of individual conduct.[4] These became both visible and cognizable – no longer lost in the fleeting passage of space, time, movement, and voice but identifiable and notable in so far as they conformed to or deviated from the network of norms that began to spread out over the space of personal existence. Behavioral space was thus geometrized, enabling a fixing of what was previously regarded as quintessentially unique into an ordered space of knowledge. In this perceptual process the phenomenal world was normalized – that is to say, thought in terms of its coincidences and differences from values deemed normal – in the very process of making it visible to science. The properties of disciplinary regimes were fundamental to the production of the person as a knowable individual.

The development of institutions and techniques that required the co-ordination of large numbers of persons in an economic manner and sought to eliminate certain habits, propensities, and morals and to inculcate others thus made visible the difference between those who did or did not, could or could not, would or would not learn the lessons of the institution. These institutions acted as observing and recording machines, machines for the registration of human differences. These attentions to individual differences and their consequences spread to other institutions, especially those that had to do with the efficient or rational utilization or deployment of persons.[5] In the courtroom, in the developing system of schooling, in the apparatus concerned with pauperism and the labour market, and in the army and the factory, two sorts of problems were posed in the early years of this century that the psychological sciences would take up. The first was a demand for some kind of human sorting house, which would assess individuals and determine to what type of regime they were best suited – a question framed in relation to delinquency, feeble-mindedness, and pauperism; later in projects for vocational guidance and selection for the armed forces. The second was the demand for advice on the ways in which individuals could best be organized and tasks best arranged so as to minimize the human problems of production or warfare – industrial accidents, fatigue, insubordination, and so forth. The consolidation of psychology into a discipline and its social destiny was tied to its capacity to produce the technical means of individualization, a new way of construing, observing, and recording human subjectivity and its vicissitudes.

Contemporaneous with the nineteenth century transformations in the organization of asylums, prisons, hospitals, and schools, new systems were devised for documenting and recording information concerning inmates – files, records, and case histories.[6] This routine notation and accumulation of the personal details and histories of large numbers of persons identifies each individual with a dossier consisting in the facts of his or her life and character accorded pertinence by the institution and its objectives. The individual entered the field of knowledge not through any abstract leap of the philosophical imagination, but through the mundane operation of bureaucratic documentation. The sciences of individualization took off from these routine techniques of recording, utilizing them, transforming them into systematic devices for the inscription of identity, techniques that could translate the properties, capacities, energies of the human soul into material form – pictures, charts, diagrams, measurements.[7]

This dependence upon means of visualization and techniques of inscription does not mark a fundamental difference between the psychological sciences and other sciences. Science not only entails techniques that render phenomena visible, so that they may form the focus of conceptualization, but also requires devices that represent the phenomena to be accounted for, which turn these phenomena into an appropriate form for analysis. Perhaps the psychological sciences differ from other sciences only in their low epistemological threshold. That is to say, so frequently the norms that enable their objects to become visualized and inscribed become part of the scientific programme of perception as a consequence of having first been part of a social and institutional programme of regulation – and to such programmes they are destined to return.

The sentence, the proposition or description in language, is not the principal mode in which phenomena are are inscribed into scientific discourse.[8] The observation statement in linguistic form is rapidly superseded by, or at the very least accompanied by, traces of a different type: images, graphs, numbers. But all the traces produced and worked on by science have certain characteristic qualities. Bruno Latour describes them as immutable mobiles.[9] Whatever the original dimensions of their subjects, be they rooms full of children or chromosomes invisible to the naked eye, the traces must be neither too large or too tiny, but of proportions that can be rapidly scanned, read, and recalled. Unlike their subjects, which are characteristically of three dimensions, and whose image is subject to variations of perspective, inscriptions are ideally of two dimensions and amenable to combination in a single visual field without variation or distortion by point of view. This enables them to be placed side by side and in various combinations, and to be integrated with materials, notes, and records from other sources. Inscriptions must render ephemeral phenomena into stable forms that can be repeatedly examined and accumulated over time. Phenomena are frequently stuck in time and space, and inconvenient for the application of the scientist's labour; inscriptions should be easily transportable so that they can be concentrated and utilized in laboratories, clinics, and other centres of accounting, calculation, and administration.

The first techniques of visualization and inscription of human differences in the psychological sciences constituted the surface of the body as the field upon which psychological pathologies were to be observed. The visual image, which in the portrait had functioned as a monument to an honoured nobility, now was to become a means of grasping and calibrating the sicknesses of the soul. Doctors of the insane in the late eighteenth and nineteenth centuries, from Lavater, through Pinel and Esquirol, Bucknill and Tuke, and up to the theorists of degeneracy such as Maudsley and Morel, reworked and systematized the ancient arts of physiognomy, utilizing the external proportions and characteristics of the body as the means of individualization of the pathological person. Tables and arrays of visual images, from line drawings to carefully contrived photographs, sought to establish a grammar of the body. This system of perception strove for a language in which the variations and combinations of the visualized body could be systematically mapped onto invisible mental characteristics. As Sandor Gilman has pointed out, the linking of these pictorial representations with case studies in textbooks on insanity and psychopathology throughout the nineteenth century performed a vital cognitive function in linking up the theoretical and the observable, materializing the theory and idealizing the object, instructing the mind through the education of the eyes.[10]

In phrenology, criminal anthropology, and other sciences of the soul, systems were constructed that sought to make other aspects of the individual similarly visible and legible to the trained eye. Such systems had only a limited life-span, not because of their internal inconsistencies or through a theoretical critique, but because they failed to provide the individualizing techniques that were to be demanded of them. The co-ordination and regulation of large numbers of persons in the expanding apparatuses of penality, industry, education, and military life produced both a demand for new techniques and vocabularies for the managing of human difference and the conditions under which they might be invented. Capacities and attributes now became evident which, while they affected performance at school, predisposed to crime, had a bearing on the success of penal regimes, or were related to efficiency in the factory or liability to breakdown in the army, were not clearly inscribed upon the surface of the body. The discipline of psychology took shape around the problem of inventing these new techniques of individualization.

The first contribution of psychology to the project of individualization was the psychological test of intelligence. The psychological test was a means of visualizing, disciplining, and inscribing a difference that did not rely upon the surface of the body as the diagnostic intermediary between conduct and the psyche. The problem for which the intelligence test would be a solution arose in the early years of universal schooling in both England and France. The figure who provoked it was the feeble-minded child.

From our contemporary perspective, the intense concern with feeble-mindedness in children that flourished in the late nineteenth and early twentieth centuries is hard to understand. The feeble-minded child, and the adult that he or she would become, appeared to be a major social threat. Eugenicists saw the feeble-minded as a central element in the degeneracy or deterioration of the race.[11] The feeble-minded were kith and kin of the prostitute, the tubercular, the insane, the unemployable, the vagrant, and the libertine – all manifestations of a degenerate constitution. Feeble-mindedness was a key element in this degeneration, for not only did it clearly run in families, but the feeble-minded were unsocializable, impervious to morality and hence to the curbs that civilization imposed upon promiscuous reproduction. They were a testament to the fact that the race renewed itself most rapidly from its inferior sections, with the consequent increase in hereditary unfitness down the generations. In short, curbing their reproduction, by segregation or sterilization, was a matter of urgency, and hence their detection and ascertainment was a priority.

Eugenicists were only one group among many who thought the 'feeble minded' needed to be correctly ascertained and dealt with in distinct institutional provisions. Some argued on financial grounds. To support them in institutions that had no capacity to improve or reform them was a drain on national resources, when there was a chance that they could be trained in such a way that they might not only contribute to their upkeep, but actually make a net contribution to industry and agriculture. Others argued on grounds of social economy. Idiots outside institutional care were open to ill use and exploitation by corrupt and criminal elements, exacerbating the 'social problem' of crime, poverty, destitution, physical ill-health, and immoral habits that philanthropists and social investigators had revealed at the heart of our great cities.[12] Together, these concerns posed an urgent question. How was the feeble-minded individual to be identified for special treatment?

The schoolroom provided further evidence of the problem. But it would also produce its solution. Universal schooling gathered together large numbers of children in the same physical space, and sought to discipline them according to institutional criteria and objectives. It thus established norms of conduct and performance that organized behavioural space and enabled divergences between children to be charted. Among the children unable to learn the lessons of the school were a group who were unlike the blind and deaf in that they appeared to possess the full complement of the senses. But they none the less did not seem to be able to benefit from instruction. These children came to be known as educational imbeciles or the feeble-minded. They accumulated in the lowest classes, unable to reach the standards set by the board of education – a source of concern to those who saw the school as a vital moralizing apparatus and an affront to those who considered education to be a right of all citizens. The problem was to find a way in which these feeble-minded children could be ascertained in a rigorous and consistent manner such that they could be separated out from the rest of the school population and segregated in specialized institutions that would seek to awaken their moral sensibilities and increase their resistance to the temptations of vice and crime. In England, France, and the United States the problem was posed in almost identical terms. Administrators sought a scientific and rational solution to the problem of individualizing the feeble-minded. But this was a task that proved rather difficult for the scientists. In the first instance, in seeking to discover these children, diagnosis was carried out by a scrutiny of the body. Children would parade before the doctor, who would seek the marks of pathology: stigmata, misproportioned limbs, unbalanced nerves or muscles, deformed palates, characteristic cranial shapes, degenerate ears.[13] But it proved difficult to align the gaze of the doctor with the requirements of the institution. Difference was no longer marking itself unambiguously on the surface of the individual; it was receding into the interiority of the soul. It would have to be made legible.

The intelligence test arose out of the attempts to make these invisible differences legible. The procedures invented were to be used as the model for a whole panoply of psychometric devices. The technique did not spring fully formed from the heads of the eugenicist proponents of mental measurement such as Francis Galton, Charles Spearman, Lewis Terman, and Cyril Burt. Nor was it simply 'invented' by Alfred Binet, upon whose name it has conferred a dubious kind of immortality. It formed through the confluence of two rather different projects of individualization.

From *Hereditary Genius*, which Galton published in 1869, proponents of mental measurement had sought to provide ways of grasping the variability of human mental powers in thought, so that their heritability and social consequences could be calibrated and acted upon.[14] The statistical concept of the normal distribution was the vital cognitive mechanism that enabled Galton to visualize human variability. The simple act of comparison of the respective amount of a particular quality or attribute possessed by two members of the population enabled the mathematization of difference. This could be represented in a simple visual form once it was assumed that all qualities in the population varied according to a regular and predictable pattern, and that the characteristics of this pattern were those established by the statistical laws of large numbers. Individual difference could be made thinkable by a simple act of inscription: cumulative acts of comparison would be combined with the figure of the norm or average for the population; when represented diagramatically they would form the smooth outline of the 'normal' curve. Intellectual abilities could be construed as a single dimension, whose variation across the population was governed by precise laws. The capacity of any individual could be established in terms of their location along that curve; the variability of the intellect had been reduced to order, made graspable through its normalization into a stable, predictable, two-dimensional trace.

The normal distribution was a visual and conceptual fusion of the laws of variability of qualities, the laws of large numbers, and the norms of social expectation. It produced a new mode of social perception of variability, a way of disciplining difference and making it socially usable. But a further step was needed before psychometrics could fulfil its social vocation. This was provided by the administrative requirements of schooling.

Eugenics sought a link between the biological, heritable, variable basis of mental characteristics and the criteria of social worth. This link that was to be forged by psychologists, who measured the senses and related these measurements with social judgements. The English eugenicist psychologists – Galton, Cattell, Pearson, and Spearman – all sought to assess intellectual ability by measuring sensory capacities, and tried to show that these were normally distributed, heritable, and correlated with social judgements as to intellect and worth. But feeble-mindedness in children became troublesome in the institution of the school, and the educational judgements of the school did not seem to coincide readily with the psycho-physiological measurements of capacities to discriminate weights and sounds favoured by the English theorists of mental measurement.

The test that Alfred Binet devised in the French context was initially conceived as merely an administrative device for identifying children for admission to special schools for the feeble-minded.[15] In order to construct it, Binet set aside his earlier work on intelligence.

In this he had concluded that intelligence could not be satisfactorily investigated by tests aiming at a diagnosis in a few hours, but required the lengthy and detailed study of particular individuals. Nevertheless, as a member of the Society for the Psychological Study of the Child, Binet sought to assist the 1904 Ministerial Commission for the Abnormal to decide on the admission of children to special schools. The commission needed a device that would enable it to make an 'exact distribution', and to permit clinicians to 'separate subjects of inferior intelligence into categories verifiable by all'.[16] The demands of rational administration triumphed where decades of detailed scientific study had led into a cul-de-sac.

Age provided Binet with the key conceptual device for ranking individuals according to their abilities; adaptation to educational requirements provided the criterion of measurement. First, rather than seeking to measure psycho-physiological properties of individual subjects and to compare these with social judgements, Binet's test used criteria that were directly educational and behavioural. They were direct assessments of the degree of adaptation of individual children to the expectation that others had of them. Combined with the observation of large numbers of children of similar ages in schools, and of large numbers of defectives in institutions, this allowed two related shifts in images of children.[17] Despite variations between individuals, norms of performance could be established for children at particular ages. And defective children could be seen to bear a striking resemblance to normal children some years younger. Binet did not need to commit himself to a view of feeble-mindedness as arrested development in order to group these under a single measure, mental level, which could be combined with chronological age to produce a simple indication of degree of defect. And this, of course, was all that was required to enable an initial assessment of children for administrative purposes.

The subsequent history of the intelligence test is not our concern here; its phases have been well documented.[18] Binet himself transformed it from a technique for diagnosing the pathological into a device for creating a hierarchy of the normal. William Stern invented the single numerical index of mental quotient, which combined chronological age and mental level into a single figure. Lewis Terman in the United States produced a refined version of the test and, with fellow eugenicists Henry Goddard and Robert Yerkes, promulgated its use in the service of campaigns for detecting the previously undetectable high grade defectives in order to allow their segregation or sterilization, and to demonstrate the need for immigration control to keep out the lower races. In the rather less flamboyant eugenic climate of Britain, Cyril Burt standardized the test in order to bring it into line with the theoretical requirements of the normal distribution and the administrative requirements of the educational authorities.[19] Group tests, non-verbal tests, and all the other varieties of psychometrics followed the same path for aligning individual conduct, social judgement, statistical probity, and administrative convenience.[20] What is significant about all this for my present concerns is not so much the details of the history and vicissitudes of testing as the new way of visualizing normality and difference, of inscribing personal powers, of administering children, and other new methods.

The technique of the test was the most important contribution of the psychological sciences to the human technologies of the first half of the twentieth century. The test routinizes the complex ensemble of social judgement on individual variability into an automatic device that makes difference visible and notable. One no longer has to observe children for long periods of time or compare large numbers one with another in the classroom and the asylum in order to reveal their similarities and differences. The test codifies, mathematizes, and normalizes difference. It is a simple technical device, but one that can be used to realize almost any psychological schema for differentiating individuals in a brief time span, in a manageable space, at the will of the expert. It has become an indispensable part of any modern programme for the government of individual differences.

The psychological test takes the powers of individuals and turns them into writing as numbers, quotients, scores, profiles. This form of writing has a clear vocation, which is the dossier, the portable cumulative record of individual worth that is central to bureaucracy and psychology alike. Its results are directed towards any institutional forum where a calculation is to be made about personal fortunes in terms of an assessment of individual capacities. In the courtroom, the classroom, the consulting room, and the interview room these inscriptions of individuality are pored over, compared, weighed in the balance. They make the individual knowable, calculable, and administrable, to the extent that he or she may be differentiated from others and evaluated in relation to them. A general science of the individual no longer appears a paradoxical project; individuality has been made amenable to scientific judgement.

With psychometrics the previously ungraspable domain of mental capacities is opened up for government. What can now be judged and administered is not what one *does* but what one *is*. These procedures for administering children on the basis of judgements of their mental capacities are not solely or even principally in the hand of legal functionaries, although they have obligatory consequences for children in terms of their school careers or distribution to different reformatory institutions. The enquiries and the judgements are psychological. They are not made in terms of a rule and its transgression, but in terms of a norm and an assessment of normality.[21] With psychometrics psychology had begun to establish its claim as the appropriate authority to adjudicate upon the lives of individuals, to administer them in such a way that would maximize their social utility and minimize the social danger their difference might represent. In the conception and technology of intelligence, for perhaps the first time, a science of the soul was combined with a strategy for the government of the individual.

Psychometrics rendered the intellect manageable. As a technique for the judgement and allocation of children and adults it would have a great destiny. The image of the normal curve, the concept of an intelligence that was unitary, variable, assessable, summable into a simple score, certainly has a wide currency. But despite the proliferation of the language of IQ into lay discourse, the market in manuals for self-assessment of IQ, and the emergence of 'user' organizations of those with a high IQ, psychometrics fits most readily into professionalized and bureaucratic modes of administration. Judgement is in the hands of experts, decisions in the hands of administrators. The consequence is that the individual is directed to one or other social or institutional location. But pretty soon psychometrics was joined by other normalized and normalizing visions of childhood, which appear softer and more benign but which have become, by this very token, more pervasive. The most powerful of these was the notion of development.

It seems perverse to suggest that, prior to the early twentieth century, children did not 'develop'. Surely their growth from infancy to maturity has always been obvious to any with eyes to see. Yet it was by no means self-evident that a systematic knowledge of childhood should be grounded in the notion that their attributes should be linked along the dimension of time in a unified sequence. Young children had been objects of philosophical interest in the eighteenth and nineteenth centuries, providing 'crucial experiments' that might reveal the presence or absence of innate ideas and qualities, or show the extent to which the attributes of humanity derived from sensations entering the sense organs.[22] But in the late nineteenth and early twentieth centuries a new scientific gaze focused upon the young child from the perspective of evolution. Observation of young children could, it appeared, cast light upon the nature of human evolution and the characteristics distinguishing man from the animals. It might reveal the extent to which human emotions and expressions were inborn or learned. It might support the doctrines of recapitulation, for in the same way as the development of the human embryo appeared to repeat the stages of the physical evolution of the human species, the development of the child appeared to repeat the stages of the cultural evolution of humans from primitive to civilized.[23] Time had become integral to the sciences of nature – why not also to the sciences of man?

From this perspective, Darwin, Preyer, Sully, Stanley Hall, Claparede, and Baldwin all observed infants and described and documented their emotions, words, and movements and the ways in which these changed over time.[24] Sully in England, and Stanley Hall in the United States, sought to incorporate parents into this movement for the scientific observation of children, and child study inspired mothers and fathers to collate innumerable observations of their own children. But the psychologists of the 1920s, while ritually acknowledging these contributions, tended to discount them. It seemed that the mere observation of children did not amount to science of children. The accounts that had been put together were too idiosyncratic, often anecdotal and unsystematic, neglecting important factors like the influence of surroundings, varying in method from person to person and hence lacking comparability. However suggestive they were in their reflections on the changing behaviour and abilities of children over time, it appeared that they did not themselves have the capacity to found a discipline of childhood psychology.

Developmental psychology was made possible by the clinic and the nursery school. Such institutions had a vital role, for they enabled the observation of numbers of children of the same age, and of children of a number of different ages, by skilled psychological experts under controlled, experimental, almost laboratory conditions. They thus simultaneously allowed for standardization and normalization – the collection of comparable information on a large number of subjects and its analysis in such a way as to construct norms. A developmental norm was a standard based upon the average abilities or performances of children of a certain age on a particular task or a specified activity. It thus not only presented a picture of what was *normal* for children of such an age, but also enabled the normality of any child to be assessed by comparison with this norm.

The gathering of data on children of particular ages over a certain period, and the organization of this data into age norms, enabled the norms to be arranged along an axis of time and seen as cross sections through a continuous dimension of development. Growth and temporality could become principles of organization of a psychology of childhood. And normalization and development enabled individual children to be characterized in terms of their position on this axis of time relative to that deemed 'normal' for their age.

The work of Arnold Gesell and his colleagues provides an exemplary demonstration of the techniques for the disciplining of human difference. Gesell's work was carried out at the Yale Psycho-Clinic, which had opened in 1911 for the assessment and treatment of children having problems at school. An early photograph captures the essential elements of this project (Plate 1). Dr. Gesell is pictured in his laboratory.[25] The date is probably in the 1920s. The laboratory itself manifests in its design and equipment the characteristics of the gaze that psychologists would, from this moment on, target upon the child. It is a dome brilliantly lit within and designed for one-way vision. Outside, able to see in without being seen themselves, are observers, probably student psychologists. While one merely watches, another writes notes with pencil upon a pad. A third, probably a technician, operates a movie camera. Within the dome is the white coated scientist. His gaze, like that of the observers within the picture, and our own, is focused upon one particular spot. At the centre of the dome, contained in a kind of playpen, sitting at a table, playing with what appears to be a small brick, is a baby. This is a photograph of Dr Arnold Gesell testing a baby.

We should not be misled by the familiarity of such a scene. It is surely something quite remarkable that this small creature should

Plate 1:   Arnold Gesell in his laboratory

Sources: Norman L. Munn, Psychology: the Fundamentals of Human Adjustment, 5th edition, London: George Harrap & Co. (1961:15).
Photo courtesy of Edward B. Gerard.

have become the focus of this complex apparatus. The child is here caught up within a complicated arrangement that will transform it into a visible, observable and analyzable object, within a particular rational scientific discourse (developmental psychology) making a particular kind of claim upon our attention, a claim to truth.

The child, no doubt, is by now an old man or woman; it left the laboratory long ago. But its traces remain in the form of records, photographs, graphs, measurements. It is these traces or inscriptions, together with those of many other similar children that have been accumulated, combined, correlated, graded, and consolidated into the object of developmental psychology.[26] For the psychologist, as for scientists elsewhere, inscriptions have a number of advantages over their subjects themselves. Some of these are immediately apparent in Gesell's own work. Children are difficult to accumulate in large numbers. Large rooms and considerable labour are required to hold them side by side, to pick out common or differentiating features. They change over time. Once dismissed from the laboratory it may be impossible to reassemble them for further examination. Only a limited number of observers can view them and thus be convinced of the value of what the psychologist has to say about them. They are unstable material for a science to work on.

Gesell solved this problem by photography. The movies were analyzed frame by frame and still photographs produced (Plate 2). These could be compared and contrasted, placed side by side and examined at will, on the stable two-dimensional plane of the desk rather than in the changing, three dimensional space of the playroom or laboratory. They could form the material of cognitive operations constrained only by the limits of the scientific imagination, operations that would be difficult to manage with the children who were their subjects. The photographs could be assembled in various combinations in order to search out regularities. 'Representative' and 'typical' pictures could be differentiated from those that were 'odd', 'unusual' or 'atypical'. They could, that is to say, be normalized. And they could then be arranged into a visual display that summarized and condensed the multifaceted actions of the children into a single array that could conveniently be deployed within scientific debate, in articles, textbooks, and teaching materials.

Having been thus arrayed, a further transformation could occur through work upon the inscriptions themselves. The photographs themselves 'showed' typical behaviours but they did not yet embody instructions as to how they were to be read. These instructions had to be displayed separately, in the form of captions: 'Throwing'; 'Train without chimney'; 'Tower of nine'. The captions function as directions; they serve to indicate those aspects of the photograph to which we should attend and those which are not relevant: the smile on the

Plate 2: Normalizing development

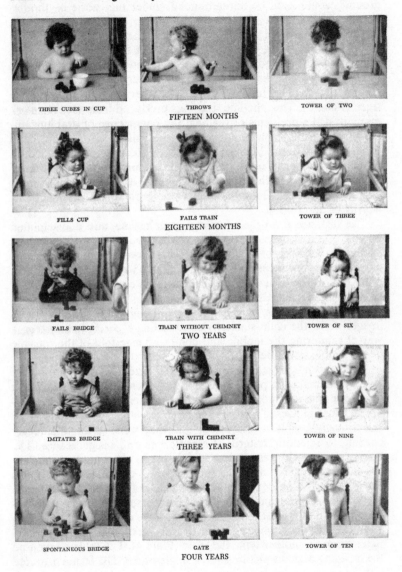

THREE CUBES IN CUP

THROWS
FIFTEEN MONTHS

TOWER OF TWO

FILLS CUP

FAILS TRAIN
EIGHTEEN MONTHS

TOWER OF THREE

FAILS BRIDGE

TRAIN WITHOUT CHIMNEY
TWO YEARS

TOWER OF SIX

IMITATES BRIDGE

TRAIN WITH CHIMNEY
THREE YEARS

TOWER OF NINE

SPONTANEOUS BRIDGE

GATE
FOUR YEARS

TOWER OF TEN

Source: Arnold Gesell, The first five years of life, London, Methuen, (1950)

face, the length of hair, the 'background'. At a later date, this 'background' would itself be 'foregrounded' under the rubric of 'the importance of context'. But here the scope of possible pertinent features of the child and its actions has been radically simplified through its rendering into a photograph, yet the trace does not yet fully contain or embed the concept it 'illustrates'. We are directed as to how to read, but directions can be misunderstood.

Graphic displays indivisibly weld together the concept and the trace (Plate 3). Thus the line drawings produced from Gesell's work minimized the problems of reading; the perspective of developmentalism was displayed as the texture of the child itself. The object so produced had, to use Michael Lynch's term, become docile; it had internalized the norms of the scientific programme in the very form of its inscription. [27] In these little drawings the child was reduced to its essential elements. Only that which was normatively pertinent was worthy of description.

The distance from the squalling, troublesome, and undisciplined infants of the laboratory, to these calm, ordered, and disciplined frames is considerable. We should not, however, think of this as movement on a dimension from the concrete to the abstract. Indeed, quite the reverse. These images are far more concrete, far more real than the child itself. Children are ephemeral, shifting, elusive, changing before one's eyes, hard to perceive in any stable fashion. These images make the child stable by constructing a perceptual system, a way of rendering the mobile and confusing manifold of the sensible into a legible visual field.

The perceptual system of a science, the gaze it constructs for itself and which makes it possible, is one in which the world impinging upon our senses is normalized in the very act of becoming perceptible. Thus, in Gesell's laboratory, the activities of the child were scientifically legible to the extent that they were differentiated according to scientific criteria of significance and insignificance. The phenomenal world was rendered thinkable by charting its coincidences and deviations from values and properties deemed normal. In this act of scientific perception, the statements of a scientific discourse are not separable from the object of discourse. The forms of knowledge have, in a crucial sense, merged with the object itself.

In Gesell's work these little line drawings exist alongside a perceptual system of another type: the table (Plate 4). The table condensed the meaning of many pictures into a single frame. The frame provided simultaneously a means of perceiving, recording, and evaluating. It provided a summation of those features of the object-child that were developmentally significant at a particular age, together with norms – percentage figures that authoritatively announce the proportion of children who can do this or that at this age. It enabled the formulation of a series of questions through whose answers, here in the form of a simple affirmative or negative, the unorthodox could be identified.

The scales, through the norms to which they were attached, introduced a new division into the lives of small children, a division between normal and abnormal in the form of the differentiation of advanced and retarded. Behavioral items that were characteristic and distinctive of different age levels were defined and organized into scales with specifications of the ages at which a given proportion of children could achieve the different levels on each scale. Non-intellectual behaviour was thus rendered into thought, disciplined, normalized, and made legible, inscribable, calculable. Norms of posture and locomotion; of vocabulary, comprehension, and conversation; of personal habits, initiative, independence, and play could now be deployed in evaluation and diagnosis. The discourse of development es-

Plate 3: Docile objects: drawings employed with the Gesell Developmental Schedules to illustrate typical behaviour at 28 weeks of age.

Source: H. Knobloch and B. Pasaminick, eds., Gesell and Amantruda's Developmental Diagnosis, 3rd edition, Hagerstown, Maryland, Harper and Row.

Plate 4: Tabulating life

24-MONTH LEVEL

(M) MOTOR		18 mos	24 mos.
M-1	RUNS: without falling............................	12	48
M-2	STAIRS: walks up and down alone..................		
M-9	LARGE BALL: kicks..............................		(59)
M-17	CUBES: tower of 6–7............................	20	56
M-22	BOOK: turns pages singly........................		

(A) ADAPTIVE			
A-2	CUBES: tower of 6–7............................	20	56
A-3	CUBES: aligns 2 or more, train....................	23	62
A-20	DRAWING: imitates V stroke......................	47	79
A-20	DRAWING: imitates circular stroke.................	32	59
A-28	SENTENCES: repeats 3–4 syllables.................		50
A-12	FORMBOARD: places blocks on board separately (F)	(28)	(63)
A-12	FORMBOARD: adapts in 4 trials...................	8	62
A-10	PERFORMANCE BOX: inserts square..............	29	70

(L) LANGUAGE			
L-2	SPEECH: has discarded jargon.....................		
L-2	SPEECH: 3-word sentence.........................		73
L-2	SPEECH: uses I, me, and you......................		48
L-6	PICTURE CARDS: names 3 or more...............	2	57
L-6	PICTURE CARDS: identifies 5 or more.............	2	55
L-4	TEST OBJECTS: names 2.........................		(74)
L-5	BALL: 4 directions correct........................		51

(P-S) PERSONAL-SOCIAL

FEEDING: inhibits turning of spoon
TOILET: dry at night if taken up
TOILET: verbalizes toilet needs fairly consistently (r)
DRESSING: pulls on simple garment
COMMUNICATION: verbalizes immediate experiences
COMMUNICATION: refers to himself by his name
COMMUNICATION: comprehends and asks for "another"
PLAY: hands full cup of cubes to examiner
PLAY: plays with domestic mimicry (doll, teddy bear, etc.)
PLAY: parallel play predominates

Source: A. Gesell. The first five years of life, London, Methuen, (1950:328)

tablished a system of perception that was capable of grasping any feature of life that could be construed as changing over time. It grasped
life in a form that could be effected through a few simple operations:
advanced or retarded? By how many months? In the table life comes
pre-digested, pre-calibrated, pre-normalized.

We should not think of these procedures of inscription as merely
allowing the documentation of a familiar reality – the developing
child – in a more convenient form. While children and their development, like persons and their peculiarities, have been the object of attention from philosophers, theologians, philanthropists, reformers,
and savants for centuries, the devices and techniques for visualization
and inscription are not merely technical aids to intellectual processes. To think this is to accord too much to a faculty of abstract
thought and too little to the technical mechanisms by which thought
operates. Technological changes are simultaneously revolutions in
consciousness. Techniques for visualizing and inscribing individual differences transform the intellectual universe of the scientist
and the practical universe of objects and relationships to which
things can be done. In short, technical developments make new
areas of life practicable.

Gesell's work was followed in the 1930s by a series of other attempts to use the same tactics of evaluation in similar situations.[28]
The children in such schools and nurseries were there, by and large,
because they had proved educationally troublesome, so it is not surprising that their social and emotional behaviour was increasingly
evaluated in terms of adjustment and the development of socially acceptable responses. The criterion of social approval and the conception of adjustment enabled the technical normalization of the
developmental scales in a manner similar to that used by Binet. They
thus provided the technique to assess the success of the efforts being
made for the practical normalization of educationally troublesome
children. We shall meet these troubled and troublesome children again
in other forums in the juvenile court and the child guidance clinic.

The scales generalized and extended some of the essential characteristics of psychometrics. But they constituted a normalizing vision
of childhood that gained an even wider purchase upon reality. For
these scales were not merely means of assessment. They provided new
ways of thinking about childhood, new ways of seeing children that
rapidly spread to teachers, health workers, and parents through the
scientific and popular literature. Baby books, teacher manuals, and
psychology textbooks began to incorporate 'landmarks of development' in tabular and pictorial form to enable anyone to evaluate a
child (Plate 5). [29] All who had dealt with children in their professional
or personal life could now have their mind instructed through the
education of their gaze. In the space between the behaviours of actual

children and the ideals of the norm, new desires and expectations, and new fears and anxieties could be inspired in parents, new administrative and reformatory aspirations awakened in professionals. With the rise of a normative expertise of childhood, family life and subjectivity could be governed in a new way.

Plate 5:   Landmarks of development

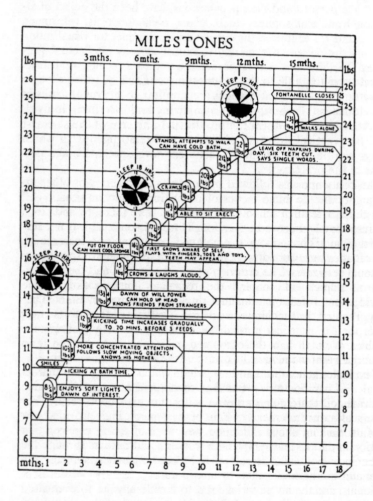

Source: M. Lyddiard, The Mothercraft Manual, London, Churchill, (1924).

Chapter thirteen

Adjusting the Bonds of Love

It is submitted that the evidence is now such that it leaves no room for doubt...that the prolonged deprivation of the young child of maternal care may have grave and far-reaching effects on his character and on the whole of his future life.[1]

John Bowlby, 1952

In the contemporary family the personal projects of individuals to live a good life, to infuse their actions and choices with meaning and pleasure, to realize their ambitions, and to give their existence a transcendental purpose in the face of certain death have become linked to social obligations for the continual reproduction and rearing of adequate numbers of healthy and well-adjusted children. Personal desires have been caught up in social networks of power and control, shaped and organized through the images and criteria provided by professional technicians of subjectivity and intersubjectivity. Projects and technologies whose initial aims were to ward off underpopulation, prevent social inefficiency, and rectify the social troubles of youth have become connected to the vocabularies and techniques that women and men themselves used to guide their lives and evaluate their conduct. And 'the family' has come to operate as a social mechanism for producing and regulating the subjective capacities of future citizens and as the privileged pathway for the fulfilment of individual wishes and hopes.

Many have investigated the intense concern with the mother–child relation in the post-war period. Analyses frequently involve reference to the socio-political interests at work in binding women to domesticity and motherhood, the self-interested entrepreneurship of professionals, and the mystifying character of the language of psychology with its references to maternal deprivation, the bonding of mother and child, and the maternal instinct. But it is worth following each of

these lines of criticism in the reverse direction. How did familialization come to be an objective around which social forces organized
themselves in the post-war years? How was an expertise of the maternal relation constituted? How did the language and evaluations of the
experts come to be introjected by individuals as norms and standards,
both rewarding and persecuting?

Already in the nineteenth century a class of dangerous children
had become visible.[2] New forms of police organization, new mechanisms for recording crimes and the use of statistical devices to chart a
kind of 'moral topography' of urban space appeared to reveal a breakdown in the moral order at the heart of our great cities. Bourgeois
philanthropists, religious organizations and social statisticians located the source of these problems in the home and the moral environment surrounding it. A series of different projects sought to turn
the home into an enclosed domestic sphere that would act as a moral
restraint upon adults and inculcate morality into children. Childhood
began to be seen as a distinct period during which bad habits could be
laid down that would have a lifelong influence. It was in the failures
of parents to inculcate morality, coupled with the contagion of bad
habits within the corrupt moral milieu of city life, that the roots of
criminality and vice were to be found.

There were many elements in the programmes for the remoralization of juveniles. The apparatus of pedagogy was to be extended
through the establishment of pauper schools and other sites of moral
training. The urban environment was to be remodelled through vi-
sionary schemes of town planning to break up the colonies and
rookeries of vice, where moral contagion spread like an epidemic disease in the miasma of degradation and sin. But specific campaigns
centred around two groups of troublesome children and sought to
persuade the state to intervene where moralization had failed. Dangerous children were those who had already offended, but in the ordinary prisons they were learning vice, not virtue; they needed to be
separated from adult criminals and sent to establishments where
they could be retrained in morality. Perishing children were inci-
pient criminals, living a life of vagrancy but not yet subject to the
law; they needed to be picked up and sent to institutions that could
train them in the habits of regular labour, discipline, obedience,
and religious observance necessary to leading a law-abiding and
moral life. In a series of Acts from 1854 onwards, reformatory
schools were established for the former and industrial schools for
the latter, and provisions were extended to include in this category
children thought to be 'in need of care and protection' or 'beyond
parental control'.

The family was construed and utilized as a possible, but not
unique, locus of inculcation of morality into children. The character

of the child was shaped by moral influences, it consisted in a set of learned habits acquired from examples in the home, among friends, and on the streets. Families whose children were inadequately moralized were to have their moralizing responsibilities removed, the children were to be relocated in reformatories that would act as substitute families inculcating correct moral principles and acclimatizing their inmates to the habits of cleanliness, work, and obedience.

A new way of construing the troubles of children began to take shape in the first decade of this century, although it was to reach its culmination only after World War II. The family was to be reconstrued in terms of a set of relations, psychological relations between mothers and fathers, parents and children, brothers and sisters. And the problems of children were to be conceived in terms spanning and linking the dangerous and the endangered along a single dimension of adjustment and maladjustment. The juvenile court and the child guidance clinic acted as crucial nodes in a new network of powers and perceptions that was woven around the child and family.

When the juvenile court was established in 1908 it brought together in one forum children who had committed offenses, those who had been found wandering or in bad company, and cases of parents or others who had ill-treated or neglected children – a continuous dimension of unfortunate children and bad families. It soon began to be argued that there was no difference between the young criminal and the neglected child in either character or appropriate treatment. The offence, that is to say, was only the outcome of neglect, and neglect, soon enough, would lead to an offence. In either case, what one was seeing was a psychological problem, the outcome of the effects of something wrong in the home on the psychology of the child. At the same time, in the schools, a class of children was coming to light that manifested minor disturbances of behaviour. In analogy to the new hygienist techniques being developed for minor physical ailments, these disturbances were construed as arising from faulty techniques of child rearing, that is, poor mental hygiene. It now appeared that major mental disturbances in adults, leading to crime and social inefficiency as well as to insanity, had their origins in minor and apparently inconsequential disturbances of emotion and conduct in childhood. Early recognition and treatment were as crucial for promotion of mental health as for physical health. Lack of mental hygiene, like lack of physical hygiene, was a recipe for future social distress. The school could be a vital site for the detection of these minor troubles, and a new class of children emerged as the object of science and administration – nervous, neuropathic, unstable, or maladjusted. Quarrelling, lying, cheating, night terrors, being too outgoing or not outgoing enough, grieving or fearing too little or too much – all these gained their importance less on their own account than as the sign they gave of serious trouble to come.

The 1933 Children and Young Persons Act, with its abolition of the distinction between reformatory and industrial schools, marks the progressive blurring of the boundaries between the delinquent and the deprived child. The juvenile court was one key node linking practices that had previously operated in relative isolation – the penal system, the educational apparatus, the organization of social assistance and psychological, medical and psychiatric expertise – into a multidimensional social network.[3] In this network, social work coupled the provision of benefits and other forms of financial assistance to families with the scrutiny of their internal economy. It also linked penality with the administrative organs of the state by collecting information from the various forces bearing in upon the child and the family, transporting facts and interpretations from one part of the network to another, translating the life of the family into the deliberations of the court and injecting a legal and administrative consciousness back into the subject household.

While the courtroom remained the key *locus* of decision, its judgement became increasingly entangled with knowledge, criteria, evaluations, and diagnoses derived from the psycho-sciences. As Michel Foucault put it in another context, 'the sentence that condemns or acquits is not simply a judgment of guilt, a legal decision that lays down punishment; it bears within it an assessment of normality and a technical prescription for a possible normalization'.[4] The judgement was only possible, the sentence only legitimate, when it could be articulated within the register of the psychological.

The child guidance clinic provided a second institutional location for this new way of thinking about and acting upon the child and the family. In the programmes of mental hygiene the child guidance clinic was to become the centre of a web of preventive and therapeutic child welfare embracing the nursery, the home, the school, the playground, and the courts. The disturbed and disturbing children from the various quarters of the social field would be directed to the clinic: backward children, nervous children, stammerers, liars, truants, the unmanageable, the neglected, and the delinquent. In the clinic the troubles of childhood would be diagnosed, norms of adjustment and maladjustment would be produced and refined, and normalization would be undertaken. Norms of adjustment, practices likely to produce adjustment, and visions of maladjustment would be disseminated from the clinics back into institutional and family life.

The most significant way of understanding these issues was that put forward by the 'new psychology'. In the new psychology the impulse to social adjustment was inscribed in the individual at the psychic level. Where Freud wrote of the unease inherent in civilization, the new psychology was a science of social contentment. Character was now no longer merely the product of training and good moral influences. It was the outcome of the organization of the instincts. When instincts were correctly channelled, a child would be produced who was *adjusted* to its social environment. The social adjustment of the individual was at the same time the natural outcome of the child's development and the normal outcome of family life. For instincts had evolved in such a way that an adjusted child was the natural outcome of a normal family. Hence the normal family could now be specified in psychological terms, and the normal adapted child construed as its product. But if the family produced conflicts in wishes or emotions, denied them expression, associated them with unpleasant feelings, or reacted in terms of their own fears, hopes, desires, or disappointments to the child's feelings, what would be produced would be *maladjustment*. And maladjustment, from bed-wetting to delinquency, had become a sign of something wrong in the emotional economy of the family.

The new psychological social workers combined with the psychologists of the clinic in writing narratives of love gone wrong, combining a number of recurrent motifs in family dramas that made childhood maladjustments understandable in terms of the emotions, desires, and disappointments of the adults who surrounded them. Parents who loved their children too much might trap them into infantility because of their own fears of losing their child. Parents who did not love their children enough, who projected their own frustrations upon them, or who favoured one sibling over another could foster delinquency as a weapon of retribution. Children who were unwanted, were the wrong sex, were not loved for what they were, might steal for the love they were denied. Abnormality had its roots in the interplay between the desires of the parents and the desires of their children, in the medium of love itself.

The strength of this perspective was that it was reversible. If families produced normal children, this was itself an accomplishment, not a given; it was because they regulated their emotional economy correctly. The production of normality now appeared to be a process fraught with pitfalls. The line between safety and danger was a narrow one; it was all too easy for major problems to develop from minor upsets if they were not handled correctly. A constant scrutiny of the emotional interchanges of family life was required, in the name of the mental hygiene of the individual and society. As the new psychology and the child guidance clinic produced a new means of representation of the psyche, the possibility opened up for the emotions and desires of all parents, not merely those of the socially troubling variety, to be inscribed within the field of social regulation. Through radio talks and child care manuals, all adults who had to deal with children were educated in this new way of visualizing the internal workings of the family and speaking about the bonds between its members. Simultaneously they were instructed in the ways in which the forces of love could be used to promote subjectivity in children: increasing confidence, helpfulness, dependability, and thoroughness at the same time as averting fear, cruelty, stubbornness, and jealousy. If parents had problems with their own emotional life, they would build these unconsciously into their attitudes and relations to their children, hence transmitting psychical disturbance across generations without the need to posit any hereditary process. Parents and teachers were now to take responsibility for regulating not just their habits and morals, but their feelings, wishes, and anxieties, if they were not to produce troubled and troublesome children.

Love was no longer merely a moral duty or a romantic ideal, it was the element in which were produced normal and abnormal children. Normality was now to be promoted not through coercion after the event – the removal of a pathological child and the disablement of the family – but by inciting the family itself to take on board the business of production of normal subjects. A new relation between subjectivity and the social order was being formed within the matrix of the family. Expertise was to enable the social obligation on the family to regulate the subjectivities of its children to be translated into the personal desire for normal children, and into a set of emotional and intersubjective techniques for securing this goal. To fulfil both social obligations and personal wishes parents were well advised to examine and regulate their own desires, to inspect and evaluate their emotions. The wish to achieve the ideal was a source of pleasure when it was satisfied, but it was also the incentive to seek anxiously for guidance and assistance from family technicians when the register of the actual diverged too much from the register of the ideal. Love and pleasure, far from representing the spontaneous and asocial humanity within us all, were to become the dimensions through which these new technologies of government could achieve their purchase upon reality.

It was in the two decades following the end of the war that this vision of the child and its family was generalized. The group life of the family, its relational economy, the dependencies, frustrations, jealousies, attachments, rivalries, and frustrations that traversed it, became both the means of explanation of the troubles of childhood and the means of construing the ideal family. The processes of emotional development of the child within its family were reconstrued as delicate and fragile, liable to distortions in so many directions that would produce pathologies in the child, ranging from naughtiness through criminality to frank insanity. And, perhaps more significantly, the mundane tasks of mothering came to be rewritten as emanations of a natural and essential state of love.

This therapeutic familialism was one element in a web of programmes and arguments that enmeshed conjugal, domestic, and parental arrangements in the post-war period. The objectives of these programmes were varied, but each entailed the revalorization of the child-centred family as a site for the emotional investment and self-realization of citizens. One mesh of this web, itself multi-faceted, was pronatalism. Many voices made up this discourse, but together they sang one song: many babies must mean happiness. The Beveridge Report of 1942 had expressed concern that 'with its present rate of reproduction the British race cannot continue', and despite the successful outcome of the war this anxiety about the effect of the selfish decision of citizens to marry late, to remain childless, or to limit themselves to only one baby remained.[5] The Royal Commission on Population, established in 1944, was the official mark of this widespread concern.[6] It was to examine the trends in the British population, their causes and their probable consequences, and to recommend measures in the national interest. The effects of a low and declining birthrate, as far as the commission was concerned, were both on 'the security and influence of Great Britain' and on 'the maintenance and extension of Western values'.[7] Thus there was a strong national case for a range of measures to mitigate the burdens of parenthood in order to prevent rates of reproduction falling below replacement level – from advice on contraception, through measures to minimize 'reproductive wastage' (stillbirths and infant perinatal mortality), to schemes for financial assistance and relief such as family allowance schemes and income tax relief. The development of services for the special benefit of children and their mothers was an essential element in their pronatal programme, for the object was to provide the social conditions that would not inhibit but positively encourage the instinctive desire for a family and the realization of its lasting satisfaction.

Proposals proliferated for the reactivation of the wish for the large family. Denise Riley indicates their breadth and variety:

> nurseries, after-school play centres, rest homes for tired housewives, family tickets on trains, official neighbourhood baby-sitters, holidays on the social services for poorer families, proper access for all to good gynecological and obstetric help, a revolution in domestic architecture towards streamlined rational kitchens and a good number of bedrooms, more communal restaurants and laundries.[8]

Pronatalism brought together proposals from distinct politico-ethical positions. Egalitarians argued the privileges available to the few, such as nurseries and proper medical care, should be extended to all citizens. Feminists argued that more children would be encouraged if measures such as contraception made parenthood voluntary and if social support was available to allow women freedom to organize their time. Eugenicists argued that positive measures aimed at encouraging the best sectors of the population to have children would maximize population fitness. The church argued that the deliberate decision to restrict a family to one child was bad for both the child and the family.

Not that what was envisaged by any of these parties was a direct engagement by the state with the production of children; this smacked of the population policies of the Nazis. Rather, what was sought was a means of encouraging citizens themselves to make a decision in favour of children, and one that would encourage the best endowed to reproduce, rather than the feckless and irresponsible individuals who made up the social problem group. Pronatalism was thus a language for debate and policy that could be articulated in many different forms and with many different consequences. Financial allowances and fiscal benefits for married couples and families with children were one element, but never amounted to a consistent family policy; the consequence of the various measures overall was to favour the married couple *without* children. Nor were the contraception measures advocated by the commission, the Family Endowment Society, and others enshrined in a coherent policy. Advice to mothers and mothers-to-be, through the radio, magazines, and books, was directed at the literate and responsible mother, and sought to shape that responsibility in particular ways. And the households of the troubled and the troublesome were subject to more direct intervention. Their problems demonstrated the need to restore and reinforce a family that was both the natural order of things and something to be maintained by expert attention.

A new image of troubled childhood joined the maladjusted child and the juvenile delinquent – the deprived child. The experiences of wartime conferred a new visibility upon this group of children and their problematic existence. The specific problems of children in wartime may have been new (evacuation, hostels, residential nurseries, day nurseries), but the analyses and remedies were constructed in the familiar terms of mental hygiene. Before the outbreak of the war the mental hygiene movement had argued that the emotional lives of citizens were a matter for public concern, expert knowledge, and professional guidance. At the programmatic level the Feversham Committee published its recommendations for a National Council for Mental Health in 1939.[9] This was to amalgamate the principal voluntary agencies, to co-ordinate them with statutory authorities, to undertake a programme of education of professionals and laypersons in the elements of mental hygiene, and to assist in the provision of out-patient clinics as the focus for a scheme of research prevention and treatment. At the outbreak of war the key organizations promoting such a policy science of mental health (the Central Association for Mental Welfare, the Child Guidance Council, and the National Council for Mental Health) formed a Mental Health Emergency Committee. [10] By 1943 these organizations, heavily funded by the Ministry of Health, had been fused into a Provisional National Council for Mental Health, which had its administrators and psychiatric social workers in each of the thirteen civil defence regions.

Wartime provided mental hygiene with new experiences and new opportunities. The war nurseries were a marvellous laboratory for the observation of children and their problems. Work on the psychiatric consequences of the institutional care of children in hospitals and foundling homes had begun in the 1930s, and descriptions of the dangers of institutional care for the psyche of the young child were well established in the pre-war American, French, and Scandinavian literature.[11] Even Rene Spitz's 'classic' paper of 1945 on the effects of hospitalization on the mental health of young children was based on work that had begun in 1936.[12] Medical debate about the wartime nurseries used existing arguments concerning the deleterious consequences of breaking up the biological unity of mother and child.[13] But the war itself conferred a new visibility upon children separated from their parents, and enabled the proponents of psychodynamic conceptions of mother–child relations to draft the children as allies in their struggle to change social policies.

Anna Freud's studies, which would be used to support many such arguments in the post-war period, were conducted in the Hampstead War Nursery, established in 1941 for London children who were made homeless by air raids, were still unevacuated or were unevacuable, or could not be cared for by their parents.[14] Unlike the other residential nurseries established by the Foster Parents Plan for War Children Inc. of New York, it was not run on institutional lines. Rather,

> It tried to re-establish for the children what they have lost: the security of a stable home with its opportunities for individual development. The only characteristic of 'institutional' life which it was powerless to avoid was the absence of the family itself.[15]

What was significant about these studies was the perception they constructed of the fragile emotional life of *normal* children. Unlike many other studies of children in clinics and institutions, these children were not inherently pathological nor did they come from pathological families. Only the force of wartime circumstances (bombing, tube sleeping, evacuation problems, physically unhealthy home conditions due to bombing, dissolution of the family through the exigencies of war) had deprived them of a normal family life. And their care was not in the impersonal atmosphere of a large institution but in small groups in houses with plenty of adult care and attention. The children were divided into 'families' of three or four, each cared for by a single worker who bathed them, put them to bed, took them for walks, gave them treats, and so forth. The children, thus normal in everything but the presence of a real family, had their emotions, responses, and patterns of behaviour under constant scrutiny by experts of the psyche.

Anna Freud herself was one of the inventors of psychoanalytic treatment with young children, and she was aided by James Robertson, a social worker later to join the Tavistock Clinic and to make films of young children separated from their mothers. The monthly reports of the nursery charted the stages of the mother–child relation – the first six months, the next eighteen months, the period from three to five – and documented the effects of separation: regression, bed-wetting, autoeroticism, greed, temper tantrums, withdrawal of emotional interest from the outside world and even hysterical symptoms, phobias, and compulsions serious enough to require psychoanalysis.

In 1942 it appeared to Freud that the choice was between the twin evils of keeping little children in the bombed area with their parents, with all the physical danger, emotional upset, and brutalization that is implied, or evacuating them to the country and imposing other shocks through separation from the parents at an age that needs emotional stability and permanency.[16] But by 1944 the problem was placed squarely in the domain of the relative instinctual satisfactions and frustrations of family and nursery life. Small infants in residential nurseries, it appeared, did develop community reaction and enjoy the companionship of children of their own age. But they searched further for objects towards which they could direct all those emotional interests that would normally be directed towards their parents. Lack of the opportunity to share bodily pleasures with the mother was behind autoeroticism, and withdrawal from the outside world into primitive self-interest and self-indulgence. Lack of satisfaction of the 'wish to be admired' led to constant seeking for admiration or the reverse. Problems in satisfying infantile curiosity led to failure to develop the wish to learn and could result in inhibitions of all kinds.[17]

Sigmund Freud had, of course, extrapolated his analysis of the psychic life of children principally from his analyses of adults. On the basis of clinical work with children, Anna Freud and Melanie Klein had proposed different conceptions of the psychodynamics of child-hood and enacted different versions of analysis with children them-selves. But for the first time the everyday life of children could be visualized through the perceptual grid of psychoanalysis; it appeared that the instinctive forces of infantile sexuality and primitive aggres-sion, repression, regression, fantasy, and the rest could actually be ob-served.[18] Not that these were visible to everyone. Anna Freud remarks that some visitors to the nursery who had read the reports expressed concern at the discrepancy between the atmosphere of peace and serenity that they found on their visits and the naughty, ag-gressive, and unrestrained children who featured in the reports. But, as Miss Freud points out, while these evanescent features of child-ren's behaviour could be ignored for everyday purposes, 'for purposes of understanding they had to be pinned down for observation'.[19] The psychic life of children no longer had to be extrapolated from limited observation of adult analysis; it had been opened directly to the psy-choanalytic gaze and rendered observable, notable, and inscribable in terms of the pertinencies of psychoanalytic theory.

Evacuation was also 'a cruel psychological experiment on a large scale'.[20] In the first phase, in September 1939, under the fear of immi-nent air attack, 750,000 schoolchildren, 542,000 mothers with young children, 12,000 expectant mothers, and 77,000 other persons left their homes in the cities for the perceived safety of the country. But, cruel as it might be, evacuation was also 'an opportunity to learn priceless lessons for future social service'.[21] Hence the Cambridge Evacuation Survey was established in October 1939, including Susan Isaacs, Margery Fry, Sybil Clement Brown (the principal pre-war ex-ponent of psychiatric social work), John Bowlby, Melanie Klein, and Lucy Fildes (one of the first psychologists involved in the pre-war child guidance movement). Revealed again was 'the crucial import-ance of family ties and of the feelings of parents and children towards one another', and the sad fact that 'the strength of the family tie, on the one hand, and the need for skilled understanding of the individual child, on the other, seem to have lain too far outside the ken of those responsible for the scheme.'[22] While 'The work of the Child Guid-ance Clinics had shown clearly that the emotional difficulties of children such as anxiety, temper, upsets in feeding, sleeping and elimination, were generally bound up with the child's relationship with his parents', the Child Guidance Clinics saw only selected mem-bers of the population.[23] What was to be crucial for psychology and social work about the evacuation was the new population it would bring within the gaze of the experts.

Evacuation appeared not merely to reveal the existence of a new group of troublesome children but actually to produce them. Some 15,000 to 20,000 children over the war were 'unbilletable' through 'difficulties of behaviour or temperament' and gradually accumulated in special hostels for 'difficult' children.[24] It was around these hostels, together with the camps and residential nurseries that also accommodated unaccompanied evacuated children, that the Provisional National Council for Mental Health introduced its own psychiatric social workers and cajoled the local authorities into appointing their own. For authors like John Bowlby, however, the experience of evacuation only confirmed what was already known. Bowlby had carried out a series of investigations into the familial experiences of juvenile thieves from 1936 to 1939, while working at the London Child Guidance Clinic. These studies had convinced him that there was a demonstrable link between early separation from the mother and juvenile theft, a high proportion of these children having been cared for by strangers for periods in their first five years of life. The link was made through the psyche of the child. The effects of separation were to produce an 'affectionless character', and it was this character disorder that lay at the root of antisocial behaviour. Or, to put it another way, antisocial behaviour was a symptom of a psychodynamic disturbance resulting from a disturbance in the child's early relation with the mother.

It was not until 1944 that these findings were to be published.[25] But as early as 1940, in the Report on Evacuation that Richard Padley and Margaret Cole edited for the Fabian Society, Bowlby was warning in dire tones that the apparent solution to the danger of aerial bombardment might be worse than the problem itself. Drawing on the results of his own work, Bowlby asserted:

> when small children are separated from home and given for long periods to the care of strangers in strange surroundings, their whole character development may be seriously endangered ... the prolonged separation of small children from their homes is one of the outstanding causes of the development of a criminal character... There are at present many thousands of young children who have been placed unwittingly in circumstances gravely jeopardising their future. Not only are some likely to develop into criminal characters as a result of their experiences, but many others may be expected to become prone to chronic anxiety or depression or to vague pains and illness of an apparently physical nature. The semi-delinquent character who is grasping, jealous and not much above petty cheating may also follow.[26]

Psychological criticisms of evacuation and residential nurseries had little influence on government policy during the war. Nor did psychology play more than a marginal role in the post-war closure of nurseries. Rather, what wartime had done was to supply new arguments and new strategic possibilities for the advocates of mental hygiene; a problem could now begin to be posed to which 'Bowlbyism' was to appear a solution. Carlos Blacker's *Report on the Mental Health Services* had been sponsored by the Ministry of Health in 1942, but it went far beyond its original aim of a survey of psychiatric out-patient services. Like many other reports in the aftermath of war, it proposed a radical reorganization of mental health services away from the emphasis on psychoses and the segregative institution, and towards a system of prevention and of rapid treatment of minor mental troubles occurring wherever possible on an out-patient basis 'in the community'.[27] The troubles of childhood were of particular concern to such a scheme for preventive mental health, not only for themselves, but because they were sure warning of greater problems to come, and they were treatable by early intervention. Hence Blacker's programme laid great emphasis on provision for the troublesome child: child guidance centres (1 for every 20, 000 children), child psychiatric clinics (3 or 4 per million population), hostels for unstable or difficult children, and colonies for mental defectives.

When, in the aftermath of war, the Expert Committee on Mental Health of the WHO emphasized in its first session, 'the desirability of concentrating especially on the therapeutic and preventive psychiatry of childhood', it was in the terms of mental hygiene that the problem was posed.[28] At the third session of the Social Commission of the United Nations in April 1948 it was decided to make a study of the needs of homeless children, those orphaned or separated from their families for other reasons and who needed care in foster homes, institutions, or other types of group care. The World Health Organization offered to contribute a study of the mental health aspects of the problem; John Bowlby, then director of the Child Guidance Department of the Tavistock Clinic, was appointed to compile the report.[29]

Subsequent discussion of Bowlby's report has usually been concerned to support or contest his now familiar assertion that the future life of a child may be gravely and irreversibly damaged by deprivation of maternal care. But this postulate, itself not novel, was only one moment in a more complex circuit that Bowlby sought to establish, a set of unshakable connections between mental health, childhood, their social consequences, the tasks of government, and the role of expertise. Refined conceptions of the psychodynamics of childhood and the relations of mothering were to be linked in an expanded project for the regulation of the relations between mother and child, one that would be prophylactic and pedagogic as much as reactive and reformatory.

Bowlby's discussion lays the groundwork for two distinct but related axes along which the charting of the psychodynamics of childhood and personality would proceed. The first was a new attention not to the gross features of the relations between mother and child but to its minutiae. This arose out of an apparent problem, that despite the similarities between the different studies discussed, the details showed a highly variable set of relations between 'deprivation' and 'personality'. Such variations were rapidly converted from a threat to an opportunity; they enabled the gross conclusions to form the basis for discussions of policy, while the details could form the basis of an expanding psychological research programme. Future research, writes Bowlby:

> must pay minute attention not only to ages and periods of deprivation but also to the quality of the child's relation to his mother before deprivation, his experiences with mother-substitutes, if any, during separation, and the reception he gets from his mother or foster mother when at last he becomes settled again.[30]

Along this axis would develop a fine-grained picture of the minutiae of mothering, an ever more tightly specified set of ideal relations between the details of a child's experiences of mothering and the course of his or her mental development. Separation in and of itself was no longer the point, for the child could experience separation even when in proximity to his or her mother. Separation began to merge with the quality of the experience of mothering itself. The stage was set for the entry of the 'sensitive mother'. We shall encounter her presently.

The second axis was a refined psychoanalytic vision of childhood in terms of the ego and object relations along the lines proposed by Anna Freud. For, as Bowlby concluded:

> the theoretical framework of developmental phases of ego functioning and of capacity to make object relationships, and of the periods within the life cycle by which they must be completed, seems to fit the clinical evidence. No doubt as understanding increases the three main phases described here will be subdivided into many subphases, and one will learn to discern the particular psychic forces which are brought into play by deprivation in each of them.[31]

Psychoanalysis was to become a theory of development, and, what is more, a theory of the role of the mother in the development of the adjusted and maladjusted ego.

The second half of Bowlby's report was devoted to the prevention of maternal deprivation, a task that was principally to take the form of the prevention of family failure, due to the mother's failure to provide the psychological conditions for normal development, to the removal of the child from the mother to strangers by medical or social agencies, or to the loss of the mother by death, illness, or desertion. While Bowlby concentrated on the latter two, he did not seek to minimize the importance of the former. These arose from ignorance or unconscious hostility of the mother deriving from experiences in her own childhood and requiring skilled treatment of the mother by child guidance workers.

What was required was a comprehensive scheme of mental hygiene. This would entail training on a large scale of professionals (physicians, nurses, and workers) in the psychology and psychopathology of human relations, in the importance of unconscious motivation and how to recognize and modify it. Crucially it would be a family service. This should involve the treatment of children and the giving of expert advice to parents, especially mothers of young children, who had got into difficulties. It should seek to support the family by marriage guidance and other measures to avoid the removal of children from the home and ensure the best possible provision for children who, for any reason, could not remain at home. Other ethical principles, such as sentimental or punitive attitudes to illegitimate children and their mothers, must be subordinated to this aim. Arrangements for adoption should be swift, use skilled experts to match the genetic potential of the child with that of the family, and subject it to psychiatric screening. Fostering was to be preferred to institutional care and should be encouraged by paying foster parents and giving them a quasi-professional status. Group residential care should be avoided for children under six. Maladjusted children should be treated at home wherever possible so that they are kept in contact with parents, and therefore treatment centres should be scattered widely through the community. Bowlby dreamed of a radically revised and rationalized child-care service, an integral part of family welfare services with wide new financial and legal powers staffed by professionals skilled in sociology and the psychology of human relations:

> a service giving skilled help to parents, including problem parents, to enable them to provide a stable and happy family life for their children... it will care for the unmarried mother and help her either make a home for the child or arrange his adoption, help mobilize relatives or neighbours to act as substitutes in an emergency, provide short-term care in necessary cases, while working towards the resumption of normal home life, and finally provide long-term care where all else fails.[32]

A powerful and humane vision indeed, and one that rapidly spread beyond the specialist literature. Bowlby presented a shortened version of his argument for a wider audience in his *Child Care and the*

Growth of Love, published as a cheap paperback in 1953 and reprinted six times in the next decade before going into a second edition. His work was extended and refined with the aid of a research group at the Tavistock clinic, and the results disseminated in research papers and films, through the training of professionals, and through popular presentations on the nature and consequences of separation and loss.[33]

Bowlby himself was to develop his views through an heretical amalgam of psychoanalysis and ethology. But the early work was the paradigm for a welter of writings during the late 1940s and 1950s that appeared to establish the naturalness of a bond of love between mother and infant that bound them psychologically into a mutually interdependent relationship in the earliest months of the child's life. It appeared that this relationship was not only natural in the sense that it derived from fundamental and unchanging aspects of the human condition, be they biological or psychological. It was also natural in that those who departed from this pattern, or who protested it, be they mother or child, were exceptional and pathological cases whose aetiology need to be explained and understood, in terms of some hereditary fault or physical problem in the child, of his or her experience in the womb or in the earliest moments of life, or of events in the mother's own childhood. And it was natural in a further sense, in that variations upon it produced all the consequences one might expect from going against nature. Separation of mother and child in the first two years of life or substitute care in an institution would damage the emotional economy of the child, leading to childhood troubles both physical and behavioral, anxiety, naughtiness, neuroses, an incapacity to form links of affection later in life, delinquency, perhaps even a criminal career or full-blown mental pathology.

In the post-war period such an analysis provided the rationale for a wide-ranging strategy for minimizing social troubles and maximizing social efficiency that sought to govern the mental health of the population through the family, through the bonds of love between mother and child. The theme was elaborated in official reports and legislation throughout the 1950s and 1960s. The Curtis Committee, reporting in 1946, was confined by its terms of reference to provision for children who had been deprived of a normal home life. In many Homes it found:

> a lack of personal interest in and affection for the children which we found shocking. The child in these Homes was not regarded as an individual with his rights and possessions, his own life to live and his own contribution to offer. He was merely one of a large

crowd, eating, playing and sleeping with the rest... Still more important, he was without the feeling that there was anyone to whom he could turn who was vitally interested in his welfare or who cared for him as a person.[34]

The child was a citizen of a democracy, a citizen with rights, and these included the right to a family life. The new visions of the psychological relations of mother and child enabled the political objective of policing the troubles of childhood to be reconciled with democratic obligations to preserve personal liberties. Authorities now had a moral and psychological obligation to try to prevent family breakdown in the first place, and to reconstruct normal family life through such devices as adoption and fostering, for children who had been deprived of their own. As Eileen Younghusband later put it:

When the children's service began it was still assumed that children must be rescued from inadequate families, the slate wiped clean and the child given a fresh start. By degrees it was realized that the parent lived on inside the child, that his identity was bound up with his origins and hence that everything possible should be done to strengthen home ties.[35]

The 1948 Children Act was the legislative index of this new democratic perception of the child and family. A Home Office Circular of 1948 stressed:

To keep the family together must be the first aim, and the separation of a child from its parents can only be justified when there is no possibility of securing adequate care for the child in his own home.[36]

Psychodynamic social work provided the knowledge and technique that could interpret and seek to rectify these failures of human relations in family life in a manner that preserved the liberties of the citizen and enshrined the reciprocal positive obligations of the state and the family to provide the best possible socialization for the child. Eileen Younghusband described the new duties of the social worker in 1950:

the social worker can no longer rest satisfied with her knowledge of the social services and her manipulation of entities like relief funds, prams, pawn tickets, ambulance services, hostels and so forth, trusting to the light of nature for her understanding of the persons for whose benefits these services exist. It is now demanded of her that she shall seek to understand the person in need, not only at that particular moment in time, but in all the major experiences and relationships which have gone into making him the person he is, with conflicts of whose origin he may be unaware, with problems whose solution may lie less in external circumstances than in his own attitudes, with tensions, faulty relationships, inabilities to face reality, hardened into forces which he cannot alter unaided.[37]

While the psychiatric casework that had been invented in the 1930s around the Child Guidance Clinics took its theoretical protocols from the new psychology, during the war it began to take on a psychodynamic character with the involvement of Susan Isaacs and other psychoanalytically oriented teachers on the Mental Health Course at the London School of Economics.[38] As Bowlby put it, psychodynamic diagnostics must lie at the base of social work with families, for

unless a social worker has a good deal of understanding of unconscious motivation she will be powerless to deal with many an unmarried mother, many a home which is in danger of breaking up, and many a case of conflict between parent and child.[39]

This perspective was enshrined in the Advanced Course in Social Case Work begun in 1950, which was run by Bowlby's Department of Parents and Children at the Tavistock Clinic, 'to give case workers in non-psychiatric settings an opportunity to gain systematic teaching in psychodynamic psychology and to increase their understanding of the effects of early influence in shaping the adult personality'.[40] What this amounted to was:

the dynamics of seeking, accepting and giving help ... discussion of reality and fantasy elements in the (worker client) relationship ... the study of transference both in its positive and negative aspects, together with the various ways in which its manifestations can be dealt with in casework situation ... the causes and expressions of anxiety ... the value of helping the client to express or admit his mixed feelings towards other figures in his earlier life ... the worker's attitudes and feelings towards the client, which may at times include over-protective attitudes or over-identification.[41]

Psychodynamic social casework was to provide the technological means for acting upon troubled and troublesome children. The training courses were set up following the recommendations of the Curtis Committee and the Provisions of the Children Act 1948 instructed aspiring social workers in the new language and technique. Clare Britton, fresh from her work with the difficult children of the wartime hostels, ran the course at the London School of Economics, and the students attended Donald Winnicott's lectures on the psychodynamics of childhood. Britton (subsequently Mrs Winnicott) was herself to train as a child analyst and later to become Director of Child Care Training at the Central Training Council of the Home Office. Child analysis became a growth area within the psychoanalytic profession, not surprisingly given the rival influences of Melanie Klein and Anna Freud, the two doyens of the art, on psychoanalytic politics in England. The Institute for the Study and Treatment of Delinquency, under the aegis of Edward Glover, a leading light of the British psychoanalytic movement, provided a further focus for research and publicity. And, during the 1950s, analysis and investigation of problem children came to centre upon one particular type of family – the problem family.

Of course, the problem family was not new. Eugenicists had constructed their genealogies of ignobility since the nineteenth century, purporting to demonstrate the coexistence in a single family line of intemperance, insanity, tuberculosis, idiocy, criminality and prostitution, their association with high rates of reproduction, and the fateful consequences. Hence it is not surprising that many of the studies of the problem family in the 1950s should have been published under the aegis of the Eugenics Society. Blacker, a stalwart of the society, began his discussion of the prevention of mental infirmities by quoting from the 1929 report of the Joint Departmental Committee on Mental Deficiency, the Wood Report. The report had argued that most mental deficiency was inherited 'primary amentia', and that it was the final stage in the inheritance of a degenerate group that had to be compulsorily prevented from propagating its own kind and dragging down the rest of the community:

> Let us assume that we could segregate as a separate community all the families in this country containing mental defectives of the primary amentia type. We should find that we had collected among them a most interesting social group. It would include, as everyone who has practical experience of social service would readily admit, a much larger proportion of insane persons, epileptics, paupers, criminals (especially recidivists), unemployables, habitual slum dwellers, prostitutes, inebriates and other social inefficients than would a group of families not containing mental defectives. The overwhelming majority of the families thus collected will belong to that section of the community which we propose to term the 'social problem' or 'subnormal' group. This group comprises approximately the lowest 10 per cent in the social scale of most communities.[42]

Wartime may have served to cast a spotlight into the dark places where this social problem group dwelt. But the eugenic analysis of the likes of Blacker was only one small part of the concern with the problem family in the post war years. It was not so much heredity, but relationships that were at the heart of the problem of the family. Throughout the subsequent twenty years, the problem family would be scrutinized by a whole series of social surveys, which charted its existence, its characteristics, and its consequences. [43] Whether initially concerned with evacuation, ill health, mental hygiene, or the neglected child, each social agency attached to the troubled family appeared to open up a line of sight on the same problem. The problem family, in touch with many agencies, had multiple problems, but the long and short of it was that there was a clear link between social disadvantage, disturbed family relationships, and socially maladjusted behaviour on the part of both adults and children. It was a deeply troubling mixture of low social status, low income, poor housing, poor physical and mental health, criminality, and child neglect. No matter from which angle the investigation began, from which agency it was mounted, and which type of problem initially concerned it, it pretty soon found all the other difficulties there as well. And not only this, but these families had many children, and hence could transmit their pathology to future generations, even if the eugenic explanation of the inter-war period was now supplanted by a psycho-social one. The human relations of the problem family were an urgent target for government action. For 'if the problem family's real difficulty is a primary failure of human relationships, then the only way in which we can hope to modify the situation is by providing the people with some form of satisfactory relationship therapy'. [44]

The human relations of the family established the matrix for both theoretical analysis and practical intervention, opening up the internal world of the home to knowledge in a new way. It is well known that the sociologists in the 1950s proclaimed the family to be the central mechanism in modern societies for the transmission of values and standards of conduct. In subsequent critiques of this functionalist sociology most people have rather neglected the significance of the linkages between psychoanalysis, sociology, and therapeutic expertise in which this work was enmeshed. For Talcott Parsons, the most notable American representative of this sociology, the importance accorded to psychiatry, clinical psychology, and other forms of expert advice and guidance in contemporary society was a response to, and an index of the strains placed on personality and human relations in modern life. Nowhere was this strain greater than on the family and marriage relations. [45] For the isolation of the nuclear family subjected it to particular stresses, to which experts could and should apply the kinds of techniques deployed by experts of human relations in industry and other areas of social life.[46]

In England, too, the language and techniques of human relations were to be applied to the family, although with a vigour directed more towards the invention of new technologies than the elaboration of abstract theoretical systems.[47] One such technology was marriage guidance. The impetus for this came from the Committee on Procedure in Matrimonial Causes, set up in the pronatalist climate of 1947 to advise on the problems caused by the increasing number of divorce cases in the aftermath of war. Among its recommendations, the report suggested a 'Marriage Welfare Service, to afford help and guidance both in preparation for marriage and also in difficulties after marriage'.[48] The recommendation was to be given further weight by another committee set up by the Home Secretary; the outcome was a form of service that was to be funded from the Exchequer but run by voluntary societies.[49] The Family Discussion Bureau was the first answer – promoted by Tommy Wilson of the Tavistock as an opportunity for training social workers in the psychotherapeutic techniques and human relations expertise to engage with family problems and develop a scientific knowledge of the psychodynamics of the family. The bureau was established in 1949 within the Family Welfare Association (the latest incarnation of the Charity Organization Society) in collaboration with the Tavistock; by 1957 it had been taken over by the Tavistock Institute of Human Relations. The result was the technique of marital therapy, which was to make the psychodynamic relations between wives and husbands a possible subject for professional analysis and management. [50]

Reports and surveys throughout the 1950s and 1960s drew repeated attention to the role of disturbed family relations in the genesis of childhood maladjustment and delinquency. The 1955 report of the Committee on Maladjusted Children, the Underwood Report, was convinced that this was a problem with very serious social implications, for mental illness inside and outside mental hospitals, divorce courts, prisons, delinquency, loss of industrial production, and the rest. And it felt the problem was more serious because it was self-perpetuating, for 'the maladjusted child of yesterday can be the maladjusted parent of today, and his offspring the maladjusted children of tomorrow'.[51]

Maladjustment in the child became the site of registration of the whole gamut of possible disturbances in the passage of the citizen towards security, happiness, independence, success in personal relations, and socially harmonious ways of living. Within the notion of maladjustment were gathered together all the problems of the school-age child, from temper tantrums to truancy, from nervousness to nastiness. Maladjustment, for the Underwood Report, could hardly be encompassed in a definition, for the disharmony between the individual and the human relations in which he must live could take such a wide variety of forms. Nor could the contribution of the factors that produce it be precisely weighed. So variable was their interplay, course, and effects that they could only be enumerated: personal relations, family environment, community influence, physical factors, even the school itself. But this diversity was not a weakness of the notion of maladjustment; quite the reverse. It was the occasion for the recommendation of an expanded network of professional expertise, skilled enough to detect and rectify the problems of childhood – a comprehensive child guidance service within each local education authority, involving a school psychological service, the school health service, the employment of educational psychologists and psychiatric social workers as well as child psychiatrists, the expansion of training facilities for the professionals of human relations and psychological disturbances, a network of treatment centres that could act on maladjusted children without necessitating their removal from the home.

Yet this was only treating the symptoms of the problem. For, as the Underwood Report recognized:

> the surest way to prevent maladjustment from arising in children is to encourage in every possible way their healthy development, particularly on the emotional side. This is, indeed, what those general practitioners of child guidance – parents and teachers – spend much of their lives in doing.[52]

Parents and teachers were now to be construed as 'general practitioners in child guidance', their tasks conceived in terms of a therapeutics of childhood, their role that of workers, in the front line of the struggle for social harmony through mental health.

On the one hand, the family tie appears as 'natural'; on the other, parents can only carry out their task effectively when educated, supplemented, and in the last instance supplanted by psychologically trained professionals. The government of children and parents alike is to be subject to the normative scrutiny of expertise, and all citizens are to be tutored in the ways of conducting their lives in order to promote the psychological conditions for social harmony and tranquillity. Such a human relations strategy for the family was to lie at the heart of all interventions upon troublesome children. The final recommendation of the Underwood Report stressed:

> The fundamental importance of the family as a whole should be borne in mind by those responsible for strengthening and developing the social services, and action designed to keep the family

together should be regarded as one of the most important aspects of prevention.[53]

The theme was echoed in interventions targeted upon the young delinquent. A series of publications throughout the late 1950s and the 1960s, emanating from the political left, sought to deploy the human relations approach in the prevention of delinquency.[54] Human needs, it was argued, do not come in specialized packages. They were intertwined in persons and families, And delinquent children were merely the most visible of a much wider group who were suffering from the problems of parents. Disease or poverty could no longer be considered to be at the heart of the problem families, for the welfare state had ensured that these problems did not have the disastrous consequences they had had in a previous era. The source of the problem must be found in the inability of parents to cope with human relations, and the transmission of problems from inadequate parents to their children. The objective, therefore, must be a family service designed to re-equip parents with the insight, skills, and capacities to enable them to cope with the complexities of modern life and the tasks of rearing children in a rapidly changing society.

Official reports and white papers throughout the 1960s stressed similar themes, blurring the boundaries between the delinquent, the troublesome and the merely naughty child, construing diagnosis as a task for skilled expertise, suggesting mechanisms for the earlier and more effective diagnosis of family failure, advocating responses to childhood troubles framed in terms of therapy rather than punishment, and suggesting reforms to the court system to enable it to function as a kind of tribunal for the interpretation of family problems and the choice of measures for the educative rehabilitation of child and parents.[55] The objective was to find a way to govern the family such that it could become an educative institution that would school the new generation in the values, conducts, and skills of citizenship. What was stressed, as Clarke points out, was the need to get the family to accept what became defined as 'its own' responsibility, promoting its agreement to having *itself* treated where problems arise with its children, forming a partnership that is at once consensual and tutelary between the family and social expertise.[56] For the problem family was precisely the one that neither had the capacities to educate itself in the obligations of family life, nor would be reformed by coercive imposition of legal sanctions. Of course, coercive legal processes had a certain role, for they could be brought into play as a last resort and a point of appeal in cases where non-cooperation becomes a problem. But their use destroyed those very human relations that social expertise had to foster – the responsibility of the family for the management of itself according to the norms of proper conduct.

When the Seebohm Committee on the Local Authority and Allied Personal Services was set up in 1965, the objective of an effective family service was built into its terms of reference – an objective that required it to confront not simply an isolated problem group but something that embraced all citizens. 'We decided', says the report,

> very early on in our discussions that it would be impossible to restrict our work solely to the needs of two or even three generation families. We could only make sense of our task by considering also childless couples and individuals without any close relatives: in other words, everybody.[57]

Its recommendation was for an amalgamation of child care, welfare, educational welfare, child guidance, home help, mental health social work, adult training, other social work services, and the welfare aspects of housing into a single department:

> a new local authority department, providing a community based and family oriented service which will be available to all. This new department will, we believe, reach far beyond the discovery and rescue of social casualties; it will enable the greatest possible number of individuals to act reciprocally, giving and receiving service for the well-being of the whole community.[58]

The organizational changes instituted after Seebohm mark a major shift in the powers of therapeutic familialism, for they established social work in a key role, knitting together the diverse administrative strands extended to the interior of the family by other agencies (education, health, housing, psychiatry and education) into a nexus that bore upon the family case as the site for a policy at once individualized and co-ordinated. In its ideal form it was to make possible a preventative, anticipatory intervention in which social work was to pick up the early signs of malfunctioning and coordinate information and action prior to any gross infraction by either the parent or the child. The aim was to maintain the functioning of the problem family rather than disrupting it by the removal of the child, not disabling the family but rectifying it under expert tutelage. Family technicians sought to align the social and the personal, soliciting the active co-operation – or at least the compliance – of family members in the re-jigging of their own human relations.

This objective also lay at the heart of the Children and Young Persons Act of 1969. This sought to reformulate the previous strategic relations between the court and casework, such that social work would be able to diagnose the family problem, co-ordinate the information that would make the family legible, and calculate the appropriate response. Through the device of the care order, the centre of decision was to be shifted away from the court, so that social work could choose from among a range of tactics, supplementing or displacing the authority of the parents, monitoring the outcome, and making appropriate adjustments.

The Children and Young Persons Act was to mark the high point of therapeutic familialism as a strategy for government through the family. Many of its key provisions were never implemented – the age of criminal responsibility was not raised, criminal proceedings were not prohibited for the under-14s, more juveniles passed through the courts, detention and attendance centres were not phased out, more custodial sentences were imposed by magistrates, and more use was made of formal cautions by the police. It is sometimes thought that the objectives of the Act were subverted by diehards of the old school, characterizing the new approach as 'soft on criminals', appalled by its namby-pamby liberalism and do-gooder mentality, defending the traditional powers of the bench and appeasing the reactionaries of the political right. But the fate of the juvenile justice system is not explicable in terms of a simple reactivation of a punitive mentality. It was part of a much more widespread shift in the techniques for governing the family and its troublesome offspring. This shift was paradoxical. On one hand, it was built upon the generalization of the norms and techniques of therapeutic familialism into the public domain through books, radio programmes, television documentaries, and the like and their introjection by citizens themselves. Yet, on the other, it came about through the disintegration of the alliance of psychologists, social workers, psychoanalysts, and political progressives who had thought in terms of therapeutic familialism.

In the 1940s and 1950s, those who rallied around the cause of motherhood and deprived children considered themselves progressive and humanitarian, in touch with the latest scientific evidence on the nature of the family and child rearing, understanding troubles rather than condemning them, emphasizing care, therapy, and reform for problem cases rather than condemnation or punishment, seeking to support mothers and their children both intellectually and financially. But in the mid-1960s this amalgam of theoretical systems, professional practices, legislative measures, social provisions, and public images – this 'maternal complex' – came under attack. Historians and sociologists challenged the universality of the mother–child bond and hence its claim to be 'natural', suggesting in one way or another that childhood as a special period of life was a modern phenomenon, that the mother's love for the child and good mothering were inventions of modernization, and the family unit based upon strong emotional ties between husband and wife, and parent and child, did not exist in traditional societies for a variety of social and demographic reasons.[59] Feminists criticized it as little more than a means of enforcing and legitimating women's socially inferior position and their exile from public life.[60] Psychologists expressed doubts about the evidence and the conclusions, questioned the general application of the findings from particular types of residential care and from small numbers of case histories, pointed to complexities and ambiguities and generally muddled the powerful simplicity of the earlier arguments.[61] Progressive psychoanalysts argued that the theses of Bowlby and Winnicott, the analyses they made, the advice they proffered, were not authentic psychoanalysis but a popularized and sanitized distortion of it.[62]

Libertarians of both left and right began to question the rationale of welfare bureaucracies in general and social work in particular.[63] The philosophical justification for the extension of the powers of social work at the expense of those of the courts had been the welfare of the child, but this welfare principle now lost its self-evident virtue. It was argued that it denied the rights of children and parents alike, subverted the safeguards that due process provides for the liberties of the subject, and had underpinned an illegitimate expansion of social workers using unproven and biased theories to justify their interventions into family life.

As far as social work was concerned, the first effect of all this criticism was the ill-fated attempt to produce a 'radical social work', whose general aim was to relocate the 'problem' of the family within a wider social and political context. As far as psychoanalysis was concerned, the response tended to be a turn towards orthodoxy in theory and method, with intensive treatment in individual sessions or family therapy, and the withdrawal of credibility from the 'debased' versions of analysis circulating in the 'helping professions'. As far as psychology was concerned, emphasis shifted from the presence or absence of a relation between mother and child to its microstructure. Detailed observation, sound recording, filming, videotaping, and other techniques were used to inscribe the minutiae of the 'interaction' between adult and child into knowledge. Gazes, sounds, words, the nature of holding and touching – all these became the focus of a refined perception of mothering that came to centre on 'the sensitive mother' and her levels of responsiveness to 'the needs of children'. And this notion was to be buttressed by a concern that came from another quarter: a renewed anxiety about the intellectual capacities of a class of problem children and their consequences. Out of all this would gradually emerge a new strategy for the government of social life centred upon the privacy of the family; the responsible, autonomous family was to be its emblem.

Chapter fourteen

Maximizing the Mind

Education does not begin or end with school. A child is learning from the day he is born, and in the first years he goes through a period of development that is more extensive than at any other time of his life. If, during these years, the child is deprived of experiences necessary to this development, the effects can be far-reaching and it is not likely to be easy for him to overcome the disadvantages of early deprivation. These early years are the years when parents are the biggest influence on a child's education. It is the home that provides the early experience through which development takes place. At school the first teacher can only begin to build on the foundations that the parents have prepared.[1]

Cynthia Mitchell, 1973

The mother, today, is to be more than a technician in child guidance. Since the early 1960s she has been increasingly allotted a vital role in the cognitive development of the child, in maximizing his or her ability to think, to reason, to read, write, and figure. She has been incorporated as an actual or potential ally into pedagogic programmes advocated by reformers. Psychological theories of cognitive development and the importance of 'the early years' have transformed the everyday life of the household into a complex of educational opportunities. The mother is to precede the teacher; her daily routines, and her responses to the wants and troubles of her children are to be conducted in the interests of her child's mental development.[2] If she plays her part well, the child's future life chances will be immeasurably enhanced; if she fails through ignorance or impatience to realize or to actualize such a learning scheme, woe betide her child when he or she enters school.

For some two centuries, perhaps more, two distinct types of education have been designed for young children, one directed at the child of the well-to-do, the other at the child from the working class.[3] The former has sought, by and large, to maximize the potential of the adult that the child will become, seeking to convince parents that a particular way of thinking about and acting upon the child in its infancy will help them promote their own lineage and secure the best future for their offspring. The latter has sought, in different ways, to minimize the threat to social well-being that the future adult might represent, by supplementing the work of the mother in various ways, and by training her in the correct ways of conducting her tasks.

Historians of 'early education' tend to take Rousseau's *Emile* as a revolutionary turning point, and to regard his emphasis upon the natural processes by which the child learned as the initiation of 'child centred' education. Irrespective of the truth of this myth of origins, from the late eighteenth century onwards, philosophers and scientists attempted to inspire the members of the advanced bourgeois family with their moral and spiritual duties to their own children. It appeared to be the duty of adults to enable each child to realize his or her human destiny, and this duty was to be fulfilled through the provision of very particular kinds of experiences in the first years of life. The very young child was a particular object of such attention, no doubt because of the oft repeated arguments that events at this time laid down habits and propensities that endured for the rest of life.[4]

Perhaps the most significant proponent of this view in the nineteenth century was Friedrich Froebel. For Froebel, education was a way of enabling man to give expression to his inner, divine nature as it developed through the stages of childhood. But more significant, Froebel translated this romantic philosophy into a set of practical procedures and devices that would achieve such moral development. These tried to utilize the play of the child for pedagogic purposes, to instrumentalize it in such a manner that the child would educate its senses through the activities it engaged in. Through the device of the kindergarten, the techniques of the curriculum, and the system of training of kindergarten teachers, this new strategy of pedagogic philanthropy was to spread slowly across Europe.[5]

In England, in the late nineteenth century, Froebel's romanticism and spirituality were to be underpinned by the appeal to science. 'Mothers', as Johannes and Berthe Ronge put it, 'had been left without the assistance of science in their nurseries' for too long.[6] The scientific techniques for educating the senses derived, at least in part, from attempts to reform and educate pathological children: those found in isolation, those born deprived of sight or hearing or of limited intellect. Jean Itard's programme of education of the senses for the wild boy of Aveyron had originated the mechanism by which philosophical doctrines concerning the nature of knowledge could be turned into instructions and exercises to enhance the capacities of individuals. Edouard Seguin developed this method into a systematic project for the education of the idiot through awakening of the senses. Itard himself used it for the education of the deaf.[7] Maria Montessori was to ask why, if deaf children did so well through programming a systematic relationship between the expression of the child's needs and the apparatus of shapes and solids that it used in its games, did 'normal' children do so badly? Thus she applied the methods first to backward children, then to poor and delinquent children in the Case de Bambini, which she set up in the Italian slums.[8] These programmes of Froebel, Montessori, and their followers sought to act upon the soul of the child through the experiences of the body, turning pedagogy into a philanthropic science by adjusting the child's experiences into a logical sequence that would reveal the laws of mathematics and the physical world, while at the same time embodying in every activity the central moral principles of love and religion.

The British nursery school movement of the early twentieth century took up some of these analyses, but wove them into a set of more prosaic and ascetic social aspirations that recast an earlier attention to the 'infant poor'. Nineteenth century philanthropists in Britain and Europe saw the establishment of infant schools as one mechanism 'for the prevention of juvenile delinquency, and for the promotion of the best interests of society.'[9] For Samuel Wilderspin, the 'infant system for developing the intellectual and moral power of all children from one to seven years of age' was a powerful moralizing device.

> By taking children at an early stage out of the reach of contamination on the streets, and removing them from the no less baneful influence of evil example at home, we may lay such a foundation of virtue as is not likely to be shaken....[10]

From the *garderies d'enfants* of mid-eighteenth century Paris, through Oberlin's late eighteenth century schools for children of agricultural workers, Cochin's *salle d'asile* of the Paris of the 1830s, the German *Kleinkinderbewahranstalten* of the same period, the aim was the same, though the methods may have differed. Robert Owen's celebrated infant school at New Lanark admitted children as soon as they could walk, for 'education should begin in the cradle', and education had a powerful part to play in creating future useful citizens.[11] Other British philanthropists, from different moral and political stances, argued for infant schools to restrain the unbridled passions of the child and cultivate its kindly affections: 'even in the mother's arms the child may be tutored'.[12] It appeared that the mothers of the poor would render great service to the nation by collaborating with teachers in implanting truthful habits of heart and mind.

Although, when it came, compulsory education in England commenced at five, younger children could be admitted when their parents desired it, and almost 300,000 children under five were in school by the 1870s, rising to a peak of over 600,000 at the turn of the century. When disquiet arose over the numbers of young children in schools, in the early years of the twentieth century, it was less on grounds of the moral consequences of the school for the children, and more on the grounds of the moral consequences for the parents, for did not this opportunity allow the feckless to avoid their proper duties towards their children? And such avoidance was doubly regrettable, for the environment of the school was unsuitable for the young child, and actually damaging his or health. Where home conditions were satisfactory (clean, well-lighted, well-ventilated, not overcramped) and the mother did her duty by the children, the home afforded advantages for the early stages of education that could not be reproduced by school or any other public institution.[13]

The question of schooling for young children became caught up in a neo-hygienic strategy, in which the health and welfare of the child were construed simultaneously as a vital national resource and as under threat by living conditions that were unsavoury, mothers who were uneducated in the skills necessary to maintain health and hygiene, and public provisions that were unsuitable for the particular nature of children. This movement was to give birth to the health visiting system, compulsory medical inspection of schoolchildren, instruction of schoolgirls in the domestic arts and much else – an extension of social machinery into the petty details of the home and the quotidian routines of the people.[14]

The attempt to target schooling for the young at children from 'unsatisfactory homes' and to make that schooling appropriate to the intellectual, moral, and physical capacities of the child was to be undercut by financial constraints. Local authorities were entitled to refuse admission to ordinary schools to children under five but were not obliged to provide the new nursery schools; in the decades that followed, expenditure in this area was often explicitly discouraged.[15] The banner of nursery education was to be taken up by the socialist movement, first in the form of socialist philanthropy and later through municipal socialism.

An early supporter of workers' struggles and a member of the International Labour party, Margaret McMillan was first made aware of the extent of ill health in the slums in the course of campaigns in Bradford for improved school medical services.[16] Returning to London in 1902, now a member of the National Administrative Council of the ILP, she became a leading member of the Froebel Society. With help from a wealthy American industrialist, she opened a school clinic in Bow, in the East End of London, and by the time the clinic moved to Deptford, as the Deptford Schools Treatment Centre, it was funded by the London County Council. The clinic provided health facilities for some 6,000 children a year, but the problem with it was that when the children returned to their homes they rapidly became reinfected. The cure that Margaret and her sister Rachel employed was fresh air.

The first open-air school had been founded in Charlottenburg, outside Berlin, in 1904. The idea was that dark, overcrowded, and ill-ventilated school conditions exacerbated the ill health of children who were nervous, debilitated, undernourished, anaemic, or tubercular; fresh air, wholesome and regular meals, and rest would reverse this process.[17] The McMillans' version of this entailed camps in which children stayed overnight in shelters open to the elements; this technique was developed into open-air nursery schools that began taking children in 1913. The pedagogy of McMillan's open-air nursery schools of the 1920s drew eclectically from Froebel, Pestalozzi, and Robert Owen, stressing the development of the aesthetic imagination of the child, its natural flowering in a nurturing atmosphere. But it was underpinned by a hygienic vision of the nature of the child and the mechanisms for ensuring his or her welfare. Physical health was a virtue in itself but was also a prerequisite for mental development; somehow the exercise of the muscles was connected to the exercise and stimulation of the mind.

As first president of the Nursery Schools Association, founded in 1923, Margaret McMillan campaigned among MPs. By the 1929 election campaign the Labour party had adopted a policy of the extension of nursery schools. As the new Labour government put it in a circular of 1929:

Open-air Nursery Schools where infants are tended, washed, fed and taught have passed the test of experiment. They are a comparatively inexpensive and entirely effective means of securing a fair start in life for infants whose home life is most depressed.[18]

And, for the Bradford ILP, the functions of nursery schools were even more radical, for 'a working class trained in the Nursery School spirit would not tolerate existing conditions, economic or social', such intolerance being 'a necessary condition of permanent advance'.[19]

Nursery school provision certainly extended in the early 1930s, but the repeated stress from the Board of Education was on the role of such institutions in the prevention of ill-health rather than egalitarianism or the class struggle.[20] By 1938 over 15 percent of children aged three and four were attending nursery schools. This was coupled with the reactivation of nursery provision for the well-to-do by Susan Isaacs, and the movement into the state schools of many teachers influenced by her argument about the significance of early education for all children. It appeared as if a pedagogic network was about to coalesce that reconciled the two axes of concern over the development of the young child, incorporating them into a systematic network of persons, institutions, and activities aiming to maximize the utility of the body and mind.

As we have seen in a previous chapter, nursery schemes expanded during the war to release mothers for employment, but later contracted for administrative and financial rather than ideological reasons. Indeed, initial suggestions from the government were that the wartime provision be reorganized into a comprehensive system embracing nursery schools, nursery classes, and day nurseries available to all who desired them. The successive reduction of central government support for nursery education during the 1950s has been well documented and analyzed.[21] But new techniques in the post-war period were to provide a refined mapping of the vicissitudes of growing up, and a transformed concern for the mind of the young child.

A series of longitudinal studies appeared to provide the empirical possibility of linking early events with future prospects. The National Survey of Health and Development originally grew out of a much more limited attempt by the Royal Commission on Population to study the functioning of the maternity services and the cost of having children. But the cohort of virtually all children born in England, Wales, and Scotland between 3 and 9 March 1946 proved more valuable than envisaged. For such surveys turned out to provide unparalleled opportunities for opening up the life and health of children and families for scrutiny, for making visible and notable the factors influencing their development for good or ill. The initial plan to study the children for five years, to examine social differences in infant and child mortality was subsumed under an expanded project. The lives of the children were documented at two and four in terms of their development, accidents, illnesses, family circumstances, and use of welfare services. When they reached school, psychological tests mapped their intellectual and educational progress. After they left school, assessments were made of their occupational aspirations and progress. To close the circle, a 'second generation' study was planned, to document the families and children of the study children themselves.[22]

This was the start of a massive enterprise to turn the romance and tragedy of human lives, loves, and deaths not into inspirational or salutary fictional narratives but into questionnaires, computer printouts, graphs, charts, tables, scores, and norms. Intrepid explorers mapped the dark continent of family life and the attitudes, behaviours, and beliefs of the natives who dwelt there. The physical development of the infant and young child was surveyed repeatedly, and charted in texts and measuring devices modelled in one way or another upon the work of Gesell.[23] The results were directed towards doctors, psychologists, students, teachers, and parents, instructing them in a normalized and normalizing vision of childhood with the express purpose of alerting them to the presence and diagnosis of abnormality. From the other direction, as it were, interview studies of family life charted class differences in the minutiae of child-rearing techniques – in infant feeding, play behaviour, discipline and permissiveness, domestic uses of literacy and the value attached to books, reading and story telling, and so forth.[24]

Two morals gradually emerged from all these stories of the family life of children. The first was that the capacity to learn, the wish to learn, and the pre-conditions for future intellectual development were inculcated or nurtured in the course of the early domestic life of the child. The second was that the social classes differed in this, that working-class families suffered, at best, from a kind of cultural lag whereby they were fated to play out the child-rearing nostrums of a past age, which progress had made redundant. Thus they stressed obedience, tidiness, and habit formation in their children – the values of Truby King but not those for the new age of liberalism. At worst, the physical, intellectual,and emotional constraints upon the family lives of the working class seemed to be positively dangerous to the prospects for their children.

These children were to become the heroes, or rather the martyrs, of a new version of some rather old morality tales. The family histories that told the doleful tale of the hereditary passage of degenerate stock down a family line were to be modernized and rewritten in terms of the malign effects of environment (in particular the family environment) upon the mental development of the young. Adults who had themselves suffered deprivation and disadvantage as children, were failures at school, got poor jobs, got married too early, brought too many of their own children into the world in poverty and squalor, were too immature or damaged to rear them well and transmitted their poor physical and mental health to the next generation. The cycle of poverty, disadvantage, and deprivation provided a narrative formula that gave meaning to a whole variety of research, reflections, and programmes to do with children, families, and social problems for the next twenty years.

The evidence seemed compelling. The 1964 report of the National Survey of Health and Development appeared to reveal clear class differences in parental interest in education and in the attainment levels and educational success of children.[25] While there were possible links with variations in social environment and school conditions, research and publication throughout the 1960s argued that the 'home' variables were the most significant, that it was parental attitudes rather than social levels that were most important in the home, that working-class families were less interested in their children's schooling, and that this was reflected in poor school performance, low levels of adjustment, and absenteeism.[26]

In this context, further longitudinal studies of childhood appeared to provide yet more confirmation. The National Child Development study, which followed the cohort of children born in England, Wales, and Scotland in the week 3 to 9 March 1958, modelled itself on the survey of the 1946 cohort. Like its predecessor, the cohort had originally been selected for the investigation of the social and obstetric factors associated with perinatal mortality. But by the early 1960s the National Children's Bureau was arguing that it provided a very valuable opportunity for a more general charting of the norms of educational, behavioural, emotional, and social development. Such a study, it was claimed, would enable deviancy and handicap to be linked to educational, environmental, and physical factors; the circumstances associated with risk could be examined; means could be worked out for identifying individuals at risk; and the adequacy of provisions for handicapped, deviant, and exceptional children could be evaluated:

> Why do some children become backward readers? Why are some children maladjusted? What are the results of a broken home? ... A longitudinal study makes it possible to say what proportion of children from broken homes become delinquent, i.e. what is the risk involved. It also holds out the possibility of identifying some of the circumstances which might counteract a potentially damaging experience. In terms of future preventive action, the white sheep are at least as important to study as the black sheep.[27]

Not content with this study of children and their families at the ages of 7, 11, and 16, which in its first ten years alone gave rise to some twenty books as well as countless articles, a third longitudinal study was undertaken. The Child Health and Education Study followed children born in England, Wales, and Scotland during the week that began on Sunday, 5 April 1970. By the time of its first report, the message of all the studies was clear. As Brian Jackson put it in his opening statement:

> The authors have taken a universal question; what gives one child born in this week a better life-chance than another born in the same week? They have then tried to pursue why some children are at risk, developmentally delayed or behaviourally deviant – and other children are not... They have looked at environmental factors and at the many different and subtle forms of family life; one-parent, large family, rooted, mobile, prospering or struggling. Simultaneously they have searched... for patterns which positively show forms of equality in life chances or universality in provision of services.[28]

The authors of this study express their premises lucidly:

The first five years of life are unique. Not only is this period critical for a child's future development and life chances, but it is also the only time when the crucial concerns surrounding his or her health, education and socialization are left almost entirely to people who, for the most part, have no special training in these vital spheres. These people are, of course, the child's parents....Some children...do not have two parents; for others their parents may be young, inexperienced, poorly educated, in poor health, emotionally unstable, immature or have inadequate financial means for supporting a family and limited scope for making a living...so some children start life with greater chances of healthy development and successful achievement than others less fortunate.[29]

It was not only in Britain that the dark continent of childhood was being explored through such longitudinal studies. By 1981 the World Health Organization was able to publish a compendium of some seventy studies from as far apart as Romania, Iceland, and Mauritius under the general title of *Prospective Longitudinal Research: An Empirical Basis for the Primary Prevention of Psychosocial Disorders.*[30]

For there is no mystery about the object of all this documentation and analysis. The aspiration of these researchers was to find a means of governing childhood to minimize maladjustment, delinquency, neurosis, psychosis, and all the other disorders of conduct, affect, and will that were now being construed as 'psychosocial'. This dream was not motivated by a repressive desire for surveillance and control. On the contrary, this was a profoundly humanistic and egalitarian project, one that searched for the causes of failure of citizenship and sought to provide the knowledge that was to ensure the extension of the benefits of society to all its members. From these egalitarian aspirations emerged the vision of an apparatus of government, at once nationally organized and with its human face in every encounter between child, parent, and professional. A new project came to bear upon the mental development of the young child, to supplement or replace the pedagogy of citizenship provided by the mother.

Throughout the 1960s official reports elaborate upon these themes. The Newsom Report of 1963 identified the problems of a group of schools in difficult social and physical environments, with low educational standards, ill health, truancy, delinquency, and little enthusiasm among pupils to remain at school after the statutory school leaving age.[31] The Plowden Report on primary education refined the analysis on the basis of a number of specially commissioned pieces of research; indeed the work of the Plowden Committee provided the initial base for the National Child Development

Study, whose first major analysis was published as an appendix to the report.[32] The investigations carried out for the committee seemed to bear out the link between material and social disadvantage and poor school performance, a link that was encapsulated in the notion, at once analytic and administrative, of 'education priority areas' where social and educational problems coincided: poverty, large families, poor housing, absenteeism, and truancy.

By the late 1960s this linkage had become the received wisdom of the sociology of education:

> Poverty can make a parent less willing to keep a child at school; can make it difficult for him to afford books and toys, or expeditions which help a child to learn; can enforce housing conditions which make the whole family strained and unhappy or make it almost impossible for parents and child to talk or play together. Moreover, even where these conditions are no longer present, the fact that they have existed in the recent past, or were a feature of the parents' own childhood, may exert an influence on attitudes, values and aspirations for a generation or more.[33]

The concerns that circulated around the disadvantaged child certainly have a profoundly egalitarian ring to them. Again and again authors emphasized that equality of educational provision meant little if children were placed by their home backgrounds in such a position that they were unable to benefit from it. They stressed the deleterious effects that poor material conditions, inadequate facilities for the care of young children, isolation, and lack of knowledge among mothers had upon both children and mothers alike. They urged investment in pre-school services for families and young children, for 'all our future'. While the cost might be great in the immediate term, the lack of such investment carried a greater, though hidden, social cost, not only in depression in mothers but, more importantly, in the children themselves: poor academic achievement, poor study habits, truancy, delinquency, disaffection.

We should not deny or minimize the genuineness of the concern for individual well-being and social justice that suffuses this work. But alongside the notion of education as an equalizing apparatus runs another conception of schooling as a socializing and moralizing enterprise. For if education was to be a vital apparatus of citizenship, it was never simply because of the intellectual capacities and qualifications it conferred. Egalitarianism also encompassed a hope that the educational apparatus would be the means of inculcating the *aspirations* of citizenship in children – the will, as well as the means, to organize their lives within a project of self-betterment through diligence, application, and commitment to work, family, and society. Thus what was revealed by all these studies of childhood was not merely a problem of inequity and waste, but one of alienation, of the production of a group of children who were unwilling or unable to respond appropriately to the values, rewards, and expectations that formed the culture of the school, and the culture of the larger society for which school was a vital preparation.[34]

It was in the United States that the first major interventions into social reality were undertaken in these terms. In the early 1960s a new social topography was constructed, which centred upon the growth of the population, its concentration in the large cities, and the racial and class distribution within these cities. Investigators found a regular pattern: the gathering together of black families in the ghetto districts in the central blocks; a surrounding ring inhabited by white working-class families, often recent European immigrants; the bulk of the middle-class population distributed in the outer suburbs. Ways were proposed by which this topography could be quantified and rates of change measured, such as Havighurst's 'status ratio' formula, which calculated the ratio of middle-class to lower-class pupils within a school, and suggested a 'critical point' beyond which schools in transition areas would rapidly descend into a predominantly 'lower-class' ratio as the remaining middle-class parents withdrew to the suburbs.[35] This dynamic was exacerbated by the shift in the expanding sectors of employment to the suburbs, increasing their attractiveness to higher-income families, reducing the local tax base and employment opportunities in the ghettos even further, while simultaneously increasing their need for services and their rates of unemployment.

Statistics and surveys appeared to support this argument. Many analysts felt that automation and other technological changes were, in any event, increasing persistent hard-core unemployment especially among blacks, and that the unemployed school drop-out would further swell this group. The drop-out himself would produce a family that would further add to those who were unemployable.[36] Political perceptions of social and racial polarization shifted from a concern with the denial of legal and civil rights in the South to social and economic inequality amounting to racial segregation in the large cities. Research reports drew repeated attention to these problems, to their potentially explosive social consequences, to the apparent failure of economic expansion to reduce them given current policies, and hence to the need to do more than rely upon further economic expansion to reduce or ameliorate them.[37]

When President Lyndon Johnson declared 'unconditional war on poverty in America' in 1964, this was the enemy he had in mind. The war was to be fought out as much on the field of research and academic argument as in the plethora of legislative activity and social programmes. The school appeared to be fundamental to poverty and the attack upon it. It both exemplified and exacerbated the problems to be faced, and was to become a crucial testing ground for explanations and solutions. Residential segregation and the zoning of school catchment areas, together with the evacuation of the white and the employed from the inner cities, led to a segregation of schooling as effective as that which had earlier offended against civil rights. Poor black children were concentrated in the under-resourced ghetto schools, with poor equipment, dilapidated buildings, low motivation, and high levels of racial tension. The attitudes of the teachers, the nature of the curriculum, the turnover of staff – all these appeared to reinforce the problems of the inner cities, ensuring for the children a slum education, with low standards of attainment and a high drop-out rate contributing to further disadvantage by reducing employment prospects still further.[38]

A burgeoning literature from radical autobiography to scholarly reports testified to the severity and disgrace of the problem. Jonathan Kozol's *Death at an Early Age,* subtitled 'the destruction of the hearts and minds of Negro children in the Boston public schools', began by quoting Eric Erikson's doctrine that 'the most deadly of all possible sins is the mutilation of a child's spirit', and ended with Langston Hughes' poem, 'Ballad of the Landlord'.[39] More prosaically, but no less devastatingly, the Coleman Report documented the evidence in painstaking but compelling detail for a disparity in educational performance between black and white children.[40]

But there was a significant shift in the analysis Coleman produced. It seemed that it was the home background of children and the characteristics of fellow pupils that were more significant than variations in schools or teacher quality. Other reports agreed; the problem, it appeared, was a 'cycle of poverty':

inadequate education, low or non-existent income, limited job opportunities, dilapidated and over-crowded housing, poor physical and mental health, an inclination towards delinquency and crime – these and many other characteristics of poverty both cause and are caused by each other, interacting in a manner which renders it virtually impossible for the disadvantages child, adult or family to break out of the 'cycle of poverty'.[41]

If education displayed and exacerbated this cycle, it also held the key to breaking out of it. The psychology of intellectual development was reoriented around this problem, and appeared to show that the earliest years, before school began, were vital in the growth of intelligence and hence to the child's subsequent success in the educational apparatus. Thus Bloom re-analyzed longitudinal studies of child development to demonstrate that the most rapid growth of intelligence occurred in the pre-school years.[42] Hunt drew on the work of Hebb,

Harlow, and Piaget to propose that a massive increase in levels of intelligence could be achieved by bringing a sound scientific educational psychology to bear upon the events of a child's early years.[43] Other suggestions, such as the notion of critical periods of development, were activated to make much the same point.

'Compensatory education' was the invention that would link up those insights and opportunities to new forms of regulation in order to break into 'the cycle of poverty'. The Head Start programme was most significant. 'Child Development Centres' were opened in poverty areas throughout the United States in summer 1965 to provide eight weeks of summer pre-school for four- and five-year-olds. In the first summer over half a million children were enrolled in over 2,000 centres, with almost 200,000 paid and voluntary workers taking part. But these centres were more than merely 'educational'; they constituted the basis of a whole new programme of intervention into the family life of young children, including health services for medical diagnosis and treatment, social services organizing aid to the child's family, psychological services, nutritional programmes, and parent participation.[44]

The rapid growth of Head Start meant, in the first instance, little innovation in the actual content of the education provided, with most Centres deploying a rather unstructured, supportive programme of 'socialization'. But a range of more specialized projects sprung up around it – Gray and Klaus's 'Early Training Project' in Nashville, Deutsch's programme run from the Institute of Developmental Studies in New York City, Weikart's 'Perry Preschool Project' in Ypsilanti, Michigan, the Nimnicht Early Education Program in Greensboro, North Carolina, the highly structured 'academic' pre-school set up by Bereiter and Engleman, Marion Blank's Individual Language Program, and so forth. An accelerating spiral of power and knowledge, a new and forceful regulatory technology, and an even more refined set of calibrations and techniques sought to manage the intellectual life of the child, its ways of speaking and thinking. They would provide the possibilities, in the decade to come, for a new way of incorporating the social aspirations of citizenship into the family machine.

Initially it appeared even highly structured and intensive work with the child itself was insufficient. On the one hand the work had to be followed through into the school itself. The Office of Economic Opportunity was precluded from sponsoring programmes occupying normal school hours, which was one more reason for the concentration on the pre-school years. But Title I of the Elementary and Secondary Education Act of 1965 released about $1 billion for compensatory educational projects at school level, funding increases in staffing, curriculum refinements, and reading programmes. On the other hand, the world outside the school was to be utilized in the service of cognitive development and school motivation. The aspirations, values, and techniques of the school were to be channelled into the home. Mothers were to be encouraged to participate in the preschool schemes, which would enable them to be more or less subtly instructed in the attitudes and responses central to an effective pedagogy. In some schemes, like the Mother's Training Program in Nashville, they were to be directly trained and used in a teaching role. However, as was frequently pointed out, the mothers most in need of instruction were also the least likely to involve themselves in this active way, hence the growth of visiting schemes and other mechanisms for instructing parents in their own homes. Other schemes sought to act on the environment more generally in the interests of the minds of children. Some used 'bussing' as a means of breaking out of the residential racial segregation of the city schools. Others sought to link up the school with other projects to mobilize and develop the community as a whole. These ranged from the sedate community and neighbourhood schools like the Adams Morgan Community School in Washington, D.C., to the free schools of Boston, Harlem, and elsewhere that fused the transformation of schooling into a radical political project with more general aspirations.

An army of psychologists was employed on various studies that attempted an assessment of the effects of all this work in the children themselves, either in the form of 'action research' or post hoc followup. The story constructed from these evaluations had a disappointing message.[45] While the children made some limited gains in emotional and cognitive capacities during the project, the general consensus appeared to be that these were lost in the first few months of schooling. In the disillusionment that followed, these negative findings were deployed in the service of many different analyses.[46] Some argued that the failure flowed from the fact that the projects did not start early enough, that they were not long or intensive enough, that they were not sufficiently tightly structured and carried out. Others argued that the results confirmed that IQ was largely inherited – the furore around Arthur Jensen's paper, 'How much can we boost IQ and scholastic achievement', is well documented.[47] A third group, mainly sociologists, argued that 'education cannot compensate for society', and that concentration on the 'disadvantaged' child distracted attention from the social and political conditions that conferred such disadvantage, conditions that educational changes alone could not significantly transform.[48] In any event, when Richard Nixon brought the major American social programmes of the 1960s to a halt in December 1971, when he vetoed a 2 billion dollar legislative programme for educational and health care for the children of low-income mothers, the progressive and liberal arguments that had once established an almost incontrovertible case for action were divided, uncertain, and weak.[49]

But it should not be thought that this American failure signalled the demise of expert activity to understand and shape the intellect of the growing child. Indeed, as the American work was already heading for disappointment, British programmes conceived in almost identical terms, though on a rather more modest scale, were just getting off the ground. Here, too, pedagogy was to be infiltrated into the home, and an expanding programme was to be initiated for acting upon the intellect of the child. And here, too, the aim was to enable the apparatus of the school to act as a socializing and moralizing machine, channelling the aspirations of the poorest and most alienated into the pathways of social integration.

The 1960s in Britain were the high point of radical hopes for, and theories of, education and schooling. The American literature on schooling and society was imported into Britain. Kozol's book was published in 1968 (fateful year) to be followed by the radical writings of Paul Goodman, Ivan Illich, Everett Reimer, and others on the links between educational reform and social transformation. And it was in April 1968, as social disorder flowed through the streets of Europe and the United States, that Enoch Powell, MP, linked immigration, urban disturbance, poverty, and unrest to a growth of resentment in Britain over rates of unemployment, urban decay, and poor housing, basing much of his argument upon his perceptions of the lawlessness and violence of the United States and prophesying streets running with rivers of blood. Within the month, as dockers and other trade unionists who were traditional supporters of the Labour party marched in the streets in favour of Powellite positions, the Labour Prime Minister, Harold Wilson, announced a new urban spending programme. This urban programme was to be directed towards conurbations with areas of multiple problems, including high concentrations of immigrant families. It was into education that much of the urban aid was channelled, in particular as suggested by Plowden to pre-school provisions.

It was also in 1968 that the 'educational priority areas' invented by Plowden were turned into a kind of reality. Five of them (Oxford, Birmingham, Liverpool, London, and the West Riding of Yorkshire) were singled out for action research projects under the general direction of A. H. Halsey, director of the Department of Social and Administrative Studies at Oxford University. Halsey summarized the aims of his project in terms derived from the Plowden Report:

   (a) to raise the educational performance of the children;
   (b) to improve the morale of teachers;
   (c) to increase the involvement of parents in their children's

education; and

(d) to increase the 'sense of responsibility' for their communities of the people living in them.[50]

What happened on the ground was somewhat modest in relation to these grandiose aims. The territory of the priority areas and their educational provisions were mapped and the previous assumptions confirmed, with qualifications. Pre-school provisions were marginally increased, principally by encouraging the expansion of provisions already provided by local authorities or by voluntary associations. Attempts were made to improve language development by the use of a structured 'kit' imported from the United States. Number conservation was encouraged in Birmingham by a method which, as it were, inverted Piagetian notions of stages of cognitive growth, transforming the means he utilized for demonstrating a child's grasp of number into pedagogic devices. Children were tested and retested to evaluate results, and their home backgrounds were documented. A Community Education Centre was set up in the West Riding, curriculum developments were undertaken, home visiting schemes were tried out, and home–school liaison teachers were appointed, to 'enlarge mutual understanding between the school and families and neighbourhood which it serves and to strengthen the help which they can give to each other, bearing in mind especially those children who need most help, and whose parents sometimes seek it least.'[51]

This was a rather meagre outcome of all this concern, one might think, and indeed beneath the pomposity and grandeur of the five volumes of reports on the EPA schemes, the statistics, charts, tables and graphs, one is struck by the sparseness of the actuality in comparison with the rhetoric. None the less, Halsey and his team were still optimistic in 1972, concluding that 'positive discrimination' could be applied through the administrative means of the educational priority area, and that 'pre-schooling is the outstandingly economical and effective device in the general approach to raising educational standards in EPAs', despite the fact that the results of all the assessments were, to say the least, equivocal.[52]

A veritable deluge of research projects, papers, and books emerged, focusing upon the issues of the disadvantaged child and compensatory education. The Schools Council, the National Foundation for Educational Research, and almost every other research organization one could think of sought to establish and evaluate the effects of intervention in the pre-school years upon the cognitive and emotional development of children.[53] It seemed impossible to think of children in terms other than 'the crucial importance of the early years', 'pre-schooling', and 'intellectual and linguistic stimulation'.

Whilst one side of this vision was turned towards the disadvantaged working-class child from the inner cities, and the social problems that alienation from schooling held in store, a second was focused upon the educational advancement of the child of the well-to-do, and the career advancement and satisfaction of the bourgeois mother. The institutional form this concern took was the pre-school playgroup, but it also was embodied in books, toys, games, and behaviours – a hundred little ways in which the sensitive and affluent mother could maximize the chances of the future success of the members of her lineage, or suffer the guilt if she refused the opportunity.

The playgroup movement of the 1960s certainly reactivated both the intellectual and the ethical aspirations of the nineteenth century, though posed now in the secular language of cognitive growth and social and emotional development.[54] When a young mother wrote to the *Guardian* in 1961, describing the arrangements she had made with a number of neighbours to form children into a group meeting regularly in their homes, she was inundated with requests from similarly situated young middle-class mothers for information and advice. Events moved rapidly – a Pre-School Playgroups Association was formed to promote local groups for children aged two and a half to five, and voluntary area organizers were appointed. By 1965 there were 500 members of the association, and by the end of the decade the numbers of members implied the existence of over 8,000 playgroups involving about a third of a million children each year.

These playgroups, and the playgroup idea, became the focus of aspirations and desires from many directions. Parents of would-be successful children needed no convincing about the importance of education, and these groups combined the ethics of the intellect with those of self-help and the neighbourly spirit. Radical groupings saw playgroups as a means of counteracting the harms of bourgeois socialization, breaking down gender stereotypes and narrow notions of education. They saw in the community playgroup a basis for collective action and libertarian struggle, involving alliances between the articulate university-educated middle classes (often bringing up their children in unconventional family settings) and the oppressed women of the working classes. This had the added advantage that, at the same time, it would inculcate progressive attitudes and values into the future generation at their most critical time of life, inoculating them against the harmful effects of state education that were to follow.

But playgroups became more than a self-help movement. The government funded playgroups in 'disadvantaged' areas, in the belief that they were a cheap form of intervention into the pre-school lives of endangered children. When established by charities like the National

Society for the Prevention of Cruelty to Children and the Save the Children Fund, they were a means of monitoring the progress of children at risk and scrutinizing their parents, as much as a way of providing temporary relief for overburdened families. Others sought to turn the playgroup into the site for a new quasi-profession of the early years, with training courses, qualifications, and new careers opening up. The mundane business of rearing children was a potential site for upgrading. The undervalued pleasures and labours of motherhood (speaking to children, playing with them, reading to them, painting with them) were to be transformed into a socially sanctioned and valued sector of scientific expertise.

It was in a speech to the Pre-School Playgroups Association in 1972 that Sir Keith Joseph, then Secretary of State for Social Services, rearticulated the links between these 'educational' initiatives and a more general project of the government of troublesome sectors of the social body. 'Why is it', asked Sir Keith, 'that, in spite of long periods of full employment and relative prosperity and the improvement in community services since the Second World War, deprivation and problems of maladjustment so conspicuously persist?'[55] His answer was to reactivate the notion of the 'cycle of poverty' in terms of a 'cycle of deprivation', a subtle but significant shift that internalized the process of transmission within the culture of the family, its ignorance, immaturity, emotional impoverishment, and despair.

Intervention into the pre-school years through the formal apparatus and agencies of the state became a province of the social services, and of those voluntary organizations that were extending their remit to 'social work' with the disadvantaged child and its family. It was a matter of provision for children 'at risk', a term that came to encompass the whole range of dangers from physical abuse, through poor hygiene, to intellectual deprivation. Pre-school provisions were integrated into the dream of prophylactic family regulation through machinery ranging from the juvenile court, through doctors, police, and social workers, to health visitors and neighbours. From Maria Colwell to Jasmine Beckford, the child 'at risk' became both opportunity and nightmare – the constant reminder of the need for further research, the refinement of expertise, new mechanisms of intervention, and yet the constant reminder of the inevitable discrepancy between rational schemes for the government of the family and the messy realities of existence.[56]

Yet in another way the pedagogic aspirations of the 1960s were maintained and extended into a concern to mould and regulate the individual relations between mother and child in the home in the interests of the cognitive and emotional development of the child. 'Education for parenthood' in schools and pre-natal classes and via health visitors diffused the norms and pedagogic techniques of developmental psychology and the pre-school into the home itself. The ideas, values, and norms of psychology were to be inserted into the lives of mothers and children through such routine social practices as infant testing and medical check-ups, and through the explosion of books, pamphlets, and magazine articles directed towards mothers.

The incorporation of the mother into a pedagogic alliance with psychological expertise and professional authority resolved a problem that had hampered and worried advocates of early education since its inception. As Gesell put it in 1925, 'The great problem is to assist the home and the parents, not to replace them.'[57] The difficulty, that is to say, was how to supplement the inefficient and socially damaging practices of the mother without destroying the responsibility of the private family for the socialization of its members. The answer was to incorporate pedagogic norms within the mother's own desires and fantasies, for them to form an inescapable and pervasive grid for calculating and judging her own behaviour and that of her child. Professionals were to define good mothering and establish its necessity for the realization of the child's potential. They were to prescribe the techniques for carrying out such practices and define the norms according to which they were to be evaluated. But the mother was to operate the regimes in the 'privacy' of her own home, under the direction of her personal wishes and fears.[58]

As the norms of intellectual growth spread outwards from the professionals into the home, entrepreneurs capitalized on the expansion of the market created by these new needs. With the aid of the books, games, toys, records, and other aids now made available for purchase, the intimate environment of the home was to be transformed into a veritable laboratory of cognitive growth. Each child was to become a little wild boy of Aveyron, the subject of a personal experiment in mental development through the programming of experience in relation to wants and needs. Every wish of the child – for food, drink, play, exercise – could be made the basis of a learning experience by interposing manipulative tasks, reasoning hurdles, or memory tests between the desire and its satisfaction. Every domestic duty could provide lessons in order and number, every conversation could become a little tutorial in vocabulary, grammar, and articulation.

Take, for example, Joan Beck's *How to Raise a Brighter Child*.[59] Its purpose was to

> report to parents about new research on the growth of children's intelligence during the first six years of life and to translate this research from scientific journals, learned symposiums, and

experimental laboratories into a form that will be useful to those who live and work with small children every day.[60]

'Translate' is precisely the term – a translation from the discourse of science to the imperatives and techniques of practice, and simultaneously a powerful translation of plausibility from the sacred domain of truth to the profane domain of runny noses and sticky fingers.

Science has, of course, all too often devalued parents, and appeared to them as a threatening and persecuting alien body of prescriptions. But science here constantly reassures parents how important they are and how much pleasure and delight lie in store for them through the use of early learning techniques. Little family dramas are played out to make the point. Four-year-old Jeanne Jenkins so impresses Mrs Jenkins' friends by her ability to read to their children at her birthday party. Four-year-old Danny plays by matching numbers of beads to numbers on cards up to 999. Little brain-damaged Debbie acquires a reading vocabulary of over 1,000 words. And all because, in each case, someone who loved the child knew and applied the new theories of early learning and brain development. Love, fun, success, duty, science, and superiority are sutured together into a chimera that is impossible to resist. 'Fathers and mothers who have tried using early-learning principles with their offspring are delighted not only with the intellectual progress of their children, but also with the new and happy relationship that follows.'[61]Children become not only brighter but well behaved and interesting. The rearing of children is no longer worthy but mundane, no longer emotionally intense and dangerous; through the appliance of science it becomes simultaneously educational and stimulating for both mother and child.

Not that this infant pedagogy entails disrupting home life with a series of 'classes' on different topics – far from it. What is entailed is the recognition that all aspects of life can be understood and shaped in terms of their effects on the child's learning. The Head Start experiments, the writings of experts from Jerome Bruner through Maria Montessori to Kenneth Wann, and a host of personal anecdotes contrasting success and failure are combined to produce a truthful, practicable, and captivating image. This image plays back into further psychological evaluations of mother–child interactions. Thus Tizard and Hughes conclude, after analysing such interchanges, that while some mothers assist their children to explore abstract concepts, responding to the children's curiosity and 'thirst for knowledge', through guiding, explaining, and building the basis of understanding, others, through ignorance, insensitivity, or lack of patience, never achieve such mutual understanding.[62] Vital cognitive tasks have now merged with household duties in new norms for the labour of motherhood, and the minutiae of 'interactions' between mother and child have become visualizable, evaluable, and manageable as never before.

In the educationally stimulating home, every aspect of the daily routine, from breakfast to bedtime, is turned to cognitive account and visualized as a learning experience, promoting thought, language, science, maths, perception, and creativity, safeguarding the brain of the child against deadening assaults of illness, boredom, and conformity. The hope for the exceptional child, combined with the recognition that your child's failure in school and life is your own responsibility, infiltrates the vocabulary, the evaluations, and the calculations of expertise into the fabric of household routine. Motherhood becomes in theory intellectually exciting, a test of personal capacities, virtually a profession in its own right; in practice it is the site of a constant self-scrutiny and self-evaluation in relation to norms of responsibility to one's child.

From a potential site of resistance to pedagogic norms, the private family was to become a site of demand for them. Thus Walkerdine cites a passage from a suggested school handout to parents on early mathematics:

> You are probably helping your child to get ready for Mathematics in many ways, maybe without realising it! Here are some of the many activities that you can do *with your child* which will help. Laying the table – counting, getting the knives in the right place, etc. Going shopping – handling money, counting items in basket. Helping with cooking – weighing, measuring... By sharing an activity with your child and by talking to him, you can begin to introduce the correct 'Mathematical' words such as big and small, few and many, longest and shortest and so on. But don't turn it into a lesson. All these things can be done incidentally as part of day-to-day events.[63]

The new techniques for the cognitive maximization of the child enable the private household to be incorporated into the educational apparatus without destroying its autonomy. 'Your child is your child, your sole responsibility, and no well-trained teacher ever forgets this.'[64] Parents' rights to bring up their children themselves are a precious freedom to be jealously guarded. 'Parents need guidance, not laws. They want to do their best for their children but there is not enough help available to them.'[65]

The expertise of childhood thus acted as a kind of relay between the developmental psychology of the academy and the microstructure of adult–child interactions in home and school, promulgating new notions of the right and wrong ways to play, converse, and interact with baby or child, instructing parents and teachers as to the correct ways to handle this now so delicate passage to maturity. The knowledge of what normal development is and how to ensure it has become esoteric; to have access to it requires reading the manuals, watching the television, listening to the radio, studying the magazines and advertisements. Normal development had become a problem, something to be achieved, necessitating continual nurturing and surveillance. The 'interaction' of the child with its environment is to be structured, organized, and managed to produce the optimal outcome. Activities, social contacts, space, colour, apparatus, artifacts, language, drawing, painting, sorting, counting, listening, singing – everything is to be so organized, programmed, sequenced, and monitored to achieve maximum psychological success. All this was necessary if one was to avoid permanently jeopardizing success not only in school but in the life that was dependent upon school success.

The mother–child relationship was to be governed in the name of the intellect, not through coercion or the disabling of personal familial responsibility, but through the wishes, hopes, and fears of the responsible, autonomous family.

Chapter fifteen

The Responsible Autonomous Family

> The State in England takes pains to leave parents free to choose, and to accept or refuse what the State offers.... [It] does recognize the fact that a good mother is the right judge of what is good for her own child, provided she is informed as to facts and educated as to needs. The trouble is...that those who actually administer the public services are by no means uniformly confident in the mother's ability to understand her child better than anyone else can.... The State is indeed wise in its policy of education of parents with non-compulsion and the next step is education of those who administer the public services.... Whatever does not specifically back up the idea that parents are responsible people will in the long run be harmful to the very core of society.[1]

> Donald Winnicott, 1944

Debates over the apparatus of child welfare during the 1970s and 1980s present a confusing picture. On the one hand, there are the repeated 'scandals' over the abuse of children by their own parents in their own homes. First physical and then sexual abuse have been successively discovered by experts, dramatized through highly publicized court cases, and been the subjects of official inquiries and reports. On the other hand there is a revival of disquiet over the way in which the powers of the state and social workers may have undermined the autonomy of the family and invaded its privacy. This has taken the form of powerful demands for family rights. While the former appears to call out for more intensive 'policing' of families, 'at risk' registers, enhanced powers for social workers, and the extension of surveillance over the family, the latter seems to cry out for the reverse. From this perspective, it is the family that knows best how to bring up its own children – it should be protected from 'nosey parkers'and 'do-gooders'. Every child has a right to be brought up in its natural family, where it will be loved and cherished in the proper domain, not in the artificial environment of a surrogate home provided and staffed by a welfare bureaucracy.

Yet this paradox is more apparent than real; or rather, the conflicts between these two poles occur upon a single terrain. The dramatic playing out of child abuse cases and inquiries in the law courts, the public press, the television documentaries and the official reports are not simply a replay of the concerns about the child rearing practices of the poor that inspired philanthropy and state welfare for the first half of the century. Outrage at neglect or abuse appears to emerge most vociferously from the very sector of society that had once seemed most problematic – the labouring classes themselves. The tabloid and popular newspapers are the ones most lurid in their representations of abuse, most judgemental in their depiction of the perpetrators as monsters and devils, and most vehement in their demands for retribution.

The public lessons drawn from scandals of child abuse do not, today, point to the need for the education and moralization of a whole class of society, a benighted portion of the social body whose ineptitude or indifference threatens the well-being of the nation. The family that has failed to grasp its therapeutic and pedagogic obligations appears today less as a sign of the amorality or ignorance of the poor than as consequence of the individual psychopathology of a tiny minority of individuals or couples, explicable in terms of their personal characteristics or family history, and requiring criminal sanction or psychiatric attention.

While the overt demand provoked by these public scandals is for repression of this pathological minority, the reverse force of this demand is even more intense. This is the message that hate, jealousy, violence, aggression, provocation, retaliation, and sexual desires outside the proper relations of conjugality and kinship have no place in the repertoire of normal feelings of adults to children in the normal family. If experienced, they cannot be admitted, if admitted, this can only be in the context of a recognition of their abnormality and hence to one required to judge and condemn or one qualified to hear, understand, advise, and reform.

The modern family was constructed through the intense subjectivization, emotionalization, and eroticization of domestic affairs. It is a machine held together by the vectors of desire, and can only function through the desires that its members have for one another, and the operation of the family as a place where desires for the fulfilment of the self can be satisfied. Yet the incitement of 'social' desires required to fuel the familial mechanism is always threatened by the simultaneous incitement of desires out of bounds, anti-social desires, which can be satisfied only at the price of the destruction of that very socialization the family is to achieve. The public spectacles of abuse, inquiry, and condemnation are intrinsically bound to this constant necessity to generate images and identifications that will re-establish and police – in the subjectivity of each of us – the boundaries between the licit and the illicit.

The public representations of illicit sexuality and violence towards women and children as arising from personal or familial pathology, or even from patriarchy itself, obscure their roots in the intense emotional fabric that constitutes the modern family. We are each addressed as a member of this consensual normality, loving our children and committed to their psychological well-being, their intellectual development, and their physical health. While the messages these scandals provoke may appear to be directed to the malefactors, in fact they address themselves to all who are induced to identify with them. The other side of outrage is a renewed spiral of psychological reassurance and suspicion about 'the normal family' itself – a psychopathology of the normal parent.

The writings of Donald Winnicott during the 1940s and 1950s illustrate something of this paradox. Winnicott, like Bowlby, was concerned to some extent with the origins of juvenile delinquency and 'the anti-social tendency' in children; he was certain this originated in a deprivation of essential features of home life, the loss of something good, and the search for that which was lost.[2] But the focus of his most widely read works, and his many broadcast talks, was the pathology of the normal child and the therapy carried out by the normal mother: 'the immense contribution to the individual and to society which the ordinary good mother with her husband in support makes at the beginning, and which she does *simply through being devoted to her infant*.[3]

Winnicott's notion of 'the ordinary devoted mother' encapsulated this perception:

> I was walking, in the summer of 1949, to have drinks with the BBC producer, Miss Isa Benzie... and she was telling me I could give a series of nine talks on any subject that might please me.... I told her...I would like to talk to mothers about the thing they do well, and that they do well simply because each mother is devoted to the task in hand, namely the care of one infant, or perhaps twins. I said that ordinarily this just happens.... Isa Benzie picked up the clue in a matter of twenty yards, and she said: 'Splendid! The Ordinary Devoted Mother.' So that was that.[4]

Despite the great humanity and sensitivity that inspires Winnicott's writing, it is precisely this therapeutics of normality that was to become the conceptual counterpart of the harsh responses to the scandals of abused children. At the heart of his work appears to lie a constant reassurance to parents, mothers in particular, concerning their own capacities. Mothers' actions in relation to their babies were not to be moulded by instruction as to detail, but rather were to be based on raising to the level of conscious understanding that which they would naturally do with their children. The aim was an 'enlightenment about underlying causes'; this appeared necessary to supplement their natural actions and provide them with a basis of security.[5]

In promoting this way of thinking about the natural expertise of the normal mother and her child, Winnicott's writings and talks provided more than reassurance. They established a perceptual system and a vocabulary by means of which mothers (and others) could speak about and evaluate their selves and their emotions and relations, and the self of the child as well. Infant feeding, for example, becomes not a task to be learned but a 'putting into practice of a love relation between two human beings'.[6] The life of the baby, and the life of the mother, become 'inherently difficult' – no wonder that, from this time forth, 'normal parents' will need support 'to give them the real and right reasons for their good intuitive feelings'. Yet, at the same time, to 'bring out the best in parents, we must leave them full responsibility with regard to what is their own affair, the upbringing of their own family'.[7] The family is simultaneously allotted its responsibilities, assured of its natural capacities, and educated in the fact that it needs to be educated by experts in order to have confidence in its own capacities. Parents are bound into the language and evaluations of expertise at the very moment they are assured of their freedom and autonomy.

This paradoxical set of demands underpins and feeds off the repetitive scandals of neglect, abuse, and violence within the pathological family. In the spectacle of public condemnation of the abnormal, the potency and pervasiveness of normality is reactivated. Thus the self-judgement of each of us against its standards is mobilized. A similar paradox underlies the opposite pole of recent debates over the family. Faced with the complex of legal powers that have come to surround the family, especially those within and around the juvenile court system, a powerful 'counter-discourse' has taken shape, which has sought to limit incursions into the freedom of the family in the name of the protection of children. This counter-discourse is so powerful because it brings together themes and arguments from different sides of the political spectrum and from different ethical stances. The whole coalesces into a concerted opposition to the present form of the child welfare system.

There is little new in the contemporary language of conservative and neo-liberal politicians and writers; they express their concerns about the dangers of welfare destroying rather than promoting family responsibilities in familiar terms.[8] But these arguments have gained a new potency because the strands of philanthropic, humanist, liberal, and socialist argument that had previously provided a powerful and polyvalent support for the principles underlying child welfare, although critical of many of its realities, have come unwoven, or rather have woven themselves into a new pattern. Far from representing an enlightened benevolence, the principles of welfare and the best interests of children are seen as representing and facilitating a coercive paternalism on the part of the state.

One element in this new pattern came from civil libertarians. They argued that these paternalistic powers assumed by the state and its agencies amounted to illegitimate intrusions into the private realm of the family, incursions that should be prevented by the legal recognition of family privacy. Civil liberties lawyers propounded these arguments from vociferous pressure groups under the general banners of 'family rights' and 'children's rights'.[9] They expressed their concerns about the implications of the complex of legal and professional powers for the civil rights of children and families. They criticized the loose standards that guided the courts in their judgements concerning children, and which supposedly enabled them to shape their decisions in such a way as to conform with the 'welfare' and 'best interests' of their youthful subjects.[10] They argued that the lack of precision in the framing and operation of the legal powers failed to specify clearly the types of conduct that provide grounds for intervention, thus violating a central legal principle that the use of the powers of the state is only legitimate when it is governed by rules that are clear, public, and announced beforehand, thus giving individuals fair opportunity to adjust their behaviour in light of a knowledge of the consequences of not doing so. In the absence of clear and precise standards, it appeared that the interpretation of the principles such as best interests or welfare was left to the discretion of the decision makers – magistrates, judges, social workers: a denial of justice for the children concerned and for their families.

The civil libertarians who argued in these terms drew support from sociological analyses of welfare, the critiques of moral panics, professional entrepreneurship, political surveillance and social control, and the arguments that the child protection apparatus represents a paternalism with ambiguous implications for the individual freedom of children and parents. Sociologists actively joined in the critique of

the rationale of welfare and in campaigns to constrain welfare policing of families.[11] So did some welfare practitioners, who expressed
disquiet over the responsibilities allotted to them and the hopes invested in them by the proponents of welfare. They argued that these
attempts to protect children under such a 'welfare' approach simply
did not work. Surveillance of families often increased their problems.
Involvement with the 'helping' professions could result in labelling,
stigmatization, and the exacerbation of deviance. Removal of children from the home, either for reformatory treatment for juvenile delinquents, or for placement in institutions or with alternative
families, exacerbated rather than reduced the problems for the child.
It seemed that the state, by its intrusion into the family, could actually
make good situations bad and bad situations worse.[12]

Radicals extended this argument by linking it to a wholesale assault upon the scientific credibility and professional expertise of
the professionals of welfare.[13] They suggested that social workers
simply did not have the ability to make objective judgements as to
the effects of various types of family regime on a child's development. Their claims to a scientific knowledge base in psychological
theories were invalid. Psychology itself had not achieved the status
of a science; it was divided into competing schools with different
analyses and implications, and few of its findings were properly
substantiated. There was no agreement on the relation between
child rearing and personality, on the causes of delinquency, on the
effects of being reared by father or mother, on the long-term consequences of child abuse. Further, individual variations among
children and their reactions meant that psychological theories
were unable to make accurate predictions as to the consequences
of specific family regimes upon particular individuals. Even if
these problems could be solved in laboratory or experimental situations (and follow-up studies showed that predictions as to child
development were wildly inaccurate), social workers simply did
not have the capacity to gather and evaluate sufficient data upon
particular children and families to allow objective conclusions to
be drawn. Instead, their 'social inquiry reports' were replete with
value judgements posing as scientific evaluations, with hearsay
and rumour posing as fact. The claims of social workers to have,
in psychology, a secure knowledge base, were merely an attempt
to provide a pseudo-scientific legitimation for their professional powers, which were accorded to them by the law and the
courts.

From the left, this analysis was tied in with a more general critique
of the biased values informing welfare, and the social control functions that underpinned it. Social workers judged families according

to norms that were highly culturally specific. In particular, the conceptions of normal families and proper child-rearing practices were those of the white, professional, middle class, from which these professions were predominantly drawn. Their clients, however, and those who come before the courts, were predominantly working class and frequently black. For the professionals, West Indian, Asian, or white working-class families were viewed not as different but as defective. Forms of parental authority, ways of disciplining children, prohibitions on certain types of activity differed among classes and cultures, yet, in an ethnocentric and discriminatory way, social workers and the courts imposed one set of norms as if they were universal. Further, the regulatory apparatus coercively imposed upon women certain doctrines of motherhood, of the naturalness and desirability of women adopting a domestic and maternal role, bolstered by dubious psychological theories of maternal instinct, mother–child bonding, and primary maternal preoccupation. The powers accorded to social workers and judges enabled them to utilize the coercive apparatus of the state to judge, control, and sanction individuals and families.[14]

It might seem surprising that this argument should have been supported by the very 'experts' whose expertise was under question. But this was precisely the position taken up by Anna Freud, writing with Joseph Goldstein, a lawyer, political scientist, and psychoanalyst, and Albert Solnit, a pediatrician, psychiatrist, and expert on children's behaviour problems:

> the law does not have the capacity to supervise the fragile, complex, interpersonal bonds between child and parent. As *parens patriae* the state is too crude an instrument to become an adequate substitute for flesh and blood parents. The legal system has neither the resources nor the sensitivity to respond to a growing child's ever-changing needs and demands.[15]

Hence they sought to modify the law to safeguard the rights of the family to bring up its children as it wishes, except in cases of neglect and abandonment, and to elaborate very restrictive criteria for state intervention, based principally upon demonstrated physical harm to the child rather than assessments as to the psychological adequacy of the family regime:

> The child's need for safety within the confines of the family must be met by law through the recognition of family privacy as the barrier to state intrusion upon parental authority in child-rearing. These rights – parental autonomy, a child's entitlement to autonomous parents, and privacy – are essential ingredients of 'family integrity'.[16]

In restricting the role of the law and decrying its attempts to act therapeutically on the family, these authors do not seek to restrict the remit of psychological expertise. Rather, they seek to alter its mode of incidence upon the family mechanism. Psychotherapy is to be a matter, not of coercion, but of freedom. Psychological knowledge still has a role in relation to the formal apparatus of government, but it is a different one: prescribing and evaluating the proper form of court proceedings and legal arrangements in light of a knowledge of the psyche of the child and the parents. But from this time forth, the ideal relation of psychological expertise to its subjects will be outside the legal domain, in the private contractual relations between individuals concerned about their families and experts seeking only to assist them in their search for adjusted selves, relationships and children.

No doubt these various attacks upon the rationale of welfare and child protection came from different directions, and the implications the critics drew were distinct and even opposed. But this was precisely what enabled them to interlock into a powerful, mobile, and polyvalent counter-discourse that sought to 'restore' to the family its 'rights' to autonomy and privacy, to reconstruct its legal status as a domain outside the powers of the law, and to decolonise the intimate environment. While there were clear divisions among the critics of welfarism as to the way in which the grounds for coercive intervention into the family domain should be specified, there was general agreement that these should be limited to cases of clear, demonstrable harm or danger to children. Such grounds should be clearly specified in codes and regulations approved by Parliament, as should the rights of parents and of children taken into care. Proper accountability in the system should be ensured by legal means, by restoring due process to the juvenile courts, and by providing for judicial review of administrative decisions either automatically or as required by parents, children, and interested parties. The coercive powers of the welfare bureaucracy were to be minimized, and the boundaries of the family as a domain of personal choice and private responsibility were to be re-established.

These arguments did not remain purely oppositional. They led to legal changes in both the United States and Britain, particularly concerning the powers of authorities to usurp parental rights by administrative decisions based on welfare criteria. In Britain, in 1984, the Department of Health and Social Security issued a code of practice that emphasized that local authorities should have as their objective maintaining the unity of the family, and that parents should be involved in decision making and informed of their legal rights. 'Progressive' local authorities incorporated such rights-based principles into their procedures, seeking to minimize the use of substitute care and to direct social work towards the maintenance and support of families, and the rapid return of children to the families from which they have been removed. Notions such as 'shared care' and 'inclusive fostering' sought to provide the rationale for the inclusion of the natural parents, wherever possible, in any arrangements for substitute care. Repeatedly it was stressed that any social work intervention should seek to promote the integrity, identity and autonomy of the family. The vocabulary of rights was used, above and beyond any legal reference, to emphasize the objective of safeguarding the privacy and autonomy of the family unit and its members.

The strategy of family privacy might appear to stand in opposition to all those attempts to police and regulate the family mechanism over the past 150 years. But the reverse is the case – its stands rather as a testament to the success of those attempts to construct a family that will take upon itself the responsibility for the duties of socialization and will live them as its own desires. No longer does the socializing project have to be implanted by philanthropy or imposed under threat by courts and social workers. At least in its ideal form, it inheres in each of us, maintained and reactivated constantly by the images that surround us – in advertising, on television, in newspapers and magazines, in the baby books. No longer do experts have to reach the family by way of the law or the coercive intrusion of social work. They interpellate us through the radio call-in, through the weekly magazine column, through the gentle advice of the health visitor, teacher, or neighbour, and through the unceasing reflexive gaze of our own psychologically educated self-scrutiny.

The modern private family remains intensively governed, it is linked in so many ways with social, economic, and political objectives. But government here acts not through mechanisms of social control and subordination of the will, but through the promotion of subjectivities, the construction of pleasures and ambitions, and the activation of guilt, anxiety, envy, and disappointment. The new relational technologies of the family are installed within us, establishing a particular psychological way of viewing our family lives and speaking about them, urging a constant scrutiny of our inherently difficult interactions with our children and each other, a constant judgement of their consequences for health, adjustment, development, and the intellect. The tension generated by the gap between normality and actuality bonds our personal projects inseparably to expertise.

No longer will the mechanisms necessary for the government of the family threaten the principles of an advanced liberal society. The autonomous responsible family stands as the emblem of a new mode of government of the soul. Each normal family will fulfil its political obligations best at the very moment it conscientiously strives to realize its most private dreams.

Part four

Managing our Selves

Chapter sixteen

Obliged to be Free

The self is a vital element in the networks of power that traverse modern societies. The regulatory apparatus of the modern state is not something imposed from outside upon individuals who have remained essentially untouched by it. Incorporating, shaping, channelling, and enhancing subjectivity have been intrinsic to the operations of government. But while governing society has come to require governing subjectivity, this has not been achieved through the growth of an omnipotent and omniscient central state whose agents institute a perpetual surveillance and control over all its subjects. Rather, government of subjectivity has taken shape through the proliferation of a complex and heterogeneous assemblage of technologies. These have acted as relays, bringing the varied ambitions of political, scientific, philanthropic, and professional authorities into alignment with the ideals and aspirations of individuals, with the selves each of us want to be.

While psychotherapy, its practitioners, its languages, and its techniques may appear very distant from issues of politics and power, the spectacular expansion of the psychotherapeutic domain since the end of World War II has been intimately bound up with a profound mutation in the rationales and techniques of government. Over less than fifty years the territory of the psyche has been opened up for exploration, cultivation, and regulation in many ways and along many channels. Psychoanalysis, in its maximal form of one-to-one, fifty minutes a day, five days a week, forty-four weeks a year for five years or more may still be largely confined to the urban, bourgeois intelligentsia. But a plethora of less expensive and less intensive therapeutic techniques have been constructed through which individuals may seek a resolution of their inner distress: analytic psychotherapy, gestalt therapy, behaviour therapy, rational-emotive therapy, person-centred therapy, personal construct therapy, and many others.

The body has simultaneously become the diagnostic object and clinical intermediary of a range of new holistic therapies, the means of access to and transformation of the alienation, repression, and fragmentation of the self in modern times. And a therapeutic movement for 'growth' and 'human potential' has taken shape, whose practices – bioenergetics, transcendental meditation, assertiveness training, and the like – promise not so much relief to the anguished as a transcendence of the mundane for those frustrated by their own normality. The vocabularies and mechanisms of psychotherapy are not merely addressed to those unable to conduct a life, but to living itself.

The vocabularies of the therapeutic are increasingly deployed in every practice addressed to human problems. In the general practitioner's surgery, in the nurse's care for the ordinary hospital patient, in the tutor's study and the personnel manager's office, the techniques of psychotherapy have found a reception, and the whole person, the self as a living, experiencing, feeling subject, has come into focus. Notwithstanding their penchant for drugs, psychotherapeutic techniques are applied in the psychiatric hospitals; in large and small groups; in encounters between nurses and patients; in sessions with clinical psychologists, art therapists, and drama therapists; even in the practices of some psychiatrists. In day hospitals and therapeutic communities, psychotherapeutic procedures are adapted in the quest for ways in which patients can be managed from dependence and maladjustment to autonomy and responsibility.[1] Social workers, marriage guidance counsellors, bereavement counsellors, and many others have spun a compex web, in a plane neither 'public' nor 'private', neither 'statutory' nor 'voluntary' in which the codes, conventions, and skills of psychotherapy are addressed to all the multifarious problems of life.

Psychotherapeutic language and advice extends beyond the consultation, the interview, the appointment; it has become a part of the staple fare of the mass media of communication, in the magazine advice column and in documentaries and discussions on television. No financial exchange need be involved, for on live radio 'phone-in' programmes we may confess our most intimate problems for free and have them instantly analysed – or eavesdrop on the difficulties that so many of our fellow citizens appear to have conducting the business of their lives.

The therapeutic imperative appears as much a matter of healing ourselves as it is of being cured. A new genre of publishing has made rapid strides. Bookshops fill with paperbacks, each advocating a different therapeutic system and educating the reader in the procedures by which he or she can be transformed from dissatisfaction to fulfilment by systematically acting upon the psyche. These are paralleled by a confessional and autobiographical literature that documents the experience of neurosis, depression, mania, even psychosis 'from the inside', and charts the ways in which the suffering authors have been brought, or have brought themselves, to some sort of psychic peace through therapy.

There is an understandable tendency among practitioners, clients, politicians, and the media to celebrate the emancipatory potential of the application of psychological discoveries to the troubles of human existence. The contemporary concern for the self appears to be a response to problems generated by modern life, a mark of the respect the west accords to the individual, and the consequence of a remarkable, if still new and fallible, scientific endeavour.

Social analysts, however, have tended to take a rather jaundiced view of the therapeutic culture of the self. Cultural critics of the 1970s saw the growth of interest in therapy and self-development among the young of America and Europe as a turning away from the feverish engagement of the previous decade with the public world and radical politics. The new spirit was condemned as a narcissistic withdrawal, a turning inward into a private cocoon wrapped in the jargon of personal fulfilment, awareness, and authenticity. Marxists especially saw the new therapies as an obsession with the self, the apotheosis of the celebration of the individual in capitalist ideology. The desire for therapy may have been a response to the psychic damage wrought by capitalism, reflecting people's desperate search for a better way of living and being. But in conditions of alienation grounded in the form of economic organization, therapy could only be a palliative. The slogans purveyed in the new therapeutic movements, the hopes of happiness they hold out, had themselves become fetishized elements in consumer culture, thriving on the very disappointment their unfulfillable promises could only accentuate.[2]

Historians also tended to see therapeutic culture as part of a modern obsession with the self, a negative phenomenon consequent upon the breakdown of some previous, more desirable state of affairs. Richard Sennett argued that the emphasis upon intimacy, personality, and authenticity in all aspects of modern culture arises from the breakdown of the distinction between public and private spheres that had made civilized life possible in eighteenth century urban society.[3] Public appearance, language, and conduct are not now valued for what they can achieve, but are interpreted in terms of the inner personality that is manifested; closeness, warmth, and the frank expression of the inner self have become the supreme values. The psychotherapeutic is intimately linked to this obsession with personal identity, to this tyranny of intimacy in which narcissism is mobilized in social relations and the self is defined in terms of how it feels rather than what it does.

Also pronouncing our culture narcissistic, Christopher Lasch argued that this intense preoccupation with the self arises not from complacency, but from the devastation wrought upon our private life by the advance of bureacracy.[4] The contemporary American has surrendered his or her skills to bureaucrats, managers, and professionals. The worker's experience and wisdom have given way before the expertise of the managers of the corporation. Parents have become dependent upon certified experts in child rearing. Even personal life and forms of self-reliance have been transformed into a set of skills to be learned from doctors, social workers, and psychologists. The regulative technology of expertise has invaded the competence of the individual and family, and produced dependence upon the state, the corporation, and the bureaucracy. The ostensible obsession of the narcissist with the self is a desperate search for the means to counter the insecurity produced by the weakening of the 'social superego' formerly represented by fathers, teachers, and preachers. Psychological man of the twentieth century searches desperately for a personal peace of mind under social and psychological conditions that militate against it.

In a similar melancholy vein, Philip Rieff linked the rise of therapeutics to the demise of what he termed 'positive culture' in advanced industrial societies.[5] A positive culture has an ordered system of significances attached to behaviour; it promises some kind of salvation of the self, through the subordination of personal relations to agreed communal purposes. The therapies of positive cultures are those of commitment – the healthy man is the good citizen, and therapy has as both its aim and its mechanism the restoration of the individual to communal values. But advanced industrial communities are no longer culturally positive. Individualism rules, the links that once bound each person into the chain of all members of the community have been severed, the possibility has emerged of everyone living a truly private life. Hence such communities offer no collective salvation; their therapies aim not at a symbolic return to the positive community but at a tightening of ego controls over inner conflict. In the absence of any belief in a positive community, the good life is the negotiation of a private life of personal relations rather than participation in a public life of shared activities and values. Therapy is a method of learning how to endure the loneliness of a culture without faith.

But these nostalgic yearnings for a past in which the private self could find itself at peace with itself and with its role in a public world are fundamentally misleading. The problem should be posed in precisely the reverse manner. The relations between psychother-apeutics and political power reveal not the devastation of the psychic autonomy and security of the self, but the fabrication of the autonomous self as a key term in analyses of social ills and cures, as the object of expert knowledge, as the target of systems of moral orthopaedics. The distinction between public and private is not a stable analytic tool, but is itself a mobile resource in these systems of knowledge and power. And the ambitions of these systems have been profoundly ethical. To locate psychotherapeutics in this way is to place it, not within a history of culture, but within a genealogy of political technologies of individuality. Such a genealogy reveals the shifting forms in which political power has come to bear upon subjects, and has sought to understand them and govern them. And it emphasizes the ways in which our authorities, in pursuing social objectives, have found it necessary and desirable to educate us in the techniques for governing ourselves. The modern self has been constituted through this web of practices of power, meaning, and virtue that have addressed it.

Social theorists from many different standpoints have questioned the universality of the contemporary western concept of the person: a bounded sphere of thought, will, and emotion; the site of consciousness and judgement; the author of its acts and the bearer of a personal responsibility; an individual with a unique biography assembled over the course of a life. From the mid-nineteenth century onwards, analyses proliferated of the rise of 'individualism' over the previous 200 years, linking it, among other things, with Protestantism, with Romanticism, with the growth of a market society based on exclusive possession, and with theories of natural law.[6] These arguments were supported by anthropologists in the twentieth century, who suggested that in many societies that they investigated the notion of the person as a unique individual was unknown.[7]

Marcel Mauss claimed that in Australian and north African societies no unified 'self' existed. Persons were not individuated in terms of a unique identity but through a name that designated a locus of rights, statuses, and duties within the clan.[8] In ancient Rome, the role, as mask or persona, acquired a more 'personal' character as it came to designate the bearer of responsibilities within a personalized legal and political system. However, personhood was by no means an inherent feature of humanity: several classes of humans, notably slaves, were neither political nor legal persons, non-human entities such as corporations and religious foundations

217

were moral persons at law.

Mauss argued that it was Christianity that furnished this juridical and political personality with an internal existence in the form of conscience, and a universality, through the relationship posited between each human and their God. The Christian soul unified body and soul, consciousness and act, culminating in the Protestant identification of person, soul, self, and consciousness. It remained for Kant and Fichte to give this its precise modern form, Kant making the individual consciousness the sacred basis of Practical Reason, Fichte making the self the condition of consciousness, science, and Pure Reason.

Mauss himself was certain that, despite variability in *categories* across history, 'there has never existed a human being who has not been aware, not only of his body, but also at the same time of his individuality, both spiritual and physical'.[9] Commentators on his essay tend to agree, suggesting that Mauss and those who have followed in his footsteps are simply charting the anthropology and history of a set of cultural beliefs about the self which, as societies become more developed, gradually come closer to capturing this universal core sense of self-awareness.[10] But this confidence is a product of the very processes it seeks to understand. 'The self' does not pre-exist the forms of its social recognition; it is a heterogeneous and shifting resultant of the social expectations targeted upon it, the social duties accorded it, the norms according to which it is judged, the pleasures and pains that entice and coerce it, the forms of self-inspection inculcated in it, the languages according to which it is spoken about and about which it learns to account for itself in thought and speech. Thus 'belief systems' concerning the self should not be construed as inhabiting a diffuse field of 'culture', but as embodied in institutional and technical practices – spiritual, medical, political, economic – through which forms of individuality are specified and governed. The history of the self should be written at this 'technological' level, in terms of the techniques and evaluations for developing, evaluating, perfecting, managing the self, the ways it is rendered into words, made visible, inspected, judged, and reformed.

Christianity was indeed crucial in the development of the modern western self. Mauss cites the changes in Christian doctrine culminating in the ideas of the Puritans and others who demanded the right to communicate directly with God, to be one's own priest, to have an inner God. But these doctrinal changes were, at one and the same time, changes in techniques of self-scrutiny, self-evaluation, in the ways in which one's conduct and one's wishes were to be made an object of avowal, inspection, and evaluation. The practice of confession, as it developed in European Christianity since the thirteenth century, was not merely an abstract doctrine about sin and the soul, or a set of cultural beliefs. It entailed a practice in which the obligation was to render oneself truthfully into discourse, and a power relation in which the confession was to be made under the authority of another who hears it, evaluates it, judges the soul, and prescribes the form of conduct appropriate.[11] The significance of the reactions against the Catholic confessional lay in their challenge to this set of techniques of the soul.

Benjamin Nelson has argued that in the later Middle Ages, three sets of ideas and institutions were fused together into a single system of spiritual direction: beliefs and cultural arrangements embracing the determination of individual *conscience*; the analysis of the ways in which the dictates of conscience should be realized in different cases or alternative situations through the technique of *casuistry*; and the management of errant, perplexed, or obsessively scrupulous consciences through the *cura animarum* or cure of souls.[12] The Forum of Conscience, to which every Christian was answerable, created a forensic tradition, and generated a mass of specialized treatises tracing the obligations of conscience in daily life, how individuals were obliged to conduct themselves in every particular eventuality from contracts to war. After 1215, when all Christians were obliged to make annual confession, such treatises became the guides to Christian souls everywhere.

The meditative tradition, on the other hand, was not for all Christians but only for those who strove for true perfection and illumination. Monks and nuns, later also especially pious lay men and women, undertook an arduous pilgrimage of the soul in an attempt to experience union with God. In the lives and writings of those such as St. Bonaventura, Meister Eckhardt, Thomas à Kempis and others, a spiritual pilgrimage is undertaken and documented in minute detail. St Bonaventura sets out a threefold way for *The Mind's Itinerary into God*. The purgative way entailed meditation, prayer, and contemplation. In meditation rites of self-examination bring the soul's moral disorder and danger to bitter consciousness, achieving detachment from sinful inclination. Prayer transforms meditation into weeping, deploring sin, and asking for mercy. Contemplation leads the soul from fear through pain, rigour, and severity to ardour, culminating in the desire for martyrdom. On the illuminative way, the soul penetrates into truth by submitting reason to the passion and suffering of Christ. On the perfective way, the soul is prostrated before God in a love that ends in perfect union.

The modern literature of psychotherapeutics abounds in narratives of similarly arduous spiritual pilgrimages, documented with the same detail and force. They too constitute manuals for the bringing of the self to happiness and perfection. But their point of address is not to a few, but, at least in principle, to us all. In this respect they are the offspring, however distant, of a transformation and generalization of medieval systems for the administration of the soul that Nelson, like Max Weber and others, considers to have been fundamental to the modernity of the west.[13] The distinction between those monks with a special calling, living outside the mundane world, systematically cultivating the path to perfection, and those other mortals living in the world but without benefit of a rule, was transcended. It was replaced by the Protestant notion of a disciplined character, both universalizing and individualizing, in which each human being was inhabited by a personal conscience and admonished to constantly scrutinize thoughts and actions for failings. The Protestant revolution begins a new era in the culture of the self and the systems for self-direction, in which the union of conscience, casuistry, and the cure of souls is rejected; in its place, each individual comes to bear the obligation of doing the will of God without the benefit of learned confessors, directors, and advisors.

The new forms of self-regulation were manifested in a range of new technologies of the self in which self-inspection comes to replace the confessional. Writing was one central technique. Not that writing was a new acquisition for technologies of the self; it extends from Socrates' letters to Augustine's confessions.[14] But for the seventeenth century Puritans, the confessional diary, completed at the close of each day, constituted what William Paden terms 'an account book of one's state of sin', which effected, through the work of writing, a measurement of the self against biblical standards.[15] The diary was a mirror of one's sinfulness, but a mirror one held oneself. The self-inscription of the diary both calibrated one's lapses and bore witness to the survival of one's faith; the self was to become both sinner and judge.

Religion was not the only self-disciplining force in the formation of modern society, nor the only mechanism that linked the self-regulation of subjects with the organization of social power. In his two-volume study, *The Civilizing Process*, Norbert Elias tries to demonstrate and theorize a relationship between the centralization of political power in the form of a state and the growth of what he terms 'civilization.[16] Drawing mainly upon texts of etiquette and manners (eating behaviour, conventions regarding urination and defecation, nose-blowing, spitting, behaviour in the bedroom, aggression) he claims to discover the progressive imposition of constraints upon the human instincts. Instinctive behaviour, he argues,

is progressively hidden out of sight, first regulated by public proscriptions, then invested with feelings of shame that are internalized
in the process of upbringing. Hence the instinctual and affective life
of humans comes more and more under the regulation of self-control, which becomes itself ever more embracing.

While Elias discovers a systematic pattern to this increase of self-
control, he argues that such systematicity does not spring from any
consciously imposed pattern but is the consequence of the increasing differentiation of social functions. On the one hand, power
becomes increasingly centralized as competition between feudal
lords eventually leads to the monopolization of legitimate force and
political authority within a given territory. On the other hand, each
individual becomes enmeshed in a web of functional dependencies
upon others for the necessities of life and labour, and must attune
his or her conduct more and more to those others if harmony is to
prevail. While there is an increasing monopolization of the legitimate use of force to constrain conduct by the state machinery, there is
a decreasing need to utilize such control as it becomes internalized
within the structure of personality in the form of self-control. A
transformation of the human drive economy transforms the 'self-
steering' mechanism of individuals, inducing self-scrutiny and in-
cessant hindsight and foresight into all sectors of life.

It is certainly true, as Elias recognizes, that political power depends not only upon the gross exercise of control of 'antisocial' acts,
but also entails the regulation of the minutiae of the emotional
economy, of ethics and the management of personal conduct. The
integration, sequencing, and co-operation of subjects in networks of
command and in the organization of institutional life raised new
problems about the behaviour of individuals and stimulated the
production of new solutions. But the linkage between the tasks of
government and the regulation of personal capacities is not merely
a functional dependence achieved through the socialization process.
It can be analyzed more directly.

In sixteenth and seventeenth century Europe, an explicit connection was established between the tasks of good government and the
techniques of producing industrious, able, obedient, and disciplined
subjects. Policing was one axis of this; policing in the sense of a
science, a knowledge and technique for producing and maintaining
the good order of the population and of every person within it.[17] Policing entailed the elaboration of a complex of regulations concerning all the details of life that might be conducive to the promotion
of happiness, tranquillity, virtue and the public good: religious adherence; weights and measures; the quality of foodstuffs and water;
the maintenance and supervision of midwives; the provision of poor

relief; the dress of servants, domestics and nurses; the control of beggars; the occupations appropriate for Jews. In short, policing concerned 'everything' in the field between the pronouncement of a law and the prosperity, health, life and conduct of subjects. It not only sought to bring these phenomena into the field of government through the elaboration of an administrative apparatus, but also required a precise enumeration of these affairs, a political topography of the condition of the country and the population. To govern required to know, to prescribe, *and* to monitor the lives of those for whom one was responsible.

But policing did not merely concern the subject in his or her outward relation to the world. In his study of Neostoicism, Gerhard Oestreich shows how the extension of the power and efficiency of the central state also demanded self-discipline and the extension of the duties of the ruler and the moral education of the army, the officials, and indeed the whole people, to a life of work, frugality, dutifulness and obedience. The result was a general enhancement of social discipline in all spheres of life, and this enhancement produced, in its turn, a change in the ethos of the individual and his self-perception.[18]

In the Neostoicist writings that played a key role in the elaboration and spread of a new set of doctrines and procedures for government and administration, an explicit relationship was established between the tasks of a ruler and the tasks of each individual, between government of a territory and government of oneself. The individual was to be taught 'to control his own life by mastering his emotions and to subordinate himself politically without resistance'.[19] Oestreich argues that 'discipline ' is the central notion in understanding the connection between the rationale of political rule and the arts of self-government. As Hobbes puts it 'Man is not fitted for society by nature, but by discipline'.[20] The army was a crucial pioneer in the invention of the techniques of obedience, but the disciplining process took place in many and varied spheres: the central state machinery itself, the church, the school, the home, the factory, and economic life. In administrative, economic, moral, and spiritual spheres the same rigour prevailed. Discipline not only consists in a way of organizing social life according to rational thought, exactitude, and supervision, it also embraces a mode of personal existence within such practices. It entails a training in the minute arts of self-scrutiny, self-evaluation, and self-regulation ranging from the control of the body, speech, and movement in school, through the mental drill inculcated in school and university, to the Puritan practices of self-inspection and obedience to divine reason.

Oestreich concludes his study with a quotation from Proudhon:

> Being governed means being under police supervision, being inspected, spied upon, directed, buried under laws, regulated, hemmed in, indoctrinated, preached at, controlled, assessed, censored, commanded...noted, registered, captured, appraised, stamped, surveyed, evaluated, taxed, patented, licenced, authorized, recommended, admonished, prevented, reformed, aligned, and punished in every action, every transaction, every movement.[21]

But what he demonstrates is a much more subtle process, in which the later development of modern democracy is dependent upon the existence of certain types of subjects, who did not require a continual external policing. The external constraint of police was to be translated into an internal constraint upon the conduct of the self, the formation of subjects who were prepared to take responsibility for their actions and for whom the ethic of discipline was part of their very mental fabric.

When the nineteenth century constitutional doctrines of liberty, rights, and the rule of law proclaimed limits upon the use of state power to intervene into the lives of citizens, they presupposed an individual endowed with personal responsibilities for the social consequences of their acts and propensities for the self-regulation of conduct. The mass of detailed prescriptions and proscriptions characteristic of police was to be dismantled. But the other face of such doctrines was the construction of a web of technologies for fabricating and maintaining those very forms of social subjectivity and self-government upon which the exercise of political power was premised. The household was to be designed and cathected as an inward-looking domestic space enjoining moral and social obligations upon its inhabitants. The school was to act as a moral technology, not merely inculcating obedience, but also seeking to shape personality through the child's emulation of the teacher, through the use of pastoral techniques to encourage self-knowledge and enhance the feelings of sympathetic identification, through establishing the links between virtue, honesty, and self-denial and a purified pleasure.

One should, of course, not underestimate the use of coercive powers to enforce morality. The surveillance and normalization exercised in the factory and the discipline of wage labour certainly acted as a powerful incentive to good behaviour. Ethical modes of self-conduct were certainly enjoined forcibly upon those who lacked them through the techniques of reformation and remoralization in prison, asylum, and workhouse. But the injunction to self-government spread beyond these normalizing apparatuses. It was embedded in the civilizing projects of urban philanthropists, the establishment of museums and exhibitions, the design of shops and streets and other 'public' places where standards of dress and conduct were expected. Not only could authorities inspect and judge citizens, but parents could scrutinize and criticize children and families could evaluate each other.[22] At stake was more than the simple imposition of a moral code under the threat of punishment, more than blind obedience to an arbitrary set of doctrines. The existence of a space of regulated freedom depended upon the generalization of a set of ethical techniques for self-inspection and self-evaluation in relation to the code, a way of making the feelings, wishes, and emotions of the self visible to itself, a way in which citizens were to problematize and govern their lives and conduct, to find a way in which, as free subjects, they could live a good life as the consequence of their own character.

The forms of political rationality that took shape in the first half of this century transformed the citizen from a mere subject of legal and constitutional rights and duties into a social being whose powers and obligations were articulated in the language of social responsibilities and collective solidarities. The individual was to be integrated into society in the form of a citizen with social needs, in a contract in which individual and society would have mutual claims and obligations. This strategy, as we have seen, was embodied in such technologies of government as social security and child welfare. It was also linked to doctrines of social hygiene and mental hygiene. New modes of self-evaluation were to be inculcated in schools, supervised through the activities of health visitors, doctors, and social workers, and spread through the writings of experts. Each individual was to become an active agent in the maintenance of a healthy and efficient polity, exercising a reflexive scrutiny over personal, domestic, and familial conduct. Citizens should want to regulate their conduct and existence for their own welfare, that of their families, and that of society as a whole.

For England, the Beveridge Report of 1942 is a kind of diagram of this mentality of government. The years after World War II, as we have seen, saw the construction of a complex apparatus of welfare and security conceived in these terms. It was linked to the birth of new knowledge and technologies for conceptualizing and regulating the bonds that tied individuals into social groups in the family, the army, the factory, and the organization, and for instrumentalizing the motivations and satisfactions that social solidarities entailed. But in the late 1950s and the 1960s a fundamental shift in political rationality began to occur.

This is, perhaps, first evident in a welter of reforming legislation that reconstructed the modes of control over the moral conduct of citizens: prostitution, homosexuality, obscenity, alcohol consumption, betting and gaming, censorship in the theatre, abortion and divorce. The *Report of the Committee on Homosexual Offenses and Prostitution*, chaired by John Wolfenden, articulated a philosophical basis for this new rationality in the language of nineteenth century liberalism.[23] 'It is not,' it argued, 'the function of the law to intervene in the private lives of citizens or to seek to enforce any particular pattern of behaviour'.[24] The law 'should confine itself to those activities which offend against public order and decency or expose the ordinary citizen to what is offensive and injurious'.[25] Within this 'public' realm it was proper for the state to use its legitimate powers to enforce good order. This no longer seemed to require regulating the wishes, feelings, and morals of subjects, to demand that authorities act directly upon vices such as homosexuality or intemperance by making punishment a symbol of moral disapproval and an agent of moral re-education. Rather, the organs of government should seek only to constrain the external manifestations of morality in 'visible' conduct. A 'private' realm of personal desires and predilections was to be delineated, to be regulated by the force of public opinion, by the pressures of civil society and personal conscience, but not by the use of the coercive powers of the state.

This shift in moral regulation was certainly contested at both the philosophical and the political level. But despite the vociferous demands of the 'moral majority' in the United States and Britain, and the occasional symbolic foray into censorship of explicit sexuality, legal measures and statutory enforcement of moral codes have taken second place to the utilization of other techniques to generate the commitment of selves to values and forms of life supported by authorities. To now bring the rigours of the law to bear upon conduct requires that it can be defined by authorities as, in some way or other, a matter of 'public' order and 'public' security. No doubt the exceptional position of homosexuality, as both public and private, a personal choice and a public problem, has to do with the similarly shifting locus of the 'family' it threatens, which exists both in the private realm and as a pillar of public security.[26]

But the same forces that de-legitimate 'public' interference in 'private' life open the details of wishes, desires, and pleasures to a plethora of new regulatory forms, no less powerful for being 'decoupled' from the authoritative prescriptions of the public powers. Television, advertising, magazines, newspapers, shop windows – the signs and images of the good life were inscribed on every surface that could carry their imprint. The new technologies of citizenship formation were to gain their power through the subjective commitments to values and ways of life that were generated by the technique of choice and consumption.

The transformation in the regime for the regulation of personal conduct and standards of judgement as to behaviour has been conjoined to a more wide-ranging questioning of welfare. From all sides of the political spectrum, 'the welfare state' has been criticized, as a bureaucratic and inefficient political usurpation of private choices and freedoms, as a violation of individual rights, and as a mechanism for policing personal life and family relations. Perhaps the most explicit statement of these new forms of political rationality is neo-liberalism.[27] The theme of enterprise that is at the heart of neo-liberalism certainly has an economic reference. An economy structured in the form of relations of exchange between discrete economic units pursuing their undertakings with boldness and energy, ever seeking the new endeavour and the path to advantage, will produce the most social goods and distribute them in the manner most advantageous to each and to all. But enterprise also provides a rationale for the structuring of the lives of individual citizens. Individuals are to become, as it were, entrepreneurs of themselves, shaping their own lives through the choices they make among the forms of life available to them.[28]

Thus, in place of the themes of collective provision and social solidarity, with the rational planning of welfare and its administration through bureaucracies, are proposed notions of security provided through the private purchase of insurance schemes, health care purchased by individuals and provided by the health industry, housing offered through the private sector and occupied through private ownership, efficiency secured not through selfless dedication and commitment of professionals but through the discipline of competition for customers. Welfare and social security no longer seem vital elements in political stability and social efficiency, necessary both to ensure a healthy and motivated population and to bind individuals into the social body. The political subject is now less a social citizen with powers and obligations deriving from membership of a collective body, than an individual whose citizenship is to be manifested through the free exercise of personal choice among a variety of marketed options.

Within this new rationality of government, a space has opened within which the precise standards of conduct, routines of life, values, and aspirations of any particular family or individual can vary. To use Jacques Donzelot's metaphor, their conduct is enabled to 'float' in relation to social norms.[29] Rather than being tied rigidly into publicly espoused forms of conduct imposed through legislation or coercive intervention into personal conduct, a range of possible standards of conduct, forms of life, types of 'lifestyle' are on offer, bounded by law only at the margins. Forms of conduct are governed through a personal labour to assemble a way of life within the sphere of consumption and to incorporate a set of values from among the alternative moral codes disseminated in the world of signs and images.[30]

Consumption requires each individual to choose from among a variety of products in response to a repertoire of wants that may be shaped and legitimated by advertising and promotion but must be experienced and justified as personal desires. Entry into family life is represented as occurring out of the love that two individuals voluntarily declare for each other; remaining within marriage is a matter of decision rather than conformity to an eternally binding undertaking; having or not having children should, it appears, be a personal choice. Leisure has been invented as the domain of free choice *par excellence*. However constrained by external or internal factors, the modern self is institutionally required to construct a life through the exercise of choice from among alternatives. Every aspect of life, like every commodity, is imbued with a self-referential meaning; every choice we make is an emblem of our identity, a mark of our individuality, each is a message to ourselves and others as to the sort of person we are, each casts a glow back, illuminating the self of he or she who consumes.[31]

The self is not merely enabled to choose, but obliged to construe a life in terms of its choices, its powers, and its values. Individuals are expected to construe the course of their life as the outcome of such choices, and to account for their lives in terms of the reasons for those choices. Each of the attributes of the person is to be realized through decisions, justified in terms of motives, needs and aspirations, made intelligible to the self and others in terms of the unique but universal search to find meaning and satisfaction through the construction of a life for oneself.

It is here that the techniques of psychotherapeutics come into accordance with new political rationales for the government of conduct. They are intrinsically bound to this injunction to selfhood and the space of choices that it operates within. They are themselves predominantly distributed to individuals through free choice in a market of expertise, rather than imposed by legal or religious obligation. They are characteristically sought when individuals feel unable to bear the obligations of selfhood, or when they are anguished by them. And the rationale of psychotherapies – and this applies equally to contemporary psychiatry – is to restore to individuals the capacity to function as autonomous beings in the contractual society

227

of the self. Selves unable to operate the imperative of choice are to be restored through therapy to the status of a choosing individual. Selves who find choice meaningless and their identity constantly fading under inner and outer fragmentation are to be restored, through therapy, to unity and personal purpose. Selves dissatisfied with who they are can engage in therapeutic projects to refurbish and reshape themselves in the directions they desire. The psychotherapies provide technologies of individuality for the production and regulation of the individual who is 'free to choose'.

Chapter seventeen

Reshaping our Behaviour

> [B]ehavioural methods (behaviour therapy, behaviour modifica-
> tion, conditioning treatment) have been shown to be effective,
> quick and appropriate ... we may be able within a measurable
> time to wipe out disabling fears, obsessive–compulsive beha-
> viours, and many other serious neurotic disorders, possibly by
> sending around the country mobile treatment trucks fitted out as
> clinics, and staffed by clinical psychologists. These so-called
> 'minor' psychiatric troubles have caused much individual pain
> and sorrow; it is time an onslaught were made on them commen-
> surate with the toll they take of human happiness.[1]

Hans Eysenck, 1975

It was no mean feat to make human conduct subject to re-shaping by
science.[2] Of course, religious injunctions and rituals, codes of manners, instructions as to household duties, pedagogic techniques, and
disciplinary apparatuses had all sought to shape and direct human
conduct. But the invention of the behaviour therapies transformed
this task into a science capable of direction by psychological expertise and thus made possible a technology of the self that could be
deployed wherever human conduct needed to be channelled into
certain patterns.

Behavioural techniques have associated themselves with the
sterile atmosphere of the laboratory, the rigour of experimental
methods and advanced statistical techniques and the objectivity and
neutrality of the white-coated psychologist. Yet they have played an
important part in the extension of psycho-therapeutics to new problems and populations in the period since World War II, the diversi-
fication of therapeutic expertise, and the proliferation of sites for
the practice of psychological engineers of the human soul. As *The
Psychotherapy Handbook* puts it, 'All human behavior falls within
the domain of the behavior therapist, and practitioners of behavioral treatment are to be found among educators and special educa-

tors, psychologists, social workers, medical professionals and para-professionals in every area of human service.'[3] And, while many associate behavioural techniques with manipulation and control, their practitioners stress their potential for enhancing skills of 'self-management' and helping clients gain control of their feelings and behaviour; they see them as consonant with profoundly humanistic values.

The idea that one could transform the experimental procedures of psychology into techniques for the reformation of conduct was not itself new.[4] Both Pavlov's experiments on classical conditioning in the early years of the century and Bekhterev's work on instrumental conditioning were rapidly seen to have implications for the study and rectification of abnormal behaviour.[5] In the United States early behaviourists such as Watson and Burnham sought to explain mental disease in terms of conditioning and to draw out the lessons for mental hygiene.[6] By the 1930s the two-faced nature of this research programme was well established. On the one hand, psychologists sought to investigate neuroses and demonstrate their origins by *inducing* 'neurotic behaviour' in sheep, pigs, rats, cats, and the like.[7] On the other hand (notably in the United States, the Soviet Union and France) they carried out experimental studies showing that abnormalities of behaviour could be *removed* by the application of conditioning techniques. Tics, fears, enuresis, sexual abberations, and hysteria all seemed susceptible to this approach. They seemed not so much 'illness' as learned reflexes that could be systematically extinguished.[8]

These developments began to make possible new ways of thinking about behavioural abnormalities. The range of problems amenable to rectification was extended to all maladjustments of conduct in institutional life, especially those of children. Rectification of these problems could, it appeared, be achieved by psychologists and not only by doctors. The methods used in conceptualizing, analysing, and treating the problems owed little to the clinical gaze of medicine. Diagnosis was through psychological investigation, treatment was not in the tradition of the hospital but on the model of the psychological laboratory. And the new way of thinking had important lessons for mental hygiene – it could be spread into the home by instructing parents in principles that were much closer to the uneducated beliefs of the lay person than to the theories of the doctor.

The programme of a behaviourally inspired clinical psychology remained little more than a dream until the 1950s. But in the postwar years psychologists began to formulate general theories of the origin of neurotic behaviour that firmly rejected the explanatory moves and interpretive procedures of psychoanalysis, which had previously been regarded as the only fully fledged alternative to medical psychiatry. From such theories, in both the United States and South Africa, methods of treatment were deduced and applied in clinical work with patients.[9] In Britain a more rigorous experimental assault was being made on the prerogatives of psychiatry and psychoanalysis. The chief protagonist was Hans Eysenck.

It was during the war that Eysenck invented his novel way of rendering the human personality into thought and making it inscribable, calculable, and manageable.[10] Eysenck, who had been trained in the techniques of psychometrics by Cyril Burt, was recruited to a research post at the Mill Hill Emergency Hospital, where he sought to apply factor analysis to the investigation of the personality. We have seen, in a previous chapter, that the failure of psychologists to develop conceptual and practical tools to calibrate dimensions of the personality other than the intellect had proved a major handicap in their advancement. Wartime provided psychologists with the incentive, the status, and the population to carry out large-scale studies of normal and neurotic soldiers. And what World War I had done for the intellect, World War II was to do for the personality.

The soldiers referred to the Mill Hill Emergency Hospital were not psychotic, mentally defective, or physically ill. Indeed 'In general the "neurosis" exhibited was not so much an illness as a simple failure to adapt to army routine and discipline.'[11] Hence, immediately, the jurisdiction of medicine was placed into some doubt. But crucially, what these subjects and these conditions enabled Eysenck to do was to combine two types of psychological work that had previously been distinctly different: large-scale factorial studies of personality through questionnaires and rating scales, and small-scale experimental studies of such aspects of behaviour as persistence, suggestibility, sense of humour, levels of aspiration, perseveration, rigidity, and irritability. Thus ratings derived from the questionnaires could be checked against experimental results to enhance validity and to refine the factorization. The whole complex was presented in a simple functional schema by combining a doctrine of fundamental psychological factors derived from Burt with an analysis of conduct derived from McDougall. This held that particular acts could be grouped together into habitual responses, which themselves could be grouped into traits that could be organized into general factors of personality.

Eysenck concluded that personality could be conceptualized in terms of a two-dimensional space generated by two axes, one of which he termed 'neuroticism' and the other 'introversion–extroversion'. A third dimension of 'psychoticism' was to be added in 1952 on the basis of studies carried out when Eysenck returned to the Maudsley Hospital at the end of the war.[12] It appeared that the diagnostic categories utilized in both psychiatry and psychoanalysis were gravely misleading, falsely unifying very different things. What was significant diagnostically was the location of any individual within this space of personality, as indicated by their 'scores' on each axis. By the use of the personality inventory he devised, these scores could be ascertained by the time-honoured techniques of psychometric testing. The 'personality' of individuals, its location on these dimensions, determined the kind of behaviour disorders they were likely to develop because these locations indicated their propensities to learn from the environments and stimulii with which they came into contact. Further, personality, thus construed, was also aetiologically crucial, for it determined the kinds and extent of stress that would precipitate behavioural abnormalities.

When Aubrey Lewis persuaded the University of London to establish an Institute of Psychiatry attached to the Maudsley Hospital, and put Eysenck in charge of the Psychology Department, he now had an institutional base from which to launch his two-fold assault on psychiatry and psychoanalysis. The stake was an independent profession of clinical psychology.[13] As we have already seen, in the period between the wars the activities of psychologists in clinical settings had been severely restricted. As handmaidens to medicine, psychologists were largely confined to carrying out psychological assessments of intelligence, which psychiatrists could utilize in their diagnostic decisions. For Eysenck, despite the growth of clinical psychology in the United States, it had not escaped from this role. Clinical psychology was subordinate to psychiatry and to medical models; it carried out diagnostic testing using projective techniques; it promoted psychoanalytic psychotherapy.

In his autobiographical essay, Eysenck sums up the conclusions he came to in the early 1950s:

1. Clinical psychology can only justify itself if it applies the laws of academic psychology and the findings of experimental study to the problems of psychiatric abnormality.
2. The psychologist must be independent; if he is dependent on the psychiatrist for his bread and butter, he will inevitably take over the latter's concepts and values.
3. Psychotherapy and projection tests do not derive from psychological theory or knowledge, and there is no independent evidence for their practical usefulness; until and unless this theory or knowledge is supplied, they should not form part of the training of the clinical psychologist.
4. The logic of the above approach leads inevitably to the devel-

opment of new treatment methods of a behavioural kind, i.e. behaviour therapy.[14]

The attack was to be mounted on two fronts: against the medical hegemony jealously guarded by psychiatrists and the psycho-therapeutic hegemony protected by psychoanalysts. Behaviour therapy would compete with psychoanalysis at the level of its diagnostic techniques, theoretical codes, and treatment modalities. Thus psychoanalysis was to be discredited at all three levels. Dynamically inspired tests of personality, like the Rorschach and the Thematic Apperception tests, were subjected to withering indictment. It was claimed that what was good in psychoanalytic theory was incorporated into learning theory, especially the motivating role of anxiety, while what was not incorporated into learning theory was no good – the speculative notions concerning the depths of the psyche which were not amenable to scientific specification. As far as therapy was concerned, the application of the rules of scientific experimentation soon showed that the claims of psychoanalysis to efficacy were unfounded.

But behaviour therapy would also compete with psychiatry. Hence Eysenck set out to show that psychiatry itself was in an unhealthy state, running together approaches to problems of completely different orders. On the one hand there was a properly medical part of psychiatry, that which dealt with the effects of tumours, lesions, and other physical conditions through physical and pharmacological treatment: this part of psychiatry was, in reality, so closely related to neurology that its existence as a distinct speciality was rather unjustified. On the other hand, a great proportion of the problems currently addressed by psychiatrists were not, in fact, diseases. Not only were no organic correlates of such disorders currently recognized, but they were not 'symptoms' of 'underlying disorders' at all. Neurotic disorders, personality disorders, and many types of criminal conduct were not 'illnesses' but problems of behaviour acquired in large part by the processes of learning, unlearning, or failure to learn. Psychiatry was inappropriate to treat such problems, for the processes involved were outside the scope of medical training and did not require the sophisticated and expensive clinical skills of the doctor. Further, psychiatry only laid itself open to ethical reproaches by incorporating such problems, which might be undesirable and antisocial but were not sick, within its domain. Here, then, was the scientific and moral space for a new expertise, the profession of clinical psychology.[15]

Behaviour therapy brought together four elements. There was a psychological conception of personality as consisting in a small number of dimensions assessable through the application of psychometric techniques. There was a theory of personality development through the cumulative building up of responses learned through the effects of conditioning upon the inherent susceptibilities of the individual. There was a theory of neurotic symptoms as patterns of behaviour learned in the normal way but, for some reason or another, maladaptive. And there was a normalizing technique based upon the principle that the processes of conditioning and deconditioning could be systematically exploited to re-socialize behaviour into patterns deemed adaptive.

Notwithstanding Eysenck's argument that susceptibility to behavioural problems could be understood in terms of individual physiological differences in conditionability, what had been produced was a way of understanding and treating conduct that did not require reference to hidden depths of the soul. It remained at the level of the problem itself – the discrepancy between the behaviour produced and the behaviour desired. But as important, it was an analysis that did not require reference to organic malfunction, for we were not dealing with illness but with the contingent mis-shaping of a psychology that was not sick, by means of processes that were themselves normal. Hence psychologists could make a claim to clinical expertise that was apparently neither a threat to nor subordinate to medicine. No longer would it be confined to administering a battery of tests to each patient, to answer the questions of a psychiatrist who knew little of psychology or of the skills of the psychologist. Behaviour therapy would allow psychologists themselves to have a say in the questions, and to claim exclusive capacities to carry out treatment. As Yates puts it:

> If the experimental method, involving as strict objectivity as possible, and the formulation of meaningful questions derived from knowledge of general psychology could be applied to the elucidation of the basic causal factors underlying abnormalities of function manifested by a single case, then it very soon became obvious that the same techniques could be applied to the *treatment* of the disorder.[16]

While clinical psychologists launched a frontal assault upon psychoanalysis, they sought to claim a corner of the market in psychopathology without explicitly challenging the jurisdiction of psychiatrists over medical matters. Behaviour therapy required, in its pristine form, not the techniques of the bedside but those of the laboratory and the skilled research worker. Of course, neither psychoanalysts nor psychiatrists took too kindly to this point of view. Analysts questioned the ethics and humanity of behavioural techniques and those of their practitioners. They cast doubt on the claims made for the success of the method, pointing to the inevitability of symptom substitution and relapse if the fundamental psychic origins of distress were not addressed, and they suggested that where behaviour therapy did work it was probably because the practitioners were carrying out a form of psychoanalytic psychotherapy without admitting it.[17]

Psychoanalysis itself had yet to establish any significant foothold within the system of official psychiatry in Britain; hence the response of psychiatrists was more important. They certainly defended their territory, insisting that all clinical treatment had to be under the direction of a medically trained professional, for only this would ensure that all possible organic disorders and diseases were properly diagnosed and treated. But beneath the troubled surface of dispute, a practical division of labour was gradually established within the psychiatric institutions.[18] Psychiatric diagnosis was initially necessary to rule out underlying organic pathology. One certainly should resist the temptation to reduce all mental disorders to mere psychological malformations of personality. But within these constraints, under medical guidance, given a tightly specified problem and a desired end state, clinical psychologists were let loose upon an aggregation of somewhat marginal categories that had now found some kind of home within the psychiatric apparatus. Alcoholics, anorexics, bulimics, phobics, obsessives, and the anxious could now have their behaviour managed back to normality through an expertly designed programme employing the systematic use of sanctions and rewards.

A variety of techniques were invented to render human conduct amenable to reshaping.[19] There was classical aversive conditioning, in which the undesirable behaviour was elicited in the patient and accompanied by some nasty experience induced by drugs, shock, or paralysis. This appeared particularly suitable for fetishism, transvestitism, homosexuality, alcoholism, sadistic fantasies, voyeurism, smoking, gambling, and alcoholism. There were the classical procedures of operant conditioning, in which behaviour that tended in the desired direction was 'rewarded' while that which was undesirable was either ignored or resulted in some 'negative reinforcement'. These techniques seemed hopeful for eliminating undesirable behaviour in children such as temper tantrums, head bumping, thumb sucking, rebelliousness, isolate behaviour, regressed crawling, hyperactivity, and the like. Additionally, there were the techniques that derived from the work of Wolpe. Systematic desensitization sought to eliminate fears, anxieties, and phobias by eliciting them in the presence of a response that was the opposite of anxiety. The subject would be placed in a series of situations, each one more anxiety producing than the last, but made to relax by using techniques previously taught or by hypnosis or drugs. Since it was often difficult to reproduce the anxiety-producing situation in the laboratory, the real situation could be replaced by the subject's imagination of the situation. Here was a technique that allowed plentiful opportunities for extension and generalization; indeed it can be used to enhance positive feelings of self-esteem, pride, and affection almost as easily as it can be applied to eliminate the negative.

A single conceptual and practical space had been established for the explanation and reformation of all abnormalities of behaviour. It was to prove an ideal mechanism for grasping in thought all those irritating and maladaptive difficulties of adjustment and antisocial behaviours that were troubling to parents, teachers, or the authorities. In the form of 'contingency management', operant conditioning could provide a set of more or less rigorously applied instructions for the organization of institutional regimes for obsessionals, anorexics, delinquents, defectives, and chronic schizophrenics, 'rewarding' desirable forms of behaviour with anything from love to food, withholding or reducing rewards for undesirable behaviour rather than reinforcing it by attention.[20] In their most systematic form of 'token economies', institutionally desired behaviour is made translatable into a universal reward of tokens, points, or money, which can be exchanged for those things that the subject considers desirable.[21] In the form of 'milieu therapy' the rationale of behaviour therapy merges with that of the therapeutic community, as the principles of reward and punishment become integrated into the very fabric of the institution, such that all aspects of the environment of the patient or inmate – from timetabling to interactions with the cleaning staff – are instrumentalized according to the calculus of reinforcement.[22] In factories, schools, and the home, indeed anywhere where those in authority seek to channel the conduct of those subject to them, these technologies offer themselves as rational solutions.[23]

Many critics see behaviourist theory and behaviour therapy as the paradigm of a psychology of social adaptation, concerned only with the overt conduct of individuals rather than with their subjective experiences and motivations, promising to shape this conduct towards ends required by power. Behaviour therapy thus symbolizes the vocation of psychology as an administrative discipline, allowing the powerful to manipulate the powerless in the interests of social control, building the domination of subjectivity into its theoretical fabric and its technical approach. Certainly authorities can and do openly use behavioural techniques for the manipulation of behaviour in institutions of various types. But to take exception to this 'hard' end of behavioural techniques would be to miss the point. For these ways of thinking and acting have gained a much broader purchase upon our reality. From giving up smoking to the management of anxiety, from sex therapy to assertion training, from reformation of the kleptomaniac to cognitive restructuring to change values, from prison workshops to management training courses, indeed wherever particular forms of human conduct can be specified and are desired, behavioural techniques may be deployed. These techniques are implicated in the expansion and reshaping of psychotherapies far beyond the psychiatry of mental illness, to provide a way of promoting the capacity to cope in accordance with social norms among new sectors of the population and in new institutional sites.

The name given to this new field of application is 'self-control': 'the systematic management of environmental circumstances and response-contingent reinforcements by the clients themselves'.[24] Self-control might sound like a reactivation of old moral nostrums, and to some extent it is. But the difference is that it is not merely a matter of 'will-power' but of the systematic management of one's natural and social environment ('stimulus situations') in order to transform the likelihood of pleasurable concomitants of particular types of conduct ('response contingencies'). The therapist instructs the 'client' in the rationale of the technique, but, more important, educates him or her in the means of self-inspection to be used: systematic self-monitoring and record keeping, showing the occasions on which desired and undesired behaviour occur, and the construction of a detailed plan programme for transforming conduct, not through airy and overambitious hopes, but through little steps, with achievable goals, each followed by rewards.

Behaviour modification, once the *bête noire* of progressives, thus becomes consonant with the liberating theologies of self assertion. It is easily transformed into a technique of self-analysis and self-help, a therapy of normality to enable us all to cope with stress, anxiety or demanding social situations, into a pathway to asserting ourselves. It is thus entirely consonant with a secular ethic of the technical perfection of lifestyle by the autonomous and responsible self. For it now becomes possible to think of all forms of social behaviour, successful and unsuccessful, not as expressions of some inner quality of the soul, but as learned techniques or social skills. And what is learned can be re-learned.

On the back cover of Linehan and Egan's pocket book of advice *Asserting Yourself*, we are informed:

> Very few of us are social all-rounders – some of us are good at getting what we want, others better at making and keeping

friends. Yet social skills are not innate; they are learned, just as car driving or tennis playing is learned.[25]

And the book aims to provide techniques of self-analysis and self-help for the 'one in ten normal adults who feels significantly hampered by some aspect of his or her social behaviour'.[26] It is for those who can't make friends, can't get on at parties, can't make sexual relationships, make lousy lovers, don't get on at work, are unable to say no, can't tell jokes, or generally feel miserable about some aspect of their life.

The authors, both clinical psychologists, are quite clear about their programme: 'an "educational" and "skills" model of human problems is taking over from a "disease" and "treatment" model', which means that the therapist's job is seen more often now as the teaching of new skills rather than the removal of not very well defined 'illnesses'.[27] This 'makes virtually all of us candidates for therapeutic intervention', though we should not all rush for professional help: 'psychologists have devised many techniques which people can put into practice by themselves in order to change their behaviour'. Even when professional help is needed, one of its first tasks is to help individuals 'come to a belief in their own ability to make changes in themselves and their lives'. Therapy is no attempt to enforce conformity but apparently part of a profoundly emancipatory project of learning to be a self.

Life has become a skilled performance.[28] You can learn to be socially sensitive by recognizing the signs by which others indicate such feelings as anxiety, interest, and boredom and by recognizing and adjusting the signs that you yourself give off through eye contact, body language, proximity, and the like. You can learn self-regulation, combining an awareness of the messages from others with a monitoring and adjustment of the messages you give off yourself in your choices of language and behaviour. You can learn how to manage social situations by combining self-regulation with previous imaginary rehearsal of the situation, anticipation of problems, and conscious preparation of the ways of handling them. You can learn to relax through behavioural techniques. You can learn the behavioural and conversational codes and techniques that psychologists have shown to succeed in influencing others and in resisting influence oneself. You can learn the arts of relationships, to show others you like them, to recognize when they like you, and to sequence the interchange of glances, words, and acts. You can learn to respect yourself.

The liberatory and democratic aspirations of these progressive behaviourist technologies for the reshaping of ourselves seem to speak for themselves. Their promises of self-assertion and self-control offer each of us access to those qualities that have ensured the success of those we envy. But these progressive principles are double edged. They institute, as the other side of their promise of autonomy and success, a constant self doubt, a constant scrutiny and evaluation of how one performs, the construction of one's personal part in social existence as something to be calibrated and judged in its minute particulars. Even pleasure has become a form of work to be accomplished with the aid of professional expertise and under the aegis of scientifically codified knowledge. The self becomes the target of a reflexive objectifying gaze, committed not only to its own technical perfection but also to the belief that 'success' and 'failure' should be construed in the vocabulary of happiness, wealth, style, and fulfilment and interpreted as consequent upon the self-managing capacities of the self.

The codification of the arts of existence as social skills, the development of a psycho-pedagogy of social competence, extends the rule of the norm by means of the power of the image. Life is to imitate the images of life, the simulacra of joy, warmth, and achievement presented in advertisements, television chat shows, soap operas and other public imaginings of personality, conviviality, and winning ways. These images provide the template against which the mundane dissatisfactions of our lives, the hesitancies and uncertainties of our speech, the embarrassed awkwardness of our intercourse with others, the clumsy fumblings of our loves and passions are to be judged and found wanting, According to this meta-world of images and values, more luminous and real than any other world we know, the self is to be reshaped, remodelled so that it can succeed in emitting the signs of a skilled performance. And of this continuous performance of our lives, we each are, ourselves, to be the sternest and most constant critic.

Chapter eighteen

Technologies of Autonomy

> Once the inner freedom to be truly herself was added to the outer freedom of running her own life as she saw fit, which she had gained during her years of analysis, she no longer needed the help of an analyst...she has become a stranger to her analyst, but not a stranger to psychoanalysis. Psychoanalysis...will remain with her all her life.[1]

Bruno Bettelheim, 1983

Western man, Michel Foucault argued, has become a confessing animal. The truthful rendering into speech of who one is, to one's parents, one's teachers, one's doctor, one's lover, and oneself, is installed at the heart of contemporary procedures of individualization.[2]

In confessing, one is subjectified by another, for one confesses in the actual or imagined presence of a figure who prescribes the form of the confession, the words and rituals through which it should be made, who appreciates, judges, consoles, or understands. But in confessing, one also constitutes oneself. In the act of speaking, through the obligation to produce words that are true to an inner reality, through the self-examination that precedes and accompanies speech, one becomes a subject for oneself.

Confession, then, is the diagram of a certain form of subjectification that binds us to others at the very moment we affirm our identity. It is tempting to derive from such an analysis the conclusion that confessional mechanisms that have spread through modern medicine, social work and psychiatry, far from representing an enlightened approach to the whole person are, at root, an extension of discipline and professional control over life itself.[3] In compelling, persuading and inciting subjects to disclose themselves, finer and more intimate regions of personal and interpersonal life come under surveillance and are opened up for expert judgement, and normative evaluation, for classification and correction. In the name of the recognition of the subjectivity of the client or patient, a more profound subjection is produced.

Perhaps. But the confessional and the other self-regulating techniques of psychotherapeutics should be seen as inhabiting the space formed by the intersection of disciplinary mechanisms with another dimension of subjectification. This concerns the different ways in which humans have been urged and incited to become ethical beings, beings who define and regulate themselves according to a moral code, establish precepts for conducting and judging their lives, and reject or accept certain moral goals for themselves. As Foucault has pointed out, there is no way of living as an ethical subject except through certain modes of subjectification, involving the monitoring, testing, and improving of the self.[4]

An account of these practices of the self might be organized in a rough threefold division.[5] There would, first, be the *moral codes*, the languages they use, the ethical territory they map out, the attributes of the person that they identify as of ethical significance, the ways of calibrating and evaluating them they propose, the pitfalls to be avoided and the goals to pursue. Second, there would be the *ethical scenarios*, the apparatuses and contexts in which the moral codes are administered and the means by which they are enjoined – in the school and the courts, in the practices of social work and medicine, in the private consultation, in the radio phone-in, in the solitary act of reading or viewing. Third, there would be the *techniques of the self*, the 'models proposed for setting up and developing relationships with the self, for self-reflection, self-knowledge, self-examination, for the deciphering of the self by oneself, for the transformation one seeks to accomplish with oneself as object'.[6]

Of course, the moral codifications embodied in psychotherapeutics are far from systematic and homogeneous. But the territory of morality for psychotherapy is nonetheless marked out by a limited set of terms: the need to work on the self to improve the quality of life, the achievement of autonomy, the release of potentiality, the opposition of a restricting dependency to a liberating freedom. Freud, it will be recalled, advertised psychoanalysis thus: 'You will be able to convince yourself', he wrote to an imaginary patient, 'that much will be gained if we succeed in transforming hysterical misery into common unhappiness. With a mental life that has been restored to health you will be better armed against that unhappiness.'[7] His successors formulate their goals very differently. Life training may be exceptional in its claim that one can change one's life in only 39 hours. It 'undertakes' that a 'learning experience' lasting from 6 pm on Friday until midnight on Sunday will 'radically enhance your ability to transform the quality of everything in your life', and all for only £140.[8] But it is only the *reductio ad absurdum* of a moral system within which contemporary psycho-therapeutics finds its meaning.

The London Centre for Psychotherapy points out that psychotherapy takes time. Yet it offers the possibility of great rewards: 'far more fulfilling relationships and greater self expression. Family and social life, sexual partnerships and work are all likely to benefit.'[9]

The British Association of Psychotherapists warns the novitiate that 'psychotherapy often means hard work and emotional stress for the patient', but its aim is to promote 'the patient's self-understanding and capacity to view the world objectively and less coloured by personal wishes, fear and prejudice'.[10] The professional advocates of behavioural psychotherapy hold only that 'the client's "symptoms" can be regarded as discrete psychological entities which can be removed or altered by direct means'.[11] But the modesty of the promise held out to this client is rather diminished by the generalization of 'therapy' to include such diverse 'symptoms' as sexual orientation, anxiety, lack of assertiveness, the wish to increase self-control of alcohol, food, smoking, and other bad habits, and the elimination of unwanted thoughts. And by the addition of such therapeutic goals as 'greater self awareness', which should not only 'facilitate the change process but should lead the client to reappraise his life style', and result in 'the development of problem-solving skills' and increasing 'overall perceived self-efficacy'.[12]

Carl Rogers' 'client-centred therapy' is clear about its ethical theme: 'To Be That Self Which One Truly Is'.[13] Hence its task is to enable its clients to change away from facades, from the constant preoccupation with keeping up appearances, from an internalized sense of duty springing from externally imposed obligations, from the constant attempt to live up to the expectations of others. In the place of such unwanted burdens, the client may hope to change towards valuing honesty and 'realness', the capacity to direct one's own life, accepting and valuing one's self and feelings, valuing the experience of the moment, a greater respect for and understanding of others, a cherishing of close relationships, a longing for more intimacy, a willingness to risk being open to all inner or outer experiences. The goal of therapy is nothing less than 'the fully functioning person', on whom the survival of the species may well depend.[14]

The moral codes of the less 'respectable' forms of therapy are equally clear. Frederick Perls, inventor of Gestalt therapy, proclaims the Gestalt outlook to be 'the original, undistorted, natural approach to life' through which each individual can 'heal the dualism of his person', recover 'his Wholeness, his Integrity', grow, mature, develop his 'self' – nothing less than 'a small contribution to that problem which might contain the possibility of the survival of mankind'.[15] Art Janov, originator of primal therapy, claims,

> There is a state of being quite different from what we have conceived: a tensionless, defense-free life in which one is completely his own self and experiences deep feeling and internal unity. This is the state of being that can be achieved through Primal Therapy. People become themselves and *stay* themselves.[16]

Become whole, become what you want, become yourself. Thomas Harris, in his 'practical guide' to the system of transactional analysis invented by Eric Berne, proclaims it to have

> given a new answer to people who want to change rather than to adjust, to people who want transformation rather than conformation ... it is enabling persons to change, to establish self-control and self-direction, and to discover the reality of freedom of choice.[17]

The autonomous self, freed from the burden of the past, can say, I'm OK *and* you're OK.

The therapies of the body offer the same hope of wholeness, self-possession, and pleasure. For Alexander Lowen, bioenergetics is 'a therapeutic technique to help a person get back together with his body and to help him enjoy to the fullest degree possible the life of the body' – breathing, moving, feeling, self-expression, and sexuality. Bioenergetics is an 'adventure of self-discovery' that has no less a goal than 'to help people regain their primary nature, which is the condition of being free, the state of being graceful and the quality of being beautiful'.[18]

Man, it would appear, is born free but everywhere lives in psychic chains. But the chains can be released, and with them the original state of grace, potential, love, freedom, and pleasure can be regained through a pilgrimage of the soul. The soul no longer journeys through the arduous rituals of religious meditation, the imitation of the sufferings of Christ, and the contemplation of the goodness of God to truth and salvation. The autonomous self will discover itself in the passage through the therapeutic.

What of the ethical scenarios for the deployment of psychotherapy? We have already become aware of the diversity of apparatuses and contexts within which encounters may take a therapeutic form: not merely the private consulting room or the visit to the counsellor for advice on problems of birth, marriage and death, but also the doctor's surgery, the consultation with a medical specialist, the social worker's visit, the ward group of the psychiatric hospital, the interview with the personnel officer, the radio phone-in. The practitioners of psychotherapy have succeeded in colonizing the professions with their own vocabularies, images, evaluations, and techniques, and in extending and increasing the sites for the operation of therapeutic encounters. But they have not simply occupied existing sites and problems; rather, a new set of problematizations has been born, new ways of reordering the experiences of living such that new issues and possibilities are transposed into the field of scientific knowledge and therapeutic rectification. They do not replace those older strategic objects around which the therapeutic activity had been deployed – the hysterical woman, the dangerous or endangered child, the pervert, the malfunctioning conjugal couple – but situate them within a wider field in which they appear both exemplary and exceptional. Without seeking to be exhaustive, four new strategic dimensions of the psychotherapeutic suggest themselves.[19]

A *subjectification of work*, involving the saturation of the working body with feelings, emotions, and wishes, the transformation of work, mental and manual, into matters of personal fulfilment and psychical identity, in which the financial exchange is significant less for the cash reward it offers than for the identity it confers upon the recipient. Hence the emergence of an entire discourse upon success and failure in jobs and careers, upon the costs and benefits of employment and unemployment, conducted in therapeutic rather than economic terms, and the correlative extension of the therapist into the organization of work, and of problems of work into the field of concerns of all therapeutic activity.[20]

A *psychologization of the mundane*, involving the translation of exigencies from debt, through house purchase, childbirth, marriage, and divorce into 'life events', problems of coping and adjustment, in which each is to be addressed by recognizing it as, at root, the space in which are played out forces and determinants of a subjective order (fears, denials, repressions, lack of psycho-social skills) and whose consequences are similarly subjective (neurosis, tension, stress, illness). Such events become the site of a practice that is normalizing, in that it establishes certain canons of living according to which failures may be evaluated. It is clinical in that it entails forensic work to identify signs and symptoms and interpretive work to link them to that hidden realm that generates them. It is pedagogic in that it seeks to educate the subject in the arts of coping. It is subjectifying in that the quotidian affairs of life become the occasion for confession, for introspection, for the internal assumption of responsibility.

A *therapeutics of finitude*, in which grief, frustration, and disappointment at the limits of life, the tragedies of passion and the omnipresence of death are reposed as issues of pathology and normality, or rather of the points of manifestation of pathological possibilities and healing potentials hidden within each normal person. Bereavement counsellors are just the most evident of those who cluster around events from the death of a loved one to the failure of a relationship, from the illness of a child to the diagnosis of a fatal disease. These become at one and the same time dangerous nodes and therapeutic opportunities. They are dangerous because around them might form problems from delinquency and antisocial behaviour, through personal and interpersonal destructiveness and failures of coping, to frank psychiatric disorder. But they are also opportunities for personal growth. In coming to terms with sadness, that is to say, in passing one's sadness through the experience of counselling or therapy, one can learn to make a new life or a good death. Finitude, through therapy, becomes a means to the discovery of the self, part of the work of life itself.

A neuroticization of social intercourse, in which our 'relationships' with lovers, friends, and colleagues are discovered as key functional elements in both our personal happiness and our social efficacy. All kinds of social ills, from damaged children to ill health, disruption at work and frustration at home, come to be understood as emanating from remediable incapacities in our 'interactions' with others. Such incapacities are themselves re-construed as the repetition of patterns engendered in the intercourse between parents and children or the consequence of other disturbances in the interpersonal domain. Therapists will take charge of this domain of the interpersonal, knowing its laws, diagnosing its ills, prescribing the ways to conduct ourselves with others that are virtuous because they are both fulfilling and healthy; in a reverse movement, the language of relationships will come to define our very conceptions of ourselves.

In each of these fields, and others that could be identified, what is at stake is a reciprocal relationship between the elaboration of a body of knowledge and practice and the production of the self itself, as the terrain upon which our relations with one another and with our bodies, habits, propensities, and pleasures is to be understood. No doubt one would be wise not to overstate the constitutive powers of psychotherapeutic discourse and practice. Their potency derives from their confluence with a whole political rationality and governmental technology of the self. But none the less it is important to recognize what is at issue in these therapeutic technologies of knowledge and power – no longer sex, not even pathology, but our autonomous selves.

Each therapeutic system and each therapeutic context has its own particularity. But what unites them is the calculated attempt to bring the subject from one way of acting and being to another. One could imagine a study of these technologies, which have been little examined, analyses tending to rely upon the programmatic representations contained in textbooks and case histories.[21] An arrangement of spaces and gazes – the psychoanalytic couch is only the most emblematic of these, in which the subject speaks only to an empty space filled with their own images, while the therapist inhabits another space, both more real because it is actual, and more fantastic, because it is merely the repository of the transference. But there are many other spatial technologies of therapy, from the frank and accepting reciprocal gaze of humanistic therapies, from Guntrip to Rogers, in which the subject is interpellated as a worthwhile person, to the circle of chairs in the therapeutic group, which constitute the subject as one responsible to its self because it is responsible to others, incorporating each person, apparently equally, into a democratic field of confession and judgement by all.

There is a technology of voices, a way of eliciting confession and responding to it through sequences of words and gestures often formulaic and specific to particular systems. The interpretive tropes of psychoanalysis, the encouraging 'M-hm' of 'non-directive therapy', the reflection back of the speaker's own words by the voice of the therapist with the implication, 'I understand that; I accept you'. To speak in the therapeutic encounter is to place one's words within a whole scientific field. The voice is the means of investigation and diagnosis. Through it a codification is reached, albeit by only one party to the interchange, of the nature of the problem and the possibility of its resolution. The voice speaks in a room filled with the murmurings of all those other voices that have spoken in the training of the therapist and in the case histories that have been studied; it finds its place in a web of words and phrases that provide the conditions for its re interpretation as a sign. Speech, by virtue of its location in this technology, becomes a therapeutic activity. No doubt it always does us good to 'get it off our chest', but never so much as in an encounter defined as one that will make us better and taking place within the powerful ambit of a tradition, an authority, a history of cases and cures.

And there is a technology of transformation, methods of persuasion or constraint – judicial, quasi-judicial, clinical, pedagogic – by which the subject is brought from one state to another. In the subtle communicative interaction of the confessional scene, the expert gently brings the subject into a relation with a new image, an image that appears more compelling because it is their own. Subjects come to identify themselves with the kind of self they are brought to display in their speech and conduct in the therapeutic scenario, to take responsibility for themselves as ideally that kind of person, to be impelled by the pleasures and anxieties in the gaps beween themselves and what they might be. They become, in the passage through therapy, attached to the version of themselves they have been led to produce.

It would be misleading to confer a spurious unity upon the heterogeneous mechanisms of persuasion. There are 'coercive interpretations' that render the utterances and observations of the subject in such a way as to enjoin agreement, calling into play 'transcendent' images of normality, family life, sexuality, caring, love for children, and personal responsibility for the normalized moral discourses of everyday life that the subject would have to be sick or pathological to reject; these seem most prevalent in medicine, social work, and work with parents and children.[22] There are 'narrativizations', most evident in analytic therapy, in which the therapist seeks to reassemble the fragments of utterances into a coherent story of a life with a sequence, a logic, causes and effects, decisions and outcomes, a story that reveals the subject neither as an accidental participant in a jumbled series of random events, an innocent bystander, or an extra in someone else's script, but as both author and actor of their own life.[23] These and other mechanisms of persuasion occupy a relay point between the scenario of therapy and the techniques of the self. Their aim is to reach out beyond the therapeutic encounter, to transform the subject through installing a permanent hermeneutics of the self. The therapeutic subject is destined to leave therapy and live their life; but the self-techniques of therapy are to accompany them always.

To interrogate the psychotherapeutic at the level of the techniques of the self that it provides is to become aware of its inventiveness, of the diversity of the procedures it has invented by means of which individuals, with the aid of experts, can act upon their bodies, their emotions, their beliefs, and their forms of conduct in order to transform themselves, in order to achieve autonomous selfhood.[24] There are techniques for examining and evaluating the self: modes of self-inspection, vocabularies for self-description, ways of rendering the self into thought. These entail attending to different aspects of the self – thoughts, feelings, posture, tone of voice – ways of marking differences and making them notable. They entail ways of disclosing the self speaking in the consulting room or the group, keeping diaries, expressing inner states through action, drama, painting, and the like. They involve different modes of engaging with the self – an epistemological mode, for example, which searches for past determinants of present states, or an interpretive mode, in which the word or act is supplemented with an account of its significance in relation to the therapist. They involve education of the subject in the languages for evaluating the self, diagnosing its ills, calibrating its failings and its advances. And they involve techniques for the curing of the self, through the purgative effects of catharsis, the liberating effect of understanding, the restructuring effect of interpretation, the retraining of thoughts and emotions.

The texts of psychotherapy give us some access to these practices, for each is a kind of instructional manual in the techniques of the self. In addition to those discussed above, we can roughly separate out three further procedures: methods of awareness, whose principle tool is the experiment on the self; algorithms of interaction, which work by making human relations calculable; narratives of feeling, which instruct us through the mechanisms of identification. Three examples will illustrate these different, but often interlocking, procedures for making the self thinkable and manageable.

Frederick Perls' *Gestalt Therapy* proceeds through a series of experiments to help reorganize our behaviour and our awareness of that behaviour.[25] They begin with the simple ones to help us 'contact the environment', for example: 'Make up sentences about what you are immediately aware of. Begin them with "now" or "at this moment" or "here and now"' (p. 44). After each a set of instructions for interpretation follow, educating us in how to make sense of the significance of our experience, and a set of little narratives of the experiences of others together with interpretations. Gradually we proceed to an awareness of our body: 'Concentrate on your "body" sensation as a whole. Let your attention wander through every part of your body. How much of yourself can you feel?' (p. 100). Thence to an awareness of emotion: 'Visit a gallery of paintings, preferably of wide variety. What emotion, however faint, does it stir in you? If a storm is depicted, do you feel in yourself a corresponding turbulence?' (p. 119). We learn how to verbalize healthily and get rid of the pathological aspects: 'Listen to your own production of words in company .... The more your concept of yourself differs from your actual personality, the more unwilling you will be to recognize your voice as your own.... Notice the modulation of your internal voice. Is it angry, wailing, complaining, bombastic?' (p. 125).

Now we can be taught to direct the awareness of which we have now become aware, for example, to change anxiety into excitement. Having learned these techniques of self-examination and self-reflection, we can learn to manipulate and work upon ourselves, despite the discomfort that it may cause. We can become aware of, and redirect, our 'retroflections': 'When a person retroflects behaviour, he does to himself what originally he tried to do to other persons or objects.... To the extent that he does this, he splits his personality into "doer" and "done to"'(p. 171). We can learn to recognize and assimilate our 'introjections': 'a way of acting, feeling, evaluating – which you have taken into your system of behaviour, but which you have not assimilated in such a fashion as to make it a genuine part of your organism' (p. 222). And we can learn to interpret and overcome our 'projections': 'the projector, unaware for instance that he is rejecting others, believes that they are rejecting him; or unaware of his tendencies to approach others sexually, feels that they make sexual approaches to him' (p. 248).

Thus we can master the mental technology of creative adjustment. Gestalt therapy provides a set of detailed techniques for self government by which we can open up the hidden roots of our behaviour to ourselves and hence render our selves transformable, in order that we may 'live more freely and fully in the Here and Now' (Frontispiece).

But techniques of self-government are not simply 'individualistic', if that implies a concentration on the sovereign, isolated ego. Steering ourself through the world involves shaping our relations with others. Hence, perhaps, the popularity of Eric Berne's *Games People Play* (600,000 copies sold in paperback alone, according to the publisher's blurb), for it provides a set of algorithms for representing pathological *interactions*, and a variety of techniques for reforming them.[26] Instruction begins with a simple representation of the psyche and its relations with others. Each individual, we are told, exhibits three types of 'ego states' in social relations, those that 'resemble parental figures', those that are 'autonomously directed towards objective appraisal of reality', and those that 'represent archaic relics, still-active ego states which were fixated in early childhood'(p. 23). If that seems complicated, we can just term them Parent, Adult, and Child, and represent the psyche in a simple diagram: three circles, one on top of the other, labelled with the three states. Thus any interaction between two individuals can be analyzed in terms of whether it is Parent–Child, Adult–Adult, Adult–Child, and so forth, not in terms of the actual participants, of course, but in terms of the psychic participants. This is a versatile inscription device for representing interactions. We put the two sets of circles next to each other and draw lines between them to show what is relating to what. Since any social interaction may involve more than one level, the picture becomes more complicated but still intelligible. Through this algorithm of encounters we can learn to recognize when it is their 'Child' speaking, or our 'Parent', we can pick up crossed lines and their consequences. In short, we have been taught a new way of seeing.

But more significant is the formulation of a language of games to characterize pathological interactions. For transactions between individuals occur in programmed forms. There are 'rituals', stereotyped, simple, complementary transactions that do not convey information but give 'strokes' to the participants, according to a social logic, which prevent offence or, rather, prevent one's spinal cord shrivelling up (p. 35). There are 'pastimes' that are semi-ritualistic, simple, complementary transactions whose primary object is to structure a period of time: for example 'General Motors' (comparing cars), 'How Much' (does it cost), or Ever Been (to some nostalgic place). These can occur in various forms – Adult–Child, Parent–Adult and so forth – and are utilized in different circumstances according to age, sex, and situation; they fulfil various important social functions like selecting friends or stabilizing positions. And there are 'games'.

'A game is an ongoing series of complementary ulterior transactions progressing to a well-defined, predictable outcome'(p. 44). But what makes it a game is that it is dishonest, it involves a catch or a snare, and it has a payoff. Berne provides us with a complete and classified repertoire of all the games that he and his associates have discovered. There are 'Life Games, Marital Games, Party Games, Sexual Games and Underworld Games', and there are some games that professionals play, such as 'Consulting Room Games'. Each category of games is further subdivided, thus among the Life Games are Alcoholic, Debtor, Kick Me, Now I've Got You, You Son of a Bitch, and See What You Made Me Do. For each game we are provided with a thesis, an aim, a set of roles, an account of the predictable dynamics, a fictional narrative of a scenario involving husband and wife or host and guests, which we are encouraged to recognize and confirm from our own experience, and an account of the advantages which it confers on the principal and other participants. We are also provided with a recipe for forestalling it, and short-circuiting it, bringing the gaming to awareness and hence making it redundant.

The colloquial designations, the simple examples, the dissection of recognizable moves: all these provide a means of rendering our own experiences in social transactions into thought and making them amenable to management. The aim of the game analysis is to render the games conscious and to disperse them, to enable the attainment of autonomy, release or recover three capacities. Awareness is the capacity to 'hear the birds sing in one's own way, and not in the way one was taught,' to live 'in the here and now' (p. 158). Spontaneity is the freedom to choose... liberation from the compulsion to play games and have only the feelings one was taught to have' (p. 160). Intimacy is 'the spontaneous, game-free candidness of an aware person' (p. 160).

If one technique of the self involves instruction in the procedures for self-awareness, and a second operates by providing algorithms that make the self visible as it engages in transactions with other selves, a third works through inciting us to identify with narratives of needs and dependencies in relationships. For example, Luise Eichenbaum and Susie Orbach's *What do Women Want* ('This book will change lives': *Women's World*) proceeds through a series of small vignettes, tales of relationships gone wrong, presented in the cloying language of romantic novels.[27] We are informed of the theme that should guide our studies of our lives at the outset. Our lives are about 'relationships' and 'what makes women and men tick is not really so different. We will show that what makes it so hard for them to relate satisfactorily is a deep confusion and misunderstanding over the dependency needs of themselves and each other'(p. 15). The text begins by providing us with the language through which we are to make our failures and successes in life intelligible. Dependency is 'a basic human need' (p. 16). But this does not mean that the ethics of this text are against autonomy. Immediately, we are re-assured:

> Psychological development theorists and psychotherapeutic practitioners know that achieving autonomy and independence rests on the *gratification* of dependency needs. It is only when a child feels confident that she or he *can* depend on others that the child grows up feeling confident enough to be independent. (p. 16).

> A man's dependency needs are hidden from sight, because women throughout his life have met them without him ever having to confront them or make them explicit.

> Women must throw off the dependent behaviour traits and stereotypes that cripple them, but ultimately this will only be possible when they receive gratification of their own needs. This means that men as well as women have an enormous task in front of them. (p. 18)

This is surely struggle enough to occupy each of us for the better part of a lifetime; to paraphrase Nietzsche, we will at least no longer be void of purpose, even if that purpose is a void.

This is not merely a morality of exhortation, it is instruction in a vocabulary for describing and accounting for our pains in life and our dealings with those whose lives are bound up with our own. It is a vocabulary that faces two ways: at once authoritative, justified by reference to the results of scientific investigation, and popular, recognizable by each of us as the common terms of description of persons and relations. Hence it leads us naturally into the stories through which we will learn to understand our own lives. We learn to apply the language of self-description through identification with the characters, and we simultaneously engage in a kind of introjection of the author's interpretation. Take, for example, the 'Cha Cha Phenomenon':

> It's Saturday afternoon. Janie and Peter are sitting in their living room reading. Janie looks over to Peter and feels waves of love for him. She loves the way he looks. She feels happy. She goes to sit next to him on the sofa, gives him a kiss. He looks up and smiles and looks back down at his book. Janie says, 'Maybe we should forget about going to the movies tonight and just make a nice dinner at home. We can open our good wine.' Peter responds, 'Well, I really do feel like seeing that movie.'[28]

The cast of this little narrative captures precisely the constituency at whom the texts and techniques are directed: young, urban, reasonably well off, disenchanted with all higher purposes, making their lives meaningful through food, wine and cinema – and 'relationships'. The point is to produce an identification, followed by an interpretation:

> This is step one of the cha-cha. Janie feels open to Peter. She makes several gestures towards him for contact. The first 'rebuff' was Peter looking down at the book after the kiss. The second move away from intimate contact was the rejection of the 'dinner in' idea. Janie felt both of these gestures as rejection.[29]

The scenes and the plot are familiar from soap operas, as are the repertoire of emotions allowed and excluded. An interiority has opened up behind our conduct, but it is a shallow interiority, occupied by the simple, wholesome needs. Love, affection, sex, dependency, attention and rejection operate here, but not rage, hate, self-loathing, guilt, envy, fantasy, and self-abasement, let alone the earlier moral imperatives of duty, obligation, social responsibility, conscience, grace, good, and evil.

The narrative of the cha-cha continues through the predictable stages, up to the point when the participants become aware of 'the space between them'. At this point, choice is offered – different responses from each of the partners are presented with their outcomes. One leads to exacerbation of the cha-cha, the other to resolution - 'expression of anger' or 'letting go of the hurt'. We hear more of Janie and Peter, get some 'background' so that we can put this little sequence into the history of their 'relationship', lest we make the mistake of thinking 'the guy only wanted to see the film'. We discover how the cha-cha manifests the tensions between fear of dependency, needs for intimacy, vulnerability, distancing, barriers, and so on. We are educated in a therapeutic discourse of the emotions, one that we can use to turn our own 'cases' into stories, and become the authors of our own plot, perhaps without the need of the counselling, the 'couple therapy' that brings Janie and Peter's story to a satisfying narrative resolution.

Thus we learn a language and a technique, a way of selecting, mapping, and interpreting certain modes of interchange as representing psychic needs and fears. We learn to make ourselves manageable not through an experimental technology of awareness, not through a logical algorithm of transactions, but through our identifications with a narrative of the emotions. If these identifications fulfil their aims, then we will be able to narrativize our own lives in terms of 'emotions' and 'relationships', our actions as manifesting 'needs', and hence obtaining the capacity to construct our own endings to the soap operas of our lives. And we learn, too, that we make, and can remake, our lives through our own choices, and that it is legitimate, desirable, indeed healthy to calculate our lives in terms of the choices that will fulfil our subjective needs.

Eichenbaum and Orbach's is a self-consciously progressive and feminist text. But we should not be misled by the rhetoric of sharing and communality which we find in these tales. We may be hoping for a life where 'People will no longer strive to be independent of one another – to stand on their own two feet – to be individualistic and competitive' (p. 203). But we are still aiming for autonomy, for 'it is only through the satisfaction of our dependency needs and the security of loving and nurturing relationships which provide us with an emotional anchor that we can truly feel autonomous' (p. 203).

The freedom promised by the folk gurus of 'anti-psychiatry' in the heady culture of the 1960s was a total liberation of subjectivity from social restrictions.[30] Their contemporary offspring promise something different: not liberation from social constraints but rendering psychological constraints on autonomy conscious, and hence amenable to rational transformation. Achieving freedom becomes a matter not of slogans nor of political revolution, but of slow, painstaking, and detailed work on our own subjective and personal realities, guided by an expert knowledge of the psyche.

Psychotherapeutics is linked at a profound level to the socio-political obligations of the modern self. The self it seeks to liberate or restore is the entity able to steer its individual path through life by means of the act of personal decision and the assumption of personal responsibility. It is the self freed from all moral obligations but the obligation to construct a life of its own choosing, a life in which it realizes itself. Life is to be measured by the standards of personal fulfilment rather than community welfare or moral fidelity, given purpose through the accumulation of choices and experiences, the accretion of personal pleasures, the triumphs and tragedies of love, sex, and happiness.

The codes and vocabularies of psychotherapeutics thus can bring into alignment the techniques for the regulation of subjectivity and the technologies of government elaborated within contemporary political rationales. It promises to make it possible for us all to make a project of our biography, create a style for our lives, shape our everyday existence in terms of an ethic of autonomy. Yet the norm of autonomy secretes, as its inevitable accompaniment, a constant and intense self-scrutiny, a continual evaluation of our personal experiences, emotions, and feelings in relation to images of satisfaction, the necessity to narrativize our lives in a vocabulary of interiority. The self that is liberated is obliged to live its life tied to the project of its own identity.

Chapter nineteen

The Therapies of Freedom

After Nietzsche's devastating criticism of those 'last men' who 'invented happiness,' I may leave aside altogether the naive optimism in which science – that is, the technique of mastering life which rests upon science – has been celebrated as the way to happiness.[1]

Max Weber, 1918

Max Weber doubted the possibility of conducting an 'ethical' life within a rationalized life order. In our times of rationalization, intellectualization, and the 'disenchantment of the world', ultimate values no longer provide a means of guiding our lives. Persons discharge their lives according to rational rules and impersonal duties rather than by virtue of a set of transcendent ethical values.[2] Complete rationalization denies a space of freedom for the conduct of one's life. Rational principles may specify how to reach certain goals, but they cannot say which goals we should strive to reach. Science, it would appear, has nothing to say about the conduct of life of the free individual. Thus Weber asks, 'What is the meaning of science as a vocation, now after all these former illusions, the "way to true being," the "way to true art," the "way to true God," the "way to true happiness," have been dispelled?' He answers with Tolstoy's words: 'Science is meaningless because it gives no answer to our question, the only question important for us: "What shall we do and how shall we live?" '[3]

Should we then conclude that our contemporary proponents of a science of autonomy, a rational solution to the question of how to live, are merely naïve or mischievous moralists? That their espousal of psychotherapy not just as a source of income but as a vocation, a way of giving life itself a meaning, is a product of bad faith? Or more, that they are moral entrepreneurs, appealing to the mystique of sciences to give the appearance of an objective foundation to ethical presumptions that are both arbitrary and functional in that they legitimate their claims to increased social power? Pierre Bordieu proposes something of this sort. This ethical avant-garde, he suggests, comes from a new petit-bourgeoisie whose objective role of servicing industry, advertising, social regulation, and cultural manipulation conflicts with their subjective aspirations to lead a good life and improve the world. They promote their own solutions to this contradiction – the cultivation of an individualized, secular art of lifestyle, consumption and pleasure – as a universal solution with a scientific basis. In strenuously promoting this new ethic they produce the demand for the services of a corps of experts that they alone can provide. Thus they turn profession of a faith – in the liberating powers of psychological doctrines – into the creation of a profession.[4]

Such a sceptical evaluation is tempting. But it would be partial. To oppose an ethics to science is to impose a distinction that substitutes critique for analysis. Rather, one could say that science today is the mode by which ethical statements come to place themselves within the true, to establish a power for the values and techniques they espouse. The overlaying of science and ethics in the psychotherapies is no less significant for its ingenuousness or its self-aggrandizement. Rather, turning Weber's own theme against himself, the interpenetration of science and an aesthetics of existence, of rationality and ethics, has become fundamental to the ways whereby individuals are governed in accordance with the economic, social, and political conditions of the present.

The location of ethical statements within the field of science is double edged. On the one hand, in freeing many questions concerning the proper conduct of life from the authoritative prescriptions and proscriptions of political, religious, and social authorities, it pluralizes the answers that can be provided, opening up a field of diversity within which each subject is obliged to locate themselves. On the other hand, in relocating these questions of the conduct of life within the field of expertise, in tying it to norms of truth and health, it binds subjects to a subjection that is the more profound because it appears to emanate from our autonomous quest for ourselves, it appears as a matter of our freedom.

Certainly the psychotherapeutic solutions to the government of subjectivity are consonant with the political rationales that are in play in the period of 'the crisis of the welfare state'. Their espousal of the morality of freedom, autonomy, and fulfilment provides for the mutual translatability of the languages of psychic health and individual liberty. Their expansion through the market mechanism frees the techniques for self-regulation from systems of bureacratic surveillance, evaluation, and regulation of personal conduct. Thus, for example the exchange of money that makes private therapy possible is no longer required to guarantee the impersonality of the relation between analyst and analysand that lies behind the intensely personal analytic encounter.[5] Rather, its rationale is now that of choice and the sovereignty of the client. It emphasizes the voluntary nature of the commitment made by the individual to his or her self-development, and manifests the willingness to accept the responsibility of a contract for freedom.

Critical theory, as Colin Gordon has put it, might dwell with a 'melancholy, aristocratic sarcasm' on the ways in which the cultural valorization of 'lifestyle' and 'quality of life' has made such terms banal. But this perspective is more than a little self-indulgent. The significance of these themes lies more in the 'space of indetermination' that they inhabit in relation to the conduct of personal existence.[6] It is through the promotion of 'lifestyle' by the mass media, by advertising and by experts, through the obligation to shape a life through choices in a world of self-referenced objects and images, that the modern subject is governed.

It is in the space opened between the imposition of controls upon conduct by the public powers and the forms of life adopted by each individual that the vocabularies and techniques of the psycho-sciences operate. In the complex web they have traced out, the truths of science and the powers of experts act as relays that bring the values of authorities and the goals of business into contact with the dreams and actions of us all. These technologies for the government of the soul operate not through the crushing of subjectivity in the interests of control and profit, but by seeking to align political, social, and institutional goals with individual pleasures and desires, and with the happiness and fulfilment of the self. Their power lies in their capacity to offer means by which the regulation of selves – by others and by ourselves – can be made consonant with contemporary political principles, moral ideals, and constitutional exigencies. They are, precisely, therapies of freedom.

The paranoid visions of some social analysts, who see in the expansion of the therapeutic a kind of extension of state surveillance and regulation throughout the social body, are profoundly misleading. [7] The new sphere opened in our reality allows the play of values and aspirations from widely varying ethico-political positions. The central feature of these new apparatuses and techniques is the decoupling they effect between the central powers and the regulation of the internal worlds of institutions, families, and individuals. Their importance flows from the pluralization of the agencies and mechanisms of regulation of individual and group life, the heterogeneity of the assemblages of power in modern societies which have come to operate through the element of subjectivity. Their significance lies less in the fact that they extend domination than in their functioning, at the same time, as practices that promote the obligation to be free. We are obliged to fulfil our political role as active citizens, ardent consumers, enthusiastic employees, and loving parents as if we were seeking to realize our own desires.

If the new techniques for the care of the self are subjectifying, it is not because experts have colluded in the globalization of political power, seeking to dominate and subjugate the autonomy of the self through the bureaucratic management of life itself. Rather, it is that modern selves have become attached to the project of freedom, have come to live it in terms of identity, and to search for the means to enhance that autonomy through the application of expertise. In this matrix of power and knowledge the modern self has been born; to grasp its workings is to go some way towards understanding the sort of human beings we are.

Notes

Introduction

1. M. Foucault, 'The subject and power', Afterword to H. Dreyfus and P. Rabinow, *Michel Foucault: Beyond Structuralism and Hermeneutics*, Brighton: Harvester, 1982, p. 214.

2. As I have argued elsewhere. 'Calculable minds and manageable individuals', *History of the Human Sciences* 1: (1988): 179–200. I have drawn on this paper in what follows.

3. Cf. J. Meyer, 'The Self and the Life Course: Institutionalization and its Effects', in A. Sørensen, F. Weinert, and L. Sherrod (eds), *Human Development and the Life Course*, Hillsdale, NJ: L. Erlbaum, 1986. I have drawn on Meyer's ideas in what follows

4. Michel Foucault has given the most illuminating consideration of this issue. See, in particular, *The History of Sexuality. Vol. 1: An Introduction*, London: Allen Lane, 1979, especially Part 5; also his essays 'On governmentality', *I&C*, 6 (1979), 5–22, and 'Omnes et singulatim: towards a criticism of political reason', in S. McMurrin (ed.), *The Tanner Lectures on Human Values*, Vol. 2, Utah: University of Utah Press, 1981. For discussion of the related notion of 'police' see J. Schumpeter, *History of Economic Analysis*, New York: Oxford University Press, 1954, and P. Pasquino, 'Theatrum politicum. The genealogy of capital – police and the state of prosperity', *Ideology and Consciousness*, 4 (1978): 41–54.

5. Foucault, 'On governmentality', op. cit., p.20.

6. On statistics, see Pasquino, op. cit., and I. Hacking, 'Biopower and the avalanche of printed numbers', *Humanities in Society* 5 (1982): 279–95. On inscription and calculation see B. Latour, 'Visualization and cognition: thinking with hands and eyes', in H. Kushlick (ed.), *Knowledge and Society*, Vol. 6., Greenwich: JAI Press 1987.

7. On the history of statistical societies in Britain see P. Abrams, *The Origins of British Sociology ,1834–1914*, Chicago, Il: University of Chicago Press, 1968; and M.J. Cullen, *The Statistical Movement in Early Victorian Britain*, Hassocks, Sussex: Harvester, 1975.

8. M. Foucault, *Discipline and Punish: The Birth of the Prison*, London: Allen Lane, 1977, pp. 184–92.

9. My discussion of 'technologies' draws on the work of Bruno Latour, Michael Callon, and John Law. See their contributions to J. Law (ed.) *Power, Action and Belief* London: Routledge & Kegan Paul, 1986.

10. See, especially, M. Foucault, 'Technologies of the self', in L. Martin, H. Gutman, and P. Hutton (eds), *Technologies of the Self*, London: Tavistock, 1988; and M. Foucault, 'The subject and power', op. cit.

Chapter one The Psychology of War

1. Some issues that emerged in the war will be treated in other chapters. In particular the analysis of psychological concerns that arose in relation to the productivity of industry during the war years will be discussed in Part II, Chapter 7. The policy of evacuation, the wartime nurseries, and other shifts in family life will be discussed in Part III, Chapter 3.

2. Two prime examples are A. Marwick, *Britain in the Century of Total War*, London: Bodley Head, 1968; and P. Addison, *The Road to 1945*, London: Cape, 1975.

3. For example H. Pelling, *Britain and the Second World War*, London: Collins, 1970, p.270 and A. Calder, *The Peoples War*, London: Panther, 1969, p.15, both cited in A. Marwick, *War and Social Change in the Twentieth Century: a comparative study of Britain, France and the United States*, London: Macmillan, 1974.

4. There are notable exceptions, which will be discussed in the course of this chapter.

5. For war and 'human nature' see K. Lorenz, *On Aggression*, London: Methuen, 1966; E. Wilson, *On Human Nature*, Cambridge, Harvard University Press, 1978; and Brigadier Sheldon Bidwell, *Modern Warfare*, London: Allen Lane, 1973. For the effects of war on those caught up in the conflict, see P. Watson, *War on the Mind*, London: Hutchinson, 1978. For war as a psychological event within a culture see Marwick, op. cit.

6. Watson, op. cit., p. 15.

7. See their entries in the relevant volumes of *A History of Psychology in Autobiography*, San Francisco, CA: Freeman.

8. Watson, op. cit., p.22.

9. See P. Buck, 'Adjusting to military life: the social sciences go to war', in Merrit Roe Smith (ed.), *Military Enterprise and Technological Change*, Cambridge, MA: Massachusetts Institute of Technology, 1985.

10. The best overview is probably, for Britain, Robert H. Ahrenfeldt's *Psychiatry in the British Army in the Second World War*, London: Routledge & Kegan Paul, 1958.

11. Leon Kamin's study is the most influential of those who accuse the founders of the American mental testing movement of racism and pseudo-scientificity. Franz Samelson suggests that the evidence is more equivocal and that not only did the psychologists have less social impact than is often suggested in the passage of racist immigration laws, but also that many of the psychologists themselves were either uninterested or ambivalent about the issue of race, and certainly not involved in invention or falsification of data to suit prejudices. Indeed they criticized others like Brigham, who did draw con-

clusions from unsound evidence and extrapolations. See L. Kamin, *The Science and Politics of I.Q.*, Harmondsworth: Penguin, 1977; and F. Samelson, 'Putting psychology on the map: ideology and intelligence testing', in A.R. Buss (ed.), *Psychology in Social Context*, New York: Irvington, 1979.

12. This account of intelligence testing in the US army draws heavily upon the account by Franz Samelson cited above.

13. Samuelson, op. cit.

14. Ibid., p. 144.

15. I discuss these processes in more detail in two papers, 'Individualizing psychology', in J. Shotter and K. Gergen (eds.), *Texts of Identity*, London: Sage, 1989; and 'Calculable minds and manageable individuals', *History of the Human Sciences*, (1988): 179–200. More generally on the role of inscription devices in social regulation, see B. Latour, 'Visualization and cognition', in H. Kuclick (ed.), *Knowledge and Society: Studies in the Sociology of Culture Past and Present*, Vol. 6, Greenwich, CT: JAI Press, 1986.

16. C. Burt, 'Psychology in war: the military work of American and German psychologists', *Occupational Psychology* 16 (1942): 95–110; P. Vernon and J. Parry, *Personnel Selection in the British Forces*, London: London University Press, 1949.

17. On the general question of the 'disciplinization' of psychology, see my paper 'Calculable minds', cited above.

18. M. Simmonheit, *Wehrpsychologie: Ein Abriss ihrer Probleme und politischen Folgerungen*, Berlin: Bernard and Graefe, 1933, discussed in Burt, op. cit. See also Ansbacher's contribution to C. Pratt et al., 'Military psychology: a selected bibliography', *Psychological Bulletin* 38 (1941), 309–510; and D. Davis, 'Post-mortem on German applied psychology', *Occupational Psychology* 21 (1947), 105–10.

19. Davis, op. cit.

20. I give some more details of the debates over and consequences of shell-shock in *The Psychological Complex*, London: Routledge & Kegan Paul, 1985, pp. 180–91, and in 'Psychiatry: the discipline of mental health', in P. Miller and N. Rose (eds.), *The Power of Psychiatry*, Cambridge: Polity, 1986. A very useful account is provided in M. Stone, 'Shellshock and the psychologists', in W.F. Bynum, R. Porter, and M. Shepherd (eds), *The Anatomy of Madness*, Vol. 1, London: Tavistock, 1985. See also P.J. Lynch, 'The exploitation of courage', MPhil thesis, University of London, 1977, and War Office, *Report of the Committee of Enquiry into 'Shell Shock'*, London: HMSO, 1922.

21. See Stone, op. cit., p. 249, for a discussion of the statistics.

22. See, for example, the contributions to Hugh Crichton Miller, ed., *Functional Nerve Disease: An Epitome of War Experience*, London: Oxford University Press, 1922, and the discussion in my *Psychological Complex*, op. cit.

23. Rose, ibid.

Chapter two The Government of Morale

1. E. Glover, 'The birth of social psychiatry', *Lancet*, 24 August 1940, p. 239.

2. A. Calder, *The Peoples War*, 1969, p. 18.

3. See M. Foucault, 'On governmentality', *I&C* 6 (1979): 5–22; see also my 'Beyond the public/private divide', *Journal of Law and Society*, 14 (1987) 61–76.

4. See D. Armstrong, *Political Anatomy of the Body*, Cambridge: Cambridge University Press, 1983.

5. Royal Commission on Lunacy and Mental Disorder, *Report*, London: HMSO, 1926, p. 22.

6. The following few paragraphs rely heavily upon R. Titmuss, *Problems of Social Policy, History of the Second World War, UK Civil Series*, London: HMSO, 1950. For further discussion of the predicted and actual effects of air war, see I. Janis, *Air War and Emotional Stress*, New York: McGraw Hill, 1951.

7. W. Churchill, House of Commons Debate, 28 November 1934, vol. 295, col. 859, quoted in Titmuss, op. cit., p. 9.

8. Ibid. p. 16.

9. Titmuss, op. cit., pp. 20–21.

10. In E. Miller et al., *The Neuroses in War*, London: Macmillan, (1940) pp.184–5. See also the contributions by the other members of the Tavistock Clinic who contributed to this volume, E. Miller, G.R. Hargreaves, E. Wittkower, and A.T.M. Wilson. See also J. Rickman, *Lancet* i (1938) 1291, and *British Journal of Medical Psychology* 17: 361. Titmuss also quotes R.D. Gillespie, another leading British psychiatrist, as describing how he and his colleagues held long discussions in the period after the Munich crisis in 1938, deciding how to meet the tremendous incidence of psychiatric disorders that were expected once the Germans began their assault. See Titmuss, op. cit., pp. 338–39.

11. For the following see Titmuss, op. cit., pp. 340–51.

12. These issues are discussed in a subsequent chapter.

13. See A. Lewis, *Lancet*, 15 August 1942; P.E. Vernon, 'A study of war attitudes', *British Journal of Medical Psychology* 19 (1941): 271–91, R. Barber, 'The civilian population under bombardment', *Nature*, 7 June, 1941, 700–1, C.P. Blacker, *Neurosis and the Mental Health Services*, London: Oxford University Press, 1946; and the discussion in I. McLaine, *Ministry of Morale: Home Front Morale and the Ministry of Information in World War II*, London: George Allen & Unwin, 1979, pp. 108ff.

14. Titmuss, op. cit., p. 347.

15. The following discussion of the work of the Ministry of Information draws heavily upon Ian McLaine's comprehensive study cited above.

16. See I.L. Child, 'Morale, a biographic review', *Psychological Bulletin* 38 (1941): 393–420.

17. See, for example, G.W. Allport and L. Postman, *The Psychology of Rumour*, New York: Holt, 1947.

18. G. Gallup and S.F. Rae, *The Pulse of Democracy: The Public Opinion Poll and How it Works*, New York: Simon & Schuster, 1940.

19. See the account in W. Albig, *Modern Public Opinion*, New York: McGraw Hill, 1956.

20. For collective psychology see G. Le Bon, *The Crowd: A Study of the Popular Mind*, London: Fisher Unwin, 1895, and the writings of William McDougall. For an influential critique of the newer position see F.H. Allport, 'Towards a science of public opinion', *Public Opinion Quarterly* 1 (1937): 7–23. Allport himself favoured a view of public opinion as nothing more than the arithmetical sum of 'individual verbalizations' – individual behaviour rather than group mind.

21. There were many different versions of this analysis, from the 'hormic' psychology of William McDougall, through Alexander Shand's theory of 'sentiments' to Gordon Allport's notion of 'dispositions' or 'neural sets'.

22. For more discussion of this, especially of the pioneering industrial investigations reported in the 'Hawthorne Studies', whose techniques were used by British political parties in the 1930s, see Chapter six.

23. See K. Middlemas, *Politics in Industrial Society*, London: Deutsch, 1979, Ch. 12. The quote is from p. 369.

24. On the science of police see P. Pasquino,' Theatrum politicum: the genealogy of capital – police and the state of prosperity', *Ideology and Consciousness* 4 (1978): 41–54. For details of the sources described, see McLaine, op. cit., pp. 51ff.

25. For details of Mass Observation, see C. Madge and T. Harrisson (eds), *Mass Observation: First Year's Work 1937–8*, with an essay on a nationwide intelligence service by Bronislaw Malinowski, London: Mass Observation, 1938.

26. See G. Watson (ed.), *Civilian Morale*, Boston, MA: Houghton Mifflin, 1942; L. Farago and L.F. Gittler (eds), *German Psychological Warfare*, New York: Putnam, 1942; D. Katz,' The Surveys Division of OWI: governmental use of research for informational purposes', in A.B. Blankenship (ed.), *How to Conduct Consumer and Opinion Research*, New York: Harper, 1946; F.H. Allport and M. Lepkin, 'Building war morale with news headlines', *Public Opinion Quarterly* 7 (1943): 211–21; F.H. Allport, M. Lepkin, and E. Cahen, Headlines on allied losses are better morale builders', *Editor and Publisher*, 9 October 1943; G.W. Allport and L. Postman, *The Psychology of Rumour*, New York: Holt, 1947. All are discussed in D. Cartwright, 'Social psychology in the United States during the Second World War', *Human Relations* 1 (1947–48): 333–52.

27. Other surveys were carried out by the British Institute of Public Opinion (BIPO), which, like Gallup's organization, had been established before the war.

28. See K. Box and G. Thomas, 'The Wartime Social Survey', *Journal of the Royal Statistical Society* 107 (1944): 151–77.

29. McLaine, op. cit., p. 262.

30. Ibid.

31. For a recent overview see T.H. Qualter, *Opinion Control in the Democracies*, London: Macmillan, 1985.

32. Pasquino, op. cit.

33. McLaine, op. cit., p. 144.

34. This is discussed further below.

35. This is illustrated by the equivocation on the publication of the Beveridge Report on the reform of the social services. See P. Addison, *The Road to 1945*, London: Cape, 1975, Ch. 8.

36. See, for example, F.C. Bartlett, *Political Propaganda*, Cambridge: Cambridge University Press, 1940.

37. For useful introductions to the use of film and radio in various countries see K.R.M. Short (ed.), *Film and Radio Propaganda in World War II*, London: Croom Helm, 1983. For details on Britain and the United States see the contributions by Pronay and Culbert, respectively.

Chapter three The Sykewarriors

1. Letter from General Eisenhower to General McLure, reproduced as frontispiece to Psychological Warfare Division, *Psychological Warfare Division, SHAEF: An Account of its Operations in the Western European Campaign, 1944–1945*, Bad Homburg, Germany, October 1945, and quoted in Daniel Lerner, *Sykewar: Psychological Warfare Against Germany, D-Day to VE-Day*, New York: Stewart, 1949.

2. The title of this chapter is taken from Daniel Lerner's valuable study cited above. This book also contains a useful supplementary essay by Richard Crossman.

3. Lerner, op. cit., p. 7.

4. Ibid., p. 329.

5. Much wartime and post-war discussion focused on this theme of unconditional surrender, and the extent to which it delayed or accelerated victory.

6. The best discussion is in Anthony Cave Brown, *Bodyguard of Lies*, London: W.H. Allen, 1976, to which my account is indebted. See also Ronald Seth's anecdotal volume, *The Truth–Benders: Psychological Warfare in the Second World War*, London: Frewin, 1969.

7. PWD SHAEF Memorandum, 'Policy and methods of black warfare propaganda against Germany', 10 November 1944, quoted in Brown, op. cit., p. 7.

8. William J. Donovan, Director US OSS, Memorandum to US Joint Chiefs of Staff, 'Overall strategic plan for US psychological warfare', 2 February 1943, quoted in Brown, op. cit.

9. Quoted in Brown, op. cit.

10. Lerner, op. cit., pp. 262–72.

11. H.V. Dicks, 'Psychological foundations of the Wehrmacht, Directorate of Army Psychiatry (British), Research Memorandum 11/02/9A. This work is extensively discussed in Lerner, op. cit., Ch. 6.

12. However they did include social scientists among their number. For example Saul Padover, who was involved in developing the techniques of prolonged interrogation issuing in reports on 'German types', was originally a historian, and had worked with Lasswell at Chicago before the war. See Saul K. Padover, *Experiment in Germany*, New York: Duell, Sloan & Pearce, 1946; and the account in Lerner, op. cit., pp. 85–87, 111, 128n.

13. See Lerner, op. cit., p. 129.

14. This discussion draws heavily on Dorwin Cartwright, 'Social psychology in the United States during the Second World War', *Human Relations*, 1 (1947–48): 333–52. The best general account of the American history is P. Buck 'Adjusting to military life: the social sciences go to war', in Merrit Roe Smith (ed.), *Military Enterprise and TechnologicalChange*, Cambridge, MA: Massachusetts Institute of Technology, 1985.

15. Cartwright, op. cit., p. 337. The research is reported in United States Strategic Bombing Survey, *The Effects of Strategic Bombing on German Morale*, 2 vols., Washington, D.C.: US Government Printing Office, 1947.

16. A.H. Leighton, *The Governing of Men: General Principles and Recommendations Based on Experience at a Japanese Relocation Camp*, Princeton, NJ: 1945. See Buck, op. cit., for a discussion of this work.

17. A.H. Leighton, *Human Relations in a Changing World: Observations on the Use of the Social Sciences*, New York: Dutton, 1949.

18. For a good account of these debates, see Richard Rhodes, *The Making of the Atomic Bomb*, New York: Simon & Schuster, 1987.

19. This work is discussed in Ch. 3 of Denise Riley's excellent study *War in the Nursery*, London: Virago, 1983, on which my discussion here draws heavily.

20. H.M. Spitzer and Ruth Benedict, *Bibliography of Articles and Books Relating to Japanese Character*, Washington, D.C.: US Department of War Information, 1945.

21. C. Kluckhohn and D. Leighton, *The Navaho*, Cambridge, MA.: Harvard University Press, 1946; C. Kluckhohn and D. Leighton, *Children of the People*, Cambridge, MA.: Harvard University Press, 1947; E. Erikson, 'Observations of the Yurok: childhood and world image', *American Archaeology and Ethology* 35 (1943): 257–301; E. Erikson, 'Childhood and tradition in two American Indian tribes', in A. Freud (ed.), *The Psychoanalytic Study of the Child, Vol. 1*, New York: International Universities Press 1945. All cited in Riley, op. cit.

22. Margaret Mead and Martha Wolfenstein (eds), *Childhood in Contemporary Culture*, Chicago, Il: University of Chicago Press, 1955, p.vii. See Riley, op. cit., p. 70.

23. T. Parsons and E.A. Shills (eds), *Toward a General Theory of Action*, Cambridge, MA: Harvard University Press, 1951.

24. For studies of the general effect of the war on the social sciences, see John Madge, *The Origins of Scientific Sociology*, London: Tavistock, 1963, Ch. 9, 'Social science and the soldier', which is principally on the four volumes by Samuel Stouffer and others published in 1949 and 1950 under the general title *Studies in Social Psychology in World War II* (New York: Wiley). These are mentioned below. See also Buck, op. cit.

25. See, for example, J. Bruner, *Mandate from the People*, New York: Duell, Sloan & Pearce, 1944; P. Lazarsfeld, H. Gaudet, and B. Berelson, *The People's Choice*, New York: Duell, Sloan & Pearce, 1945; A. H. Leighton, *The Governing of Men*, Princeton, NJ: Princeton University Press, 1945; B. L. Smith, H. D. Lasswell, and R. D. Casey, *Propaganda, Communication and Public Opinion*, Princeton, NJ: 1946; Many further references to articles and books are cited given in Lerner, op. cit.

Chapter four Groups at War

1. Privy Council Office, *The Work of Psychologists and Psychiatrists in the Services: Report of an Expert Committee*, London: HMSO, 1947. The expert committee of nine people included the director-general of each of the services, together with Lord Moran (Churchill's physician), Professors F.C. Bartlett from Cambridge, D.K. Henderson from Edinburgh, A.W. Walters from Reading, and Dr. Aubrey Lewis, clinical director of the Maudsley Hospital.

2. In addition to the report cited above, an anodyne overview of the issues discussed in this section is contained in the chapter on psychological medicine in the relevant volume of the official history: V.Z. Cope (ed.), *Medical Services – Medicine and Pathology, History of the Second World War, United Kingdom Civil Series*, London: HMSO, 1952. Two other very useful overviews that focus on psychiatry but also deal with some general issues are J.R. Rees, *The Shaping of Psychiatry by War*, London: Chapman and Hall, 1945, and R.H. Ahrenfeldt, *Psychiatry in the British Army in the Second World War*, London: Routledge & Kegan Paul, 1958.

3. Ahrenfeldt, op. cit., p. 15.

4. Ibid., p. 31.

5. This work is discussed in Part II.

6. Ahrenfeldt, op. cit.

7. Full details of the employment of psychological personnel in the different branches of the British services as of 1943 are given in Appendix I to the *Report of an Expert Committee*, cited above. As far as professionally trained psychologists are concerned, the Admiralty employed a senior psychologist and ten industrial psychologists. The Director of Selection of Personnel in the Adjutant General's Department at the War Office had a staff of 19 psychologists (together with a small number in other research and medical departments), and the Air Ministry employed four civilian advisors. There were, however, over 1,500 non-psychologists who were given limited psychological training and employed in the testing programmes of the various branches of the services. I do not discuss here the role of psychologists in the selection of personnel for specialized tasks such as radar operation, the development of specific tests of aptitude for such jobs, and the work on factors such as temperature and rest periods that might influence performance. The Cambridge Psychological Laboratory, and the wartime work of Donald Broadbent, were important here. See Broadbent's contribution to G. Lindzey and G. Murphy, *A History of Psychology in Autobiography, Vol. 7*, San Francisco, CA: Freeman, 1980.

8. Ahrenfeldt, op. cit., pp. 40f. The work was also extended to other tasks, for example the selection of paratroops. A similar scheme was developed by the Admiralty for the selection of Royal Navy manpower – Alec Rodger of the NIIP was the senior psychologist here. See A. Rodger, 'The work of the Admiralty psychologists', *Occupational Psychology* 19 (1945): 132–39. For an account that gives details of the different testing and classification procedures used by the psychologists, see P.E. Vernon and J.B. Parry, *Personnel Selection in the British Forces*, London: University of London Press, 1949.

9. J.R. Rees, 'Three years of military psychiatry in the United Kingdom', *British Medical Journal* 1 (1943): 1–6; quoted in Ahrenfeldt, op. cit., p. 50.

10. The flavour of these can be gained from the following: E. Ginzberg, J.L. Herman, and S.W. Ginzburg, *Psychiatry and Military Manpower Policy: A Reappraisal of the Experience in World War II*, New York: Columbia University Press, 1953; E. Ginzberg and D.W. Bray, *The Uneducated*, New York: Columbia University Press, 1953; E. Ginzberg, J.K. Anderson, S.W. Ginzburg, and J.L. Herman, *The Ineffective Soldier: Lessons for Management and the Nation*, New York: Columbia University Press, 1959.

11. S.A. Stouffer et al., *Volume 1: The American Soldier: Adjustment During Army Life*, New York: Wiley, 1949; *Volume 2: The American Soldier: Combat and its Aftermath*, New York: Wiley, 1949; *Volume 3, Experiments in Mass Communication*, New York: Wiley, 1950; *Volume 4: Measurement and Prediction*, New York: Wiley, 1950. These studies have been much discussed, as, for example, in John Madge, *The Origins of Scientific Sociology*, London: Tavistock, 1963.

12. Stouffer, op. cit., Vol. 2, pp. 130–31.

13. E.A. Shils, 'The study of the primary group', in H.D. Lasswell and D. Lerner (eds), *The Policy Sciences – Recent Developments in Scope and Methods*, Palo Alto, CA: Stanford University Press, 1951, p. 64. Cf. the good discussion of this material in C. Sofer, *Organizations in Theory and Practice*, London: Heinemann, 1972.

14. See the discussion of the work of Elton May in Chapter six.

15. For discussion of officer selection see Ahrenfeldt, op. cit., Ch. 3; Vernon and Parry, op. cit., Ch. 4; and B.S. Morris, 'Officer selection in the British army', *Occupational Psychology* 23 (1949): 219–34. For the American work, see Office of Strategic Services Assessment Staff, *Assessment of Men*, New York: Reinhart, 1948.

16. Details of the disputes are provided in Ahrenfeldt, op. cit., pp. 62–76.

17. The techniques of psychiatric interviewing were developed by J.D. Sutherland, who was both a psychiatrist and a psychologist and who was a member of the first experimental board, and Eric Trist, later senior psychologist at the Research and Training Centre. See Rees, op. cit., p. 71.

18. See N. Rose, *The Psychological Complex*, London: Routledge & Kegan Paul, 1985, and N. Rose, 'Psychiatry: the discipline of mental health', in P. Miller and N. Rose (eds), *The Power of Psychiatry*, Cambridge: Polity, 1986, pp. 63–64.

19. Although Eysenck's work on the factorization of personality and its assessment was carried out in England, at the Mill Hill Emergency Hospital. This will be discussed in Chapter seventeen.

20. K. Lewin, *Dynamic Theory of Personality*, New York: McGraw Hill, 1935; K. Lewin, *Principles of Topological Psychology*, New York: McGraw Hill, 1936; J.L. Moreno, *Who Shall Survive? A new approach to the problem of human interrelations*, Washington, D.C.: Nervous and Mental Diseases Publishing Co., 1934.

21. Ahrenfeldt, op. cit., p. 61.

22. W.R. Bion, 'The leaderless group project', *Bulletin of the Menninger Clinic*, 10 (1946): 77–81. The technique and its development are discussed in Ahrenfeldt, op. cit., pp. 60f. and Vernon and Parry, op. cit., pp. 61f. For

Bion's theoretical developments see his 'Experiences in groups', *Human Relations*, Vols. 1 – 4, reprinted in *Experiences in Groups*, London: Tavistock, 1961.

23. Office of Strategic Services Assessment Staff, *Assessment of Men*, New York: Reinhart, 1948.

24. The following paragraphs draw upon my chapter, 'Psychiatry: the discipline of mental health', in Miller and Rose, op. cit., and P. Miller and N. Rose, 'The Tavistock programme: governing subjectivity and social life', *Sociology*, (1988): 22, 171-92. See W.R. Bion and J. Rickman, 'Intra-group tensions in therapy: their study as the task of the group', *Lancet* 245, 27 November 1943, pp. 678–81. Cf. Bion's own reflections in his *Experiences in Groups*, op. cit., and F. Kraupl Taylor, 'A history of group and administrative therapy in Great Britain', *British Journal of Medical Psychology* 31 (1958): 153–73.

25. For a good discussion, see Sofer, op. cit., pp. 203–6.

26. T. Main, 'The hospital as a therapeutic institution', *Bulletin of the Menninger Clinic* 10 (1946): 67.

27. See M. Jones, *Social Psychiatry*, London: Tavistock, 1952.

28. See, for example, A.T.M. Wilson, M. Doyle, and J. Kelnar, 'Group techniques in a transitional community', *Lancet* 1 (1947): 735–38, and A. Curle, 'Transitional communities and social reconnection: a follow-up study of the civil resettlement of British prisoners of war', *Human Relations* 1 (1947): 42–68.

29. Jones, op. cit.

Chapter five The Subject of Work

1. L. Baritz, *The Servants of Power*, New York: Wiley, 1965; H. Braverman, *Labour and Monopoly Capital*, New York: Monthly Review Press, 1974; M. Rose, *Industrial Behaviour*, London: Allen Lane, 1975. There are many other books that stress the same themes. See, for example, R. Edwards, *Contested Terrain*, London: Heinemann, 1979; M. Burawoy, *Manufacturing Consent*, Chicago, Il. University of Chicago Press, 1979.

2. F.W. Taylor, *The Principles of Scientific Management*, New York: Harper, 1913.

3. Of course, not all sociological analysts of industrial relations put the matter in such stark terms. The writings of Alan Fox on conflicts of interest in the workplace have been influential in the British context. See, for example, A. Fox, 'Industrial relations: a social critique of pluralist ideology', in J. Child (ed.), *Man and Organization*, London: Allen & Unwin, 1973.

4. See P. Miller and T. O'Leary 'Hierarchies and American ideals 1900–1940', *Academy of Management Review*, forthcoming (1989). Cf. Gareth Morgan, *Images of Organization*, Beverly Hills, CA: Sage, 1986.

Chapter six The Contented Worker

1. E. Cadbury, *Experiments in Industrial Organization*, London: Longmans, 1912, quoted in J. Child, *British Management Thought*, London: Allen & Unwin, 1969, p. 37. I have drawn extensively on Child's account in this section.

2. Marx's own writings on the wage form in *Capital* remain the best account of this analysis.

3. For this next section see Child, op. cit., Ch. 2, and M.M. Niven, *Personnel Management 1913–63*, London: Institute of Personnel Management, 1967.

4. For one overview that remains instructive, though not perhaps in the sense the author intended, see T.H. Marshall, *Social Policy*, London: Hutchinson, 1965. See also the discussion in Chapters 5 and 6 of N. Rose, *The Psychological Complex*, London: Routledge & Kegan Paul, 1985. The attempts to create a national market for labour via the labour exchange, and the corollary individualization of the labourer that was involved, were also of significance in the governmentalization of subjectivity. I discuss this in *Psychological Complex*, pp. 83–89.

5. For discussion of this see my 'Socialism and social policy', in D. Adlam et al. (eds), *Politics and Power: 2*, London: Routledge & Kegan Paul, 1980, on which the following comments are based.

6. See Marshall, op. cit., Chs. 3 and 4.

7. See John Keegan, *The Face of Battle*, Harmondsworth: Penguin, 1978, Ch. 4.

8. Quoted in C.S. Myers, *Industrial Psychology in Great Britain*, London: Cape, 1927, p. 14.

9. Ibid., pp.14–15.

10. C.S. Myers, cited in P. Miller, 'Psychotherapy of work and unemployment', in P. Miller and N. Rose (eds), *The Power of Psychiatry*, Cambridge: Polity, 1986. See also E. Farmer, 'Early days in industrial psychology: an autobiographical note', *Occupational Psychology* 32 (1958): 264–67.

11. My account of Myers' career is indebted to L. Hearnshaw, *A Short History of British Psychology 1840–1940*, London: Methuen, 1964. For an analysis of psychology in this period, see my *Psychological Complex*.

12. Hearnshaw, op. cit., p. 245. On shell-shock and World War I, see Part I.

13. *The Nature of Mind*, 1930, quoted in Hearnshaw, op. cit., p. 210.

14. Hearnshaw, op. cit., pp. 275–82 gives a good overview of the work of the NIIP.

15. C.S. Myers, op. cit. For what follows I have also drawn upon P. Miller, 'Psychotherapy of work and unemployment', op. cit.

16. For a full discussion of the psychology of individual differences and the strategy of mental hygiene, see my *Psychological Complex*.

17. Farmer, op. cit.

18. The new psychology is discussed in detail in my *Psychological Complex*, op. cit., Chs. 7 and 8.

19. Myers, op. cit., pp. 29–30.

20. M.S. Viteles, *Industrial Psychology*, New York: Norton, 1932, and V.E. Fisher and J.V. Hanna, *The Dissatisfied Worker*, New York: Macmillan, 1932. My discussion of the American experience is indebted to Miller, op. cit.

21. See E. Mayo, *The Human Problems of an Industrial Civilization*, New York: Macmillan, 1933. Mayo himself was not directly involved in the experiments at the Hawthorne Plant, and the claims he made for them differed in significant respects from those of the researchers themselves. For a discussion of Mayo, see M. Rose, op. cit., and P. Miller, op. cit.

22. The most detailed accounts of the actual studies are F.J. Roethlisberger and W.J. Dickson, *Management and the Worker*, Cambridge, MA: Harvard University Press, 1939, and T.N. Whitehead, *The Industrial Worker*, Oxford: Oxford University Press, 1938.

23. Roethlisberger and Dickson, op. cit., p. 269.

24. See the discussion in Part I.

25. Roethlisberger and Dickson, op. cit., p. 151.

26. E. Mayo , op. cit., quoted in Miller, op. cit., p. 152. This danger of fragmentation of social solidarity under the influence of the advanced division of labour and the growth of individualism was, of course, a concern of many writers in the first three decades of the twentieth century, most notably Emile Durkheim.

27. Child, op. cit.

28. See K. Middlemas, *Politics in Industrial Society*, London: Deutsch, 1979.

29. Ibid.

30. See A. Fox, *History and Heritage: the Social Origins of the British Industrial Relations System*, London: Allen & Unwin, 1985. I am grateful to Peter Seglow for comments on Whitleyism.

31. S. Webb, *The Works Manager Today*, London: Longmans Green, 1917, p. 157, quoted in Child, op. cit., p. 53.

Chapter seven The Worker at War

1. W.K. Hancock and M.M. Gowing, *British War Economy History of the Second World*, *War UK Civil Series*, London: HMSO, p. 541, quoted in K. Middlemas, *Politics in Industrial Society*, London: Deutsch, 1979, p. 274.

2. See Middlemas, op. cit., Ch.10 for a discussion of the wartime period. Despite my disagreements with his analysis of corporatism, I have drawn heavily upon his research here.

3. Cited in M.M. Niven, *Personnel Management 1913–63*, London: Institute of Personnel Management, 1967, p. 96.

4. Quoted in Niven, op. cit., p. 98.

5. Quoted in Niven, op. cit., p. 107.

6. Middlemas, op. cit., p. 280. Not that the existence of such machinery eliminated all industrial conflict. The key exception was the coal industry, which was racked by disputes throughout the war. See Middlemas, pp. 280ff, and L. Harris, 'State and economy in the Second World War', in G. McLennan, D. Held, and S. Hall (eds), *State and Society in Contemporary Britain*, Cambridge: Polity, 1984.

7. The phrase is that of Bevin's biographer, Bullock, quoted by Middlemas, op. cit., p. 302.

Chapter eight Democracy at Work

1. R. Dahl, 'Worker's control of industry and the British Labour Party', *American Political Science Review* 41 (1947): 875–900, quoted from p. 900.

2. Ibid.

3. Ibid.

4. See, for example, T.F. Rodger, 'Personnel selection', in N.G. Harris (ed.), *Modern Trends in Psychological Medicine*, London: Butterworth, 1948.

5. Cf. C. Sofer, *Organizations in Theory and Practice*, London: Heinemann, 1972, pp. 199–203. See also J. Munro Fraser, 'New-type selection boards in industry', *Occupational Psychology* 21 (1947): 170–78.

6. J. Tomlinson, 'Industrial democracy and the labour party', unpublished typescript, September 1985.

7. P. Inman, *Labour in the Munitions Industry. History of the Second World War, UK Civil Series*, London: HMSO, 1957. Cripps moved from President of the Board of Trade in September 1947 to Minister of Economic Affairs and then, in November, to Chancellor of the Exchequer.

8. Tomlinson, op. cit.

9. Ibid.

10. Details of the work of the Human Factors Panel are given in the Annual Reports of the Committee on Industrial Productivity for 1949, Cmd. 7665, and 1950, Cmd 7991.

11. Tomlinson, op. cit.

12. For the managers see L. Urwick and E.F.L. Brech, *The Making of Scientific Management, Vol. 3*, London: Management Publications, 1948; C.H. Northcott, *Personnel Management: its Scope and Practice*, London: Pitman, 1945; F.J. Burns Morton, *Foremanship – a Textbook*, London: Chapman and Hall, 1951. See also the discussion in J. Child, *British Management Thought*, London: Allen & Unwin, 1969, upon which I have drawn heavily, and V.M. Clarke, *New Times, New Methods and New Men*, London: Allen & Unwin, 1950. For the psychologists see J.A.C. Brown, *Social Psychology of Industry*, Harmondsworth: Penguin, 1954; G.R. Taylor, *Are Workers Human*, London: Falcon Press, 1950; R.F. Tredgold, 'Mental hygiene in industry', in N.G. Harris (ed.), *Modern Trends in Psychological Medicine*, London: Butterworth, 1948; R.F. Tredgold, *Human Relations in Modern Industry*, London: Duckworth, 1949; C.A. Mace, 'Satisfactions in work', *Occupational Psychology* 22 (1948): 5–16; and C.A. Mace and P.E. Vernon (eds), *Current Trends in British Psychology*, London: Methuen, 1953.

13. J.A.C. Brown, *Social Psychology of Industry*, Harmondsworth: Penguin, 1954.

14. Ibid., p. 130.

15. Ibid., p. 126.

16. G.R. Taylor, *Are Workers Human?* London: Falcon Press, 1950, p. 20.

17. Brown, op. cit., pp. 162–63.

18. Ibid., pp. 172–73.

19. Interestingly Middlemas argues that the management of public consent which began to be systematically undertaken by the Conservative party in the inter-war years drew heavily on the analyses of the Hawthorne experiments in terms of social and economic groups. See K. Middlemas, *Politics in Industrial Society*, London: Deutsch, 1979. esp. p. 354.

20. Ibid., p. 127.

21. Taylor, op. cit., p. 52.

22. Brown, op. cit., Ch. 8.

23. Taylor, op. cit., pp. 12–13.

24. R. Fraser, *The Incidence of Neurosis among Factory Workers*, Industrial Health Research Board Report no.90, London: HMSO, 1947.

25. Tredgold, 'Mental hygiene in industry', op. cit, p. 364.

26. Ibid., p. 365.

27. This research is summarized in L.S. Hearnshaw, *The Shaping of Modern Psychology*, London: Routledge & Kegan Paul, 1987, pp. 206–9, who gives extensive references to the relevant papers.

28. The Tavistock Institute, and the Clinic, are the subject of a forthcoming study undertaken by myself and Peter Miller, to be published by Tavistock Publications, which was itself initially an outgrowth of the Tavistock. Some preliminary indications of the direction of this study are contained in P. Miller and N. Rose, 'The Tavistock programme: governing subjectivity and social life', *Sociology* (1988): 22, 171–92. Other accounts of the work of the Tavistock, on which I have drawn here, are R.K. Brown, 'Research and consultancy in industrial enterprises', *Sociology* 1 (1967): 33–60, and S.G. Grey, 'The Tavistock Institute of Human Relations', in H.V. Dicks, *Fifty Years of the Tavistock Clinic*, London: Routledge & Kegan Paul, 1975.

29. M. Rose, *Industrial Behaviour*, London: Allen Lane, 1975 pp. 163–64. Rose describes these studies and gives references to them.

30. E. Jaques, *The Changing Culture of a Factory*, London: Tavistock, 1951, pp. xiii–xiv.

31. Ibid., p. 300. This theme was later developed at length by I. Menzies in her 'Case study in the functioning of social systems as a defense against anxiety', *Human Relations* 13 (1960): 95–122.

32. Ibid., pp. 308ff.

33. E.L. Trist and K.W. Bamforth, 'Some social and psychological consequences of the longwall method of coal getting', *Human Relations* 4 (1951): 3–38; E.L. Trist et al., *Organizational Choice: Loss, Recovery and Transformation of a Work Tradition*, London: Tavistock, 1963. See also A.K. Rice's 'Report of the Ahmedabad experiment, a study of the intersection of social, economic and technical change in an Indian textile mill carried out from 1953', in *Productivity and Social Organization*, London: Tavistock, 1958.

34. See, for example, W. Brown and E. Jaques, *Glacier Project Papers*, London: Heinemann, 1965.

35. Brown, *Social Psychology of Industry*, op. cit., pp. 122–23.

36. Taylor, op. cit., p. 120.

Chapter nine The Expertise of Management

1. J.H. Goldthorpe, 'Industrial relations in Great Britain: a critique of reformism', *Politics and Society* 4 (1974); reprinted in T. Clarke and L. Clements, *Trade Unions Under Capitalism*, London: Fontana, 1977, p. 184.

2. National Institute of Industrial Psychology, *The Foreman: A Study of Supervision in British Industry*, London: Staples Press, 1951; National Institute of Industrial Psychology, *Joint Consultation in British Industry*, London: Staples Press, 1952.

3. Department of Scientific and Industrial Research and Medical Research Council, *Final Report of Joint Committee on Human Relations in Industry 1954–57*, London: HMSO, 1958, p. 9.

4. Department of Scientific and Industrial Research and Medical Research Council, *Report of Joint Committee on Individual Efficiency in Industry 1953–57*, London: HMSO, 1958.

5. D. McGregor, *The Human Side of Enterprise*, New York: McGraw-Hill, 1960, quoted from D.S. Pugh, ed., *Organization Theory: Selected Readings*, 2nd edn., Harmondsworth: Penguin, 1984, pp. 325–26.

6. Ministry of Labour, *Industrial Relations Handbook*, revised edn., London: HMSO, 1961. Previous editions came out in 1944 and 1953.

7. P. Ribeaux and S.E. Poppleton, *Psychology at Work*, London: Macmillan, 1978, p. 11.

8. Michael Rose summarizes the arguments against human relations, and gives ample references, in his *Industrial Behaviour*, London: Allen Lane, 1975.

9. J. Child, *British Management Thought*, Allen & Unwin, 1969, pp. 172ff discusses a number of the important papers, as does M. Rose, op. cit. See, for one example, J.H. Goldthorpe, 'Attitudes and behaviour of car assembly workers', *British Journal of Sociology* 17 (1966): 227–44.

10. J. Woodward stressed the first, in her *Industrial Organization*, London: Oxford University Press, 1965, and D.S. Pugh and the 'Aston Group' the second. See D.S. Pugh and D.J. Hickson, *Organizational Structure in its Context: The Aston Programme I*, London: Gower, 1976.

11. The most significant of these was the Royal Commission on Trade Unions and Employers Associations 1964–1968, which was chaired by Lord Donovan. See also the various reports of the Prices and Incomes Board published over this period. Detailed references follow as appropriate.

12. Royal Commission on Trade Unions and Employers Associations, 1965–1968, *Report*, London: HMSO, p. 262.

13. See, for example National Board For Prices and Incomes, Report no. 65, *Payment by Results System*, Cmnd 3627, London: HMSO, 1968, and Report no 83, *Job Evaluation*, Cmnd 3772, London: HMSO, 1968.

14. British Standards Institution, *Glossary of Terms on Work Study*, London: British Standards Institution, 1959.

15. C. Sofer, *Organizations in Theory and Practice*, London: Heinemann, 1972, p. 97. Sofer was one of the instigators of the Tavistock version of these methods. His book is a good source of information on their conceptual and practical background. On Lewin and laboratory training methods see A.J. Marrow, *The Practical Theorist: the Life and Work of Kurt Lewin*, New York: Basic Books, n.d.; R. Lippitt, *Training in Community Relations*, New

York: Harper & Row, 1949; and L.P. Bradford, J.R. Gibb, and K. Benne (eds), *T-Group Theory and Laboratory Method: Innovation in Re-Education*, New York: Wiley, 1964.

16. Sofer, op. cit., p. 96.

17. E.L. Trist and C. Sofer, *Explorations in Group Relations*, Leicester: Leicester University Press, 1959. The account that follows is derived from this book, which documents the First Leicester Conference.

18. J.D. Sutherland, in Trist and Sofer, op. cit., pp. 56–57.

19. Ibid., p. 60.

20. The analysis of group dynamics promulgated by the Tavistock and at the conferences was to come under the expanding sway of systems thinking, whose principal exponent was A.K. Rice, moving from the small to the large group and opening the group to relations with the world outside. See A.K. Rice, *Learning for Leadership*, London: Tavistock, 1965, and E.J. Miller and A.K. Rice, *Systems of Organization*, London: Tavistock, 1967. This was to enable the work on group relations to align with the project of organizational change discussed in the next chapter.

Chapter ten The Production of the Self

1. P. Ribeaux and S.E. Poppleton, *Psychology and Work*, London: Macmillan, 1978, p. 306.

2. See N.Q. Herrick and M. Maccoby, 'Humanizing work: a priority goal of the 1970s', in L.E. Davis and A.C. Cherns, *The Quality of Working Life: Vol. 1: Problems, Prospects and the State of the Art*, New York: Free Press, 1975. I draw the account that follows from the essays in this volume, together with N.A.B. Wilson, *On The Quality of Working Life*, Manpower Papers no. 7, London: HMSO, 1973; M. Rose, *Reworking the Work Ethic*, London: Batsford, 1985; and A.T.M. Wilson, 'Quality of working life: an introductory overview', manuscript.

3. Herrick and Maccoby, op. cit., p. 66.

4. F.E. Emery and E. Thorsrud, *Democracy at Work*, Leiden: Martinus Nijhof, 1976.

5. See A. Myrdal, *Towards Equality*, Stockholm: Prisma Press, 1971, and D. Jenkins, *Job Power*, New York: Doubleday, 1973.

6. N.A.B. Wilson, op. cit.

7. A.T.M. Wilson, op. cit..

8. M. Rose, *Reworking the Work Ethic*, London: Batsford, 1985, p. 108.

9. See, for example, E. Trist, 'The socio-technical perspective', in A. van de Ven and W.F. Joyce (eds), *Perspectives on Organizational Design and Behaviour*, New York: Wiley, 1981.

10. G. Hunnius, 'On the nature of capitalist-initiated innovations in the workplace', in T.R. Burns et al. (eds), *Work and Power: The Liberation of Work and the Control of Political Power*, London: Sage, 1979.

11. Michael Rose in *Reworking the Work Ethic*, op. cit., Ch. 8, provides a useful analysis and critical discussion of these critiques, upon which I have drawn here.

12. For example R. Sennett, 'The boss's new clothes', *New York Review of Books*, 22 February 1979, pp. 42–46, discussed in Rose, op. cit.

13. I. Berg et al., *Managers and Work Reform: A Limited Engagement*, New York: Free Press, 1979, discussed in Rose, op. cit.

14. F.E. Emery and E.L. Trist, 'The causal texture of organizational environments', *Human Relations* 18 (1965): 21–32.

15. W.H. Whyte, *The Organization Man*, New York: Simon & Schuster, 1956.

16. Chris Argyris's *Integrating the Individual and the Organization*, New York: Wiley, 1964, provides one of the clearest accounts, and the significant figures are taken from him, pp. 4–5. References to the authors cited are: G.W. Allport, 'The trend in motivational theory', *American Journal of Orthopsychiatry* 23 (1953): 107–19; G.W. Allport, 'The open system in personality theory', *Journal of Abnormal and Social Psychology* 61 (1960): 301–10; K. Lewin et al 'Levels of Aspiration', in J. McV. Hunt (ed.), *Personality and Behaviour Disorders*, New York: Ronald Press, 1944; A. Maslow, *Motivation and Personality*, New York: Harper, 1954; C. Rogers, 'A theory of therapy, personality and interpersonal relationships', in S. Koch (ed.), *Psychology: A Study of a Science, Vol. 3*, New York: McGraw Hill, 1959; J. Bruner, 'The act of discovery', *Harvard Educational Review* 31 (1961): 26–28; E. Fromm, *The Art of Loving*, New York: Harper, 1956; V.E. Frankl, 'Basic concepts of logotherapy', *Journal of Existential Psychiatry*, 3 (1962): 113–14.

17. Argyris, *Integrating the Individual*, op. cit., p. 4.

18. See, for example, V.H. Vroom, *Work and Motivation*, New York: Wiley, 1964.

19. F. Herzberg, *Work and the Nature of Man*, London: Staples, 1968.

20. D. McGregor, *The Human Side of Enterprise*, New York: McGraw-Hill, 1960, quoted in D.S. Pugh (ed.), *Organisation Theory*, Harmondsworth: Penguin, 1985, pp. 326–27. Italics removed.

21. Ibid., p. 328.

22. C. Argyris, *The Impact of Budgets on People*, New York: Controllership Foundation, 1952, quoted in P. Miller and T. O'Leary, 'Accounting and the construction of the governable person', *Accounting, Organizations and Society* 12 (1987): 235–65, on which these remarks are based.

23. C. Argyris, *Personality and Organization*, New York: Harper, 1957.

24. C. Argyris, in the *Research News Bulletin* of the National Institute of Industrial Psychology, October 1961, quoted in M. Niven, *Personnel Management 1913–63*, London: Institute of Personnel Management, 1967, p. 150.

25. C. Argyris, *Integrating the Individual and the Organization*, New York: Wiley, 1964.

26. Ibid., pp. 33–34.

27. See, for example, C. Argyris and D. Schon, *Organizational Learning: a Theory of Action Perspective*, New York: Addison-Wesley, 1978.

28. The phrase is the sub-title of T.J. Peters and R.H. Waterman's best-selling book, *In Search of Excellence*, New York: Harper & Row, 1982.

29. Ibid., p. 60.

30. Ibid., pp. 72–73.

31. See, for example, C. Garfield, *Peak Performers: The New Heroes in Business*, London: Hutchinson, 1986; V. Kiam, *Going for it: How to Succeed as an Entrepreneur*, London: Collins, 1986; W. Avis, *Take a Chance to be First: The Secrets of Entrepreneurial Success*, London: Macmillan, 1986. See also the review of this and other 'excellence' material by Patrick Wright, 'Excellence', *London Review of Books*, 21 May 1987.

32. These techniques of the self are discussed in detail later in this book. See also the discussion in C. Lasch, *The Culture of Narcissism*, London: Abacus Press, 1980, esp. pp. 41ff and 63ff, and J. Donzelot, 'Pleasure in work', *I&C* 9 (1982): 1–28, esp. p. 24.

33. This is the title of the lame British imitation, W. Goldsmith and D. Clutterbuck, *The Winning Streak*, London: Weidenfeld & Nicolson, 1984.

34. See, for example, T.R. Pascale and A.G. Athos, *The Art of Japanese Management*, New York: Simon & Schuster, 1981.

35. D. Wilson, *The Sun at Noon*, London: Hamish Hamilton, 1986, quoted in P. Wickens, *The Road to Nissan: Flexibility, Quality, Teamwork*, London: Macmillan, 1987, p. 38.

36. Wickens, op. cit., p. 183.

Chapter eleven The Young Citizen

1. T.H. Marshall, 'Citizenship and social class', in *Sociology at the Crossroads*, London: Heinemann, 1963. The phrase quoted is from p. 72.

2. B.S. Turner, *Citizenship and Capitalism*, London: Allen & Unwin, 1986, esp. pp. 92–96. Cf G.M. Thomas and J.W. Meyer, 'The expansion of the state', *Annual Review of Sociology* 10 (1984): 461–82.

3. See, for example, I. Gough, *Political Economy of the Welfare State*, London: Macmillan, 1979.

4. For two examples of this literature, see A. Platt, *The Child Savers*, Chicago, Il: University of Chicago Press, 1969; N. Parton, *The Politics of Child Abuse*, London: Macmillan, 1984. See also the overviews given in M. Freeman, *The Rights and Wrongs of Children*, London: Pinter, 1983, and R. Dingwall, J.M. Eekelaar, and T. Murray, 'Childhood as a social problem: a survey of legal regulation', *Journal of Law and Society* 11 (1984): 207–32.

5. This picture, of course, obliterates many conceptual and political distinctions. For examples of this literature see: A. Oakley, *Sex, Gender and Society*, London: Temple Smith, 1972; L. Comer, *Wedlocked Women*, Leeds: Feminist Books, 1974; E. Zaretsky, *Capitalism, The Family and Personal Life*, London: Pluto Press, 1976; E. Wilson, *Women and the Welfare State*, London: Tavistock, 1977; J. Lewis, *The Politics of Motherhood: Child and Maternal Welfare in England 1900–1939*, London: Croom Helm, 1980; J. Lewis, 'Anxieties about the family and the relationships between parents, children and the state in twentieth-century England', in M. Richards and P. Light, *Children of Social Worlds*, Cambridge: Polity Press, 1986.

6. These paragraphs draw on my article 'Beyond the public/private division: law, power and the family', *Journal of Law and Society* 14 (1987): 61–76. For some of this literature see M. Stacey,' The division of labour revisited', in P. Abrams et al., (eds), *Development and Diversity: British*

Sociology 1950–1980, London: British Sociological Association, 1981; M. Stacey and M. Price, *Women, Power and Politics*, London: Tavistock, 1981; E. Gamarnikow et al., (eds), *The Public and the Private*, London: Heinemann, 1983. Much of the recent debate refers back to M. Rosaldo, 'Women, Culture and Society', in M. Rosaldo and L. Lamphere, (eds.), *Women, culture and society*, Stanford: Stanford University Press, 1974. See also S. Ardener (ed.), *Women and Space*, London: Croom Helm, 1981, and J.B. Elshtain, *Public Man and Private Woman*, Brighton: Harvester, 1981. The argument has been particularly influential in disputes over the legal regulation of families: see F. Olsen, 'The family and the market: and study of ideology and legal reform', *Harvard Law Review* 96 (1983): 1497; K. O'Donovan, *Sexual Divisions in Law*, 1985; M. Freeman, 'Towards a critical theory of family law', *Current Legal Problems* 38 (1985): 153; A. Bottomley, 'Resolving family disputes: a critical view', in M. Freeman (ed.), *State, Law and the Family*, London: Tavistock,1984.

7. For a useful discussion see J. Minson, *Genealogies of Morals*, London: Macmillan, 1985, Ch. 5.

8. J. Donzelot, *The Policing of Families*, London: Hutchinson, 1979.

9. I discuss philanthropy further in N. Rose *The Psychological Complex*, London: Routledge & Kegan Paul, 1985.

10. These are discussed in detail for England in my *Psychological Complex* and for France in Donzelot, op. cit.

Chapter twelve The Gaze of the Psychologist

1. M. Foucault, *Discipline and Punish*, London: Allen Lane, 1979, p. 191.

2. This chapter is based upon the argument made in my paper, 'Calculable minds and manageable individuals', *History of the Human Sciences*, 1 (1988): 179–200.

3. Foucault, op. cit.

4. This discussion is indebted to M. Lynch, 'Discipline and the material form of images: an analysis of scientific visibility', *Social Studies of Science* 15 (1985): 37–66.

5. More details of these are given in N. Rose, *The Psychological Complex*, London: Routledge & Kegan Paul, 1985, and the chapters by Peter Miller and myself in P. Miller and N. Rose, *The Power of Psychiatry*, Cambridge: Polity, 1986. See also D. Garland, *Punishment and Welfare*, Aldershot: Gower, 1985.

6. Cf. M. Donnelly, *Managing the Mind*, London: Tavistock, 1983, Ch. 7.

7. For the concept of inscription devices see B. Latour, 'Visualization and cognition: thinking with hands and eyes', in H. Kushlick (ed.), *Knowledge and Society*, Vol. 6, Greenwich, CT: JAI Press, 1986.

8. For a discussion of some problems in Foucault's archaeology arising from his assumption of an equivalence between a statement and a sentence, see B. Brown and M. Cousins, 'The linguistic fault', *Economy and Society* 9 (1980): 251–278.

9. Latour, op. cit.

10. S. Gilman, *Seeing the Insane*, New York: Wiley, 1982. See also M. Shortland, 'Barthes, Lavater and the legible body', *Economy and Society* 14 (1985): 273–312.

11. I have discussed this at length in *The Psychological Complex*, London: Routledge & Kegan Paul, 1985. For other discussions of the feeble-minded and eugenics see G.R. Searle, *Eugenics and Politics in Britain 1900–1914*, Leyden: Noordhof, 1976; D.A. MacKenzie, *Statistics in Britain*, Edinburgh: Edinburgh University Press, 1981; C. Webster (ed.), *Biology, Medicine and Society 1840–1940*, Cambridge: Cambridge University Press, 1981, esp. Chs. 5, 6, 7 and 8.

12. This was the line taken by philanthropists impressed by the work in the first half of the nineteenth century by Séguin in France, Saegert in Germany, and Guggenbühl in Switzerland. Sidney Howe led the campaign for the education of idiots in the United States; in England the campaign for state action to counter the burden of the idiot was led by the Charity Organization Society; it was this line of argument, rather than the eugenic perspective, that dominated the *Report of the Royal Commission on the Care and Control of the Feeble Minded*, Cd 4202, London: HMSO, 1908. These debates are discussed in *The Psychological Complex*, op. cit., Ch. 4.

13. The leading advocate of this system in Britain was Dr Francis Warner. See *The Study of Children and their School Training* London: Macmillan, 1897. His scheme was incorporated into the standard texts, and was still included in the 16th edition of A. Newsholme and J. Kerr, *School Hygiene*, London: George Allen & Unwin, 1924. The use of the body as a means of diagnosis of mental pathology can be traced back to physiognomy, and was popularized in phrenology, but it was refined and codified as a diagnostic technique by doctors of the insane in the eighteenth and nineteenth centuries, from Lavater, through Pinel and Esquirol in France, to Bucknill and Tuke in England. It was utilized by theorists of degeneracy such as Maudsley and Morel, and refined in the science of criminology of Lombroso and his successors. See S. Gilman, *Seeing the Insane*, New York: Wiley, 1982, and my 'Calculable minds and manageable individuals', *History of the Human Sciences* 1 (1988): 179–200.

14. For a discussion of the work of Galton and his followers, see R.S. Cowan, 'Francis Galton's statistical ideas: the influence of eugenics', *Isis* 63, (1972): 509–28, and R.S. Cowan, 'Nature and nurture: the interplay of biology and politics in the work of Francis Galton', *Studies in the History of Biology* 1 (1977): 133–208. See also D. Mackenzie, *Statistics in Britain 1865–1930: The social construction of scientific knowledge*, Edinburgh: Edinburgh University Press, 1981.

15. On Binet, see T.H. Wolf, *Alfred Binet*, Chicago, Il: University of Chicago Press, 1973.

16. Quoted in ibid., p. 141.

17. See *The Psychological Complex*, op. cit., pp. 127–28.

18. See G. Sutherland, *Ability, Merit and Measurement: mental testing and English education 1880–1940*, Oxford: Clarendon, 1984.

19. For the details, see L. Hearnshaw, *Cyril Burt: Psychologist*, London: Hodder & Stoughton, 1979.

20. See G. Sutherland, op. cit.

21. This theme is elaborated in various places in Foucault, *Discipline and Punish*, op. cit.

22. See the discussion of the 'Wild Boy of Aveyron' in *The Psychological Complex*, op. cit.

23. For a good discussion see D. Riley, *War in the Nursery*, London: Virago, pp. 43–59.

24. C. Darwin, 'A biographical sketch of an infant', *Mind* 2 (1877): 285–94; W. Preyer, *Mental Development in the Child*, tr. H.W. Brown, New York & London: Arnold, 1894; M. Shinn, *Notes on the Development of a Child*, California: University of California Studies, 1893; J. Sully, *Studies in Childhood*, London: Longmans Green, 1895. G. Stanley Hall, 'The contents of children's minds', *Princeton Review* 11 (1883): 249–72; W. Stern, *Psychology of Early Childhood*, tr. A. Barwell, London: Allen & Unwin, 1924. On the Child Study Movement, see D. Riley, op. cit., 1983 Chapter 3.

25. For representative samples of Gesell's many works, see A. Gesell, *The Mental Growth of the School Child*, New York: Macmillan, 1925, and *Infancy and Human Growth*, New York: Macmillan, 1928.

26. I discuss these processes more theoretically in my paper, 'Calculable minds and manageable individuals', op. cit. See also Latour, op. cit, and Lynch, op. cit.

27. Cf. Lynch, op. cit.

28. See the reviews in C. Buhler, 'The social behaviour of the child', in C. Murchison (ed.), *Handbook of Child Psychology*, Worcester, MA: Clark University Press, 1931; M. Collins, 'Modern trends in child psychology', in F.C. Bartlett et al. (eds), *The Study of Society*, London: Kegan Paul, Trench, Trubner, 1939; and C.J.C. Earl, 'Some methods of assessing temperament and personality', in Bartlett, *The Study of Society*, op. cit.

29. See the discussion in C. Hardyment, *Dream Babies: Child Care from Locke to Spock*, Oxford: Oxford University Press, 1984, Chapter 4.

Chapter thirteen Adjusting the Bonds of Love

1. J. Bowlby, *Maternal Care and Mental Health*, Geneva: World Health Organization, 1952, p. 46.

2. The following paragraphs draw upon the discussion in Chapter 8 of N. Rose, *The Psychological Complex*, London: Routledge & Kegan Paul, 1985.

3. J. Donzelot, *The Policing of Families*, London: Hutchinson, 1979, esp. Ch. 4.

4. M. Foucault, *Discipline and Punish*, London: Allen Lane, 1979, pp. 20–21.

5. W. Beveridge, *Social Insurance and Allied Services*, London: HMSO, 1942, p. 154. On post-war pronatalism, see J. Weeks, *Sex, Politics and Society: The Regulation of Sexuality since 1800*, London: Longmans, 1981, Ch. 12, and D. Riley, *War in the Nursery*, London: Virago, 1983.

6. *Report of the Royal Commission on Population*, Cmd 7695, London: HMSO, 1949. See also Mass Observation, *Britain and Her Birth Rate*, London: John Murray, 1945; M. Abrams, *The Population of Great Britain*, London: Allen & Unwin, 1945; J.C. Flugel, *Population, Psychology and*

Peace, London: Watts, 1947; G.F. McCleary, *The Menace of British Depopulation*, London: Allen & Unwin, 1945; R.M. Titmuss, *Birth, Poverty and Wealth*, London: Hamish Hamilton, 1943; R.F. Harrod, *Britain's Future Population*, London: Oxford University Press, 1943; Fabian Society, *Population and the People*, London: Allen & Unwin, 1945; E. Hubback, *The Population of Britain*, West Drayton: Penguin, 1947. I am grateful to Weeks, op. cit., for these references.

7. Weeks, op. cit., p. 232.

8. Ibid., p. 167.

9. Feversham Committee, *The Voluntary Mental Health Services*, London: n.p., 1939.

10. See R. Titmuss, *Problems of Social Policy*, London: HMSO, 1950, pp. 378–87.

11. D. Riley, op. cit.

12. R. Spitz, 'Hospitalism: an inquiry into the genesis of psychiatric conditions in early childhood', *The Psychoanalytic Study of the Child* 1 (1945): 53–74.

13. Editorial, 'Loneliness in infancy', *British Medical Journal*, 19 September 1942, p. 345, quoted in Riley, op. cit., pp. 112–13.

14. A. Freud, Foreword to new edition of *Infants Without Families and Reports on the Hampstead War Nurseries 1939–1945*, London: Hogarth Press and Institute of Psycho Analysis, 1973, p. xxiv. The first annual report on the Hampstead War Nursery was published as D. Burlingham and A. Freud, *Young Children in War-Time: A Year's Work in a Residential Nursery*; London: George Allen & Unwin for The New Era, 1942. *Infants Without Families: the Case for and Against Residential Nurseries* was also published under the joint authorship of Burlingham and Freud, by George Allen & Unwin in 1944.

15. Freud, *Infants Without Families*, p. xxv.

16. Ibid, p. 208.

17. Ibid, p. 599ff.

18. Of course this is not strictly true. Melanie Klein was not the only analyst to both observe and analyze her own offspring in these terms.

19. Freud, op. cit., p. 585.

20. K.M. Wolf, 'Evacuation of children in war-time – a survey of the literature, with biography', *Psychoanalytic Study of the Child* 1 (1945): 389–404.

21. S. Isaacs, ed., *The Cambridge Evacuation Survey*, London: Methuen, 1941, p. 3.

22. Ibid., p. 7.

23. Ibid.

24. Ministry of Health, *Hostels For 'Difficult' Children*, London: HMSO, 1944; Titmuss, op. cit., p. 383.

25. J. Bowlby, 'Forty-four juvenile thieves: their character and home life', *International Journal of Psycho-Analysis* 25 (1944): 19–53, 107–28.

26. J. Bowlby, 'Psychological Aspects', in R. Padley and M. Cole (eds), *Evacuation Survey: A Report to the Fabian Society*, London: Routledge, 1940.

27. C. Blacker, *Neurosis and the Mental Health Services*, London: Oxford University Press, 1946. See also World Health Organization, *Report of the*

Third Expert Committee on Mental Health, Geneva: 1953. See my 'Psychiatry: the discipline of mental health', in P. Miller and N. Rose (eds), *The Power of Psychiatry*, Cambridge: Polity, 1986.

28. See Riley, op. cit., pp. 115–6 and World Health Organization, 'Separation of the Pre-School Child from the Mother', Expert Committee on Mental Health, *Report on the Second Session*, Geneva, 1951.

29. J. Bowlby, *Maternal Care and Mental Health*, Geneva, World Health Organization, 1951. Page references are to the second edition, 1952. The chief of the Mental Health Section of the WHO was Ronald Hargreaves, one of the Tavistock Clinic's wartime team; the principal discussion forum while the Report was in preparation was a research team at the Tavistock, including James Robertson (ex-Hampstead War Nursery), which was studying the effects on personality development of separation from the mother in early childhood. Another important influence, according to Bowlby himself, was Eric Trist of the Tavistock Institute of Human Relations.

30. Ibid., p. 48

31. Ibid., p. 58.

32. Ibid., p. 151.

33. These are discussed in H.V. Dicks, *Fifty Years of the Tavistock Clinic*, London: Routledge & Kegan Paul, 1970. For example: James Robertson's films *A two-year-old goes to hospital* (1952) and *Going to hospital with mother* (1958); J. Bowlby, M. Ainsworth et al., 'The effects of mother- child separation: a follow-up study', *British Journal of Medical Psychology* 29 (1956): 211–47, and Bowlby's own *Attachment*, London: Hogarth Press, 1969.

34. Home Department, Ministry of Health and Ministry of Education, *Report of the Care of Children Committee* (Chairman: Myra Curtis) Cmd 6922, London: HMSO, 1946, para. 418.

35. E. Younghusband, *Social Work in Britain: 1950–75*, London: George Allen & Unwin, 1978, pp. 36–37.

36. Home Office Circular no. 160, 1948, quoted in Younghusband, op. cit., p. 41.

37. In C. Morris (ed.), *Social Case Work in Great Britain*, London: Faber & Faber, p. 193, quoted in Yelloly, *Social Work Theory and Psychoanalysis*, London: van Nostrand Reinhold, 1980, p. 101.

38. N. Timms, *Psychiatric Social Work in Great Britain, 1939–1962*, London: Routledge & Kegan Paul, 1964; Younghusband, op. cit., pp. 190–94.

39. Op. cit., p. 157.

40. Yelloly, op. cit., p. 80.

41. N.K. Hunnybun, 'A contribution to casework training', *Case Conference* 2 (1955), quoted in Yelloly, op. cit. p. 80.

42. Board of Education and Board of Control, *Report of the Joint Departmental Committee on Mental Deficiency*, London: HMSO, 1929, Pt. III, para. 91, quoted in Blacker, op. cit., p. 103.

43. See, for example, A. Bowley, *The Problems of Family Life*, Edinburgh: Livingstone, 1948; R. Wofinden, *Problem Families in Bristol*, London: Eugenics Society, 1950; C.P. Blacker, *Problem Families: Five Enquiries*, London: Eugenics Society, 1952; Institute for the Scientific Study of Delinquency, *The Problem Family*, London, 1957; A.F. Philp and N. Timms,

The Problem of the Problem Family, London: Family Service Units, 1962; A.F. Philp, *Family Failure: a study of 129 families with multiple problems*, London: Faber, 1963. See also J. Clarke, 'Social democratic delinquents and Fabian families', in National Deviancy Conference (ed.), *Permissiveness and Control*, London: Macmillan, and J. Lewis, 'Anxieties about the family and the relationships between parents, children and the state in twentieth century England', in M. Richards and P. Light (eds), *Children of Social Worlds*, Cambridge: Polity Press, 1985. The evidence for the existence of such families is reviewed in M. Rutter and N. Madge, *Cycles of Disadvantage*, London: Heinemann, 1976.

44. Dr. Ratcliffe, speaking to the Institute for the Study and Treatment of Delinquency, quoted by Yelloly, op. cit., p. 108.

45. T. Parsons et al, *Family, Socialization and Interaction Processes*, Glencoe, IL: Free Press, 1955. Parsons, of course, developed his arguments in the School of Social Relations at Harvard, along with many of the American wartime social psychologists of human relations discussed in an earlier chapter.

46. One notable exception is C. Lasch, *Haven in a Heartless World*, New York: Basic Books, 1977.

47. e.g. A.T.M. Wilson, 'Some reflections and suggestions on the prevention and treatment of marital problems', *Human Relations* 2 (1949): 233 52; H.V. Dicks, 'Clinical studies in marriage and the family,, *British Journal of Medical Psychology* 26 (1953): 181–96.

48. *Report of the Committee on Procedure in Matrimonial Causes*, Cmd 7024, London: HMSO, 1947.

49. Harris Committee, Cmd 7566, London: HMSO, 1948.

50. See H.V. Dicks, *Marital Tensions*, London: Routledge, 1967.

51. Ministry of Education, *Report of the Committee on Maladjusted Children*, Chairman: J. Underwood, London: HMSO, 1955, para. 16.

52. Ibid., para. 482.

53. Ibid., p. 151.

54. E.g. D. Donnison and M. Stewart, *The Child and the Social Services*, Fabian pamphlet, London: Fabian Society, 1958; D. Donnison, P. Jay, and M. Stewart, *The InglebyReport: Three Critical Essays*, Fabian Pamphlet, London: Fabian Society, 1962; Longford Study Group, *Crime: A Challenge to us All*, London: Labour Party, 1966. These are all discussed in J. Clarke, op. cit., which I have drawn on heavily in the following paragraphs.

55. Home Office, *Report of the Committee on Children and Young Persons* (Chairman Viscount O. Ingleby), Cmnd 1191, London: HMSO, 1960; Home Office, *The Child, theFamily and the Young Offender*, London: HMSO, 1965; Home Office, *Children in Trouble*, London: HMSO, 1968.

56. Clarke, op. cit., p. 91.

57. *Report of the Committee on Local Authority and Allied Personal Social Services* (Chairman: Lord F. Seebohm), Cmnd 3065, London: HMSO, 1968, para. 32.

58. Ibid., para. 2.

59. P. Aries, *Centuries of Childhood*, London: Cape, first published in English in 1962, was republished by Penguin in 1973 and deployed in this cause, to be followed by many others more directly written to this end.

60. L. Comer, *Wedlocked Women*, Leeds: Feminist Books, 1974, was one of the first.

61. M. Rutter's *Maternal Deprivation Reassessed*, Harmondsworth: Penguin, was first published in 1972 and reprinted six times during the 1970s.

62. J. Mitchell's *Psychoanalysis and Feminism*, London: Allen Lane, was published in 1974.

63. One of the first English discussions of the concept of children's 'rights' is the National Council For Civil Liberties' *Children Have Rights*, London, 1972. The literature expanded enormously in the late 1970s and 1980s. For a review see M. Freeman, *The Rights andWrongs of Children*, London: Francis Pinter, 1983.

Chapter fourteen Maximizing the Mind

1. C. Mitchell, *Time for School: A Practical Guide for Parents of Young Children*, Harmondsworth: Penguin, 1973.

2. V. Walkerdine, *Democracy in the Kitchen*, London: Virago, forthcoming. I would like to thank Valerie Walkerdine for letting me see this book in draft; I have drawn upon a number of its arguments in this chapter.

3. The main secondary sources I have drawn upon here are T. Blackstone, *A Fair Start: The Provision of Pre-School Education*, London: Allen Lane, 1971, and N. Whitbread, *The Evolution of the Nursery–Infant School*, London: Routledge & Kegan Paul, 1972.

4. For a critical analysis of the evidence for this view, see A.M. and A.D.B. Clarke, *Early Experience: Myth and Evidence*, London: Open Books, 1976.

5. F. Froebel, *The Education of Man*, New York: Appleton, 1906 (originally published in 1826).

6. J. Ronge and B. Ronge, *English Kindergarten*, London: Hudson, 1855, p. iii, quoted in Blackstone, op. cit., p. 26.

7. See my discussion in N. Rose, *The Psychological Complex*, London: Routledge & Kegan Paul, 1985, Ch. 1. See also H. Lane, *The Wild Boy of Aveyron*, London: Allen & Unwin, 1977, and *When the Mind Hears*, New York: Random House, 1984.

8. See M. Montessori, *The Montessori Method*, London: Heinemann, 1912; W. Boyd, *From Locke to Montessori*, London: Harrap, 1914; E.P. Culverwell, *The Montessori Principles and Practice*, London: Bell, 1913. See also the discussion in V. Walkerdine, 'Developmental psychology and the child-centred pedagogy', in J. Henriques et al. (eds), *Changing the Subject*, London: Methuen, 1984.

9. *Wesleyan Methodists Magazine*, 1823, quoted in Blackstone, op. cit., p. 15.

10. S. Wilderspin, *The Infant System for Developing the Intellectual and Moral Power of all Children from One to Seven Years of Age*, London: Simkin and Marshall,1840 p. 38, quoted in Blackstone, op. cit., p. 14.

11. *Westminster and Foreign Quarterly Review*, 1847, quoted in Blackstone, op. cit.

12. *Manchester Times*, quoted in Blackstone, op. cit., p. 20.

13. Board of Education, *Report of the Consultative Committee upon the School Attendance of Children Below the Age of Five*, London: HMSO, 1908.

14. See *The Psychological Complex*, Ch. 6.

15. The 1908 Education Act, and the repeated circulars and reports in the two decades following on Local Education Authority expenditure, discussed in the sources given in note 3.

16. See especially the work of Margaret and Rachel McMillan: M. McMillan, *The Nursery School*, London: Dent, 1930. See N. Whitbread, *The Evolution of the Infant–Nursery School*, London: Routledge & Kegan Paul, 1972.

17. Cf. D.G. Pritchard, *Education and the Handicapped 1760–1960*, London: Routledge & Kegan Paul, 1963.

18. Circular 1054 (Health): 1405 (Education).

19. Quoted in Blackstone, op. cit., p. 47.

20. *Report of the Consultative Committee on Infant and Nursery Schools*, London: HMSO, 1933; Board of Education, *Nursery Schools and Nursery Classes*, London: HMSO, 1936.

21. See especially D. Riley, *War in the Nursery*, London: Virago, 1983.

22. An overview of the survey is contained in E. Atkins, N. Cherry, J.W.B. Douglas, K.E. Kiernan, and M.E.J. Wadsworth, 'The 1946 British Birth Cohort: an account of the origins, progress and results of the National Survey of Health and Development', in S.A. Mednick and A.E. Baert (eds), *Prospective Longitudinal Research: An Empirical Basis for the Primary Prevention of Psychosocial Disorders*, Oxford: Oxford University Press for the World Health Organization, 1981. For references to the various publications from the survey, see below. See also M. Wadsworth, 'Evidence from three birth cohort studies for long-term and cross-generational effects on the development of children', in M.P.M. Richards and P. Light, *Children of Social Worlds*, Cambridge: Polity, 1986.

23. For example, the work of J.M. Tanner, who invented such handy inscription devices as the Harpenden Pocket Stadiometer for the convenient measurement of children's height. See his *Education and Physical Growth*, London: University of London Press, 1961. See also R.S. Illingworth, *The Development of the Infant and Young Child: Normal and Abnormal*, Edinburgh: Livingstone, 1960; A.H. Bowley, *The Natural Development of The Child*, Edinburgh: Livingstone, 1st ed 1942, 4th ed 1957.

24. The classic examples being the work of the Newsoms: J. Newsom and E. Newsom, *Infant Care in an Urban Community*, London: Allen & Unwin, 1963, and *Four Years Old in an Urban Community*, London: Allen & Unwin, 1968. Of course, these formed only one part of a massive enterprise of studying the working-class family, its transformations under conditions of rapid urban development and mobility, and the consequences, typified by the work of Willmot and Young.

25. J.W.B. Douglas, *The Home and the School*, London: MacGibbon and Kee, 1964.

26. This research is summarized and discussed in a number of books published in the 1970s, when this thesis was beginning to come into question. See M. Kellmer Pringle and S. Naidoo, *Early Child Care in Britain*, London: Gordon and Breach, 1975; M. Rutter and N. Madge, *Cycles of Disadvant-*

age: A Review of Research, London: Heinemann; A.M. Clarke and A.D.B. Clarke, *Early Experience: Myth and Evidence*, London: Open Books, 1976; R.K. Kelsall and H.M. Kelsall, *Social Disadvantage and Educational Opportunity*, London: Holt, Rinehart & Winston, 1971.

27. The history of this study is described in K. Fogelman and P. Wedge, 'The National Child Development Study (1958 British cohort)', in Mednick and Baert, op. cit. The quotation that follows comes from R. Davie, N. Butler, and H. Goldstein, *From Birth to Seven*, London: Longman with the National Children's Bureau, 1972, pp.11–12.

28. B. Jackson, Prologue to A.F. Osborn, N.R. Butler, and A.C. Morris, *The Social Life of Britain's Five-Year-Olds: A Report of the Child Health and Education Study*, London: Routledge & Kegan Paul, 1984, p. xxv.

29. Ibid, p. 3.

30. Mednick and Baert, eds., op. cit.

31. Central Advisory Council for Education, *Half Our Future* (the Newsom Report), London: HMSO, 1963.

32. Central Advisory Council for Education, *Children and Their Primary Schools*, The Plowden Report, London: HMSO, 1967.

33. O. Banks, *The Sociology of Education*, London: Batsford, 1968, p. 74.

34. See Kelsall and Kelsall, op. cit., p. 24 ff.

35. R.J. Havighurst, 'Urban development and the educational system', in A.H. Passow (ed.), *Education in Depressed Areas*, New York: Teachers College Press, 1963. The tradition of studies of urban subcultures in the United States is, of course, a long one, and particularly focused on class and race zoning and the emergence of poor and delinquent subcultures.

36. A. Little and G. Smith, *Strategies of Compensation: A Review of Educational Projects for the Disadvantaged in the United States*, Paris: Organization for Economic Co Operation and Development, 1971, p. 20.

37. Little and Smith, ibid, contains a comprehensive review of these studies.

38. See Little and Smith, ibid., for a summary of the plethora of studies documenting the links between race, high drop out rate, and low educational performance.

39. J. Kozol, *Death at an Early Age*, New York: Houghton Mifflin, 1967.

40. J.S. Coleman et al., *Equality of Educational Opportunity*, Washington DC: Government Printing Office, 1966.

41. 'The North Carolina Fund: Programmes and Policies, November 1963', quoted by P.Marris and M. Rein, *Dilemmas of Social Reform: Poverty and Community Action in the United States*, London: Routledge & Kegan Paul, 1967.

42. B.S. Bloom, *Stability and Change in Human Characteristics*, New York: Wiley, 1964.

43. J. McV. Hunt, *Intelligence and Experience*, New York: Ronald Press, 1961.

44. S.H. White, 'National Impact Study of Head Start', Harvard University, Laboratory of Human Development, mimeo, 1969, quoted in Little and Smith, op. cit., p. 50.

45. For an example of the first, see W.L. Hodges, B.R. McCandless and H.H. Spicks, *Diagnostic Teaching for Preschool Children*, Arlington, V:

Council for Exceptional Children, 1971. The most comprehensive evaluation of the latter type was V.G. Cicirelli et al., 'The Impact of Head Start on Children's Cognitive and Affective Development', Washington, DC: Westinghouse Learning Corporation, 1969. See also D.G. Hawkridge et al., *A Study of Selected Exemplary Programmes for the Education of Disadvantaged Children*, Washington, DC: U.S. Department of Health, Education and Welfare, 1968. These and other studies are reviewed in Kelsall and Kelsall, op. cit.

46. Daniel Moynihan gives an account of the 'politics of disillusionment' in the War on Poverty in *Maximum Feasible Misunderstanding: Community Action in the War on Poverty*, New York: Arkville Press, 1969.

47. The American debate over the article is contained in two *Harvard Educational Review* reprints: no. 2, 'Environment, heredity and intelligence', and no.4, 'Science, heritability and IQ', both published in 1969.

48. S. Baratz and J. Baratz, 'Early childhood intervention: the social science base of institutional racism', *Harvard Educational Review* 40 (1970): 29–48.

49. See, for example, the pieces collected in J.L. Frost (ed.), *Revisiting Early Childhood Education*, New York: Holt, Rinehart & Winston, 1973.

50. A.H. Halsey, *Educational Priority: EPA Problems and Policies*, Vol. 1., London: HMSO, 1972, p. 57.

51. Ibid., p. 125.

52. Ibid., p. 180.

53. For some examples of the projects funded by the Schools Council, see M. Chazan, A. Laing, and S. Jackson, *Just Before School*, Oxford: Blackwell for the Schools Council, 1971, and M. Parry and H. Archer, *Pre-School Education*, London: Macmillan, 1974. For the National Foundation for Educational Research, see H. Williams, 'Compensatory Education in the Nursery School', in M. Chazan (ed.), *Compensatory Education*, London: Butterworths, 1973.

54. For the playgroup movement, see W. van der Eyken, *The Pre-School Years*, Harmondsworth: Penguin, 1974.

55. For a discussion of this speech, its assumptions and bases, see Rutter and Madge, op. cit., Ch. 1.

56. On the history of concern with child abuse, see N. Parton, *The Politics of Child Abuse*, London: Macmillan, 1985.

57. A. Gesell, 'Pre-school development and education', *Annals of the American Academy* 71 (1925), quoted in Blackstone, op. cit., p. 48.

58. C. Urwin, 'Constructing motherhood: The persuasion of normal development, in V. Walkerdine, C. Urwin, and C. Steedman (eds), *Language and Childhood*, London: Routledge & Kegan Paul, 1986. See also D. Ingleby, 'Professionals as socializers: the "Psy Complex" ', in A. Scull and S. Spitzer (eds), *Research in Law, Deviance and Social Control* New York: JAI Press, 1985.

59. J. Beck, *How to Raise a Brighter Child*, originally published London: Souvenir Press, 1968; republished by Fontana in 1970 and reprinted many times during the next decade.

60. Ibid., p. 7.

61. Ibid., p. 23.

62. Cited in Walkerdine, op. cit., Ch. 1.

63. Ibid., Ch.4.
64. Mitchell, op. cit., p 250.
65. Ibid.

Chapter fifteen The Responsible Autonomous Family

1. In a radio broadcast entitled Support for Normal Parents, included in Winnicott, *The Child, the Family and the Outside World*, Harmondsworth: Penguin, 1964, pp. 174–5.

2. See 'The anti-social tendency (1956)' in D.W. Winnicott, *Through Paediatrics to Psycho-Analysis*, London: Hogarth Press and Institute of Psycho Analysis, 1975.

3. Winnicott, op. cit., p. 10.

4. In a lecture to the Nursery School Association, quoted in M. Davis and D. Wallbridge, *Boundary and Space: An Introduction to the Work of D.W. Winnicott*, Harmondsworth: Penguin, 1983, pp. 129–30.

5. Winnicott, *The Child, the Family and the Outside World*, op. cit., p. 186.

6. Ibid., p. 30.

7. The first quote is from ibid., p. 125; the others from ibid., p. 176.

8. F. Mount, *The Subversive Family*, London: Jonathan Cape, 1982.

9. One of the first compilations was A. Morris et al., *Justice for Children*, London: Macmillan, 1980. The same authors edited various other texts on the same themes. This material is well discussed in M. Freeman, *The Rights and the Wrongs of Children*, London: Pinter, 1983.

10. A. Morris, H. Giller, E. Szwed, and H. Geach, *Justice For Children*, London: Macmillan, 1980, was the first of a series of texts edited by these authors along these lines.

11. E.g. L. Taylor, R. Lacey, and D. Bracken, *In Whose Best Interests*, London: Cobden Trust/Mind, 1980.

12. For a review of this material see N. Parton, *The Politics of Child Abuse*, London: Macmillan, 1985.

13. Cf. M. King (ed.), *Childhood, Welfare and Justice: A Critical Examination of Children in the Legal and Childcare System*, London: Batsford, 1981.

14. E.g. R. Bailey and M. Brake, *Radical Social Work*, London: Arnold, 1975;

15. J. Goldstein, A. Freud, and A. Solnit, *Before the Best Interests of the Child*, New York: Free Press, 1979, pp. 11–12. See also *Beyond the Best Interests of the Child*, New York: Free Press, 1973.

16. Goldstein et al. *Before the Best Interests of the Child*, op. cit., p. 9.

Chapter sixteen Obliged to be Free

1. Cf. my chapter, 'The discipline of mental health', in P. Miller and N. Rose (eds), *The Power of Psychiatry*, Cambridge: Polity, 1986.

2. Cf. J. Kovel, *A Complete Guide to Therapy*, Harmondsworth: Penguin, and his later book *The Age of Desire*, New York: Pantheon, 1981.

3. R. Sennett, *The Fall of Public Man*, London: Faber, (1977) 1986.

4. C. Lasch, *The Culture of Narcissism*, London: Abacus Press, 1980.

5. See in particular P. Rieff, *The Triumph of the Therapeutic*, London: Chatto & Windus, 1966.

6. For a review, see S. Lukes, *Individualism*, Oxford: Blackwell, 1973.

7. For a review of some of this material, see A. Marsella and G. White (eds), *Cultural Conceptions of Mental Health and Therapy*, Dordrecht: Reidel, 1982.

8. M. Mauss, 'Une category de l'esprit humaine: la notion de personne, celle de "Moi" ', *Journal of the Royal Anthropological Institute* 68, (1938): 263–81, translated as 'A category of the human mind: the notion of person; the notion of self', in M. Carrithers, S. Collins, and S. Lukes (eds), *The Category of the Person*, Cambridge: Cambridge University Press, 1985. The elements of Mauss's argument are also developed in a rather different way in the writings of Durkheim. See also the collection of articles in K.J. Gergen and K.E. Davis (eds), *The Social Construction of the Person*, New York: Springer Verlag, 1985.

9. Mauss, op. cit., p. 3.

10. See the collection edited by Carrithers et al., op. cit.

11. See M. Foucault, *The History of Sexuality*, Vol. 1, London: Allen Lane, 1979.

12. B. Nelson, 'Self-images and systems of spiritual direction in the history of European civilization', in S. Klausner (ed.), *The Quest for Self-Control*, New York: Free Press, 1965.

13. Ibid., p. 71. The classic argument is made in Max Weber, *The Protestant Ethic and the Spirit of Capitalism*, London: Allen & Unwin, 1930.

14. Michel Foucault, 'Technologies of the self', in L. Martin et al. (eds), *Technologies of the Self*, London: Tavistock, 1988.

15. W. Paden, 'Theatres of humility and suspicion', in ibid., p. 70.

16. N. Elias, *The Civilizing Process*, 2 vols., Oxford: Blackwell, 1978, 1986.

17. On police see G. Rosen, 'Cameralism and the concept of medical police', *Bulletin of the History of Medicine* 27 (1953): 21–42; M. Foucault, 'On governmentality', *I&C* 6 (1979); M. Foucault, 'Omnes et singulatim: towards a critique of political reason', in S. McMurrin (ed.), *The Tanner Lectures on Human Values*, Vol. 2, University of Utah Press, 1981; M. Foucault, 'The political technology of individuals', in L. Martin et al. (eds), *Technologies of the Self*, London: Tavistock, 1988; P. Pasquino, 'Theatrum politicum: police and the state of prosperity', *Ideology and Consciousness* 4 (1978): 41–53.

18. G. Oestreich, *Neostoicism and the Modern State*, Cambridge: Cambridge University Press, 1982, p. 7.

19. Ibid., p. 164.

20. Ibid., p. 269. See my discussion in the Introduction, and M. Foucault, *Discipline and Punish*, London: Allen Lane, 1979.

21. Quoted in G. Oestreich, op. cit., p. 272.

22. Cf. M. Foucault, *Madness and Civilization*, London: Tavistock, 1965; M. Foucault, *Discipline and Punish*, London: Allen Lane, 1977. On school-

ing as a moral technology see especially I. Hunter, *Culture and Government: the Emergence of Literary Education*, London: Macmillan, 1988. On museums as citizen-forming technologies, see T. Bennett, 'The exhibitionary complex', *New Formations*, (1988): 73–102.

23. Home Office, *Report of the Committee on Homosexual Offenses and Prostitution*, Cmnd. 257, London: HMSO, 1957. The era of permissive legislation is sometimes thought to end with the non-implementation of the recommendations of the Wootton report which advocated liberalization of the legal constraints of the use of certain classes of drugs: Home Office, *Report of the Advisory Committee on Drug Dependence*, London: HMSO, 1968. The key pieces of legislation over this period were the Street Offenses Act 1959, the Obscene Publications Act, 1959, the Suicide Act 1961, the second Obscene Publications Act 1964, the Sexual Offenses Act 1967, the Family Planning Act 1967, the Abortion Act 1967, and the Divorce Reform Act 1969.

24. *Report of the Committee on Homosexual Offences*, op. cit., p. 24.

25. Ibid., p. 87.

26. Cf. my 'Beyond the public/private division: law, power and the family', in P. Fitzpatrick and A. Hunt (eds), *Critical Legal Studies*, Oxford: Blackwell, 1987.

27. For example F.A. Hayek, *The Constitution of Liberty*, London: Routledge & Kegan Paul, 1960; R. Nozick, *Anarchy, the State and Utopia*, Oxford: Blackwell, 1974; L. von Mises, *Omnipotent Government*, New Haven: Yale University Press, 1945; M. Friedman, *Free To Choose*, Harmondsworth: Penguin, 1980.

28. Cf. C. Gordon, 'The soul of the citizen: Max Weber and Michel Foucault on rationality and Government', in S. Whimster and S. Lash (eds), *Max Weber, Rationality and Modernity*, London: Allen & Unwin, 1986, p. 314.

29. J. Donzelot, *The Policing of Families*, London: Hutchinson, 1979, Ch. 5.

30. In the remarks that follow on the obligations of selfhood, I have drawn on John W. Meyer's insightful argument 'The self and the life course: institutionalization and its effects', in A. Sørensen, F. Weinert, and L. Sherrod (eds), *Human Development and the Life Course*, Hillsdale, NJ.: L. Erlbaum, 1986.

31. Cf. J. Baudrillard, 'The system of objects and consumer society, in M. Poster (ed.), *Selected Writings*, Cambridge: Polity, 1988; See also C. Campbell, *The Romantic Ethic and the Spirit of Modern Consumerism*, London: Blackwell, 1987.

Chapter seventeen Reshaping our Behaviour

1. H.J. Eysenck, *The Future of Psychiatry*, London: Methuen, 1975, p. 25.

2. In what follows I draw upon my paper, 'Psychiatry: the discipline of mental health', in P. Miller and N. Rose (eds), *The Power of Psychiatry*, Cambridge: Polity, 1986.

3. C.V. Binder, 'Behavior modification', in R. Herink (ed.), *The Psychotherapy Handbook*, New York: New American Library, 1980.

4. For the following I have drawn upon the useful historical account in A. Yates, *Behaviour Therapy*, New York: Wiley, 1970.

5. I.P. Pavlov, 'Neuroses in man and animals', *Journal of the American Medical Association* 99 (1932): 1012–13; I.P. Pavlov, *Conditioned Reflexes and Psychiatry*, New York: International University Press, 1941; V.M. Bekhterev, *General Principles of Human Reflexology*, New York: International University Press, 1932. For what appears to be the first overview in English of the development of Soviet psychiatry in the twentieth century, see J. Wortis, *Soviet Psychiatry*, Baltimore, MD: Williams & Wilkins, 1950.

6. E.g. J.B. Watson, 'Behaviorism and the concept of mental disease', *Journal of Philosophy, Psychology and Scientific Methods* 13 (1916) 587–97; W.H. Burnham, 'Mental hygiene and the conditioned reflex', *Pediological Seminary* 24 (1917): 449–88.

7. E.g. H.S. Liddell, 'The experimental neurosis and the problem of mental disorder', *American Journal of Psychiatry* 94 (1938): 1035–43; J.H. Masserman, *Behaviour and Neurosis*, Chicago, IL: University of Chicago Press, 1943.

8. E.g. K. Dunlap, *Habits: Their Making and Unmaking*, New York: Liveright, 1932; F.B. Holmes, 'An experimental investigation of a method of overcoming children's fears', *Child Development* 7 (1936): 6–30; O.H. Mowrer and W.A. Mowrer, 'Enuresis: a method for its study and treatment', *American Journal of Orthopsychiatry* 8 (1938): 436–47; L.W. Max, 'Breaking up a homosexual fixation by the conditioned reflex technique: a case study', *Psychological Bulletin* 32 (1935): 734; R.R. Sears and L.H. Cohen, 'Hysterical anesthesia, analgesia, and astereognosis', *Archives of Neurology and Psychiatry* 29 (1933): 260–71.

9. J. Dollard and N.E. Miller, *Personality and Psychotherapy*, New York: McGraw-Hill, 1950; J. Wolpe, *Psychotherapy by Reciprocal Inhibition*, Stanford, CA: Stanford University Press, 1958.

10. See Hans Jurgen Eysenck, in G. Lindzey, ed., *A History of Psychology in Autobiography, Vol. 7*, San Francisco, CA: Freeman, 1980, and H.B. Gibson, *Hans Eysenck*, London: Owen, 1981. Eysenck replaced Eric Trist, who had gone to work on the War Office Selection Boards.

11. E. Slater, 'The neurotic constitution: a statistical study of two thousand soldiers', *Journal of Neurology, Neurosurgery and Psychiatry* 6 (1943): 1–16 quoted in H.J. Eysenck, *Dimensions of Personality*, London: Kegan Paul, Trench, Trubner, 1947, p. 2.

12. H.J. Eysenck, *The Scientific Study of Personality*, London: Routledge & Kegan Paul, 1952.

13. The principal sources for what follows, as well as Yates, op. cit., are the following by H.J. Eysenck: 'Function and training of the clinical psychologist', *Journal of Mental Science* 96 (1950): 710–25; 'The effects of psychotherapy: an evaluation', *Journal of Consulting Psychology* 16 (1952): 319–24; *The Scientific Study of Personality*, London: Routledge & Kegan Paul, 1952; 'Learning theory and behaviour therapy', *Journal of Mental Science* 105 (1959): 61–75; and H.J. Eysenck (ed.), *Behaviour Therapy and the Neuroses*, London: Pergamon Press, 1960.

14. Eysenck in Lindzey (ed.), op. cit., p. 164.

15. The argument is rehearsed in a punchy manner in Eysenck's pamphlet, *The Future of Psychiatry*, op. cit.

16. Yates, op. cit., p. 17.

17. E.g. E. Glover, 'Critical notice of Wolpe's "Psychotherapy by reciprocal inhibition" ', *British Journal of Medical Psychology* 32 (1959): 68–74, and his 'Comment on Wolpe's reply', *British Journal of Medical Psychology* 32 (1959): 236–38; L. Breger and J.L. McGaugh, 'Critique and reformulation of "learning theory" approaches to psychotherapy and neurosis', *Psychological Bulletin* 63 (1965): 338–58.

18. C.f. Central Health Services Standing Mental Health Advisory Sub-Committee, *The Role of Psychologists in the Health Services* (The Trethowan Report), London: HMSO, 1977.

19. For a review, see Yates, op. cit., Ch. 4.

20. E.g. W. Yule and J. Carr, eds, *Behaviour Modification with the Mentally Handicapped*, London: Croom Helm, 1980.

21. Cf. A.E. Kazdin, *The Token Economy: A review and evaluation*, New York: Plenum, 1977.

22. See my discussion in 'Psychiatry: the discipline of mental health', op. cit.

23. Many further examples are given in A. Anastasi, *Fields of Applied Psychology*, 2nd edition, New York: McGraw Hill, 1979.

24. Ibid., p. 359

25. M. Linehan and K. Egan, *Asserting Yourself*, London: Century, 1983.

26. Ibid., p. 137.

27. This and the following quotations are from ibid., pp. 9–11.

28. For some examples of this literature see S. Spence and G. Shepherd (eds), *Developments in Social Skills Training*, London: Academic Press, 1983; Linehan, M. et al, 'Assertion therapy: skill training or cognitive restructuring?', *Behaviour Therapy* 12 (1979): 372–88; M. Combs and D. Slaby, 'Social skills training with children, in A. Kazdin and B. Lahey, *Advances in Clinical Child Psychology*, Vol. 1, New York: Plenum, 1977; L. Minkin et al., 'The social validation and training of conversational skills', *Journal of Applied Behavioural Analysis* 9 (1976): 127–39; A. Bandura, 'Self-efficacy: towards a unifying theory of behavior change', *Psychological Review* (1977): 191–215.

Chapter eighteen Technologies of Autonomy

1. B. Bettelheim, Afterword to M. Cardinal, *The Words to Say It*, London: Picador, 1984.

2. M. Foucault, *The History of Sexuality. Vol. 1: An Introduction*, London: Allen Lane, 1979.

3. This seems to be the line of argument in recent work in medical sociology. D. Armstrong, 'The patient's view', *Social Science and Medicine* 18 (1984): 737–44; W. Arney and B. Bergen, *Medicine and the Management of Living*, Chicago, Il: Chicago University Press, 1984; D. Silverman, *Communication and Medical Practice*, London: Sage, 1987.

4. Cf. M. Foucault, *The History of Sexuality. Vol. 2: The Use of Pleasure*, London: Viking, 1986, esp. pp. 25–32.

5. I have adapted this schema rather loosely from Foucault's argument cited above.

6. Foucault, vol. 2 op. cit., p. 29.

7. J. Breuer and S. Freud, *Studies in Hysteria, Standard Edition of the Collected Works of Sigmund Freud*, London: Hogarth Press, 1953–73, Vol. 2, p. 305.

8. Promotional literature, July 1987.

9. London College for Psychotherapy, brochure, 1987.

10. British Association of Psychotherapists, *What is Psychotherapy*, pamphlet, London: 1987.

11. D. Mackay, 'Behavioural Psychotherapy', in W. Dryden (ed.), *Individual Therapy in Britain*, London: Harper & Row, 1984, p. 276.

12. Ibid., passim.

13. C. R. Rogers, *On Becoming a Person*, London: Constable, 1961, esp. Ch. 8.

14. C. Rogers, in W.B. Frick, *Humanistic Psychology: Interviews with Maslow, Murphy and Rogers*, Columbia, OH: Merril, 1971, quoted in B. Thorne, 'Person-centred therapy', in Dryden (ed.), op. cit., p. 114.

15. F. Perls, R.F. Hefferline, and P. Goodman, *Gestalt Therapy*, New York: Bantam, (1951) 1977, pp. xiv, xi.

16. A. Janov, *The Primal Scream. Primal Therapy: the Cure for Neurosis*, New York: Putnam, (1970) 1980, p. 21.

17. T.A. Harris, *I'm OK – You're OK*, London: Pan, (1967) 1973, pp. xii–xiv.

18. A. Lowen, *Bioenergetics*, Harmondsworth: Penguin, (1975) 1976, pp. 43–4.

19. Cf. Foucault, *The History of Sexuality. Vol. 1*, op. cit., pp.104–5.

20. See P. Miller, 'Psychotherapy of work and unemployment', in P. Miller and N. Rose (eds), *The Power of Psychiatry*, Cambridge: Polity, 1986.

21. Some recent autobiographical accounts are illuminating. See M. Cardinal, *The Words to Say It*, London: Picador, 1983; N. Herman, *My Kleinian Home*, London: Quartet, 1985; D. Wigoder, *Images of Destruction*, London: Routledge & Kegan Paul, 1987; A. France, *Consuming Psychotherapy*, London: Free Association, 1988; R. Dinnage, *One to One: Experiences of Psychotherapy*, London: Viking Penguin, 1988.

22. I take this formulation from Silverman, op. cit., Ch. 6.

23. Cf. Paul Ricoeur's essay 'The question of proof in Freud's psychoanalytic writings', in *Hermeneutics and the Human Sciences*, J.B. Thompson (ed.), Cambridge: Cambridge University Press, 1981.

24. Cf. M. Foucault, 'Technologies of the Self', in L. Martin et al. (eds), *Technologies of the Self*, London: Tavistock, 1988.

25. All the quotes that follow are from Perls et al., op. cit. The numbers in parentheses are page numbers.

26. E. Berne, *Games People Play*, Harmondsworth: Penguin, 1968. The numbers in parentheses in the discussion that follow are page numbers.

27 L. Eichenbaum and S. Orbach, *What Do Women Want?*, London: Fontana, 1984. The puff from *Women's World* is printed on the front cover. Eichenbaum and Orbach are also authors of *Outside In, Inside Out*, Harmondsworth: Penguin, 1982, and Orbach is author of *Fat is a Feminist Issue*,

London: Hamlyn 1978 and *Hunger Strike*, London: Faber, 1986. Together they are co-founders of the Women's Therapy Centre in London, and the Women's Therapy Institute in New York.
  28. Ibid, pp. 78–79.
  29. Ibid.
  30. The classic examples were T. Leary, *The Politics of Ecstasy*, London: Paladin, 1970, and D. Cooper, *The Dialectics of Liberation*, Harmondsworth: Penguin, 1968.

Chapter nineteen The Therapies of Freedom

  1. M. Weber, Science as a Vocation, in H. Gerth and C. Wright Mills, *From Max Weber*, London: Routledge & Kegan Paul, 1948, p. 143.
  2. Cf. W. Hennis, 'Max Weber's Theme: Personality and Life Orders', in S. Whimster and S. Lash (eds), *Max Weber, Rationality and Modernity*, London: Allen & Unwin, 1987.
  3. Op. cit.
  4. P. Bordieu, *Distinction: A social critique of the judgement of taste*, London: Routledge & Kegan Paul, 1984.
  5. Cf. P. Rieff, *The Triumph of the Therapeutic*, London: Chatto and Windus, 1966, p. 87.
  6. C. Gordon, 'The Soul of the Citizen: Max Weber and Michel Foucault on Rationality and Government', in Whimster and Lash (eds), op. cit. See also C. Gordon, 'Question, ethos, event: Foucault on Kant and enlightenment', *Economy and Society* 15 (1986): 71–87. I have drawn on Colin Gordon's suggestive comments throughout this chapter.
  7. See, for example, the Habermasian nightmare sketched by John Keane in the introduction to his *Public life and Late Capitalism*, Cambridge: Cambridge University Press, 1984. For an incisive account of the difference between Habermas' and Foucault's approach to these issues, see P. Miller, *Domination and Power*, London: Routledge & Kegan Paul, 1987.

Index